To Laura McManus

I hope all the
commotion isn't
stopping you from
having as much
fun as I did.
With warm regards,
Hedley

September 2, 1989

RIGHT PLACES, RIGHT TIMES

ALSO BY HEDLEY DONOVAN

ROOSEVELT TO REAGAN:
A REPORTER'S ENCOUNTERS WITH NINE PRESIDENTS

RIGHT PLACES,
RIGHT TIMES

Forty Years in Journalism
Not Counting My Paper Route

By Hedley Donovan

FORMER EDITOR-IN-CHIEF,

TIME INC.

HENRY HOLT AND COMPANY
NEW YORK

Published by Henry Holt and Company, Inc.,
115 West 18th Street, New York, New York 10011.
Published in Canada by Fitzhenry & Whiteside Limited,
195 Allstate Parkway, Markham, Ontario L3R 4T8.

Library of Congress Cataloging-in-Publication Data
Donovan, Hedley.
Right Places, Right Times: forty years in journalism,
not counting my paper route / Hedley Donovan.
p.   cm.
Includes index.
ISBN 0-8050-0564-1
1. Donovan, Hedley.   2. Journalists—United States—Biography.
3. Editors—United States—Biography.   4. Time Inc.—History.
5. New York (N.Y.)—History.   I. Title.
PN4874.D68A3   1989
070.4'1'092—dc20
[B]   89-31360
                                                             CIP

FIRST EDITION

Designed by Claire M. Naylon
Printed in the United States of America
1   3   5   7   9   10   8   6   4   2

TO MY COMPANIONS
OF THE OLD TIME INC.

CONTENTS

Contents

ACKNOWLEDGMENTS

I am of course the world's leading authority on the subject of this book, so I was essentially my own research assistant. I did, however, take some precautions. In my former place of business, Time Incorporated, I turned to many friends, now or formerly employed there, for all kinds of help: tracking down the stray fact, co-brooding about a difficult judgment on people or public issues. I thank Richard Clurman, Richard Duncan, Elaine Felsher, Barbara Foy, Otto Fuerbringer, Murray Gart, Thomas Griffith, Ralph Graves, Andrew Heiskell, William Hooper, Harry Johnston, Ben Lightman and his staff, Leo Lionni, Marshall Loeb, Carol Loomis, Henry Luce III, John McDonald, Jason McManus, Elizabeth Luce Moore, Marsha Porcell, Wyndham Robertson, Gilbert Rogin, Hugh Sidey, Richard Stolley, Strobe Talbott, Christiana Walford. A few colleagues, despite more urgent paper on their desks, were kind enough to read considerable stretches of manuscript.

And although it sometimes seems as if everybody once worked for Time Inc., we know logically this can't be true, and accordingly, I am indebted for further facts and critique to several citizens of other places: Edmund Delaney, Katharine Graham, Edward Hidalgo, Jack Howard, Jane Reed, Harrison Salisbury, Barbara Staempfli. For permission to quote from the John Shaw Billings diary, I thank Allen Stokes of the University of South Carolina.

I am grateful to two sympathetic Sheilas, who rendered my handwritten MS into typescript and professed to like what they were deciphering. These are Sheila Drouet and Sheila Tunney.

I want to thank my agent, Carol Rinzler, who gave me friendly comments on early drafts, not unmixed with incitements to do better. And Carol led me to a fine editor, Marian Wood of Henry Holt, who made me work harder than I had meant to. My thanks, too, to Kathleen Brandes, vigilant proofreader and keeper of the stylistic proprieties.

My sister, Elizabeth Donovan Edmonds, a Time Inc. employee before I was, read much of the MS and found it promising. (She was once a college instructor in English.) She also helped me button down a significant aspect or two of family lore, significant at least to Elizabeth and me.

And an affectionate salute to Elnora Boone, friend and housekeeper to the Donovans for many years, who maintained the vital support systems while this book was being written and never disturbed the mess in my study.

PREFACE

My friend Frank Pace, Arkansas raconteur, former secretary of the army and former director of the Budget Bureau, said the best job in the world is president-elect of the United States. If that is right, and it probably is, I claim the second-best job in the world is editor-in-chief of Time Incorporated. Among other advantages, it lasts longer than president-electdom, that glorious but brief eleven weeks of fame and power without responsibility.

I was chosen by Henry Robinson Luce to succeed him as editor-in-chief of Time Inc. in 1964, and I held that richly privileged job until 1979. I, in turn, chose the third editor-in-chief of Time Inc., Henry Anatole Grunwald. (I have a middle name—Williams—but never used it or the initial in bylines or mastheads. Grunwald liked the resounding Henry Anatole, and Luce liked Henry R.)

This book is chiefly about my career in that remarkable institution housed in the Time and Life Building, situated at Sixth Avenue and 50th Street in mid-Manhattan. What a company that was! Much written about—journalistically (fair enough) and in novels and plays, satirized and romanticized, a celebrated coiner of money, much coveted by merger makers and takeover artists, courted by presidents and commissars, attacked for years from the Left, then from the Right, as a sinister manipulator of public opinion, cherished by tens of millions of readers, often voted among the Ten Best Companies to work for in the United States, also struck against once and denounced from time to time by angry employees who couldn't believe that Time Inc., of all people, should care about costs and earnings per share. And through it all, one of the significant cultural and political forces, and certainly one of the journalistic form-givers, in twentieth-century America.

And what a roll call of talents, what a cast of characters: the formidable Henry Luce, of course, brilliant and richly idiosyncratic; and offstage, the brainy, beautiful Clare (off the Time Inc. stage, that is; spectacularly visible on other stages); the unforgettable photographers, no 9-to-5 types among them—Margaret Bourke-White, Alfred Eisenstaedt, Gjon Mili, Gordon Parks, Carl Mydans, Walker Evans, to name a few; a Stalinist cell in *Fortune*, of all places; the courtly C. D. Jackson, gifted salesman, promoter, publisher, friend and adviser to Dwight Eisenhower; the gruff and great *Life* editor Ed Thompson; Charles J. V. Murphy, of *Life*, *Fortune*, and the Duke of Windsor's memoirs (so grand, as one Murphy admirer said, that the ghostwriter made the duke look a little seedy); James Agee; Archibald MacLeish; John Kenneth Galbraith; the robust Australian art critic Robert Hughes; Dan Jenkins of *Sports Illustrated*, *Semi-Tough*, and *Baja Oklahoma*; the world-class *Time* punsters Jesse Birnbaum and Stefan Kanfer (also a gifted Ping-Pong player); Loudon Wainwright, Sr.; Theodore White; Joan Didion; and the drunken *Fortune* writer who claimed he was going to shoot one of my predecessors as managing editor. (The writer had a gun, and the managing editor prudently locked himself in his office.)

This book is about my life with these people, and the excitements, accomplishments, and shortcomings of the journalism we practiced. And about those tough moments when the boss must choose among two or three highly qualified people for just one desirable promotion, and the very unusual bicameral hierarchy that evolved in Time Inc., hence the very unusual position of the editor-in-chief, and how "succession" was managed—once for me, once by me.

The great issues of the day offered the editor-in-chief of Time Inc. an ample platform for his own views (including the continuous opportunity to be wrong) and an ample test of his skills in fashioning some approximation of consensus among independent and powerfully opinionated people. In that role, I confronted in my own office all the controversial questions about American journalism that have made the press itself a major "issue" in our day: questions about the effects of bigness on diversity and about the anomaly of a private profit-seeking corporation performing a quasi-constitutional role; questions about quality, bias, and, above all, accountability.

A part of the "public relations problem" all journalists face is that theirs is such outrageously entertaining work. The customers suspect this, and the suspicion contributes to the resentment of the press. It is one thing for people of some gravity, such as clergy or doctors or judges, to perform weighty offices in our society, but why should the very workings of our democracy depend in some measure on these unbuttoned types who so shamelessly enjoy their jobs—i.e., journalists? In fact, the press will never be entirely beloved, and shouldn't seek to be, but it must learn how to acknowledge error, and how to confront the question: Who elected you to tell me what to think? The question stared the editor-in-chief of Time Inc. full in the face, every day.

And in the absence of any certifying authority—medical association, bar association, a bishop conferring ordination—who is to define the ethical standards of the journalist? This question, too, was always on my desk—or sitting across the desk from me. My colleagues considered me stern in the ethics department, but I never went so far as the elder Pulitzer, who held that an editor can have no friends. So in this book I will offer my own ground rules on journalistic relationships—with advertisers, with pressure groups, with government, with the subjects of the news itself, some of whom may indeed be friends. How close should a reporter get to his sources? Who is using whom? When is the right time for the press to hold something back? And the post-Watergate cult of investigative reporting—can the press be *too* skeptical?

So who elected me? Well, Harry Luce elected me, and he felt that in a sense God had elected him. Or at least that he was answerable to God, not just at Judgment Day but at the office—not to the Time Inc. board of directors, or the stockholders, certainly not to the advertisers, and not even to the readers.

I had somewhat different views of the chain of command. I considered myself responsible first to myself. "Aha!" I can hear Luce saying. "That's just what I meant." "Myself" in this context can only be my conscience, and that can come—even to those who don't know it—only from God. But unlike Luce, I went on to acknowledge further responsibilities: to the board of directors, who could, at least theoretically, fire me, and who did, at least theoretically, speak for the stockholders. And of course to the readers, our raison d'être, who could fire me by not buying our magazines. But not least to my staff, who couldn't fire me, but to whom I was bound in the closest kind of professional comradeship.

I begin this memoir with the mysteries of managing those Time Inc. editorial people, members of a difficult and glorious breed, the intellectuals. Then I tell something of how I got to be a manager of intellectuals: a brilliant choice of parents, and exposure to some splendid institutions of higher learning—the University of Minnesota, Oxford, the *Washington Post*, the U.S. Navy, *Fortune* magazine. It always helps, of course, to be in the right place at the right time, and more than once I was. It is useful to have physical stamina, a high level of energy, steady nerves, and a good digestion. These blessings do not necessarily admit you to the ranks of intellectuals, but they certainly help if you are called upon to boss them.

December 1988
New York

After this book was in type, my editor allowed me to break open a few pages to take brief note of various events in China, Poland, Russia, and Time Inc.

June 1989
New York

RIGHT PLACES, RIGHT TIMES

I

Managing the Unmanageable

Over three decades of my professional life, I earned some good salaries for trying to manage the almost unmanageable: intellectuals. And now and then I was also rewarded in coin better than dollars: a glimpse of trust and respect, perhaps even affection, felt by some highly creative people.

I did my administering of intellectuals as associate managing editor, then managing editor of *Fortune* (1951–59), and as editorial director, then editor-in-chief of Time Inc. (1959–79). But journalism is hardly unique. This craft or trade or art of managing intellectuals— it is definitely not a science—must be practiced, well or badly, in the planning, forecasting, and research departments of corporations, banks, brokerages, government agencies; in universities, colleges, schools; in scientific and medical laboratories, think tanks, foundations, and many kinds of public-service organizations; even in the hierarchical branches of organized religion; even in some areas of the military; even on Capitol Hill.

I am defining the "intellectual," as the roll call above makes clear, rather liberally. More rigorous definitions are possible: e.g., intellectuals are Claude Lévi-Strauss; the editors of the *New York Review of Books*; the Fellows of All Souls; and some (not all) of the tenured faculty of Harvard, Columbia, and Berkeley. Roughly 750 people.

A former president of Columbia, Dwight Eisenhower (1948–50), used to repeat with relish a definition of an intellectual that he had heard somewhere—"A person who takes more words than necessary to say more than he knows." I'm afraid Ike was only half-kidding (though he was intelligent enough to esteem profoundly the mind of a genuine Eisenhower intellectual—his brother Milton). I prefer the definition of Albert Wohlstetter of the Rand Corporation, the Santa Monica think tank: "An intellectual is a fellow who turns answers into questions."

For my purposes here, I am defining intellectuals as people who by both inclination and occupation deal mainly with ideas rather than things, who have minds of some depth or originality, and who have a considerable compulsion to share their thinking with others— on paper or out loud. Some twenty years ago, Professor George Stigler, the University of Chicago economist, arrived at a guess—he didn't say exactly how—of one million full-time intellectuals in the United States. Considering the expansion of the "knowledge industry" over the past twenty years, and the doubling in the numbers of college graduates and holders of advanced degrees, one might extrapolate that there are now two million American intellectuals. Who can disprove it?

Whatever the total, I think it is indisputable that a large majority of intellectuals are on somebody's payroll. Only a few are self-employed—novelists, poets, critics, J. D. Salinger, Alexander Solzhenitsyn, the thinkers and brooders off on their own. The vast majority of American intellectuals have an employer—who may be IBM, the CIA (yes), Bell Labs, Time Inc., Princeton, the Heritage Foundation, Young and Rubicam, the Naval War College, the *Washington Post*. So the intellectuals have a boss—and the boss has them.

The essential tension in the management of intellectuals arises, of course, from the employer's urgent need for creative, independent people and his equal need to keep them under some degree of discipline. He needs to give leadership to people who would generally be repelled by any notion that they had a leader. He is presiding over a kind of institutionalized anarchy, and he needs at least a few good bureaucrats to help him keep the show on the road. He needs from his intellectuals work not easily defined, measuring up to highly subjective standards, delivered more or less on time.

The boss may come home at 8 P.M. and over cocktails tell his wife (as I did now and then) that he has become an unlicensed psychiatrist, a glorified babysitter, a section of the Wailing Wall, and so on. Indeed Dorothy Donovan would sometimes ask, on picking me up at the Port Washington station of the Long Island Railroad, "How was it at the Wall today?"

During the years that I tried to master this branch of management, I did begin to discern certain patterns and principles. I arrived at fifteen or twenty working rules. Some of what I think I learned applies primarily to journalism, perhaps especially to Time Inc., but much of it I believe has broader relevance.

YOU DIDN'T HAVE TO DO THIS: The management of intellectuals can be very hard work, but that's for others to notice, not for the boss, ever, to say out loud at the office. Nobody is making him do this if he didn't want to. (I feel the same way about presidents of the United States.)

I once had an idea for an executive short story. There's this boss who is constantly complaining that his job leaves him no time "to think." His sympathetic board of directors gives him a year's leave of absence on full pay. He goes off, and then finds he can't think of anything.

BE YOURSELF BUT: The boss in an organization of intellectuals is going to be far better known to his staff than an industrial manager is to his. The organization of intellectuals is likely to be smaller and much more informal, and a high proportion of the staff will be social peers of the boss—fellow scholars, fellow journalists, professional colleagues. So the boss is going to be seen and studied from very close up, by smart people who love gossipy shoptalk. Intellectuals may not be any quicker at spotting phoniness than blue-collar workers, but when they do, the conversation can be merciless. For the boss, the moral is: No Airs—Be Yourself.

Surely no boss in twentieth-century America could have been more supremely himself than Henry Luce. His patterns of thought and speech, the fierce concentration, the gestures and quirks, the whole style of the man were totally distinctive, and none of it was put on. His staff loved to talk about Luce—in fear, awe, amusement, affection.

Be yourself but . . . There is always room for improvement. Over the years, Luce learned to temper his considerable arrogance and to sand down his erratic manners. He never did try to master the social grace of seeming interested in something that bored him—perhaps this was a constructive rudeness in the management of intellectuals, if not in the drawing room.

I always prided myself on a lack of affectation; when I came home from three years at Oxford it was widely agreed that no trace of an English accent had invaded my Minnesota speech. During my years as a Time Inc. executive, I think I stayed pretty much myself, but I did try to work on the weak spots. One of these, I immodestly note, was an apparent excess of modesty. Once after I had spoken at a staff dinner, one of our vice presidents, Larry Laybourne, button-holed me to say it was a pretty good speech, but I had talked too much about Luce, whom I had succeeded some years earlier. Since the occasion was the fiftieth anniversary of *Time*, I thought several references to the Founder were in order. "Look," said Laybourne, "Harry was a great man, but you're the boss now—people want to hear *you*." I tried to keep that in mind. Over the years, colleagues might have felt I got it all too clearly in mind.

BOSSING INTELLECTUALS IS A HIGH CALLING: The individual who undertakes this job is seeking to organize/improve/protect an environment in which creative people can do something close to their best work. Creative people may not always be so grateful as their boss thinks they should be. All the many ways that employees can be suspicious, resentful, or critical of the boss are accentuated when the employees are intellectuals. They can be temperamental, cantankerous. After a long day with them, the boss is entirely entitled to tell his wife what a pain these prima donnas can be. But it is still true that one of the greatest possible executive satisfactions is to feel you have helped bring out or bring along an intellectual talent. Sensitively managed, even large and complex organizations can stimulate and liberate creative individuals. The manager of intellectuals must never imagine he created the talent. It had to be there (mainly in the genes, I happen to think).

I experienced three dimensions of the bossing of intellectuals. As managing editor of *Fortune*, I was right out there on, so to speak, the factory floor. I was dealing directly with the creative professionals who turned out the magazine—researchers, photographers, artists, writers. The beginning of wisdom was that I was not passing on layout—I was passing on an Art Department. And I was not editing inanimate copy— I was editing a living writer. There was much more to it than that, of course, but that was where I felt my work started. Later, as editor-in-chief of Time Inc., I had the job of editing the editors—not their magazines, of course, a physical and mental impossibility for one editor-in-chief overseeing four or five or six magazines, but editing the M.E.s, managing their management. In between managing editor and editor-in-chief, I had an instructive interlude as Henry Luce's deputy, editorial director of Time Inc., in immediate charge of a staff of one, my secretary, but with considerable if inexact influence over all the editorial premises. An executive personage whose authority is not entirely clear can appear in steel or chemicals, but he probably has an easier time in the intellectual industry, where ambiguity is part of the work.

LOYALTY DOWN NO LESS THAN UP: This traditional ideal in military command is at least equally critical in the management of intellectuals. The good colonel will stand up for his people—not blindly, but giving them always the benefit of the doubt, awarding credit liberally, deflecting blame onto himself when that is halfway plausible. The good boss of intellectuals will do the same, vis-à-vis *his* bosses; or, if he has no boss, vis-à-vis the outside world. Intellectuals tend to be skeptical, little given to hero worship. They need to know their boss practices loyalty down. With loyalty down comes a real sensitivity to subordinates' opinions of the boss—equal perhaps to his avid interest in what the next layer up thinks of him.

THE FIRST-CLASS MIND IS AN INDEPENDENT MIND: It is never totally for hire. The intellectual does not automatically agree with the boss and he would not be of much use if he did. But in an organization of intellectuals—a college, perhaps, or a magazine—it happens from time to time that a position must be taken that cannot please everybody. In my experience as editor-in-chief of Time Inc., the most divisive issue internally was the Vietnam War, which many of the staff had turned against before their top editors did. Two presidential endorsements were unpopular with many of the staff—Nixon in 1968 and, much more so, Nixon in 1972. In these situations, the most to be hoped is that the losers will respect the *process* by which the decision was reached. The best test of this comes the next time a controversial decision is to be made: Do all those whose opinions would be relevant believe they will get a fair hearing?

THE TRICKY BUSINESS OF DELEGATING: Delegating is a fine art in any field, but in the management of intellectuals, it can be especially tricky business. The bosses in organizations of intellectuals themselves rose from one of the disciplines or professions or crafts now within their executive care. It can be hard for some of them to overcome their previous competitiveness with the people they are now managing. In Time Inc., I saw some sad cases of middle-level bosses who could not seem to grasp that outstanding work by one of their staff, far from threatening them, reflected well on them. So the boss who appoints these sub-bosses must watch for that hazard. But, having been a sub-boss, he must guard against the same unlovely symptoms in himself. A manager of managers—or, as I was, an editor of editors—must be able to find his chief professional satisfaction in the quality of the managing that is going forward under his general oversight. He must know how to share his authority without diluting it. He must keep the controls and sanctions that enable him to be finally accountable—to the owners of the business, or the trustees of the university, or whoever appointed him.

THE BOSS AS BOTTLENECK: This is a much more serious hazard in an organization of intellectuals than in routine operations where there are precedents for everything and deputies and subdeputies can safely make almost any decision. The bottleneck was a persistent problem for the Time Inc. magazines. Luce once asked me to critique the editorial management structure of *Life*. I reported back to him that the managing editor, Ed Thompson, "towers an undesirable distance above his Asst. M.E.s and chief department heads. The kind of dominance Ed has on *Life* would be appropriate to a magazine with a staff of 50 or to a factory of 5,000 people manufacturing valves to standard specifications. It's an expensive way of operating a staff of circa 200 creative and professional people. . . . I wish *Life* had one or two more men of something approaching Ed's stature. Not just so there will be several people to choose the next M.E. from, at some later day, but for the sake of the magazine right now. I would not expect them to have all the same specific likes and dislikes Ed has—I would hope they didn't—but they should approach Ed's general quality of imagination, taste and judgment. There should be a strong presumption that work assigned and supervised by these men is going to end up in the magazine. . . . Today too much work goes forward at *Life* on the chance the M.E. *might* like it."

In later years, I think most of the M.E.s whom I appointed arrived eventually at a sound balance between the decisions that could be decentralized and those that couldn't. One or two never could get the hang of it, but offered compensating strengths.

CHANNELS, CHARTS, AND WHEN TO FORGET THEM: Luce would go outside channels whenever he felt like it, to the amazement—and anxiety—of freshman writers or ad salesmen who found themselves suddenly invited to tell the Proprietor what was wrong with Time Inc. These forays were generally invigorating to Luce as well as his workers. Not being the Proprietor, I was more circumspect. I did feed a good many lunches to relays of brand-new writers and researchers, usually with one of their bosses present, sometimes not. And I did a lot of listening, all over the building.

Maybe somewhere there was a Time Inc. editorial-organization chart, but if so, I never saw it. I sent editors on short rotation tours away from their own magazines and brought them in and out of my own office as acting deputies. It made for some healthy ferment, in my head among others. The rotations also helped break down the clannishness of the individual magazine staffs. The good side of the clannishness is of course esprit de corps. The manager's life is full of trade-offs.

Luce and I were both extremely frugal about staffing in editorial headquarters. We permitted ourselves some amusement at the proliferation of vice presidents on the business side of Time Inc.—up to twenty-five or so at one time. The argument, as at banks and ad agencies, was that customers liked to think they were dealing with somebody senior. Luce for a few years did indulge a weakness for personal editorial advisers in particular fields. He had a personal art director, a very talented man whose advice, through no fault of his own, was not especially welcome to the line art directors of the magazines. Likewise, a Middle European thinker about world politics whose ideas did not impress the line thinkers on *Time, Life*, and *Fortune*.

TELLING GOOD FAT FROM BAD: The lack of absolute measurements of quality in the work of intellectuals imposes peculiar responsibilities on the manager of intellectuals. In the budgeting for a magazine, for instance, the manager must calculate whether the final 15 percent of his costs adds perhaps only 5 percent to the final quality of his product, but also whether this 5 percent is perhaps an essential edge over the competition. The locating of fat in intellectual organizations, and the distinguishing between good fat and bad fat, is interesting work, as the lean, mean new owners of CBS, NBC, and ABC were discovering in 1987–88.

"FAIR," EVEN IF UNREASONABLE: Again because of the subjective standards of performance, it is especially desirable that a manager of intellectuals be perceived as "fair." He will never convince everybody, intellectuals being intellectuals, but he needs to have a very large majority—say, 90 percent of his staff—convinced that his criteria of quality, be they difficult to define or even unreasonable, are applied evenly. Better to be an impartial son of a bitch than a boss who plays favorites.

The roughest and toughest Time Inc. executive of my day was James Shepley, president of the company (partly my doing) for a dozen years. His blowtorch style of argument was applied with absolute impartiality to anybody, his technical superiors included, and he was a highly effective executive. (It helped that he was very smart.)

REMIND THEM WHY THEY LIKE WHAT THEY ARE DOING: A very high proportion of intellectuals consciously chose their line of work rather than drifting into it or feeling there was no alternative. But they also complain a lot; they can expect the impossible. They need to be reminded why they chose these careers in the first place, why those still look like smart decisions.

At Time Inc. gatherings, I devoted many speeches to the theme that journalism is an enormously exciting trade and that it had never been more so than today—1955, or 1964, or 1979, whenever. My audiences basically thought so, too, but I felt we had to keep renewing our mutual understanding of this truth. Despite the tense and draining aspects of the job, these are fabulous times to be a journalist, I said in speeches in a good many different "times." To be sure, the journalist always thinks that; otherwise he wouldn't be a journalist. Indeed, I was also doing a bit of personal image–tending in these speeches. Along with my modesty, another character defect was an inability to project professional excitement. (My successor, Henry Grunwald, described me as a man of "massive calm.") I felt it desirable to assure my colleagues that I, too, appearances to the contrary, was fired up by journalism.

DON'T BE STINGY WITH CRITICISM: It goes without saying that the manager must be generous with praise, but the judicious application of criticism to very touchy people is more challenging work. There are three messages that must be implicit in successful criticism of intellectuals. First, you can do better work than this; in fact, some of this is very good; I just wish more of it were as good as the best of it. Second, the same standards are being applied to your peers. And last, I myself want to be held, by you and others, to these standards.

These messages can be conveyed with varying degrees of subtlety or directness, but it obviously helps if there is a presumption that the boss himself could perfectly well do the work in question if he didn't have to attend to so many other things. For this presumption to prevail, the boss needs a proven track record, as an individual performer, in some of the work he now oversees.

I remember a meeting in the early 1960s of *Time* news bureau chiefs from all over the world. At lunch, the managing editor of *Time*—in effect their principal customer—offered these correspondents a tactful compliment and a clear summons to do a better job. He said that the men out in the field were almost invariably better than the files they sent to New York. Speaking at dinner that evening, I ventured that the men in the field *and* the editors and writers in New York were almost invariably better than the printed magazine. I added, of course, "That means they're really quite something, because the magazine is awfully good." The correspondents were delighted, not all the New York editors equally so.

I don't believe I was consciously imitating Henry Luce, whose deputy I then was. But Luce was a master, at least in conversation, at aligning himself with the sergeants and lieutenants against the colonels and brigadiers.

CHEWING-OUTS ARE PRIVATE OCCASIONS: It is rudimentary that the CEO does not chew out the senior vice president, sales, in front of the salesmen. The protocol is a little less clear-cut among journalists, academics, and the other contentious citizens of the intellectual world. Certainly the direct personal rebuke is not to be dropped into some general critical commentary on quality. But much of the work of intellectuals goes forward in "collegial" dialogue—and, just as on the campus, the collegial talk can get heated, even rancorous. In front of junior faculty, the full professor doesn't hesitate to take apart, intellectually speaking, the mistaken assistant professor. Comparable exchanges took place every day at Time Inc.

The art, of course, is to keep the argument on some spirited but impersonal level and never let it sound *ad hominem*. Easier said than done. I recall an occasion when forthright colleagues told me I had crossed the line. I hastened to make apologies and reassurances to those I could have offended. And I remember an excruciatingly uncomfortable hour, in close quarters in a company airplane, when I had to listen to one upper-level Time Inc. boss bawling out, unmercifully, one of his people. This impropriety was compounded by the fact that my wife was traveling with me and had to hear all this. I could have stopped it all at once, and should have, but didn't want to make *my* junior lose face in front of *his* junior. I chewed him out later. Privately.

KNOW WHEN TO BE THE AUTOCRAT: A high degree of permissiveness pervades most organizations of intellectuals. Consultation is continuous; consensus is sought; direct order-giving is frowned upon. Still, there come times when the place can no longer be a democracy. A decision must be made, and not all votes can count the same.

On *Fortune* in the mid-1970s we were debating (for about the fourth time in thirty years) a shift from monthly to biweekly publication. The business management was convinced it made publishing sense. I became persuaded they were right. The editorial staff was overwhelmingly opposed. I set about trying to persuade the key people. I perhaps won over a few, but I also heard barely veiled threats to resign and was told of tears and widespread malaise. I decided we should go ahead.

In a speech to the *Fortune* staff shortly after the decision, I said that converting to a fortnightly was almost like creating a new magazine, and "starting a new publication is about as exciting a thing as any of us can do professionally. . . . A lot of people spend a lifetime in journalism without getting in on that." I made no apologies for the fact that the new rhythm was expected to increase profits. "Nothing could be more appropriate philosophically than for *Fortune*, which for twelve times a year, now about to be twenty-six times a year, has celebrated the enterprise system, to be itself a very successful enterprise. That would make utter logical sense and close a beautiful circle."

Nobody resigned from *Fortune*, and on the whole the shift has worked well. At least a few of the old-timers, still working at *Fortune* today and still exercising their constitutional freedom of speech, would still say the boss was wrong.

KEEP THOSE IDEAS COMING: Intellectuals tend to have a lot of ideas as to how their employer could do a better job. New ideas will be intermingled with, often inseparable from, griping about the present state of affairs. The boss must get used to this. These tendencies to assist management should be encouraged, and receipt of the ideas, bad and good, unfailingly acknowledged. This idea flow is in fact essential to institutional vigor and renewal. The boss needs the ideas of his staff even more than they need the outlet and recognition.

When I first went to work at *Fortune*, newly out of the U.S. Navy, my most frequent lunch companions were three other beginning *Fortune* writers, also fresh from several years of military service, hence expert at griping about the brass: George Hunt, from the Marine Corps, later to be managing editor of *Life*; William H. Whyte, Marine Corps, later assistant M.E. of *Fortune*; and Edgar Smith, U.S. Army, later assistant M.E. of *Fortune* and M.E. of *Architectural Forum*. We talked mainly about the many ways *Fortune* should be better run, so clear to us after a few months there; about new kinds of stories and departments for *Fortune*; and sometimes about inspirations for brand-new magazines. From time to time we ventured, individually, to share these insights with our bosses. They listened, occasionally bought an idea, and, not incidentally, taught us something about being a boss.

A *Fortune* writer once complained that his story suggestions to a previous managing editor seemed to disappear into a bottomless pit. The editor hinted in a friendly way that that was the right place for them. "At least let me know you saw them on their way down," said the writer. A modest enough request.

KNOW WHEN THE JUNGLE DRUMS ARE COMING CLOSER: Within an organization of intellectuals, there is a more or less steady level of grousing, as in an army barracks, though the vocabulary is less monotonous. But the boss must know, firsthand or through his scouts, when the drums are getting louder. Something may need looking into. In Time Inc. in the early 1970s, for instance, the editors were slow—and I was among the slowest—to sense the new force and urgency in the complaints of women about their promotion opportunities. We had many good traditional answers, but they weren't good enough anymore; things had changed.

One hard-boiled school of thought holds that some kinds of people problems get magnified when there's somebody to listen to them. The theory has undeniable appeal to anybody trying to manage intellectuals, but it must be resisted. Some problems do get magnified, no doubt, by being told, but some explode if not told, and a boss can't tell which are which without listening. Then there is the very gratifying discovery, familiar to the executive returning from vacation, that certain problems simply went away while he was gone. Some, of course, were handled by his deputies; the rest, never fear, will be back.

DON'T LUMP THE INTELLECTUALS TOGETHER: For convenience, I have written here of "the intellectual," but in dealing with intellectuals in real life, the manager must comprehend—and appraise—their work with far more precision. Just within Time Inc., editors, writers, photographers, reporters, foreign correspondents, art directors all have their separate motivations, anxieties, excitements. The different professions and subprofessions want it recognized that they *are* different, and the highly individualistic personalities within each line of work want to be seen as such. The individual intellectual may be highly competitive with, even hostile to, some of his fellow intellectuals—including the guy in the next office.

There are obvious differences in the psychology of the intellectual working for a risk-taking corporation—perhaps assigned to a new magazine launch that could be a flop—and an intellectual working in the more protected environments of academia or government. Understand that the risk-takers need some shields, and that the protected from time to time could do with a jolt of danger.

PAY THE INTELLECTUALS WELL: They are worth it. Time Inc. was very generous in this regard, and as a boss I always felt I had ample resources from the company to reward the deserving. But once more, the inexact standards applying to our people's work made salary determinations, so cut-and-dried in many other places, almost an aesthetic judgment. I labored over our payroll.

A MIGHTY DETAIL: A flow of fresh talent is so important to organizations of intellectuals that the boss should get fairly deep into this "detail" himself, no matter that he has good deputies assigned to it. I spent a lot of time at it. I was proud of my hirings as managing editor of *Fortune*, though my predecessor did better. (But he had twelve years at it, and I just six.) I always stressed to writers I hired for *Fortune* that we were both taking a big chance. The job was very different from most other forms of journalism—and neither of us could be sure it would work out. I said it was a fifty-fifty chance—nobody declined—and about two out of three did make it.

We didn't use personality testing in hiring (or assigning or promoting). I could never take it seriously after a beautiful demolition job that William H. Whyte, Jr., did in *Fortune* (October 1954), including a box on "How to Cheat." Apparently the tests are coming into vogue again (*Fortune*, March 30, 1987). Not at Time Inc., I hope.

As Time Inc. editor-in-chief, I put a new stress on recruiting, shocking several of our editors who liked to think everybody worth hiring would sooner or later seek out Time Inc. I also wanted some firsthand feel of "the market." I continued to interview a good many job candidates myself, sending along the best to whichever seemed the appropriate Time Inc. magazine, discouraging some people from journalism altogether, now and then telling others to get some experience on a newspaper, out somewhere, and come back and see us in two or three years. This led to some warming, if unexpected, reunions—"Hi, Mr. Donovan, I did what you suggested"—and indeed to an occasional addition to our payroll. I think it is impossible for a manager of intellectuals to know too much about what kind of people are attracted and not attracted to his organization—and I mean as the place is today, not as he remembers the organization that hired him.

II

Not Everyone Can Be from Minnesota

As a small boy, I put in a fair bit of time wondering, Who am I, also Why am I me instead of someone else? (Reasonable questions to this day.) As I came to hear a little history, family and American, I picked up an unsettling piece of news. It seemed that my grandfather Donovan, as a young man in Ohio, had tried for a congressional appointment to West Point, but lost out to a friend of his named George Custer. If Grandfather had won that appointment, would I be alive at all? Yes, I finally concluded; I had to believe Grandfather would have been too smart to get beaten by the Indians. And I did get born, on May 24, 1914, in Brainerd, Minnesota.

The *New York Times* front page of that date (I was given a facsimile on my sixty-fifth birthday) reports that the U.S. expeditionary forces Woodrow Wilson had sent to Veracruz were preparing to march on Mexico City. Seven German army aviators lost their lives in an aerial competition dedicated to Kaiser Wilhelm's brother Henry. In an obscure corner of Europe, there was a bloody little rebellion against a king who had thought to "civilize the Albanians." Nothing on the page suggested that the civilized states of Europe were about to shed more blood than the most ferocious Albanian could dream of. I am prewar, just barely.

My father was Percy Williams Donovan, a mining engineer who studied at the University of Minnesota, then at Columbia, where he took his degree. His father, David, had fought in the Civil War (even if he didn't get to Little Bighorn), did some schoolteaching, and presently became a penniless Congregationalist minister, raising his family of eight children in a succession of little towns in southern and western Minnesota.

Donovans trace back sooner or later to County Cork, Ireland. My great-great-grandfather, Dennis Donovan, owned a linen mill there on the Arrigmideen River (Silver Stream). His oldest son, James, was a studious lad intended by his parents for the priesthood; James didn't like the idea and ran away to America. Jack Kennedy once asked me how come with a name like Donovan I wasn't a Catholic; so did Francis Cardinal Spellman and Archbishop Amleto Cicognani, once papal delegate to Washington. I enjoyed telling them the saga of James Donovan—and the happy ending: A vocation is finally discovered! James's son David becomes a Congregationalist minister! (Kennedy lost interest in my little recitation very rapidly; the prelates stayed amused a bit longer.) And Grandfather David, liberated from the bonds of Rome, married Mary Leslie, from a line of lowland Scots who had settled in Northern Ireland. ("The dregs of Scotland," as Oliver Cromwell called the families he recruited to colonize the Ulster Plantation, a garrison against the unruly Irish papists.) Her people came to the American colonies in the eighteenth century. Her grandfather was a doctor in Ohio, her father a lawyer there. She bore David ten children, two died in infancy, and she herself died at forty-four. My father was not quite five then, and all his life he spoke of her with grief and reverence. I never knew my grandfather, either: He died the year after I was born.

My mother, Alice Dougan, was a city girl, growing up in Minneapolis, where her father was stationmaster for the Great Northern Railroad. She graduated from the University of Minnesota and taught high school English and Latin before she married.

Her father was Hedley (hence my name) Vicars Dougan, so christened by a patriotic Scots-Irish family in Canada, in honor of a British army hero of the Crimean war, Captain Hedley Vicars. My mother's ancestors were almost entirely Scots; there were a few of English stock here and there on the family tree. Back there somewhere, we suspected a Dugan had changed the name to the tonier-sounding Dou*gan* to fend off any possible confusion with the really Irish (and generally Catholic) Dugans. So Hedley Vicars Dougan, down from Canada, married Mollie Knox, child of one of the earliest families to arrive in the frontier settlement of St. Paul, Minnesota. My grandfather Dougan died in his early fifties of TB; Mollie Dougan lived on into her nineties, much of the time in our house. She had been a noted beauty, and even as an elderly woman was very attentive to jewelry, hats, corsets, and the like. As the only grandparent I knew, she was an important figure in my life, an adult personage utterly different from my father and quite different from her daughter, my mother. She created new interests and variety when she was staying with us (and some tensions, as even a child could notice).

To keep Grandmother busy—after she ran out of mending, menu suggestions, card games with the children—my mother suggested she set down some reminiscences. There is more than a faint suggestion of duress in the title of the resulting work, "The Story of My Life Written by Request of My Daughter." But she wrote charmingly of the raw little cities of St. Paul and Minneapolis in the years of her youth. Her mother, Elizabeth, the heroine of the story, had been a "very lovely" young woman, sought by many beaux. One named Felix wrote her, "My hand trembles badly, but my heart trembles more." So, "the family from henceforth called him 'Trembling Felix.' " Her mother later "formed quite an attachment," Grandmother wrote, "for a young man who afterward became a prominent Judge. Unfortunately, his habits were not strictly temperance, and therefore not approved by the family." In 1852, she married Robert Knox, a fine-looking man of six feet four inches, who soon disappeared into the West to hunt for gold. He "made one or two trips home and sent money at uncertain intervals. He had no bad habits that I know of, but just could not seem to get ahead." So Elizabeth Knox ran a boardinghouse to support her family.

My own parents must have known something about birth control, though they never mentioned the subject to me. My brother David was about two and a half years older than I, and my sister Elizabeth the same span younger. I liked being the middle child. My mother said the first child sometimes gets spoiled—though not David, of course—and the youngest child sometimes feels left out of things— not Elizabeth, of course—so the middle was the perfect place to be.

In Brainerd, my father was a district manager for the E. J. Longyear Company, a mining exploration firm with headquarters in Minneapolis. He was in charge of contract drilling and surveying work on the Cuyuna iron range, northeast of Brainerd. His best friend there was Dr. Rudolph Beise, the mayor of Brainerd, who delivered me at home one Sunday morning, free of charge. When I was seven or so and asked how much the job had cost, I was told—instead of the usual it's-not-polite-to-ask-about-those-things—that my father had tried to give Dr. Beise $25, but he wouldn't accept anything. Very nice of both of them, I thought.

Brainerd, first known as "The Crossing," was founded when the Northern Pacific Railroad, on its imperial way from Lake Superior to the Pacific Ocean, built a trestle bridge there across the Mississippi River. In 1872, the last public lynching in the Brainerd region took place outside the Last Turn saloon. Two Chippewas were hanged.

By 1914, the population was about 10,000. Apart from the nearby iron deposits and timber properties, Brainerd was chiefly famous for being a division point on the Northern Pacific. In later years, Brainerd became famous for being the next town up the road from Little Falls, where Charles Lindbergh was born. My father didn't think much of Lindbergh's father, Congressman Lindbergh, who was a kind of radical agrarian, also said to be pro-German.

But my father was as proud as every other Minnesotan when the younger Lindbergh flew the Atlantic in 1927. At thirteen, I was moved to enter a schoolboy essay contest, "What Lindbergh Means to Me," winner to ride in Lucky Lindy's car in a great homecoming parade. I received an honorable mention and had my piece printed in the Minneapolis *Tribune* (key point being that "Lucky" was misleading—it took courage and skill). A dozen years later, things came full circle, back to my father's view; then, as a reporter for the *Washington Post*, I covered Colonel Lindbergh's strongly isolationist testimony on Capitol Hill, which followed his inspection of Nazi Germany's new air force.

My family moved from Brainerd to Minneapolis when I was two, leaving an attractive bungalow with a backyard sloping down to the modest little gorge of the Mississippi. As I came to know Brainerd firsthand in the 1920s, it became an immensely romantic place to me—not because I had been born there, but because it was the gateway to the Great North Woods. When the family would drive up there from Minneapolis, as we did for many vacations, I felt a powerful excitement for the last hour or two of the daylong trip—125 miles north to Brainerd, another dozen miles to the Beise cottage at Gull Lake, about seven hours by my father's intensely cautious driving in the cars and on the roads of that day. (Garrison Keillor's "Lake Wobegon" countryside lies about halfway from Minneapolis to Brainerd, off a bit to the left.) I became infatuated with maps on these trips, studying our route as I sat next to my father, who could explain the geological reasons for the geography. We lightened the journey by naming state capitals, rivers beginning with S, and so on, and guessing the populations of various places (I was second only to my father in this skill, my mother laughably weak). It was a bit before Brainerd that Minnesota changed—from the grain-and-dairy countryside to something more exhilarating. There was even a stretch of six or eight miles somewhere near Little Falls, where the highway and the railroad tracks and the telegraph poles marched exactly parallel on a straight line north into infinity. This dramatic image at the farthest edge of the prairie announced to me we were Getting There. (We could easily have had two flat tires earlier in the day, and we certainly would have had a vast picnic lunch.)

Then at Brainerd the lakes began to be everywhere. Minnesota's state slogan, "Land of Ten Thousand Lakes," turns out, uniquely for this art form, to be an understatement. According to one tabulation by the U.S. Coast and Geodetic Survey, there are 12,035 lakes in Minnesota. Most of them lie north and west of Brainerd. This glacial north country was a land of pure, sweet water, icy before Flag Day; agates and arrowheads to be hunted on the beaches; low granitic hills and ridges; majestic pine forests where the air was always moving; birch, blueberries, poison ivy, and savage mosquitoes; the teeming bass, pike, perch (all a bore to fish for, my family agreed, but great to eat); and fox, deer, beaver, woodchucks, loons, skunks, black bear, and, once in a while at night across a lake, the spine-shivering howl of a wolf.

I was last in Brainerd for the town's centennial in 1971. I made a speech on the admirable stamina of middling-small towns remote from any big city. Brainerd had grown to all of 11,000, but the town somehow looked smaller and flatter than it used to. I took Dorothy swimming in Gull Lake, and we got to ride in an official car in the centennial motorcade. Senator Walter Mondale was also allowed to ride, even though he was born shamefully close to out-of-state—in a tiny place called Ceylon, Minnesota, just next to the Iowa line.

The Donovans moved to Minneapolis when my father was promoted to manager of all the Longyear contract drilling operations, in the United States and abroad. Over the years he supervised drilling for mineral explorations all over North America, for the Roan Antelope copper field of Northern Rhodesia, for the borings for the first New York subway line under the East River, and for the Golden Gate Bridge in San Francisco.

The Minneapolis house my father bought for $7,000 was at 2412 Bryant Avenue South, in a quiet neighborhood of elm-lined streets known as Lowry Hill. Our forty or fifty blocks (bordered by commercial streets where trolley cars ran) included half a dozen vacant lots prized for football, baseball, soccer, even mini track meets, and some duplexes and four-family apartments, but it was mainly a place of single-family houses—a few rather grand, most quite homely, solidly built in the "Queen Anne" style of 1890–1910. The neighborhood went downhill during the Depression of the 1930s, recovered only a little after World War II, then suffered an invasion of raffish rooming houses and hippie communes in the 1960s. It has since undergone considerable gentrification, and a neighborhood association even publishes architectural brochures, with suggested walking tours, detailing various treasures of the Queen Anne period.

The first thing I am positive I remember firsthand, all on my own, is Armistice Day, November 11, 1918. Not a bad place for a journalist to start remembering. My father was driving the family car up Lowry Hill, a brick-paved street leading toward our neighborhood, and all the Packards and Nashes and Hupmobiles in Minneapolis seemed to be chugging along beside us, trailing strings of tin cans. My father was too staid to attach tin cans to our Oakland, but we all loved the racket the other cars were making. My father had marched once a week with the Minnesota National Guard, and though he had three children, he was still under forty, so if the war had gone on through another winter, he might have been "called." Now the war was over.

The Donovan house was perched up a dozen feet from street level (the slopes were tough to mow), a broad frame house on a narrow lot, no more than fifteen feet from the neighbors on either side. A front porch ran the width of the house, and on a summer evening it was a pleasant place for grown-ups to engage in the somewhat mystifying rite of "visiting"—though if you needed light for cards or reading or Ping-Pong, the price was a certain amount of moth and mosquito traffic through and around the screens. Inside, the center hall was maybe twelve by twenty, as big as the living room to one side of it and bigger than the library on the other side—uselessly big, except for occasional dancing, light gymnastics, dramatic offerings, or lights-out games of "Murder." These were high-ceilinged rooms with handsome parquet floors. In the library were a Victrola circa 1918, some oak Mission-style furniture, now chic (though the Volunteers of America grumbled mightily at having to haul it away in the 1960s), a fake fireplace with a little gas grill, a stained-glass window above it, and shelves holding perhaps three hundred books. This would have been one of the larger home libraries in Minneapolis in that era. There were three or four good pieces in the living room, handed down from "both sides," plus the standard-issue furniture that newlyweds would have bought in the 1910s. The dining room was a dark place with walnut paneling and built-in sideboard and silver cupboards, glassed-in china shelves, and a heavy oval table good for homework or two-handed card games around the rim. The big kitchen, with its pantry and icebox (we were never the first on the block to acquire some newfangled appliance), was old-fashioned even for its time. The full basement was a dusty, musty sort of cave with a hand-tended coal furnace, a laundry, and a whole room stocked with preserves. Second floor: four bedrooms, one to a corner, again the superfluously big hall, one bathroom for the whole family, its ancient fixtures never modernized in the fifty years my parents lived there. The full attic had a maid's room that could be a furnace in the summer.

The all-important backyard, when I came home on visits as a grown man, was postage-stamp scale. But to a boy, of course, it was big enough for two-player variants (or three- or four-) on baseball and football. It was the site of many a snow fort and an occasional igloo. A tent might be pitched there in the summer, and for several seasons it "hosted" (as the sports pages might now say) one of the trickiest four-hole miniature golf tournaments in the Upper Middle West. Twenty-five cents to enter. Having laid out the course, I was appropriately the champ; I don't think anybody else ever shot a five. Somehow the backyard also accommodated a couple of scruffy flower beds (my parents were not avid gardeners) and a few gallant clumps of rhubarb and asparagus, which did surprisingly well in the hostile athletic environment.

The Minneapolis of the 1920s was a privileged time and place to be growing up. We had real *seasons*, to say the least, there at the center of the continent. It was gratifying to me to learn in school that Minneapolis stood precisely halfway between the Equator and the North Pole. We were perversely proud of our arctic winters and scorching summers, which could yield a swing of 130 degrees or more in a year's temperatures. The weather was a dependably bountiful source of conversation (as it also is, of course, in less favored places). I liked the smell of fresh mud in March and April, of the blossoming lilacs of late May (hauntingly timed for Memorial Day and the several dozen of the GAR who could still march). Although the summer was not productive of memorable smells, everything was leading up to

October and the glorious smoke of the burning leaves, now alas forbidden by the know-it-all environmentalists. And then: no smell, no sound, the excitement of the first snowfall, which could come as early as Armistice Day. Later on, for a foot or more, school might be let out for a day.

Walking around in Lowry Hill, there were a few houses you didn't loiter in front of, because of exceptionally fierce dogs or crabby old ladies or an unpleasantly dark and empty look. I didn't believe in haunted houses and once accepted a dare to go into the backyard of an especially gloomy place, but I didn't stay long. Definitely to be avoided was the yard, front or back, of the dread Day brothers. It sometimes seemed as though there were seven or eight of these red-headed Irish terrors, but in fact I suppose there were only about four. Age for age, they could beat the tar out of any boy in the neighborhood.

Fistfights, except against a Day, were a rather popular recreation. For a brief period of glory in grammar school, before I skipped grades and got younger and smaller than my classmates, I was the tyrant of the recess period. A wiry little fellow named Eddie, with pale skin that bruised very easily, enjoyed our schoolyard fights so much that he and I had an understanding we would meet at a certain street corner for another round on our way home to lunch. Our mothers finally made us stop. "Fought" is a frequent entry in my schoolboy diary; one day, "Fought a gang," presumably with allies.

The Minneapolis public schools, as I now appreciate, were excellent, though I imagine my parents at the time thought this was simply the way schools ought to be, what the taxpayers were entitled to expect. My mother, having been a teacher herself, was professional in her reaction to my teachers. She thought most of them were splendid; once in a while, after a term was over, never before, she would confide that Miss So-and-So had seemed "a bit of a goose" or perhaps "a bit of a ninny." There were of course no "security" problems in that innocent age. What passed for disciplinary disturbances were the occasional wave of whispering or giggling, suppressed by one sharp glance from authority, and the stray "bad boy" sent to the principal's office, the lad then notably subdued for at least the next several weeks. Classes were big—twenty-five to thirty pupils. But the dedication of the teachers, and their untroubled confidence that they were doing exactly what the city of Minneapolis, the state of Minnesota, and the United States of America had entrusted them to do, in behalf of the civic future, gave them easy control over a large roomful of children who essentially believed the same things.

Many of those wonderful women (fewer men) remain unforgettable to me. Years later, when I was managing editor of *Fortune*, wandering the corridors in the evening, I might come upon an exceptionally disorganized and disheveled office of some writer or researcher, protected by ceiling-high ramparts of old newspapers and government reports, and I could not resist squeezing myself into the room and leaving a note: " 'A disorderly desk is the sign of a disorderly mind.'—Clara F. Hubachek, 5th Grade Arithmetic teacher, Douglas School, Minneapolis, c. 1924." Nothing changed in those *Fortune* offices, of course, and the staff knew I was just showing off. I myself was fantastically neat as a boy; I'm not sure Miss Hubachek would be entirely pleased with my desk today.

Minneapolis had a magnificent park system, the jewels being seven lakes within the city limits. Two of them were within a few minutes' ride by bike from our house, and they offered beaches and tennis courts much patronized by the Donovans; rowboats and canoes for hire; sailing, picnic spots, athletic fields, iceboating, hockey rinks, and modest ski slopes.

The Twin Cities Rapid Transit Company operated a fine fleet of big yellow streetcars, fare five cents. It was a ten-minute run downtown. Riding in the opposite direction out to the end of the line, and after a transfer or two, a boy could get into good hiking and exploring country. Another splendid nickel's worth was a ride to the old powder magazine at Fort Snelling, once a garrison in the Indian wars; the nearby Minnehaha Falls (the "laughing waters" of *Hiawatha*); and Longfellow's Gardens, the city's rather pathetic zoo. If you really wanted to make a day of it out in that far corner of the city, you could also watch a dashing fellow in helmet and goggles climb into an open-cockpit plane and take off from Wold Chamberlain Field, named after two Minnesota aviators of the Great War. (I don't want to exaggerate the allure of the streetcars; I preferred to be driven to these places, and sometimes was.) For a dime you could go to St. Paul, which we did sometimes to eat large dinners with relatives, or to go to the State Fair in September, some of the relatives living conveniently close to the fairgrounds.

The Boy Scouts were another special world. The mix of American frontier and Indian legend, the lore of the trail and campfire, with a touch of tradition from the imperial outposts of England (where the Scouts were invented), all had powerful romantic appeal to a twelve-year-old boy. I was an avid, ambitious member of Troop 98, Panther Patrol. We hiked all over the countryside, sometimes slept on the ground, and came home reeking of woodsmoke and citronella. I went to camp (cots and tents with decks) for two weeks every summer, progressed through the various tests and ranks and honors in which Scouting was so prolific, and in due course, age fifteen, became an Eagle Scout.

I had been mustered into Troop 98 by Everett Helm, who needed to produce one live recruit so he could advance from Second Class to First Class Scout. Ev was my oldest friend, and I was happy to oblige. We met about 1920. (And I most recently had lunch with him in 1986 in Vicenza, Italy.) I was running to school one morning when I overtook this boy, equally late, who was just strolling. He asked what was my hurry. This led to introductions, and to many years of backyard games, tennis, trading of stamps, and hoaxes played upon Ev's sweet and gullible mother.

With another grade-school friend, Radcliffe Edmonds, I founded a poker club, and we spent a good many happy hours drafting its constitution. The Edmondses were a very hospitable family, at least as serious eaters as the Donovans, and almost as competitive. They played poker right there at home, the whole family, a worldliness that greatly impressed me. My father felt poker was somewhat disreputable, I think because he associated it with gambling; he didn't play cards for money. (The disapproval of gambling did not extend to the stock market. When, around age eighty-eight or so, he first discussed his will with me and asked me to take a look at his investments, I was awed at some of the crazy cats and dogs, mainly in mining, he was holding.) The Edmondses were more affluent than we—from real estate, not poker. The families were very congenial—especially, a bit later, Rad's younger brother Peter and my sister Elizabeth. They were married in 1940.

Five blocks away from 2412 Bryant was the family church, Trinity Baptist, a rough-cut gray-stone building of Romanesque inspiration, inviting and in no way overpowering in a residential neighborhood. I was both invited and not invited. I was proud that my mother and grandmother and great-grandmother Elizabeth Hall Knox had been among the founders of the church, a courageous breakaway congregation. They had split from the First Baptist Church of Minneapolis, a citadel of the Fundamentalist theology that they deplored. Trinity was literally Baptist (I was immersed at age twelve), but also tolerant and questioning in a very modern liberal Protestant mode. My father, as a Congregationalist, another of the liberal free-form Protestant denominations, had no reluctance in signing up with

Trinity after his marriage. He became a trustee, usher, and all-purpose pillar of Trinity for the rest of his long life. My mother taught Sunday school and, more challenging, adult Bible classes, and she served on every sort of church committee.

I considered it a grave injustice that the Donovan children, almost alone in Trinity, were expected to go to both Sunday school and church services. To my father, this schedule seemed almost pagan compared with the Sabbaths of his boyhood, growing up as a minister's son. He did admit that one of the Trinity ministers of my boyhood was a bit longwinded, and, for that matter, not very interesting. This man could go on forty-five, fifty, sixty minutes. My father, engineer that he was, counted the congregation head by head and discreetly timed the sermons. Around age thirteen or so, we were finally excused from Sunday school—not church of course, but by then Trinity had called to its pulpit an eloquent and thoughtful Welshman, Dr. David Bryn-Jones. He was a Fabian Socialist and a pacifist, views not particularly congenial to the Trinity congregation. But his flock listened respectfully to sermons (twenty-five to thirty minutes) touching on Mahatma Gandhi, disarmament, social justice. There were occasional grumblings (not from my parents)—"What does this have to do with the Bible?" To Dr. Bryn-Jones, it had everything to do with the Bible.

Trinity, some years after I was squirming in the Donovan pew, dropped the "Baptist" from its name, acknowledging that it had become an interdenominational church. This pleased my liberal parents (theologically liberal, that is), but they would not have been pleased, years later still, when the dwindling Trinity congregation (having lost the elder Donovans and all their contemporaries) voted to merge with a nearby Presbyterian church. Not that they had anything against Presbyterians; indeed, the Calvinists, along with liberal "northern" Methodists (plentiful in Minneapolis), liberal Lutherans (scarce), Congregationalists, and low-church Episcopalians, made up the Elect. (My father's sister Leslie married a high-church Episcopalian clergyman; well, these things happen.) But Trinity to my parents had been an extension of their own family; they would have been stricken to see it disappear.

Devout as they were, they maintained a considerable reserve about their faith. There was much conversation around our dinner table about Trinity Church as an activity, a club in a way. Sermons were reviewed as rhetoric and for biblical scholarship. The imperfections of other faiths came up from time to time. Biblical lore was brought into play in various parlor games. But there was almost never any baring of personal belief. Though a child's questions would be answered, briefly, nobody sat around talking about God or Jesus, or reading the Bible. I got the impression that some things were just too sacred to talk about, and perhaps also that these matters had been attended to on Sunday morning.

Maybe this was why I didn't feel I should talk about it when it really hit me, perhaps age eight, that even I would die someday. It was Christmas night and my father had asked me to take some letters (he wasted no time in starting on his thank-yous) to the mailbox a couple of blocks away. It was one of those nights so clear and cold your eyes ached; millions of stars were out; where the walks hadn't been shoveled, the snow creaked underfoot. All the weeks of Christmas excitement were over, and I wondered whether I had felt this sad the previous Christmas night and the one before. For each Christmas I could remember I was now one year older, and it suddenly came to me that some Christmas night I would not be living any longer, and those stars would still be up there forever. I felt more cheerful the next morning.

It was a provincial and utterly secure childhood. We had no doubt it was better to be American than anything else (though we thought well of the English and Canadians). It was obviously much better to be Protestant than Catholic, and from Minnesota than from any other state.

We grew up with a strong sense of history—of the family, of the country—and a healthy array of prejudices. The Great War was only yesterday, and the Frontier was very recent history in the Minnesota of my parents' childhood years. For some reason the American Revolution was less in favor than the Civil War. Although both sides of the family could trace back to soldiers in the Revolution, it was considered faintly laughable that my grandmother took the DAR seriously. (My mother considered Lincoln the greatest president, Washington only runner-up because he had so many advantages.) The American Revolution was perhaps too eastern. We were anti-German and wary of Indians (American). The South was a kind of foreign country we had once defeated in a war. When my father heard that David and I had been to a revival of D. W. Griffith's *The Birth of a Nation*, he said, "That must have been pretty poor stuff." No, we said, it was exciting. But wasn't it pretty much on the side of the South, and even the Ku Klux Klan? Well, yes, sort of.

My parents were admiring of the few Jews we knew (there weren't that many to know in Minneapolis), in particular a brilliant rabbi who sometimes preached at our church. (And, as one of my Catholic-fearing aunts frequently reminded us, Christ was a Jew.) My father would occasionally lapse into a rustic style of referring to a Jew as a "Hebrew," not in hostility but more in designation of somebody foreign, even exotic, in the little towns of his boyhood—like a Greek or Arab or Chinaman. His ethnic jokes, completely clean and in wretchedly rendered dialect, tended to be about "this old German farmer" or "this young Swede" on his first visit to Minneapolis. He was told most of these jokes by his drill crews, who were mainly Scandinavian and found him a fair and friendly boss. Nobody who knew him at all would have dreamed of telling him a dirty joke, and friends who were prone to profanity tried to suppress it when they were with him.

Because of slavery and the Civil War, we had an abstract and sentimental sort of sympathy toward Negroes, although life never required us to do anything about it. Occasionally a black Southern Baptist minister might preach in our church, and over Sunday dinner the Donovans might indulge in a gentle critique. "Well," I can recall my mother commenting, "he was certainly *sincere*." Visiting black choirs and glee clubs were mightily admired for their hymn-singing prowess. Football, basketball, and baseball teams in Minnesota public schools and colleges were all-white—not because of discrimination but because of the acute shortage of blacks. There could not have been more than a few hundred blacks in Minneapolis in the early 1920s. Forty years later, visiting with Lyndon Johnson in the White House shortly after the historic passage of his Civil Rights bill, I heard him musing on the anguish of some of his fellow Southerners (and, by inference, on his own courage): "Of course you and Hubert [Humphrey] have it easy on this one—what do you folks have out there in Minneapolis, 1 or 2 percent colored?" Two percent was about right in the mid-1960s.

The closest thing to a ghetto was a neighborhood of north Minneapolis (south and southwest were the genteel directions), where several thousand Indians, mainly Sioux and Chippewa, lived. Despite Prohibition, the men there did in fact tend to get drunk on Saturday nights. This colored my teetotaling father's attitudes, none too tolerant to begin with.

Apart from affection for the uncles, aunts, and cousins condemned to live there, we were generally anti–St. Paul. The rivalry between the "Twin Cities" could be deliciously childish. The Minneapolis newspapers might report, "St. Paul Man Held in Rape," but on the other hand, "Twin Cities Man Wins Literary Award," referring to some St. Paul writer—maybe F. Scott Fitzgerald. St. Paul was older, but Minneapolis had overtaken it in population and economic muscle. St. Paul was considered "wet" during Prohibition and somewhat gamy in its politics, circumstances that my father tended to attribute to the city's sizable Irish Catholic population. The Roman Catholic cathedral in St. Paul, to his annoyance, had a dome much like that of the nearby state Capitol. He was not entirely mollified when my mother suggested both domes were much indebted to St. Peter's. The archbishop's flock also included Rhineland Germans, Bohemians, and Italians. Minneapolis, on the other hand, was heavily Scandinavian. The business and social leaders of both cities were overwhelmingly WASP. The two cities melded with each other, and together with their suburbs added up to a "metropolitan center" of perhaps a million by 1930. But with entirely separate downtowns a dozen miles apart, the feel was of two smaller places of quite distinct personalities.

My own family's social position was, I suppose, upper middle-class, though we would not have talked about it that way. My parents had many friends in the layer above, through business, church, and university connections and through my grandmother's friendships, going back to the 1860s and 1870s, with some of the girls who became the dowagers of the first and second generations of Minnesota wealth. By the time of my childhood, the Minneapolis society pages might report the doings of "Mr. So-and-So III." But any family with an income of $10,000 or $15,000 a year (and a WASP name) could become more or less instantly "socially prominent." We were not. My father never told us his salary, but from various triangulations I gathered it might be somewhere around $6,000 or $7,000.

It went a long way. We ate very well, and kept a live-in maid until the depths of the Depression. My father always wore tailor-made suits (which, to be sure, saw very long years of service). The family was not without some sense of position, it must be admitted, vis-à-vis many of our fellow Minnesotans. When my grandmother would ask who my brother or I had gone out with the previous night, she would often inquire, "Do we know her people?" Sometimes, alas, we didn't.

I never heard my parents express resentment of people who "had money" unless they just loafed around, which was not common in Minneapolis. My father especially respected wealth accumulated in mining, lumbering, and flour milling in the Minnesota of 1890–1920. My parents didn't consider their children in any way deprived because they didn't go to private school; if anything, they thought we had a bit of an edge there. They were pleased and never noticeably envious when we were invited to dinner at any of the fashionable clubs we didn't belong to, or for a few days' visit out at "the Lake"—Minnetonka—where more prosperous families kept summer houses.

The wonderful thing about social hierarchy in a Middle Western city of that day was that it was a snapshot of a moment in time, not an abiding order. I like to think that is still mainly true in America. Inherited money and position surely matter, sometimes unreasonably so, but they matter less than the urges and hunches and talents that can still propel somebody upward in a rush. My father twice came close to getting rich—once in oil, once in molybdenum. He would not have been entirely comfortable with all the consequences. My mother would have adapted more easily.

My parents disliked the idea of paying handymen for jobs the children could do perfectly well, and there was a strong presumption, furthermore, that work was good for the young. So we mowed and raked the grass ("lawn" would be an exaggeration), helped my father change screens and storm windows, helped my mother with her prodigious spring housecleaning routines, shoveled tons of snow, then spread ashes from our coal furnace on the sidewalks and the apron outside our one-car garage back by the alley. I occasionally picked up an odd job in the neighborhood in these same specialties—thus benefiting the family balance of payments. For a time I delivered groceries by bicycle on Saturday afternoons, sometimes coming home with as much as $1.50. I had earned the bike as well as a fielder's mitt by peddling the *Saturday Evening Post* door to door. Easier money was posing for B.V.D. ads, at a dollar per appearance, plus carfare, my entrée being a friend whose father worked for the Munsingwear Company. I doubt if my pictures ever made print; otherwise, the catalogs would surely be among my memorabilia.

At age twelve, I took on a more serious job, delivering the *Minneapolis Journal* every afternoon and Sunday mornings. David and I shared Route 78, about 140 customers, including a few miserable types who could make a boy come back three evenings in a row to collect the $1.05 they owed for a month of papers. The alarm clock made a hideous noise at 5 A.M. on a Sunday in February, and I felt oppressed by the paper route in general, since it tied me down every afternoon. Various substitutes filled in for me now and then, but I couldn't stay on at school often enough to work on the *West High Weekly*, or try out for teams. These would have been only intramural teams, not "varsity," because—another grievance of sorts—my parents had encouraged my skipping of those grades in grammar school. So in high school I was a fourteen-year-old sophomore with sixteen-year-old classmates—quite a gap in all departments, especially in regard to girls, in front of whom it would have been fantastically desirable to be on the hockey team.

To my father, however, my paper route looked like a very minor inconvenience compared to the daily chores of his austere boyhood. He liked to see me earn my own spending money. My last year or so on the paper route, I invested most of my earnings in Cream of Wheat common stock, a local issue he thought well of. It was in the 30s when I bought it in 1928–29, and I sold it at 7 in 1932, to help scrape together university tuition fees. I claimed to have been the youngest capitalist wiped out in the Depression.

For all the relentless housekeeping at 2412—the dusting, cleaning, polishing; the beating of rugs; the "airing-out" of this place and that—my parents had scant interest in any theoretical improvement in the decor, furniture, appliances they had started out with. An ugly lamp they had bought in 1911, for maybe $10, was still functional in 1929—why disturb it? When I much later ventured to give a lamp or a chair for a birthday, it was promptly and proudly put to use, but my parents never would have bought it themselves. Perhaps it was just a feeling there were so many other things more important.

The Donovans were intensely competitive. David and I were close enough in age to be fairly evenly matched in some games, and the accompanying arguments were very much a part of the sport. We had some gift for co-inventing games—two of our favorite creations were "Football-on-Ice" (doubtless invented over the years by thousands of other Minnesota boys) and the "Naval Splash Fight," with an elaborate scoring system rich in possibilities for controversy. David and I wrangled more or less continuously for years. My father got so tired of listening to us that he bought us boxing gloves and sent us down to the basement whenever the decibel level got too high. I got in some pretty good pokes; I somehow cared more. It was not until we were young men at the university together, and fraternity brothers, that we became good friends. We began to put away a good deal of beer together, and sometimes double-dated.

Elizabeth and I were closer from the beginning, and competitive only at indoor games. She was timid about dogs, and for a couple of years was allowed to walk to school with me, though I required her to keep several paces to the rear, lest any of my friends think we were *together*. I find in my diary a callous entry: "Shoved Liz in a few snowbanks." We spent endless hours together, playing cards, working on my stamp collection (she was content to be secretary), and treating each other to sodas and sundaes at Brodie's drugstore.

My parents never played favorites. They were unfailingly "supportive" (jargon they would not have used) of us all and, what is perhaps less common, courteous to us, respectful of a child's privacy, and willing to let us be different from each other and from themselves. (As a result, perhaps, we tried to be quite a bit like them.) They were proud, but not gushy, about good report cards and other childhood triumphs. My father could be stern once in a while, especially if money was being misspent. The harshest thing my mother could bring herself to say, and it was very effective, was that she was "disappointed."

The affection was expressed more in action, atmosphere, and tone of voice than in words face-to-face. In their letters, however, the tenderness was unrestrained. My father was a classic letter writer from out of the nineteenth century. He was warm and sentimental in correspondence—not just with his wife and children, but with his numerous brothers and sisters, and their spouses and children, for whom he became, by longevity and love of letter writing, Donovan Central. They all wrote back, of course, and we children were encouraged to pitch in. (He loathed long-distance sociabilities over the phone, and if trapped into such, tended to shout, irritably. People were wasting money, at one end of the line or the other, and it wasn't really satisfactory "visiting" anyway.)

One of the doting aunts sent my father a brisk letter I had written her when I was six. He was a great saver of family memorabilia (also of string, literally). So, being my father's son, I still possess this letter: "Dear Eddy [a familiarity that would not have been allowed a little later] I want to send you a letter and I would like to send you a letter and here it is I must stop now Love from Hedley." It was Aunt Eddy, whom we often visited in the pretty little town of Redwood Falls, Minnesota, who said, "I like to see a boy *eat*." I frequently gave her that satisfaction. David and Elizabeth had certain things they wouldn't eat, and my father was notorious for a long list of dishes he wouldn't touch. So it was a matter of rejoicing that Hedley would eat anything, and the aunts and uncles were generous in their praise. Perhaps too generous, it occurred to me in my fifties and sixties.

Not all the aunts and uncles were college graduates, but they knew the Bible and the Book of Common Prayer, *Pilgrim's Progress*, Milton, and Shakespeare. The literacy of their letters would shame some of my recent graduate students at the John F. Kennedy School of Government, Harvard University.

In a show of hands once in grade school, I was embarrassed to be the only child whose parents were both university graduates. (In Minnesota today, I am sure my schoolmates and I would be protected by some law from any such invasion of privacy.) As a child, I was observant enough to know my parents were very smart, and various adults also told me so. I was impressed when some of these family friends said my father really ought to be governor or president; he was brighter than President Harding (true enough), then brighter than President Coolidge, then at least as bright as Herbert Hoover. My father and his fellow mining engineer Hoover, whom he greatly admired, might have been a tie in brains, both excellent, and in popular political appeal, both deficient.

I would call my mother an intellectual by the rather liberal definition proposed in the previous chapter, an intellectual turned housewife. I prize a little red morocco notebook of hers, the journal of a very sensitive and perceptive young woman of twenty-one seeing Europe for the first time. Literary England—the Poets' Corner in Westminster Abbey, Stratford, Wordsworth's Lake Country—moved her deeply. She knew a good deal about the art and architecture she was looking at, certainly more than I did when I first went to Europe. Hers was the Victorian Grand Tour (just the summer after the queen died): steamer trunks packed with enough clothes for four months away from home, my mother chaperoned by her mother; also in the party were two female cousins and an Aunt Sadie and a prosperous Uncle Jake. (I think he was treating.) There are some sharp little asides in the journal: The horses on Rotten Row in Hyde Park "looked beautiful and highly bred. I can't say as much for the ladies riding them." And there is a poignant note struck more than once: In Paris or Venice or Florence, she goes back one last time to some museum for a last look at a particular Botticelli or Rubens or da Vinci, in case she never gets back to Europe again. Alas, it was a wise precaution.

My father's mind had a greater logic and precision; hers was wider ranging, more attracted by challenge, more hospitable to the new. I would say he was not quite an intellectual, a ruling that would not have troubled him. His superb memory was widely celebrated in the Longyear Company, at the church, among friends and family. David also had a fabulous memory and was fond of quoting some psychologist as saying that memory was synonymous with intelligence. I tended to think of my mother, Elizabeth, and myself as having respectably good but not sensational recall. So I was surprised at the *Washington Post* and in the U.S. Navy, but most especially in Time Inc., among so many people who had been so well informed so many years, to find I was considered someone to settle bets. But I do think there is an ability (or it's worth cultivating) to slough off a lot of stuff that comes into your head today that you know isn't going to matter tomorrow—and imprint an extra time or two the things that might matter longer, or are simply fun to know.

Some University of Minnesota professor studying selected Minneapolis families settled down in our living room one evening and gave us all I.Q. tests. I gathered we came out well, though the children weren't told the numbers. In school, David and I got mainly A's and Elizabeth nothing else. At West High School, I had some problems with French (one C) and physics (one B) and terminal difficulties with chemistry. I didn't mind the smells, but at the end of only two weeks, I grasped that each day built on the one before, and that I had lost the thread at about Day 4. I somehow wangled a transfer to biology, where things were more comprehensible.

We all loved words. My mother had taught us each to read before we went to kindergarten. As we grew up and she had a little more spare time, she wrote lovely poetry, some published in the local papers, and gave book and play reviews and creative-writing classes in women's clubs in Minneapolis and St. Paul. Her potboilers, so to speak, were comedies suitable for amateur dramatic groups: *Rummage to Rhythm*, *Meeting to Music*, and others in like vein—spoofs of the school and church clubs that were performing them. They were published by the Samuel French Company—in New York!—and the pleasant little royalty checks kept coming for years. My father sold several roadside jingles to Burma Shave, at $100 a jingle. We were all delighted when we came upon one of his verses spaced out along a Minnesota highway, the punch line always being something like "Until he got wise and used Burma Shave" (after earlier business or romantic disappointments). Otherwise, my father had very little poetry in him. He was an excellent reporter, observant and clear and direct in style. His letters, reports to his company, and even papers for professional journals were full of vivid descriptive detail and nice touches of wit. He was addicted to detective stories. Mother (a much faster reader) liked those, too, but also read new fiction, drama, serious works of theology. The house was full of magazines: the *Saturday Evening Post*; the old *Life* (the gentle weekly humor magazine whose name was bought by Henry Luce for his *Life*); the *Literary Digest*, later destroyed by its 1936 poll showing Alf Landon defeating Franklin Roosevelt; the *Saturday Review of Literature* (my mother devoured the Double Crostics); the *Atlantic Monthly*; *Boy's Life*; *American Boy*; and *The New Yorker* and *Time* soon after they started up.

My brother and I sometimes corresponded in a tolerable imitation of early *Time*-speak. When I went to work for Time Inc., Dave (another string saver) gave me a birthday letter I had written him a quarter-century earlier. "Ever since a beet-red David Donovan was sharply spanked [a bit of obstetrical lore I had picked up from *Time*], pronounced male. . . ." And so on.

The magazines were habit-forming. I also read more history books and biography than school demanded. When we had all finished some detective story, and it was duly returned to the public library, we would discuss who had guessed right, and whether the denouement was "fair."

I first had the thrill of seeing my own words in print when I was about ten, and landed a few items in the *Colfax Parrot*, which was run by a neighborhood boy who had a miniature printing press in his basement. This success could have been a textbook case of improper pressure on editors, because I was in fact an advertiser in the *Parrot*. My friend Ev Helm and I had founded the Helm and Donovan Stamp and Stone Company, and we ran ads in the *Parrot* offering stock in our company at ten cents a share. We took in two dollars or so from the senior Helms and Donovans and friends of theirs, before Ev's father told us we might have to register our issue at the state Capitol.

I began to get published more regularly in the *Jeffersonian*, my junior–high school paper, and in fact rose to the rank of assistant editor. When I was elected to a Rhodes scholarship, the paper reminisced: "He knew that school is a workshop; so he was governed accordingly. He wasted no time, completed assignments, was punctual, in fact he was cooperative. As a result of this splendid fundamental work . . ." etc. I suspect this treacly item was the work of a teacher rather than a legitimate student journalist. The *Jeffersonian* was respectful but less effusive when I became editor-in-chief of Time Inc. Under a headline reading "Reporter Steps Up," the paper said, "Hedley Donovan was selected home room reporter by his class for the *Jeffersonian* the first year that Mr. McRae sponsored it. Because of his fine contribution the first semester he was selected as Assistant Editor the second semester. Just recently Mr. Donovan was named Editor-in-Chief of the Time-Life corporation." End of item.

At eleven, I wrote a letter of six pages single-spaced (as later copied by my father's secretary, for distribution to all defenseless relatives) describing a camping trip back and forth across the Continental Divide, traveling by Model T Ford and sleeping in a tent. This was a special treat planned by Aunt Mary and Uncle Nat, whom David and I visited for one summer in Colorado. Uncle Nat ran a general store there in the little town of Florence, and we were allowed to do some clerking, which seemed more like fun than work, especially since Uncle Nat couldn't resist giving us a bit of the merchandise from time to time. Aunt Mary was my favorite aunt (a very tough call), and I think my father's favorite sister, though he never would have revealed any such ranking. She was a pert, sparkly, playful woman (she looked a little like Helen Hayes)—never solemn, as my father could be—a bright graduate of Carleton College in Northfield, Minnesota. Uncle Nat was not a good driver, as I noticed in the Rocky Mountains, and all of us were devastated when he and Mary were killed in an automobile accident a dozen years later.

The Colorado trip was my first venture out of Minnesota, not counting bits of Wisconsin very close to Minneapolis. Dave and I took the thirty-six-hour train trip alone, armed with notes to conductors and Pullman porters and a $5 tip for each night. The second night out, I was too excited to sleep much; I got up at dawn and saw the peaks of my first mountains begin to break the horizon.

Along with letter writing, diary keeping, and schoolboy journalism, there were occasional ventures into the short story. A powerful work of this period, "Garner, Dog of the North," related the adventures of a mineral prospector in Canada, and the timely help his dog gave him in dealing with some runaway criminals as well as a bear. My own children once came across the manuscript and insisted on reading various passages aloud; they professed to find "Garner" hilarious, but I think they were secretly jealous.

I was about ten when I decided, as so many people do, to write a whole book. The plot revolved around long-ago smuggling between England and France. I'd been slogging away for eight or ten pages and was beginning to run into trouble, so I consulted my mother. What would be a good thing to smuggle? What would the ladies have been wearing in those days? How fast could a horse go a hundred miles? Things like that. My mother listened in a polite way and then gave me some excellent literary advice: When you write a book, it's a good idea to choose a subject you know something about. This made such a lasting impression that I didn't try a book again until I was sixty-seven.

My father was loyal and conscientious to the ends of the earth, and famously honest, to the last decimal of a penny. He had only two character defects (my mother had none). He could be grimly censorious about people whose moral code was less rigorous than his own and unfeeling about misfortunes he felt they had brought upon themselves. He suffered from a certain lack of Christian charity. The other flaw was that he was a bad loser at games. What with all the bridge, Mah-Jongg, hearts, "Guggenheims" (categories), Canfield, Twenty Questions, Parcheesi, Checkers, and charades going on at 2412, there had to be some losers at something almost every evening. At bridge it was his general conviction that given a decent partner and a halfway even break in the cards, he *ought* to win. It was unwise for anyone (especially my grandmother) to say it's only a game. And I can remember him sulking all through one Saturday evening because Michigan (through a fluke, to be sure) had beaten Minnesota at football, 7–6. Whoever first said, "Show me a good loser and I'll show you a loser" (recent scholarship suggests it was not Leo Durocher), would have liked his attitude. On into their late eighties, I could hear him complaining about my mother's luck at Scrabble. When my sister, Elizabeth, beats me these days at backgammon, as she usually does, and I groan about the incredible dice she always throws, she will say fondly, "Oh, you remind me so much of Daddy."

My parents each had a well-tuned sense of humor, and they encouraged youthful sallies at being funny. When I was six or so, my father told me the first joke I ever heard, and I still like it. First man: "Has your wife been entertaining this winter?" Second man: "Not very." Life was real and life was earnest, all right, but the Donovans also found plenty to laugh about.

We were all fans of the great Hollywood comedians of the 1920s, Chaplin and Keaton, Harry Langdon, and, above all, Harold Lloyd. My father, flouting all his frugal instincts, went *twice* to some Harold Lloyd movies. Happily, my parents were as infatuated with the movies as their children. There were seven first-run theaters in downtown Minneapolis, and two neighborhood houses within walking distance. We saw Westerns, epics, murder mysteries, all faithfully added up in my diary at the end of a year: twenty-five movies in 1926, twenty-seven in 1927. Of *The Little Shepherd of Kingdom Come*, the diary says, "Better than it sounds." Somewhere about that period there had come a breakthrough when my father lifted his previous prohibition of Sunday moviegoing. The ban on Sabbath cardplaying had already gone; as soon as I learned to play bridge, David already having learned, 2412 had its own built-in game. Then, too, road-show theatrical companies would come to Minneapolis for a stand of a week or two, and we were taken to plays such as *Merton of the Movies* and *Seventeen*, and also, for my mother, the real stuff: *Macbeth* and *Merchant of Venice*.

My father was a Republican regular of regulars. I don't think in his seventy-odd years of voting he was ever remotely tempted by any Democratic candidate for any office. But for a man of such fixed views, he was remarkably mild in asserting them, and particularly tolerant of political deviations in his children. We were encouraged to hold forth about politics and public issues, and no views were thrown out of court just because you were only thirteen. My father was even forgiving when my mother dropped sly hints she might have voted for Franklin Roosevelt against Alf Landon in 1936. Roosevelt had done "*some* good things," I later heard her say, and though Governor Landon seemed to be a fine man, was he really qualified? She would never say for sure.

My parents were Puritans, in a sense, about sex, generally embarrassed about the subject with young children, but also lovingly encouraging to adolescents groping toward growing up. I was told how babies are born when I was about five, and how they are conceived when I was about eight. My parents didn't volunteer this information; it was drawn out under questioning. I took their word for all this, though for several years I couldn't understand *why* a man and a woman (especially my parents!) would be willing to do such a thing, even if they did want to have children. The grand insight—

that God had arranged for it to be fun—came to me in school one day when I was about twelve. The ostensible subject of the hour was Latin, but I was actually studying a girl named Harriet, a ripe thirteen or so. She had been sitting just a couple of desks away for months, but suddenly that morning she seemed very noticeable. Everything made sense. Latin, as people were always saying, was a splendid foundation. Presiding over our class was Miss Mildred Blank (really), surprisingly young and good-looking for a schoolteacher and given to surprisingly low-cut dresses. Boys often found it necessary to go to her desk for help with a difficult text. At about the same time, I reported in my diary a midyear addition to the ninth grade of "around 15 homely girls." Only a few days later, however, a cryptic entry: "Girls not so bad."

Also about then, my parents forced me to attend dancing school. Secretly, I came to like dancing school, and especially a beautiful girl named Rosemary, the best dancer in the class. She allowed me to walk her home once or twice, and I considered that I was in love. I never got up the courage to ask her to the movies. One evening forty years later, her face came back to me. I was on a flight from Honolulu to Los Angeles, sitting with Bernhard Auer, the publisher of *Time*, and I told him that the lovely creature serving our cocktails looked exactly like my first love. The next time she came back, Bernie, with his bold salesman ways, asked where she was from, and she said originally from Minneapolis. Bernie beamed. "Why, so is Mr. Donovan!" She showed a gracious interest in this none-too-remarkable coincidence. I forged on, "Is your mother by any chance named Rosemary?" She froze and said, "Yes, but my mother doesn't run around." End of true ghost story.

My father had a gallant style with the ladies and a sharp eye for good looks—as an usher in church, in the little dancing club he and my mother belonged to, and with the girls (and eventually the wives) my brother and I brought home. He was flirtatious in an utterly innocent way. I once urged him to go to a certain coffee shop at the Chicago World's Fair, which I had just visited and he was about to visit, simply to see the dazzling redhaired waitress who worked there. He did, and reported by postcard that she was everything I had claimed, but he couldn't say much for the food.

I graduated from West High School a couple of weeks after I turned sixteen. In my picture in the yearbook, I look about twelve, though the line under the photo—one of those yearbook literary motifs was at work—says, "And he looks quite through the deeds of men" (*Julius Caesar*, Act I, Sc. 2). My date at the Senior Prom was Betty Cobb: "She moves a goddess and looks a queen" (*Iliad*, Bk. III).

The University of Minnesota in the early 1930s was another favored time and place. To be sure, I would have liked to be taking the Pullman to Chicago and Boston, to go to Harvard, instead of taking the trolley, one morning in September 1930, to register as a Minnesota freshman. My parents and I thought Harvard the best university in the country, my father's Columbia perhaps the runner-up; Yale and Princeton seemed a bit unserious, a sketchy impression based on some of the Minneapolis alumni we knew. But these were idle rankings, since my family could not afford to send me "East."

The University of Minnesota at the time was among the four or five state universities included on most lists of the ten or twelve best American universities. There were a number of small private colleges in Minnesota, several very good, but no private university. "The University" (everybody knew which) was the dominant institution in the state, more important than any corporation or bank. There was no single religious institution (the Lutherans, by definition, had no Vatican) as important. Education was indeed the secular religion of Minnesota, and the university stood at the pinnacle of the faith.

The tone of the campus was earnest and industrious, like the state itself—in part, no doubt, the effect of all the Scandinavian and German genes; in part, perhaps, a product of the character-building climate. Anybody who was up and moving about anywhere in Minnesota on a January morning was, in a Darwinian sense, among the fittest. The Legislature believed that every child in this blessed state deserved a chance to go on to the university; the only admission requirement was a diploma from a Minnesota high school. This academic egalitarianism went only so far. The taxpayers having given them their chance, the slower students were flunked out by the hundreds during freshman year. Total enrollment was somewhere around twelve thousand, then one of the biggest in the country.

Per dollar, the education was unbeatable. Tuition was $135 in my freshman year. I lived at home and, through family and friends, could get part-time jobs that would have been much harder to find elsewhere. Perhaps half the students were trying to "work their way through." I did so mainly by tutoring.

Economies became more urgent as the Depression deepened. For many months in 1931–32, the E. J. Longyear Company had virtually no work; nobody explores for new mineral deposits when existing mines are closing down. I remember my father reluctantly asking me not to buy a new suit I had admired, telling me that he had taken a series of cuts that brought him down to 30 percent of his 1929 salary. He was deeply wounded by the Depression, as were so many self-reliant and frugal Americans. It wasn't just the cuts in his income, or worse, the hardships of the Longyear men who had to be laid off. It was the breakdown of a system he believed in.

But at the university, it was a kind of Hard Times Golden Age. The Depression injected an urgent contemporary content into academic studies of history, politics, economics. Minnesota seemed to amplify and anticipate some national political trends. The old strain of agrarian radicalism merged, as unemployment grew, with the new discontents in the cities and on the iron range. But Minnesota had also been one of the most stoutly Republican of all Middle Western states (it never went for a Democratic presidential candidate until 1932), and the forces of conservatism—cultural, political, economic—were still very strong. For the politically conscious students, there was a lot to listen to. And they could stimulate each other (and alarm their elders) in an extracurricular welter of panels, conferences, protest meetings.

Yet, along with all the scrimping, and all the intellectual seething, the "collegiate" spirit was still very much alive. The rah-rah mood of the late 1920s had faded only a little. Fraternities and sororities still mattered greatly. My father was delighted, despite the expense, when my brother and I were both asked to join his old fraternity, Delta Upsilon. (As "legacies," we almost had to be asked.) I experienced the traditional rigors and indignities of Hell Week before initiation, and the next year the chapter voted to abolish it. I voted to abolish it and was also proud to have gone through it. In each of my college years, I spent almost as much on fraternity dues and parties as on tuition and books. All sorts of clubs and dormitory councils and "honor societies" put on tea dances, "smokers," and get-togethers. There were black-tie Junior Proms and Senior Proms, and the men leading the Grand March were expected to turn out in white tie and tails. By tradition, at least a few men would wear their formal costume to class the morning after a prom. There were the equally traditional pajama parades and pep rallies. The fraternities and sororities all had their own rounds of dances—informal in the chapter house, formal at a hotel or country club—and in the spring, weekend house parties at some lake resort. The parties were all officially dry until the repeal of Prohibition in December 1933, but in dark corners and parked cars there might be swigs of "moon" or the almost equally lethal spiked beer—pure alcohol procured by some medical student and poured into the neck of a near-beer bottle. The university even maintained a polo team in the depths of the Depression (subsidized, to be sure, by the War Department, via the ROTC).

I arrived at the university with no set ideas about a career. Some years earlier, as I got past the stage of wanting to be a motorcycle policeman, my parents would occasionally suggest I might be a minister. I thought not, and they didn't persist. My father never pressed his own profession on me; I admired it but preferred to think of geology as a possible hobby. I was vaguely attracted to architecture, and less vaguely to law. I had always liked to draw the district attorney role when we played "Murder" at home or in Scout camp. My scoutmaster, a lawyer, had even told me I had a good legal mind. But I can remember sitting in the University of Minnesota library on a lovely April afternoon in my sophomore year, the girls finally dressed for spring, and sensing that I didn't want to read all those thick tan-and-black books piled up in front of a law student I knew.

What I did like to read, most of all, was history. I had some superb professors in history (chauvinists claimed the Minnesota department of that day was second only to Harvard): Ernest Osgood on the West in American History, Lawrence Steefel and Harold Deutsch in Modern European, and Herbert Heaton, a witty, English economic historian. Admiring these men so much—respected scholars as well as effective teachers—I aspired to become a history professor.

My minor was political science. I didn't then perceive the pretentiousness ("science" indeed!), of the name but I lapped up the content—politics and government. To think they gave credits for letting you study this! I especially liked a lively iconoclast named Benjamin Lippincott, who seemed only a little older than his students; in fact, he married one of them. Ben was accused by a couple of state senators of being a Communist. He explained to the president of our university, who bore the splendid name of Lotus Delta Coffman, that no, he was a "Social Democrat." Dr. Coffman, more sensitive to this nuance than the senators, solemnly asked him to sign an affidavit to that effect. Ben did. Why not?

Another man I admired on the political science faculty was Harold Quigley, one of the first serious American scholars in Japanese and Chinese political institutions—the audacity of this specialty, for that time and place, cloaked by a shy and formal classroom style. I enrolled in one of his courses in Far Eastern government, in innocent curiosity about the subject, and this would turn out within a year to have a considerable influence on the rest of my life.

While Professor Quigley and the others were paid to teach me, I was learning almost as much from the college newspaper, the *Minnesota Daily*. I wrote editorials for the *Daily*—about 275 of them in four years. It was "The World's Largest College Daily," because all students were perforce subscribers; the paper came with the registration fee. A fraternity brother who was on the *Daily* recruited me as a freshman to write editorials; I rose in the paper's hierarchy and became assistant editorial chairman, then editorial chairman (in charge of the editorial page) in my senior year. That job even paid a salary—a useful $25 a month.

We were moved often to write on international affairs and American political and economic issues, and I must admit some of the stuff still reads rather well today. We took a generally boosterish stance on the university and university events and teams. Certain officials of the administration—in particular the prim-looking Dean of Men, E. E. Nicholson, and the formidable Anna Dudley Blitz, Dean of Women—tended to appear in our columns as figures of fun. Anna Blitz was famous for snatching cigarettes from the lips of students walking about the campus. I can't remember whether this was an enforcement of some rule or whether perhaps the Dean was way ahead of her time. Some of our wit was witty, some was ponderous. We could be smug and preachy, even as some grown-up editorial pages.

I landed one editorial on a grown-up page in April 1932. I had written a piece tweaking New York Governor Franklin Roosevelt for refusing to admit he was trying to get himself nominated for president. From the eminence of my seventeen years, I commended to FDR the candor of his fellow Democrat Albert Ritchie, governor of Maryland, who was quoted as saying, "Sure I'd like to be president, who wouldn't?" The editor of the *Minnesota Daily* thought this was too partisan for a state-university paper. I mentioned the episode to my father, who mentioned it to Carl Jones, the publisher of the very Republican *Minneapolis Journal*, while they were riding downtown on the streetcar. Mr. Jones said he'd like to see this piece of mine, and the next day he published it as his lead editorial, word for word. For days I kept expecting some check in the mail, $10 maybe, but the *Journal* apparently felt I had simply performed a young man's civic duty. FDR was president when I became chairman of the *Daily* editorial page, and we took an admiring line about most of his policies and about the tonic effect of his personality.

We published many editorials of a generally pacifist persuasion. I was strongly under the sway of "revisionist" historians who argued that all the major European powers, not just Germany, were to blame for the war of 1914–18. Even America, through its international banks and munitions makers, bore part of the guilt. And through the films and novels of this period—and the influence of some of my professors and perhaps of the Reverend Bryn-Jones—I saw the Great War as pointless slaughter, settling nothing, sowing the seeds of another war. But I was also fascinated by that war, I have to confess, *as a war*. Professor Deutsch gave a remarkable seminar for a dozen of us on how the war worked—the railroad capacities that governed the mobilization timetables; the structure of a division, army by army; the quality of the commanding generals. Some were stupid butchers, but not all; try to know which ones you're talking about.

The national pacifist mood was reinforced in Minnesota by the traditional isolationism of the Middle West and the provincial Protestant millenarianism. I remember a speech at the university given by Frank Kellogg, of St. Paul, former secretary of state, Nobel Prize–winner and the principal author of the Paris Pact of 1929, duly signed by sixty-two nations, which he sincerely believed had outlawed war for all time. It was now 1934, the Japanese had taken over Manchuria, and there was talk of trade sanctions or quarantine against them. A student got up and asked if there was a danger of war. "There is no more chance of war with Japan," Kellogg said, "than a war with Timbuktu."

I was not a conscientious objector. In 1933, the Oxford Union took its famous stand "that this House in no circumstances will fight for King or country." The "Oxford Resolution," which was later said to have helped convince Hitler that the British ruling class had gone soft, quickly crossed the Atlantic and was debated on many American campuses, including Minnesota ("flag" replacing "King"). I voted against. I argued in a *Daily* editorial that "Thinking persons . . . would be loath to surrender the right to fight in any strictly non-aggressive war for self-defense." We all got a chance, as it turned out—the young men of England a couple of years sooner than the Americans.

Those of us who were intensely interested in political issues were perhaps 10 percent of the student body—up from 5 percent, I would have guessed, in the more tranquil twenties. One indicator was attendance at the Students Forum, which put on weekly speeches on public issues by various professors, politicians, agitators. I was chairman of the forum in my senior year, and we bragged that total attendance in 1933–34 was 30 percent higher than in any previous year. Our meetings sometimes drew audiences of a thousand. That was the turnout for Minnesota's magnetic Governor Floyd Olson, leader of the Farmer Labor party, which stood well to the left of the New Deal. (The 1936 platform of the Farmer Labor party began, "Whereas capitalism has failed . . .") The unmagnetic Republican Senator Thomas Schall also packed them in, and was lustily booed for references to "The National Ruin Act" (the NRA) and "Frankenstein Roosevelt."

I arranged pro and con speeches on Hitler, and these also were SRO. Finding a Hitler apologist was not easy, but Baron René de Staël was game. He was my most exotic friend, one of the "Baltic barons," descendants of Swedish and Prussian nobility who had settled in the Baltic provinces of Imperial Russia. René had fought in the czarist army in the Great War, then with the Whites in the Civil War, and eventually wound up as a graduate student at the University of Minnesota and a tutor in German. He was kin to various princely families of Germany, including the Hohenzollerns, and to Madame de Staël of the salon. He had an aristocratic disdain for the manners and origins of the Nazis, but he believed that only a strong Germany could save Europe from Bolshevism. At the forum, he was calm under heckling, and an audience that thought he was talking dangerous nonsense rather admired his courage. I was about ready to close down the questioning and let our speaker escape, when a man stood up and demanded, "What would happen if Jesus Christ came to Germany today?" René said, "I don't know. What would happen if He came to Minneapolis?" René got a small smattering of applause for this, and it seemed a good place to adjourn.

Among the junta that ran the forum, the staff of the *Minnesota Daily*, and various other campus groups of political bent, there was extensive overlap. The *Minnesota Daily* editorial columns had a tendency to speak well of other organizations in which I was involved. Among my friends from that era were Phil Potter, managing editor of the *Daily*, later the distinguished White House correspondent for the *Baltimore Sun*; Eric Sevareid (Arnold Sevareid in those days), who wrote the best-read feature in the *Daily*, a chatty column called "Bubbles off the Beaker"; Bill Costello, who wrote an incredibly erudite series of ten editorials on the gold standard, not the best-read feature in the paper; and Dick Scammon, a gargantuan fellow with an insatiable appetite for elections. When Boss Scammon and I were arranging for my election as chairman of the forum, we had in hand at least fifteen votes on the twenty-member committee, but Dick couldn't resist calling the election for a day when one of the other five, a spirited leftist lady, was going to be in New York attending, as he said, some "Young Stalinist" rally. Dick was much more liberal than I, but implacable toward Communists, of whom we might have had two dozen at most on the whole campus. He went on to become the leading U.S. authority on historical voting patterns.

The social fault lines on the campus ran between those politically minded students and everybody else; between students from the Twin Cities (Duluth was borderline) and those from the smaller towns and farms; and between "the Greeks" and the large majority who did not belong to fraternities or sororities. But "class" behavior was not predictable. During a bloody Teamsters strike in 1934, by the famous Trotskyite Local 544, a delegation of young Minneapolis businessmen appeared at a meeting called by the Intrafraternity Council to try to convince fraternity men to join the special deputies who were riding trucks running the picket lines. The "Greeks" were notably unenthusiastic about this opportunity, and furthermore rebuked the Intrafraternity Council for dabbling in the strike. I was among many who spoke to this effect and couldn't resist asking, "Are you going to hold a meeting for 544?" Because of the strike, the liberal-to-leftish *Minnesota Daily* lamented, with no ironic intent, that "students preparing for one of the busiest social weekends of this year" (just before Senior Prom) couldn't get their tuxedos and dress shirts back from the dry cleaner.

All social, political, ethnic, and religious elements were in passionate agreement on the importance of Minnesota's winning at football. In my editorial-writing role, I could virtuously deplore "overemphasis" in big-time college athletics, or even manage a gallant editorial compliment to a team that had beaten Minnesota fair and square. But there was no denying that it felt very good walking along Fraternity Row from the stadium to the D. U. house, milling with happy friends, when the Gophers (pitiful nickname) had beaten the Badgers (Wisconsin), the Hawkeyes (Iowa), or, above all, the hated Wolverines (Michigan). The university football team had an extraordinary hold on the loyalties and emotions of the whole state of Minnesota in the 1920s and 1930s. If the university was the single most important institution in the state, unifying and almost venerated, the football team was its flag. It was a powerful legend, of a sort that still flourishes in some states in the South, but now vanquished in

Minnesota by the arrival of the Vikings, the pros; perhaps by some advances in general sophistication; perhaps also, it must be admitted, by the university's long string of mediocre-to-dreadful teams.

In the physical exam for entering freshmen, a doctor asked each of us what sports we were interested in. A skinny sixteen, six feet and 140 pounds, I modestly said I might try out for football. Perhaps I thought I was taking the Oath of Allegiance. The doctor looked at me again, paused, and said, "You'd get killed." Another pause, and then: "I mean that." I did get plenty of exercise, however, playing for my fraternity's teams—ice hockey, touch football, tennis, baseball. The D. U. hockey team would in fact have been a respectable varsity at a middling-size college (south of Canada).

Midway through my junior year, I realized I was in danger of graduating too soon. The university gave extra course credits for A's and B's, and I had been collecting enough of these to get my degree in three years.* I was planning a run at a Rhodes scholarship, and I figured my credentials would be improved by my elevation to chairman of the Students Forum and editorial chairman of the *Daily*—both assured if I stayed for a senior year. My parents were a little shocked at my audacity, but I cut down my course load enough to make sure I couldn't graduate.

The Rhodes steeplechase was something to satisfy the most competitive soul. First, a candidate had to compete for a nomination from his own institution—the University of Minnesota was entitled to five nominees. The five then competed against the nominees of the private colleges of Minnesota and against Minnesota men attending MIT, say, or Dartmouth, who figured the competition in their home state would not be as tough as in the New England district. In my year, a field of twelve candidates was narrowed down to two nominees for the state of Minnesota. These then went up against the two semifinalists from each of five other Upper Middle Western states—twelve excited young men trying for four Rhodes scholarships. A selection committee, mainly Rhodes scholars of previous years, saw us in separate

---

*I was elected to Phi Beta Kappa in the spring of my junior year. My sister Elizabeth also became a junior-year Phi Bete at Minnesota. We agreed not to lord it over people who weren't let in until senior year. My brother David was elected to the equivalent honors fraternity in the Business School. My father had been Sigma Xi, the honors society in engineering. Mother claimed she would have been Phi Beta Kappa except for missing some classes during her long European trip. No way of knowing, Elizabeth and I would tell her.

interrogations over a very long day in Des Moines. One committee member was Harold Quigley, the university's Far Eastern authority, and from another member I came to know later, I gathered that Quigley had been a stout friend in court. Another committee member had been irritated by the brevity of many of my answers (especially when he asked me why I read *The New Yorker*, and I said, "It's funny."). Quigley apparently persuaded him that I was not being rude but just from Minnesota.

I had a very pleasant senior year, carrying only one course and being a Big Man on Campus. After I became a Rhodes scholar, I became a still Bigger BMOC. Now it was safe to graduate, and I did in June 1934, magna cum laude, short of summa by two B's and one C (French again). The new B.A.s proceeded across the football field to the Triumphal March from *Aida*, which I still like.

III

Oxford

On a morning in September of 1934, at the Greyhound Bus terminal in Minneapolis, my parents saw me off for what we all understood to be three years—the term of the Rhodes scholarship. The family finances were most unlikely to permit them a visit to me, or me a vacation trip home—except at the sacrifice of some opportunity to see more of Europe, which they (and I) would have thought quite wrong. In the years I was in England, it did bother me when prosperous friends of my family, who had been urged to look me up on their European trips, wrote my parents glowing reports on my diligence as a tour guide. I always wished I were showing Oxford to my father and mother. But at the bus station in Minneapolis that morning, they put on a splendid show of Donovan reserve, in contrast with the parents of Everett Helm—taking the same bus, only going so far as Harvard, and only for a year—who carried on in extravagantly emotional style. Indeed, I wrote my parents to thank them for their restraint and also for refraining from any farewell advice—for declining (a pretty display of my mastery of *Hamlet*) "the Polonius role."

When my bus crossed into Indiana, I was east of Chicago for the first time in my life, and when, many tedious hours later, I arrived at my brother's apartment on Ferry Street in the oldest quarter of Schenectady (he had gone to work for General Electric), I was for the first time in eighteenth-century America. A few days later, visiting in the garret of what was reputed to be the oldest house in Cambridge, Massachusetts, I was even lodged, to my discomfort, in the seventeenth century. I went on to New York and found the famous sights almost familiar, one by one, and the place on the whole barely believable.

I met my fellow Rhodes scholars of the class of 1934, and on a rainy Saturday evening we sailed for England on the *Transylvania*, a small liner of the old White Star–Anchor service. We stood at the rail to watch the lights of Long Island retreat and then decided that the first Atlantic swells were no reason not to eat dinner. Three evenings later, a spectacular sunset turned the October sky an intense coppergreen, and Cape Race, Newfoundland, floated for a few magic minutes as a black line above the distant western horizon, a last look at North America.

I am still grateful that my first crossing of the Atlantic took so long. The excitement built: Finally, eight days out, landfall off Londonderry, Northern Ireland, then the next morning the *Transylvania* docked amid the splendid smells and noises of Liverpool harbor. (How vastly more dramatic than today's approach to Heathrow, barely one bad meal and one bad movie away from JFK.) From Liverpool, the last lap was by toy train through brilliant countryside—Cheshire, Shropshire, Warwickshire, Oxfordshire, the autumn weather on its best behavior—to the first glimpse of those celebrated spires.

I liked Oxford right from the start. I had been well briefed by older Rhodes scholars back in Minnesota on the various shortcomings of Oxford food, plumbing, heating; on the challenges of the climate and the standoffishness of the English. Some of my American contemporaries were surprisingly ill-informed about these matters and remained vexed for months that Oxford was so unlike their hometowns and native universities. A few never did forgive Oxford.

I was wise enough to know I was beginning a once-in-a-lifetime experience. I even counted, by the three academic terms a year, all through my time at Oxford: only two (three) terms used up, seven (six) still to go. Basically, I was being paid to have a good time. (That was also true of my later life in journalism, but journalism is much harder work than Oxford.) The Rhodes scholarship paid £400 a year, close to $2,000 at the $4.89 exchange rate of that day. Not lavish by the rather special perspective of Oxford, admiring as it was of aristocratic extravagances, but a comfortable income for a bachelor student at the prices of fifty years ago—and certainly so by comparison with the Minneapolis economy I had just left. Rhodes scholars were treated as guest members of the gentry, and were much entertained at elegant balls in London, at theater-supper parties, for weekends and longer in the country. At least a few of our hostesses, under the harmless delusion that all Americans were rich, thought we were especially suitable escorts for their daughters. It must be recorded that little came of all the careful arrangement of place cards, at least in terms of matrimony.

I had the redoubtable stamina of age twenty for marathon parties, two-day third-class rail trips across Europe, whatever. I could collect an Oxford degree without too much exertion and complete seven years of university education just after turning twenty-three. I was no longer aggrieved that my parents had let me skip those grades back in grammar school.

My college was Hertford, pronounced "Hartford" or, still more English, "Harford," but never "Hurtford." It was one of the smaller of the twenty-five men's colleges, with about 150 undergraduates in residence, plus Principal, Dean, Chaplain, and fifteen or so Fellows or dons, i.e., the faculty. Hertford had been founded as Hart Hall "around" (as one diffident account has it) 1282. When I went back to Hertford for a few days of festivities in June 1983, we found it convenient to consider each of those very evenings the seven-hundredth anniversary. This would have made Hertford the third oldest of Oxford's colleges had all the others been willing to accept the most lenient interpretation of Hertford's rather colorful history. The chief difficulty to be swallowed here is a period in the nineteenth century when the college was broke, totally without pupils, and bereft of all but two dons, one half mad, who elected himself principal. The college was not restored to full respectability until the 1870s.

Hertford would have ranked toward the lower end of any discriminating list of the most beautiful Oxford colleges. The college did incorporate bits of the thirteenth-century town wall; an interesting octagonal chapel (fourteenth- to sixteenth-century); scattered samples of Elizabethan, Jacobean, Georgian, and Victorian architecture; and, connecting its two quads, a curious arched bridge of Clipsham stone, 1913, which some crusty Oxonians thought a vulgar imitation of the Bridge of Sighs. The bridge was beginning to be a cherished landmark by the time (many hundreds of times) I was tearing up and down the steps, already slightly hollowed. Along the way, Hertford and its ancestral endowments had been home to William Tyndale, translator of the Bible; Thomas Hobbes of the *Leviathan*; John Donne; Charles Fox; Alexander Briant, Jesuit martyr and saint; Whig prime minister Henry Pelham; and Evelyn Waugh.

The Hertford principal of my day, in the view of much of Oxford, was at the least half mad. He was C.R.F.M. Cruttwell—"Crutters," of course—a brilliant scholar steeped in the classics and a classic misogynist. Female undergraduates who had the temerity to look in on his lectures were driven off by sudden obscenities, the more disconcerting because of his gift for looking past people, male or female. He regularly addressed the unfortunate women who worked in the principal's lodgings as "you drab." He had been badly wounded and perhaps psychically damaged in the Great War, which did not stop him from writing what is still the best one-volume history of that war, taking his last line from Sophocles: "Many are the marvels, and nothing is more marvelous than man." He was a good tennis player despite his game leg, an enthusiastic golfer and notoriously shifty scorekeeper, a demented motorcar driver even by Oxford-don criteria, and occasionally a reeling drunk, coming home to Hertford only by clutching hand over hand the iron railing around a nearby university building. He had been Evelyn Waugh's tutor, and they despised each other. Waugh ever afterward would plant in his novels an unattractive (and/or lower-class) character named Cruttwell. The principal in turn ticked off Waugh as "a silly little suburban sod with an inferiority complex and no palate—drinks Pernod after meals." I didn't study with Crutters but for some reason didn't offend him (though he was not exactly pro-Yank) and was invited often to his lunches and sherry parties.

I relished some of the fusty Oxford regulations that were just waiting to be broken. Undergraduates were not to patronize pubs—not because the university opposed drink (it was on sale in the colleges) but because of the ancient history of town vs. gown, the medieval battles in which "Oxford Clerkes" and townspeople sometimes killed each other. Two young dons were tapped each year to be junior proctors, and they made nightly rounds of Oxford's pubs, attended by blue-suited "bulldogs" or "bullers," most of them ex-army or ex-police, fit fellows who had done some running or boxing in their day. They couldn't cover every Oxford pub every night, but even so, you felt a bit of a daredevil drinking in forbidden premises. If a proctor did chance upon you, his salutation was: "Excuse me, Sir, are you a member of the University?" "Yes." (He could tell just by looking at you.) "Please step outside. Your name and college, please?" At that point, your choice was to give your name and get billed for a £1 fine— or run for it. It was dishonorable to give a phony name. Once I meekly gave my name, another time I ran for it (successfully). If you had five or six friends breaking out all at once, the bullers couldn't nab everybody. If a buller did catch up with you, it was bad form to resist—gentlemen don't fight with the lower orders—and foolhardy, physically and financially. You could get beaten up, and heavily fined, or possibly suspended.

A further incitement to lawlessness was the nightly locking-up of the colleges. The gates were closed at 9:10, after Great Tom, the lordly bell at Christ Church, had tolled 101 times. The night porter would let you in, but from 11 to midnight it cost a fine of 9d. (about 20 cents). After midnight, the fine was £1, and at that price it was worth climbing in. Every college had its climbing routes, some given mock mountaineering names, like the North Face. From time to time the college authorities would lay new fields of broken glass and barbed wire on top of the historic walls and knock out any little grips and footholds that had been devised. The approach into Hertford, leading up a drainpipe, was not considered especially difficult by gymnastic types, though it gave me trouble. Climbing in with friends, I was usually allowed to go first, starting from the shoulders of somebody who was better at shinnying. A town constable coming upon such a tableau would look the other way; a proctor would report you. If an undergraduate simply didn't return all night, his "scout" (the servant who made up his rooms in the morning) was bound on pain of losing his job to notify the dean. This could lead to suspension for a term.

My scout was Walter Honey, who looked after eight of us, one staircase worth. We each had a bedroom and a sitting room with a small coal-burning fireplace, the only source of heat. Honey would arrive in the morning with a pitcher of hot water for shaving, light the fire, and announce the time and weather, sometimes grim. Oxford was essentially the same temperature indoors and out, but it was psychologically warming to dress in front of a fire. For a bath, I had a thirty-yard dash across the quad in bathrobe to a steamy cavern full of huge and ancient tubs. The toilets were behind the quad in a kind of shed, only partly roofed. Snow could fall in there, though I must admit it seldom snowed in Oxford.

To classes and to dinner in hall we wore beat-up black gowns covering the backs of our stout tweed jackets. If you forgot your gown or arrived late for dinner, you could be "sconced." The chief waiter would bring the message: "Mr. So-and-So presents his compliments and wishes to know whether you will have beer or cider." Beer. The servant then would bring Hertford's solid silver sconcing bowl, a vessel holding almost two quarts (at your expense). In the unlikely event you could down the contents bottoms-up, the sconcer then had to order the same, and try to floor it. Protests about this or that aspect of a sconce could be referred in writing to High Table, where the dons sat, but only in Latin. Protests were rare. I never protested, and never got around the whole pail, though I came respectably close. At some colleges you could be sconced for mentioning a woman's name at the dining table, or speaking in a foreign language, or discussing politics or religion. In the British army, fashionable regimental messes imposed fines for some of these offenses; Hertford put on no such airs.

To prevent the Rhodes scholars from huddling together for warmth, they were scattered all through the Oxford colleges. Thirty-two American Rhodes scholars were elected each year (and still are), and about the same number from the British Commonwealth, mainly the "Dominions" in my day—Canada, South Africa, Australia, New Zealand—now much broadened to include India, Pakistan, Kenya, even Zambia (once Northern Rhodesia). I formed very close friendships with the Hertford Rhodes scholars of 1934–35—bright, vigorous fellows carrying around a lot of local color: Missouri, Quebec, Colorado, Texas (astrophysics, history, medicine, economics). It was good, too, to have so many friends from the *Transylvania* in the other colleges, leading to lunch, sherry, dinner invitations back and forth. Among those American Rhodes scholars of my year: John Oakes, who became editor of the editorial page of *The New York Times*; Eugene Booth, a physicist who later commanded Columbia University's cyclotron and coaxed from it the first lab-made meson beam; Daniel Boorstin, legal scholar, historian, prolific author, Librarian of Congress; Oscar Gass, a terrifyingly bright economist with no interest whatever in the "manly sports" Cecil Rhodes thought his scholars should be good at (they should also have brains, character, and leadership qualities for "the world's fight"); George McGhee, petroleum geologist, ambassador to Turkey and Germany, undersecretary of state; and John Templeton, founder of investment funds, donor of the Templeton Prize in religion, benefactor of Templeton College (for business management) at Oxford, now a British subject and, indeed, Sir John. McGhee and Templeton each said in Oxford days that they planned to be millionaires by the time they were thirty, a remarkable ambition among Rhodes scholars of that New Deal era. McGhee made it; I'm not sure about Templeton, but if he didn't have his million by thirty, he soon had it many times over.

I also wanted to know the natives in Hertford College and found it was not too difficult if you didn't rush things. You might meet somebody at a sherry party, talk with great rapport for twenty minutes, then have him look right through you on the street the next day. Practically unconstitutional in America, but in Britain it was a shy and in a strange sense tactful protocol: He will not *presume* that you would wish to know *him* any better, so he is respecting your privacy as well as his own. I was content to wait these things out (and could also project a bit of reserve myself), and after a while found many warm friends in Hertford. They tended to be "hearties" (as opposed to aesthetes or swots—lingo of an earlier day), respectable students but not brilliant; lighthearted, recklessly courageous, strenuous at sports. They taught me enough rugby so I could play on Hertford's second team, sometimes the first if enough people were sick. I played on the college tennis teams—sometimes first, sometimes second. The playing fields of the colleges were stretched along two or three miles of glorious riverside meadows—grass courts, long white flannels, and ginger beer for tennis, cold mud for rugby. I was elected to the Firkins, an unserious club that played cricket against nearby village teams, carrying beer from the local pub out to our positions in the field, where otherwise nothing much might happen for half an hour.

We cycled often into the lovely countryside around Oxford. May and June could be magnificent, of course, but I also loved the lights and moods of March and April, when so much was going on in the vast, windy English skies. (The sky in Minnesota had tended to be sunny or not sunny.) I was struck that such a small country could offer such long views in a wonderfully rich variety of landscapes. There were no more than two million cars in all of Britain in those days; cyclists pretty much owned the country roads. A great day's run was out to Burford in the Cotswolds, lunch at The Lamb, back home by a different route, maybe fifty miles or more, enough to feel back in Oxford that we had earned our pint or two.

My British friends were impressed because I played ice hockey, which they considered an unbelievably fast and dangerous game—though not as I played it, I tried to tell them. They were also impressed because the Oxford teams got free tours of Switzerland, Austria, and Bavaria during Christmas vacations. When I played against Cambridge in my third year, I won my "half-blue," equivalent to an American varsity letter (only "half" because ice hockey was a minor sport; full blues were for the big British games—rugby, cricket, rowing, one or two others). A band of Hertford friends and their girls came to Harringay Arena in London to see the Cambridge game. We lost, but I had one brief moment of glory. The Cambridge captain, ex-McGill

University and the best player on either team, was bearing down on our goal with a teammate in tandem, 2-on-1 against me, the only defense in the neighborhood. I somehow broke up their play, and from the stands came a cry: "Well played, Hertford!"

I was asked to join the Hertford Dining Club, the only mildly snobbish thing in a generally unpretentious college. We put on white tie and tails once a term to eat our way through a long printed menu, drink three or four wines, sing bawdy songs. In the latter stages of a party, English undergraduates had an irrepressible urge to smash furniture and throw things out windows. "The sound of County families baying over broken glass," as Evelyn Waugh once wrote. My frugal upbringing prevented me from breaking anything on purpose, but did not spare me my share of the post-dinner bill for general damages.

Guy Fawkes Night, November 5, the anniversary of the papist "Gunpowder Plot" against the Houses of Parliament in 1605, was a traditional time for fireworks and general hell-raising. Somebody could be depended upon to climb the Martyrs' Memorial and put a chamberpot on top. The Victorian Gothic spire was fairly easy climbing; the trick was to get up and down fast enough not to get caught by proctors or police. I have a beautifully printed NOTICE, bearing the Oxford coat of arms, dated October 31, 1936:

> The Vice Chancellor and Proctors desire to warn members of the University that they will regard as a very serious offence any case of ASSAULT committed against the persons of either Constables or Citizens. The throwing or letting off of FIREWORKS in or into any public place is strictly forbidden.

I also cherish two notes dated June 20, 1936:

> The Junior Proctor presents his compliments to Mr. H. Donovan and begs to say that the Proctors regret that they are unable to give him permission to attend the private dance at Shillingford Hotel on Monday the 22nd. June.

Then only a few hours later:

> The Junior Proctor in presenting his compliments wishes to say that in view of special circumstances—which have only just come to his knowledge—his communication forbidding attendance at the pri-

vate dance at Shillingford Hotel on Monday next the 22nd. June may be considered as cancelled.

The Shillingford Hotel was a charming country inn on the banks of the Thames. The dance was being given by the parents of one of my Hertford friends in honor of his sister. I believe the proctors had belatedly learned the family was impeccable, even influential.

Female visitors had to leave Hertford before Great Tom pealed 101. Otherwise, still another fine, against her host. A memorandum on the Conduct and Discipline of Junior Members of the University stated:

> A woman undergraduate may not enter the rooms of a man under-graduate, either in College or in lodgings, without special leave previously obtained from the Principal of her Society. [There were four women's colleges.] She must be accompanied by a companion approved by the Principal.

Though the memorandum was dated 1934–35, the authorities had pretty much given up on this one. I'm afraid I never saw an officially approved companion.

In the 1970s, Hertford was the first of the men's colleges to admit women. Now they all do. The women are said to have had a civilizing effect on the young men, though I had my doubts one recent evening when I saw (and heard) my old dining club holding its spring party. The club was now called the Pelham Club, in honor of Hertford's one prime minister, and it now had a woman member, very pretty. The young men seemed inspired to even crazier feats than in my day— in particular, running leaps from one Hertford roof to another—six feet or so across, forty feet down to the pavement.

The adjustment to Oxford was perhaps easier for Americans interested in history, politics, literature, and law than for those pursuing medicine or hard science. For me, Britain itself—its glories, peculiarities, and absurdities—was very much a part of what I was learning and living.

Britain in those years was a Great Power, one of seven as I had been instructed at the University of Minnesota, in many ways The Greatest. (The others, according to various criteria of military and economic strength, population, and geographic position, were the

United States, France, Germany, Japan, Russia, Italy, in more or less that order.) America had greater intrinsic strength than Britain, but it was much more inward-looking, not very organized or experienced or even interested in applying its power to international affairs. Britain in those years had a navy ranked with ours, a small but proud and crisply trained professional army, and more serious air power than ours (though the RAF was about to be overtaken by Hitler's Luftwaffe).

It was the whole amalgam of military and industrial force—the red-colored bases, colonies, and dominions all over the globe; and the banking, shipping, and commercial currents that came together in "The City" of London—that made the British Empire the preeminent world power. Walking along Whitehall or Downing Street, a young history student from Minnesota felt he was at the center of his subject matter. I wouldn't have felt that way on Pennsylvania Avenue (where I had not yet been), nor would professional diplomats or journalists. When an international crisis erupted, as it regularly did in my Oxford years, the diplomatic/journalistic quest for a "reaction" would lead first to London.

During my time in England, the common definition of the "good old days," among the upper and middle classes, would have been "before the war," the war of 1914–18. Not a few of the working class would have agreed; among other things, you knew where you stood. Taxes were low, privilege was secure, and sons and brothers and husbands had not yet been to the trenches.

The Great War was still a haunting presence when I lived in England. Armistice Day, not Good Friday, was the most solemn date on the calendar. Crepe-paper poppies ("In Flanders Field") were sold on every street corner for the benefit of wounded veterans. Everything came to a stop—traffic, business, schoolrooms, the wireless—for two minutes at 11 A.M. on November 11. And on July 1, 2, and 3, for years after the appalling Battle of the Somme, there came the sudden surge of "In Memoriam" notices in the London *Times*: "BRAITHWAITE. In memory of Val Braithwaite M.C., Lieutenant, The Somerset Light Infantry, killed in action near Serre on July 1, 1916, aged 20, and in honor of the Men of his platoon who were killed with him." I read these affirmations, column after heartbreaking column, with immense respect.

But for all the grief held sacred in so many homes, War I was inevitably receding, and War II had not yet come to look certain or even likely. Britain between the wars, if not the legendary "long garden party" of the Edwardian age, was a generally comfortable and confident country. Coming from a society (and a family) just inching up from the depths of the Depression, I was struck by Britain's recovery. There were still the "depressed areas" in South Wales, Lancashire, Clydeside, but these places had also been ailing in the 1920s. John Maynard Keynes wrote in the *Atlantic Monthly* in 1932: "Great Britain is decidedly the most prosperous country in the world."

Keynes notwithstanding, the Labour party was bitterly critical of Britain's economic and social order, and the partisan politics of the day was class warfare translated into parliamentary give-and-take. Republican vs. Farmer-Laborite rhetoric in Minnesota was tame stuff compared with this, because Middle Western unemployed and foreclosed farmers didn't think of themselves as any sort of proletariat. I spent at least two hours a day reading the London papers, from Right to Left, and fascinating evenings at the public meetings of Oxford's rich spectrum of political clubs—October (Communist), Socialist, Labour, Liberal, Conservative, Fascist. At these meetings, and on London visits to the gallery of the House of Commons, I heard the Conservative prime minister Stanley Baldwin; Ramsay MacDonald, the turncoat Socialist who became a "national coalition" prime minister; and two Tory P.M.s-to-be, Neville Chamberlain and the much-mistrusted Winston Churchill. (He was considered "erratic.") I heard Labour leaders Clement Attlee, Sir Stafford Cripps, and Herbert Morrison, and the disarmingly pleasant crackpot Sir Oswald Moseley, fuehrer of the British blackshirts.

Many of these politicians were pleased to appear before the Oxford Union, the university's debating society, and indeed many had been members of the union (or its Cambridge equivalent) in their student days. The pros and cons, usually two students and one older personage for each side, came on in white tie and tails, to consider: Does capitalism have a future? Is Hitler dangerous? Should Britain stay on in India? The debate would be replete with parliamentary punctilio and the polished insults of Westminster, and at the end the student audience would "divide," just like the Commons, as to which side won. The union had bad food and pleasant reading rooms, like many grown-up English clubs, and unlike them, was stoutly egalitarian: any student could join (for a trifling fee) and any member could apply to debate. Whether he got invited or, more important, got invited a second time, was up to the officers. Despite my fondness for arguing, I never applied to speak: I preferred debating on paper, or close up, with friends. But I enjoyed listening to the union, and the proceedings could be highly entertaining: "That this house regrets the voyage of Columbus." "That this house will be as seditious as it pleases." Both motions carried, as I recall.

The greatest modern clash of the British classes, the General Strike of 1926, was still a recent point of reference. From dons I heard occasional reminiscences of those days when hundreds of Oxford undergraduates went to London, Southampton, Hull, drove lorries and tramcars, and helped unload ships. A sharp contrast to the Minnesota fraternity men. A Hungarian count then resident at Hertford gets a line in the college history for saying, "I know nothing of this struggle but am certainly against the lower classes."

I was fascinated, as Americans tend to be, by the monarchy, and took care not to go gaga over it. Despite Alfred, William the Conqueror, the fabulous Henrys, Good Queen Bess, and all the rest, the monarchy that I saw in the 1930s was essentially the invention of Victoria, her grandson George V (never mind his naughty father Edward VII), and the British Establishment of the late nineteenth and early twentieth centuries—the political leaders, the aristocracy, the Church of England, Oxford and Cambridge, the London *Times*. Their creation was the sober and almost powerless sovereign at the service of his people, the regal cement helping hold together a deeply divided society. The Socialists revered the monarchy almost as much as the Tories did; elderly Labour politicians would accept a peerage or a knighthood with as much alacrity as a Conservative.

I went up to London on a lovely May day in 1935 to see the clockwork pageantry of George V's Silver Jubilee. Then as now, the British did those things beautifully. The *Times*'s stately two-column headlines told it all:

SUNSHINE CROWNS THE JUBILEE

THE GREAT THANKSGIVING

VAST CHEERING CROWDS IN LONDON STREETS

TRIUMPHAL PROGRESS TO ST. PAUL'S

BEACONS ON A THOUSAND HILLS

George died only the next winter. (Fifty years later, we learned that his doctors let him die a little early so the first announcement would be handled with dignity in the morning *Times*. The popular afternoon press had less taste.) I went to Windsor to watch the funeral procession move along High Street toward St. George's Chapel in the ancient castle. Rudyard Kipling had died only the week before, another punctuation mark in an imperial history that had only a few more years to run. I saw the boyish Prince of Wales, now Edward VIII, marching behind the gun carriage bearing his father's coffin, attended by most of the remaining crowned heads of Europe.

That summer in London, while Edward, decked out in scarlet tunic and Guardsman's black busby, was leading a mounted procession, a deranged Scot pointed a pistol at his king. The *Daily Herald* printed a huge photo-diagram of the event: "Police Officer Picking Up the Revolver," "Equerry Leaving Procession to Investigate," and—this the crucial point—"The King, Unmoved by the Incident, Continues at the Head of the Procession." All was well.

But then, only months later, the Wallis Simpson affair broke. As a subscriber to the saucy American journal *Time*, I had been thoroughly informed about the king's romance, and circulated each new issue of the magazine to Oxford friends who could read none of this in their newspapers. Some wondered whether the American journalists were not vastly exaggerating the business—possibly out of some perverse pride because "the woman" was American. They were dismayed, with all of Britain, when Prime Minister Baldwin finally made it official. A kind of "King's party," led by two anti-Baldwin figures, Churchill and Lord Beaverbrook, was proposing that Edward be allowed to marry Mrs. Simpson and remain king, she remaining a commoner, a morganatic marriage as practiced occasionally by Continental royalty. But as one headline in the *Times* obiter-dicted: "No Such Word in British Law as Morganatic."

In the end, the shy and proper George VI succeeded his willful brother, and the Royal Family carried on. Within a few months, I could see the majestic Queen Mother Mary (an implacable critic of her oldest son's behavior) laying the cornerstone for an extension of Oxford's Bodleian Library—nobody can match the House of Windsor at ribbon-cutting and trowel-clapping. And I once saw George's daughters, Elizabeth and Margaret, getting into practice by patting sand castles on a beach near Eastbourne, watched by several hundred of their subjects and three governesses.

I was a devoted fan of Colonel Blimp. The great *Evening Standard* cartoonist David Low had invented—or, more precisely, realized— this walrus-mustached fellow who said outlandishly insular and reactionary things at his club, in the steam baths, on the grouse moors.

I collected Blimpisms from real life, though it was hard to match Low's stuff. Once, I was sitting next to a retired colonel (there did indeed seem to be thousands of them in England) at a Rhodes House dinner in Oxford. Quite oblivious to my name, he told me that "the whole mess in Ireland" (there had been some recent IRA activity) had come about because "England has never really taken a firm line with those people." Or was he in fact oblivious, I wondered afterward. An unpleasant thought (though I despised the IRA as much as he did). At a lunch party in Devon at the time of Mussolini's invasion of Ethiopia, a retired brigadier looked at me as though I were a chap who could be trusted with a military secret, and confided almost in a whisper: "The Abyssinians should keep to the hills, you know, and roll stones down on the Italians at night." A lady at the same lunch said to the whole table: "Isn't all this killing dreadful, even if they are blacks?" Another lady, at tea in Bristol, was astonished and genuinely distressed when I had to tell her that cricket was hardly played at all in the States. And then there were the invincibly wholesome girls who were caused to materialize for Anglo-American dances at Rhodes House, and the occasional forthright compliment: "But you don't *seem* like an American."

A charming aspect of Britain's self-image was the notion of a deep national modesty. Thus Sir Edward Elgar, in "Pomp and Circumstance": "How shall we exalt Thee/Who are born of Thee?" Or a columnist in the London *Daily Telegraph*, recommending Charles Laughton in *Les Misérables*: "This is the very soul of acting, and—can we for once be a little proud?—England bred it." The *Evening News*: "London, for all its shortcomings, is the hub of civilisation." An ad by the Great Western Railway urged early holiday reservations, because many overseas visitors at the coronation (George VI in 1937) "will stay to learn the beauties of our incomparable country. (Why should we be modest, having so much of which to be proud?)."

I came across some wonderfully touching and foolish verses in a rather scholarly quarterly devoted to imperial history and "constitutional" considerations about the empire. The poem is called "On First Looking Into Rhodes' Will," and it ends:

> And now whene'er in outposts of the world
> The British flag is to the winds unfurl'd,
> The youth of Empire stiffen at the sight
> And gently murmur: "Cecil Rhodes was right."

The sort of thing of which the *New Yorker* might have said Murmurs We Doubt Ever Got Murmured.

But I confess I admired the empire—Colonel Blimps, Lady Blimps and all—and I have remained incorrigibly Anglophile all my life. Britain in those years I lived there had come as close as any nation ever had to reconciling liberty and order. All the more remarkable because of a class structure far more confining than any such categories in our American democracy. The shared legal and political liberties were part of an implicit contract, as I understood it, between the all-too-clearly defined classes. At all levels, Britain was a remarkably civil society. The national sense of history was strong, and the profound respect for tradition, though it had its deadening effects, was surely a source of stability. There was a lot for me to try to figure out.

If the countries on the Continent seemed a little less complicated than Britain, it was perhaps because I was not fluent in any of their languages. (I read French quite well, after all that trouble in Minnesota, but didn't converse easily. I could read German laboriously, and get by conversationally.) The generous Oxford vacations—six weeks at Christmas, six weeks at Easter, more than three months in the summer—made it easy to experience Western Europe with some intimacy and now and then mount more exotic expeditions. I considered going one summer to the Soviet Union, and I find in one of my Oxford letters to my parents (all saved by my father) this P.S.: "Mother, keep cool about Russia. If I go, it means there is enough to eat there." She must have been reading somewhere about famine in the Ukraine. (Not all Jewish mothers are Jewish.)

I couldn't fit in the USSR, but I did get to one out-of-the-way place: South Africa, for the unlikely purpose of playing ice hockey. Johannesburg was putting on an "Empire Exhibition" in honor of its fiftieth anniversary, and the city invited the Oxford and Cambridge hockey teams to come and inaugurate the first artificial ice rink in Africa. (First, and probably only, even today, if it still exists.) We accepted. It was all expenses paid, seventeen days at sea on the old Union Castle Line, another thirty-six hours by rail from Cape Town, then two weeks of hockey and parties. The locals were more impressed with our hockey than they should have been and entertained us nonstop. The city seemed half American boomtown, half intensely British colonial (the Boers not yet dominant). The third half, of course, was the black workforce, who kept the country functioning, including the sweat-gleaming men I saw seven thousand feet down in a gold mine on The Rand.

I traveled often in Germany in those years just after Hitler came to power. It was almost too pat that at dusk on my first day there I should listen to Brahms and Beethoven at an outdoor concert in Bonn, look across the Rhine to the brooding hills beyond, and share the soaring music with a rapt audience that included a number of brown-shirted storm troopers. I went to the Berlin Sportspalast to hear the notorious Julius Streicher—gauleiter of Franconia and publisher of the Jew-baiting *Der Stürmer*—incite a crowd of twenty thousand. But Nazi authority was still not completely pervasive, and you could have some surprisingly candid conversations in taverns and trains. Totally frank conversation required careful introductions and arrangements. I had a letter to a Jewish bookstore owner in Berlin who had had to close down his business and told me of his plans to move his family out of Germany in stages, the children first ("What is there for them here?"), then his wife, then his elderly parents ("if they will go"), then himself. I sat on a park bench in Kassel with a Rhodes scholar named Adam von Trott und zu Solz, who had gone from Oxford into the German foreign service. (Cecil Rhodes had dreamed of an alliance between the English-speaking nations and the Germans and provided in his will for two German Rhodes scholars a year. After the Great War hiatus, they started coming to Oxford again, mainly aristocrats from families of military and diplomatic background.) Von Trott, though we had just met, was debating in front of me whether he should seek a posting abroad or work against the Nazi regime from inside. He eventually did some of each, and was one of the conspirators in the plot of July 20, 1944, which barely missed killing Hitler. He was among those the Gestapo hanged by piano wire in a Berlin jail.

I liked Germany and the Germans, the scenery, the friendliness, the efficiency (I freely admit), the beer, the music, Munich. I was irritated by American tourists breezing through for a week or so, who somehow gave Hitler credit that Germany was so agreeable. "I didn't see any Jews being beaten up," I was told more than once. But I also marveled at how swiftly—historically speaking—"national character" can change. The states of western and southern Germany shared none of the Prussian military tradition, and as late as the mid-nineteenth century, they were thought of as rather dreamy, poetic places. Now their people were cheerfully allowing themselves to be converted into a garrison state. And France, following Napoleon's defeat at Waterloo, changed in little more than a century from the terror of Europe to the somewhat soft and corrupt society I visited in the mid-1930s, though I had no idea the country could fold as fast as it did in 1940. National character and the perceptions thereof, foreign and internal, have fascinated me ever since my Oxford days, and I later had opportunities to grapple with these questions journalistically, including the deepest one of all: What is an American?

On the last of my visits to Nazi Germany, in the Rhineland in January 1937, I met more people who were critical of the regime than I had on previous trips, and saw more evidence of economic strains imposed by Hitler's rearmament. I began to indulge in the fantasy that Hitler might be overthrown by the army because of his reckless foreign policy. "England and France have most of the cards," I wrote my father, "if they only knew it."

Italy and the Italians were irresistible. It was endearing that they took fascism so much less seriously than the Germans did. In Rome, I hung around the Piazza Venezia all through the morning of some Fascist anniversary, because it was rumored that Mussolini might come out on the famous balcony and throw us a salute. He didn't, and I as a stern anti-Fascist was more disappointed than the amiable Italians strolling in and out of the crowd. In Italy, unlike Germany, I was never asked, "So what do you think of our leader?" The Italians didn't especially care what an American thought, or even what Italians thought; these things come and go; Mussolini was politics. Few Germans would have said Hitler was just politics.

I took coffee in many a *piazza, platz,* and *place,* and generally preferred outdoor sightseeing to the indoor work. I was once celebrated in a column in the *Paris Herald Tribune* as the all-time record-holder at going through the Louvre. "This youth is said to have done the museum in seventy minutes flat . . . and to have modestly stated at the finish that it was not so much, since he had a slight tail wind." In later, less vainglorious days, I put in the proper three-hour tours.

I was also supposed to be studying, of course. I was "reading" (majoring in) modern history, seeking the degree B.A. Oxon. in two years, instead of the usual three for the British undergraduates. Most of the work for an Oxford history degree would be different from my Minnesota studies, so I didn't feel I was entirely loafing, and I hoped in my third year to start some postgraduate research.

Hertford gave me two first-rate history tutors: Each became a lifelong friend. One was Tom Boase, a medievalist, an art historian, and an astute collector. The first Utrillo originals I ever saw were in his Hertford rooms. He later became director of the Courtauld (art) Institute in London, then president of his old college—I think the most beautiful of all in Oxford—Magdalen. When I took my wife, Dorothy, on her first trip to Oxford, in the early 1950s, I was delighted that we could stay with Tom in the president's lodgings in Magdalen, far grander than the principal's quarters in Hertford (if I could have drummed up an invitation there). But Tom Boase, back in the mid-1930s, was trying to prepare me for the rigors of exams in six or seven centuries of English history I had known nothing about. He had his work cut out for him. He was an affectionate and sharp critic of the weekly essays students brought to their tutors, and I think I learned at least as much writing from him as history.

Boase was dean of the college, which imposed disciplinary duties he didn't enjoy, but the post carried academic prestige and was a good stepping-stone. The dean and the principal were not too congenial. Tom wasn't amused by Crutters's foul mouth and brutal rudenesses, but he respected the man's intellect and felt compassion for the war damage. (Tom himself had won the Military Cross in Flanders at age nineteen, later lost an eye in the war, and in World War II dropped behind enemy lines on an intelligence mission.) Two little books told a good deal about Boase and Cruttwell. The Duckworth publishing house, for a biographical series, commissioned Tom to do St. Francis of Assisi. The last words of this gentle book are: "The Christian thought of the world has found in this man a most especial holiness." Duckworth got Cruttwell to do the Duke of Wellington. Crutters did not fail to include choice examples of the duke's legendary curtness. When his cavalry commander, Lord Uxbridge, riding alongside him at Waterloo, was hit by a cannonball, he cried out, "By God, I've lost my leg!" Wellington said, "Have you, by God!"

Cruttwell and Boase were both devout communicants of the Church of England. The principal's faith was sorely tested, however, by the chaplain of Hertford, who was a member of the Buchmanite "Oxford Group," a kind of show-and-tell subculture within the Protestant churches of the day. Crutters could barely stand the sight of the chaplain; I found him quite inoffensive, and I had a warm friendship with one of his circle, Robin Mowat, a fellow history student. The Groupers made gentle, unsuccessful efforts to proselytize me. They would not have dared—much as they believed he needed to be more "open" and more "loving"—to try to convert the principal.

My other Hertford history don was Felix Markham, whose field was modern European and in particular the Napoleonic era. (At Oxford, modern history, as opposed to ancient, began with Anglo-Saxon England and the Norman Conquest, 1066; until just before my student days, it stopped at 1815. Then the university generously acknowledged a whole additional century, 1815 to 1914.) Felix was a sleepy-looking man who could say very stimulating things, invariably followed by his own appreciative "Ha!" He and Boase were both bachelor dons in the old Oxford tradition. They were fond of tennis, theater, and music; entertained generously; and took a keen interest in Hertford's highly regarded wine cellars.

Students might attend lectures in any college at the university, and would usually follow their own tutor's recommendations as to which would be useful. But attendance was entirely optional. The essence of the education was in the tutorial system: reading recommended by one's tutors—much of it presumably to be done during those long vacations—essays related to the reading, and the tutor's comments on the essays.

The idea was not so much to learn history (or any other specific subject) as to learn how to think and how to express your thinking. The rest was detail. The educated man (especially if he read "Greats," the classics of Greece and Rome) could do anything—govern a colony, run a Whitehall department, see to a diocese, even manage a bank if life dealt him such a lot.

The tutor might grade his pupils' essays—*alpha, beta,* and so on— but these marks did not count toward the degree. Nor were any American-style "course credits" accumulating along the way. For the degree, everything rode on the finals, or "Schools," two or three years' work found worthy or wanting over a few long June days of exam-writing. An undergraduate could content himself with a "pass" degree or, as most did, go for the degree with honors, which came in four ranks. The tension in Schools was not so much whether you would get the degree—practically everybody would—but with which honors. In modern history, the Schools consisted of ten three-hour exams. No true-false stuff. "Candidates are recommended to attempt *not less than four questions*" from a list of a dozen or more possible essay topics. I still have the topic sheets of 1936, with checks against the questions I attempted (never more than the minimum four). It is clear to me even today why I declined certain invitations—"Compare the monasticism of Bede's time with that of Dunstan's"—but mystifying why I chose others, except that I did finally have to do four of them. As we moved out of the Middle Ages, I grew more comfortable, and began to enjoy the implicit contest with the examiners. "Examine the part played by poetry and fiction in the national European movements of the nineteenth century." A nice one.

I got a Second. Tom Boase, who had pipelines to the examiners, wrote to me in Italy: "It was a very respectable Second, Hedley, with some *alpha* about." From my class of American Rhodes scholars, the twenty of us reading for the B.A. (the others were doing law, medicine, or the D.Phil.) produced a perfect bell curve: five Firsts, ten Seconds, five Thirds, and fortunately no Fourths.

I calculated that over two years I had averaged about an hour a day in studying for the B.A., figuring in all those wonderful vacations when it seemed so much more interesting to see Europe than to read about medieval land tenure. I mentioned this statistic in later years to my children, who were somewhat scandalized. More years later, I found myself in a *People* article about Rhodes scholars. I was flattered to be shown (in my ice-hockey getup) along with such notables as Senator Bill Bradley and Kris Kristofferson in their Oxford settings, but was startled to see in cold type the confession that I had studied only an hour a day there. My son Mark works for *People*.

In my third year I tried for a B.Litt. degree (equivalent to an American M.A.). My topic was the "negotiated peace" efforts during the midphase of the Great War: two probes by Woodrow Wilson, one German initiative. I even put in a morning's work on my thesis during the Oxford ice-hockey trip to South Africa. I took the train from Johannesburg to Pretoria and called on Field Marshal Jan Smuts, the old Afrikaner hero of the Boer War who had become a statesman of the British Empire. He knew something of the peace feelers of 1916 because he was then a member of the War Cabinet in London, and he gave me his recollections with grave courtesy. It was my first interview with any national leader.

Eventually, I churned out a smallish book, forty to fifty thousand words. My faculty adviser was E. L. Woodward, an eminent historian and Fellow of All Souls. Woodward thought my thesis was excellent, but alas, this view was not entirely shared by my examiners, who put me through a *viva* (as in *viva voce*) of two or three hours. One was Constance Headlam-Morley, a diplomatic historian who was inclined to give me the degree. But the senior examiner, Professor Alfred Zimmern, was not, and his vote governed. (Their deliberations were later relayed to me by the ever-knowing Tom Boase.) Zimmern had been in the British Foreign Office during the war, and he felt my views were rather too evenhanded as between the British and the Germans. He may have been right. World War II, though it hadn't happened yet, would tend to bear him out. The *viva* had begun badly when Zimmern complained that some of my citations of American memoirs didn't seem to check out. It turned out he was using British editions in the Bodleian, while I had worked from American editions I owned, and the pagination was a little different. I may have been a little haughty in suggesting that the original New York edition of a work by an American author could be considered reasonably authentic. I offered to cycle out to my rooms and bring back the books, but this was declined.

The thesis does not read too badly today (and is still available for publication). I concluded that the peace feelers of 1916–17 never had a chance, and the only statesman who took them at all seriously was the naive American president, though there was realpolitik in his purpose: to stop the war before the United States had to get into it. British and French leaders, no less than the German General Staff, believed the war had to be fought through to total victory. "The Great War had acquired a terrible momentum." Britain had to demonstrate to Germany that she was impregnable, in particular against the U-boats. This view virtually excluded any compromise peace, "for it attached as much importance to the fact that the peace should be wrung from a defeated Germany, as to the terms of peace themselves." For all the belligerents, "the longer the war lasted, the greater the advantages which had to be won to justify the fresh sacrifices." A compromise peace would have seemed "a mean conclusion to heroic efforts."

My third year at Oxford was also the time to begin job hunting. In pursuit of my ambition to be a history professor, I sent an application to Harvard for a fellowship or teaching-assistant job. Cruttwell, Woodward, and my tutors gave me very generous letters of recommendation. These were all handwritten, and I hastily sent them all off to Harvard without making copies. As I applied to more places—Columbia, Chicago, and so on—I had to go back to my dons for more letters, and they tended to be less glowing the second and third time around. In Cruttwell's original (eventually returned to me by Harvard), he had verged on the effusive: "clear-cut and robust mind . . . thoroughly manly fellow . . . got on extremely well with the undergraduates . . ." and much more. His final version read, in its entirety: "Donovan is a quite sensible fellow who has got on well here."

Eventually, I applied to a dozen or more American universities, but the best offer I could stir up was $600 a year as a teaching assistant at Harvard. I decided to look for work in journalism, my second-choice profession. If I could find a newspaper job, perhaps I could take some postgraduate courses part-time and try to save enough money to go back to school full time for the necessary Ph.D. I had a skimpy scrapbook of newspaper stories that I could show prospective employers. During my last two years at Oxford, I had earned all of £20 or so as Oxford "stringer" for the United Press, filing for the hometown papers when somebody from North Carolina or Kansas won his blue in rugby or debated at the union or got arrested on Guy Fawkes Night. And I had all my old *Minnesota Daily* editorials if anybody wanted to look at them. So in July 1937, I sailed for New York on the *Queen Mary*, third class, to deal with the awkward years between the Rhodes scholarship and Social Security.

IV

Two Terms in Washington

I moved from Oxford to Franklin Roosevelt's Washington and worked there for eight years. My first four years (roughly Roosevelt's second term) were spent as a newspaper reporter, my second term (Roosevelt's third) was a four-year tour as an officer in Naval Intelligence.

FDR dominated the Washington of his day in a way no president has since. The city was much smaller and more intimate, of course, and perhaps easier to dominate. Roosevelt was not a modest man, but the presidency was a more modest institution. He was more approachable than recent presidents, living and working without imperial trappings, but still, a more commanding figure than any of his successors. For many of us in Washington, Roosevelt was not only the first president of our adult lives, but the president just as he should be. One could disagree with some of his policies, and I did. I was a card-carrying independent even then, and along with two of the Democratic bulwarks I found unattractive—the Southern reactionaries and the Northern city machines—I declined to be totally mesmerized by FDR. But one could deplore his deviousness and still be compelled by the style. This was the President of the United States as he should look and sound: a world figure we could be proud of, a man without fear or doubt. He would not have disagreed. Roosevelt was not in awe of his office; as Richard Neustadt of Harvard has put it, Roosevelt's philosophical concept of the presidency was simply himself as president.

As a reporter, I had some firsthand exposure to Roosevelt and his Cabinet, his Brain Trust, and assorted idealists and bureaucrats of the New Deal. In the navy, I caught intermittent inside glimpses of the Roosevelt administration's direction of the American effort in World War II. My job in intelligence gave me more war information than readers of *The New York Times* had between 1942 and 1945, and much less than is now available in the public library.

The reason I arrived in Washington in 1937 was that nobody would hire me at a living wage in New York. I had tried most of New York's then-numerous dailies (also *Time*), but one of the Hearst papers had just folded, so in addition to the general Depression difficulties in getting a job at anything, I was up against two hundred experienced newspapermen newly out of work in Manhattan. The *Daily News* offered me $17.50 a week as a copy boy. This was better than Harvard's $600 per annum (I had always been handy at arithmetic), but it still seemed skimpy. I went on to Washington and saw Felix Morley, a Rhodes scholar who presided over the *Post* editorial page. He passed me along to the managing editor, Alexander F. Jones.

Casey (inevitably) Jones was not flamboyant enough to be from out of *The Front Page*, but he was of the school generally known as hard-bitten. However little he might be paying some cub reporter at the *Post*, he could always cite how much less he was paid when he was breaking in on small Wisconsin papers. I don't know whether he cared much one way or the other that I had been to Oxford, but he was pleased when it turned out I was the same polite Donovan boy his wife had always spoken so well of when I was delivering the afternoon paper to their front step in Minneapolis, where Casey was then City Editor of the *Journal*. He hired me at $25 a week, and for some reason was entirely willing to do without my services for a month while I went out for a reunion with family and friends in Minnesota.

The *Washington Post* before it got rich and famous was the kind of place you should have paid to work, if you had any money, and Casey and the paper's proprietor, Eugene Meyer, would not have thought that totally inappropriate. It took me only a few weeks of cub reporting to abandon all thought of saving up to pursue a Ph.D. and a career in academia. Journalism was what I wanted to do. And for learning that trade there couldn't have been any more instructive place in America than Roosevelt's Washington.

An absolutely accurate cliché about journalism, as I realized right away at the *Post*, is that you meet such interesting people. (Once you have outgrown the youthful urge to overthrow all clichés, it is clear enough that clichés got that way by being true.) Some of these very interesting people are in fact other journalists, and whenever two or three are gathered together, as is often the case, they can overtax the willingness of nonjournalists to listen to all the fascinating shoptalk. This is a lifelong social hazard to the journalist, along with the professional hazards of writing for other writers and editing for other editors.

The *Post* had been bought for $825,000 in 1933, at a public auction held on the front steps of the paper's dignified old gray stone palazzo on E Street. The *Post* was in bankruptcy, mismanaged and nonmanaged by its profligate publisher, Edward McLean, Jr. Ned had inherited a profitable paper from his father, and he pretty well wrecked it during the Roaring Twenties, an epoch for which he and his wife were perfectly cast. Evalyn Walsh McLean was a Colorado mining heiress (she wrote *Father Struck It Rich*) and she owned and often wore the Hope Diamond. Ned played golf and poker with President Harding and the "Ohio Gang" and was involved on the fringes of the Teapot Dome scandal. The McLeans entertained on the grand scale; Ned drank on the grand scale and frequently checked into drying-out retreats. In 1929 he had turned down Eugene Meyer's offer of $5 million for the *Post*. When the trustees for the estate of Ned's father finally put the paper up for sale four years later, the canny Meyer did his bidding through a dummy. His $825,000 acquisition would fetch at least $825 million today, or, who knows, double that. I know the paper isn't for sale, but this isn't a firm offer either.*

Eugene Meyer was the first man of national stature I ever came to know, and I was fascinated. He came from a prosperous San Francisco banking family, of Alsatian Jewish background, and had made a fortune in his own right before he was thirty. Among other Wall Street triumphs, he became one of the founder-owners of Allied Chemical. This man—who was said by his awed employees to be worth at least $50 million—could often be seen after some dinner party, roaming the *Post* City Room in black tie and asking $50-a-week reporters (or even $25—he was democratic in that way) what they were working on tonight, who they had interviewed, had they gotten anything the

---

*In late 1988, the stock market was valuing the whole Washington Post Company, including *Newsweek* and several other properties, at close to $2.5 billion. The jewel of the empire was of course the paper.

other papers didn't have. He was trying to learn how to be a newspaper owner.

Meyer felt he had made a fool of himself in the first year or two after he bought the paper by signing up stars the *Post* couldn't really afford and giving them contracts (!) at astronomical salaries (like $25,000). By the time I was hired, this famous splurge was over. Meyer didn't like to be laughed at, and he was determined to look like a hard-boiled publisher in front of other publishers. But he also wanted to put out a serious and responsible Washington paper, in part so he could be a personage, in part to advocate certain public-policy stances—sobriety in fiscal and monetary matters, respect for civil liberties, internationalism in foreign policy. Meyer was a medium-liberal Republican. He had held high federal banking posts under Presidents Coolidge and Hoover—chairman of the Farm Loan Board and chairman of the Federal Reserve. He quit the Fed in anger when FDR ditched the gold standard. At home, out of work, he spotted some dust on the banister and complained to his wife Agnes (so their daughter Katharine relates): "This house is not well run." Agnes said, "You better buy the *Post*." He was a vain man, pontifical at times, deeply principled and public-spirited. He once told me there were not more than twelve men in the world who fully understood how money was created, and he was one of them. Was I another? I said I knew it wasn't the Bureau of Engraving (just like it isn't the stork), and that the Federal Reserve definitely had something to do with it. I don't believe I made the top twelve.

I had been on the paper barely a month when Meyer invited John Oakes and me to dinner at his grand embassy-style residence on Crescent Place. Oakes, one of my Oxford contemporaries and a nephew of Adolph Ochs of *The New York Times*, had arrived on the *Post* at the same time I did, and it was a matter of some satisfaction to Meyer, though he didn't say so, that two Rhodes scholars, especially one of royal publishing blood, had just come to work for him. He fed us very well in a dining room decorated by Rodin and Cézanne, broke out the brandy, pushed back his chair, and said expansively, "Well, when do you young men think you will be worth your salaries?" With his cigar, comfortable paunch, broad, bland face, and glinting pince-nez, he could have been a benevolent caricature of a George Grosz caricature of a capitalist. I mustered enough audacity to say, "It would be hard not to be." John was aghast at Meyer's question, and I think at my answer as well.

As Meyer's editorial viceroy, Casey Jones sat in one corner of the

City Room, all too visible to his staff, and they to him. He would knead one long-suffering eyebrow as he frowned over the final edition of that morning's *Post*, along with the competing papers, and various pieces of the day's early copy. (My God, is that something of mine he's looking at?) He would frequently call in one of the editors or reporters for comments out of the side of his mouth, and there was not a whole lot of laughing at his desk. The staff speculated that his ulcers must be savage. He had sharp news instincts and laudable journalistic standards, the latter in tension with the frugal budget he was allowed. The tension was not about ethical standards—Meyer and Jones were in agreement there, and uncompromising; the question was how much journalistic quality was possible with how few dollars. The fact that Eugene Meyer only a couple of years earlier had been spending so openhandedly on the *Post*, and could again if he wanted to, doubtless had something to do with Casey's angst.

Meyer in fact was personally making up deficits of about $1 million a year. One year he said the loss exceeded his dividend income from Allied Chemical and all the rest of his holdings. (The *Post* did not finally come out of the red until 1943, too late for me.)

The *Post* was one of five daily papers in Washington—next to the last in circulation and about the same in general esteem (except for Morley's distinguished editorial page). Its morning competitor was the much jazzier *Herald*, edited by Eleanor ("Cissy") Patterson of the *Chicago Tribune*–New York *Daily News* clan, and owned by Hearst. The afternoons were the Hearst *Times*; the *Daily News*, a lively Scripps-Howard tabloid; and the rich and sedate *Evening Star*, overflowing with classified ads and District of Columbia news. The *Post* had the most handsome format of the lot, though it was riddled with typographical errors. Its top reporters could occasionally outdig and outwrite the opposition, but in general the troops were spread very thin. We were about thirty reporters in all—beat men and "general assignment."

I was put into the general-assignment pool, reporters available for any sort of local news that turned up—civic banquets, fires, obituaries, suicides, odd new beasts at the zoo, stabbings, shootings (though big crime stories were usually handled by the men on the police beat), bad accidents, the weather when out of the ordinary. On one of the nonordinary days, I decided to interview the chief of the U.S. Weather Bureau, which had not anticipated such an early snow. (Piddling by Minnesota standards—a few inches a few days after Thanksgiving—but a sensation in Washington.) Along the eastern seaboard, the weatherman confided to me, "If you predict weather tomorrow pretty much like today, you will be right three times out of four." I have often suspected that this principle is at work in other earthly matters.

My immediate boss was John Riseling, the City Editor. John often got the summons to Casey's desk, then might tell some reporter to forget what he was doing. "The Boss wants us to get right on" such-and-such. "Phone in by six and lemme know what it looks like." Riseling was a wiry little man, German–Irish Catholic from Philadelphia, three or four newspapers in his past, lightly educated, and loaded with what are now called "street smarts." He was the perfect boss for the greenest of beginners.

One slow day in my first weeks on the *Post*, I was handed the files on three or four of the City Desk's accumulated feature-story tips and suggestions—there's this old guy out in Silver Spring, Maryland, who owns this letter proving it wasn't Booth who shot Lincoln; there's this woman in Georgetown whose cat tries to answer the telephone; etc. I checked them out, by taxi and phone, and told Riseling I didn't think there was a decent story in any of them. Privately, I was wondering if this might be my last day on the *Post*, drawing pay and producing nothing printable. John thanked me for thinning down the files and said it's a good day's work to knock down a lot of stuff that doesn't belong in the paper. "Just don't make a specialty of it."

Riseling made me write faster than I knew how to. When one of the four nightly deadlines was approaching, as the successive editions were made up, he would stand a moment by the desk of any laggard. "Come on, Donovan, we're not putting out an annual." As soon as you turned that story in, he was likely to say, "While you're resting, gimme four or five paragraphs on this" (a snippet from one of our suburban correspondents, a handout from some civic organization).

The first time John gave me a by-line—"you better sign this"—for a series on D.C. philanthropic rackets, he was bothered by my schoolboyish Hedley W. Donovan. "It's your name, of course, but it's better music without the W. The Hedley is enough." This summed up John's fatherly feeling that a Protestant Donovan was an exotic animal; that Hedley, clearly not a saint's name, was pretty fancy, but children don't name themselves; and that this young fellow might have further use for the right by-line. (I never used the W again.) One quiet night a year or two later, Riseling told me to be sure I stayed in journalism—this was a word he rarely used, and it meant he was going to be a little solemn. I was expecting some praise for my prose or analytic powers, which I thought rather well of. "The thing is," John said, "you're honest. A lot of people in this business aren't."

The wooden desks in the *Post* City Room were scarred on all available edges by cigarette burns, the hot varnish doubtless enhancing the properties of the nicotine. A few *Post* reporters actually wore their hats indoors (but not with press cards stuck in the bands— that would have been like the movies). There were real live copy boys, and you caught one by yelling, "Boy!" Along with the incessant phone and typewriters, the police short-wave radio was running: "Domestic trouble in the 600 block of R Street Northwest. . . . Three-car collision Eighth and Pennsylvania Southeast . . . ," and on and on, day and night. In later years as a *Fortune* writer, when I found my little private cell somewhat too antiseptic, I would open the door to let in some corridor chatter.

Washington was a Southern city, notwithstanding all those Union generals, and Admiral Dave Farragut as well, guarding the squares and circles. Blacks as a group were "Negroes" in the pages of the *Post*, but an individual black involved in a crime or accident was "John Doe, 24, colored." Riseling knew the racial makeup of the city block by block, but there were some shifting borderline areas. If he sent out a reporter to cover a shooting in one of these places, his first question when you phoned in was, "Colored?" If yes, "Come on back in." A black man killing his wife got two paragraphs on page twenty-nine. A white man made page one.

The staff could not be duplicated today on any halfway-serious metropolitan newspaper, which is perhaps just as well. Fewer than half the reporters were college graduates. They gave very little business to psychiatrists or divorce-court lawyers. There were two women on the news staff (not counting the all-female "Society" department), and no minorities. ("What do you mean?" Riseling would have said, "I'm Catholic, and the owner is Jewish.") Some of the staff were of the old itinerant breed who would work in one city for a couple of years, then move on to another paper when bills piled up or general restlessness set in. ("Woman trouble" was sometimes mentioned.) They were great storytellers, often better over a bottle than in print. We also had ex-drinkers, a difficult calling in the City Rooms of the 1930s. One of my best friends among the older reporters (i.e., men in their thirties) was a courtly Virginian named Scott Hart, a Civil War buff and a fine self-educated stylist. Scott liked to organize possum hunts, wonderfully vague expeditions in which a dozen or so of us reporters, wives, and dates armed with beer, bourbon, and flashlights would spend half the night slogging through Virginia swamps and thickets selected by our leader. He would sometimes recruit a disreputable dog or two, but I don't recall that a possum was ever treed.

The paper's star reporter was Edward T. Folliard, his face "the map of Ireland," who had gone from a D.C. high school into the navy in World War I. Eddie could cover anything—a presidential election, a Declaration of War, a first-class murder—and he took a generous pleasure in the progress of younger men, passing along useful tips and tactics from his own experience. One that I never quite mastered: If you're interviewing some supposedly tough character, look him up and down slowly, at least once, before you ask your first question. It's important that he should think you know quite a bit already. (But don't stare at him too long—you don't want him to freeze.)

I tried to soak it all up. I had a year or two of the normal flow of local news and features. One Indian-summer day, I did a piece on working farms within the District of Columbia (the Census Bureau had said there were eighty-nine of them), and I learned the hard way what poison ivy looks like in October—lovely golds and scarlet. I required extensive medical attention, submitted a claim to the D.C. Workmen's Compensation Commission for an industrial injury, and was indignant to be refused. The *Post*, less surprisingly, also declined to pay. Another unreimbursed expense was coffee for eight U.S. marines at the drugstore next door to the *Post*. My hospitality came about because of Orson Welles's "War of the Worlds" broadcast reporting an invasion from Mars. I wrote the roundup story on local "reaction" and was weaving together all sorts of stuff being phoned in from all over. Our Alexandria, Virginia, stringer called in with a report that marines in the barracks at Quantico were crying and praying in terror. At the *Post* around noon the next day, I saw a squad of marines approach the City Desk—an imposing sight. I couldn't hear what was said, but the copy boy holding down the desk pointed to the back of the room where I was sitting. The marines advanced on my desk and the lead sergeant said, "Mr. Donovan?" There was no point in denying it. Over coffee they convinced me there had been no unseemly praying and crying at Quantico, and I included this good news in my second-day follow-up story.

I was allowed sometimes to be cultural. I did a few book reviews, and essays for a column on the editorial page called "The Post Impressionist." I even impersonated a music critic at some of the midsummer concerts of the National Symphony, given in a pretty Potomac park innocently known as Watergate. The regular critic was on vacation and the *Post* figured I would do the reviews on my own time for free tickets (all too true). Some *Post* readers had loftier standards. One Frederick F. Fletcher, signing himself A.M., Litt.D., Phil.D., wrote: "Permit me to express my surprise at your critique of Efram Kurtz's interpretation of Tchaikowsky's Sixth Symphony. Of all the uninspired, banal interpretations . . . For one thing, and I am sure you must have noticed it, his phrasing in the fourth movement . . ." I had not noticed it. (I was aware, of course, that "Frederick F. Fletcher" could be an inside job. In those carefree old days the occasional fraternal prank could find its way into print. When the ambitious Society Editor of the *Post* finally overcame Casey Jones's reluctance to spend a couple of hundred dollars so she could cover John Roosevelt's wedding, her front-page story of this elegant event in Nahant, Massachusetts, bore the by-line in the first edition: By Hope Ridings Miller, *Post* Racing Editor. Nobody on the Copy Desk knew how it could have happened.)

Even as an all-purpose City Desk reporter, I had many chances at the bigger stuff (as I saw it), because national and international matters mingled promiscuously with local news. Washington was not Minneapolis. I covered senators and Cabinet officers addressing local dinners; President Roosevelt dedicating a new federal building; Eleanor speaking, shrilly and movingly, to a gathering of social workers; interesting foreigners coming through town—Alexander Kerensky, Batista, King George VI, and Queen Elizabeth. The embassies were a lively half-local, half-international beat that I covered for a while—the German mission's smooth Nazi apologetics; the Czech ambassador responding to Hitler, the Finns to Stalin.

I was initiated quite early into the ways that supposedly competitive reporters for rival papers might violate the spirit of the Sherman Anti-Trust Act. On Saturdays, I was often sent up to Capitol Hill to cover the Senate and House committees that dealt with District of Columbia affairs. Since Washington then had no elected government of its own, these committees were in effect the board of aldermen. It was not the most challenging beat in town—even on weekdays when the regular man was covering—and Saturday was a slow news day in Congress. Midmorning, the Saturday Hill-District men for the Washington papers would convene in one of the Capitol press galleries. The *Star* man was the dean of this specialized little corps, and he would propose in an informal way what the news that day should be. We might agree, for instance, to go together and interview Jennings Randolph of West Virginia, chairman of the House

D.C. Committee, who came to his office on Saturdays to present us that very opportunity. Within the code of our cartel, it was understood that you could say you were also trying to run down "something else," but it was considered sneaky to spend the whole day up there without any collegial conversation. My competitors were being genuinely friendly with me, and they also wanted to make sure this kid didn't disturb the peace. I didn't, up there on the Hill, but after lunch the *Post* might send me downtown to do the Saturday fill-in at State or Navy or Justice, and, depending on how much of my stuff got printed, this could lead to embarrassment for the other Saturday Hill-District men, whose editors might ask how come the *Post* guy has the Jennings Randolph story and also the interview with this admiral? My colleagues (as I thought of them) tended to blame the *Post*, fortunately, rather than me.

Along these same cartelistic lines, it was also in my *Post* local-news days that I developed a quasimonopoly in crowd counting. Covering various dinners and conventions, rallies, demonstrations, parades, I arrived at some rough-and-ready techniques that stood up well alongside "police estimates." In due course, reporters for the other papers would ask me, "How many people would you say are here?" If I said about four thousand, they wouldn't use precisely that number, but they certainly weren't going to say two thousand or seven thousand. I think a scholarly analysis of Washington newspapers in 1938–39, whatever competitive excesses might be revealed, would show a remarkable harmony in crowd estimates.

That long-ago Washington was a great place to live. I settled for a year in a circa 1910 townhouse converted to a rooming house, at 1921 K Street, now (perhaps appropriately) the site of the national headquarters of the American Association of Retired Persons. My old neighborhood of inexpensive bars, restaurants, and lodgings is today Lobbying Central, dozens of squat office buildings housing every conceivable special interest, and many you could not have conceived, and all the law firms feeding off them, and pretentious restaurants to be entered (unless on expense account) at your own peril. But in 1937, I could cross K Street to Parchey's and get a nice lunch for sixty-five cents before going to work at noon or two, whatever my shift. On my days off—Tuesday and Wednesday at first—I walked all over Washington (it was safe to walk anywhere at any hour), sometimes lugging the five-pound WPA guidebook (still a very useful reference work). John Oakes had the same days off, also a car, and we made many runs out into the countryside—from the meandering

Patuxent River in Maryland to the Blue Ridge Mountains of Virginia.

After only six months on the *Post*, I had accumulated such a stupendous amount of overtime—maybe $300 worth, under the newly enacted wage and hour legislation—that Casey Jones called me into his office and said the paper really needed people who could get their work done in forty hours. To clean up these past offenses, however, I could take equivalent time off. So I joined a Rhodes scholar contemporary from Virginia, Willeroy Wells, on a tour through the Carolinas, Georgia, Tennessee, and back to Virginia. I was seeing the South (not the Washington outpost) for the first time, and it was an educational use of my overtime. There was a particularly tender moment in Richmond with a beautiful girl whom Wells had lined up as a date for me. (He had provided for himself equally well.) We were driving past some Civil War cemetery when I was foolish enough to say that I believed some Minnesota troops had fought in the nearby battles. Yes, said my date, they're still here.

Our second year on the *Post*, Oakes and I left our rooming houses and founded a bachelor household on S Street, swiftly filled with Harvard Law School graduates coming to work in the federal agencies or as law clerks to Appeals Court or Supreme Court judges. Chief Justice Harlan Stone and Justice Felix Frankfurter were occasional dinner guests at S Street. My housemates, considerably less solemn than their subsequent careers may sound, included William P. Gray, later to be a federal district judge in California; Porter McKeever, foundation executive and biographer of his old friend Adlai Stevenson; Edwin E. Huddleson, a San Francisco lawyer who was one of the founding fathers of the Rand Corporation and the nonprofit Aerospace Corporation; and Allison Dunham, to be a law professor at the University of Chicago.

After we operated S Street for a year, so many more friends, connections, and classmates had arrived that a second house was rented, called "Hockley," a big place across the river in Arlington. Those with cars tended to go to Hockley, those without to stay on at S Street, but the two houses, with eighteen to twenty bachelors in all, coalesced for touch football games, parties, and picnic expeditions. This spectacular deposit of young men naturally attracted the attention of hostesses, makers of "lists," and mothers of the eligible, so the invitations poured in: dinners and dances, brunches, lunches, "tea" meaning cocktails, tea meaning just that. Much of the inviting came from "cave-dweller" country, the world of ambassadors, admirals, and generals who had married into money, and the widows, children, grandchildren of former senators, Cabinet officers, Supreme Court justices. Official rank, present or past, counted at least as much as money in the Washington social hierarchy, though the ideal, of course, was to have both. The requirements could be waived for a single young man with a dinner jacket and passable manners. Most of the S Street–Hockley syndicate, even the most populist, accepted most of the invitations.

The *Post*'s penuriousness had great advantages for a bachelor reporter who could get himself invited out to a decent meal now and then. Talented reporters with wives and children could be lured away from the *Post* to better-paying jobs at the Washington bureaus of the New York papers—to *Time* or the *Reader's Digest*, to radio news, or lobbies, or government PR offices. So at age twenty-five, with only two years' reporting experience, I found myself moved up to the "national desk," full-time. That could have taken six or eight years on a more prosperous paper.

The shoestring staffing of the *Post* also made it possible for a very junior reporter to play at being a pundit for the Sunday paper. The Sunday "Brains" section included the editorials, columns, some syndicated material, and several staff-written pieces banged out in all-night stints starting around 6 P.M. Friday—after you had written for the daily paper. It was perfectly ethical to get a head start on your Sunday piece by working late Thursday night. Because I had been at Oxford, I was the Sunday paper's authority on British politics and politicians.

I claim to have invented in my Sunday mode what has become one of the most tiresome clichés of modern journalism. I had been assigned a profile of Winston Churchill when he became first lord of the admiralty in the early days of World War II. I browsed through the files, reached back to some episode from Churchill's Boer War experience, and began my story: "Forty years and a half dozen wars ago . . . a young subaltern . . . ," and so on. Today you can hardly read any paper without encountering this wretched device: "Six months and $3 billion earlier . . . ," "Two hours and four martinis later . . . ," etc., etc. If anybody can establish a use of this construction prior to the *Washington Post* of September 10, 1939, my conscience will be much relieved.

For two years I wrote dozens of *Post* Sunday pieces reviewing the war news. Eddie Folliard would also be writing about the war, and we ran a congenial little military desk. "I am right so often," Eddie confessed to me on one of those long Friday nights, "it sometimes frightens me." He usually was, too, though poor Eddie—poor all of us—could hardly wait for the French army to chew up the Germans in the spring of 1940.

For the daily paper, I was now based in the Capitol press galleries, along with John Oakes and our mentor, Robert Albright. Bob usually handled the biggest stories. John and I divided the rest—there was more than enough to go around, and if I had been following a particular committee or piece of legislation that became the biggest news of the moment, Bob would always insist that I should stick with the story. He and the national-desk editor, William Nessly, were old pros but modest about it—gentle, sober guides to the young, and against the generally racy backdrop of our business, they seemed almost like professors in a nice denominational college.

When the war was beginning in Europe, much of the news on Capitol Hill still had to do with the New Deal. That dispensation was past its glory days—FDR's first term—but the momentous changes it had brought were now being adjudicated in the courts, on picket lines, in congressional hearings, in elections. Roosevelt had "lost" the midterm elections of 1938—not only had the Republicans made big gains in the House and the Senate, but, even more tellingly, he had failed to "purge" a number of conservative Democrats in the primaries. (The frugal *Post* had allowed me to cover parts of the New Deal campaign in neighboring Maryland against an offending Democratic senator.) Roosevelt, the masterful politician, was also profoundly polarizing—more so, I would argue, than any president since. Roughly two-thirds of the country loved him; one-third hated him (leaving not much standing room for some of us wishy-washy independents). In later presidencies, sizable portions of the American electorate had, or came to have, dislike or contempt for Johnson, Nixon, Carter, Reagan, but none of these presidents courted that reaction. A somewhat chilling aspect of Roosevelt was that he welcomed the hatred—he could use it in his business—and in this, there were faint but unpleasant resonances with European politics of the 1930s. (Nixon knew the usefulness of haters but didn't have enough lovers to play FDR's game.)

All these aspects of Roosevelt and his opposition were on daily display on Capitol Hill. I covered a Roosevelt tax bill, farm credit bills (a mind-numbing interest of Eugene Meyer's), legislation to raise the national-debt limit to the shocking sum of $65 billion (it approached $2.7 trillion in 1988), to compel a balanced budget, to advance the St. Lawrence Seaway. (A picturesque Illinois senator had warned that the Seaway "would give Great Britain a military avenue through the United States.") I covered congressional hearings on the behavior and biases of the National Labor Relations Board and other new regulatory agencies, and the proceedings of the famous House Un-American Activities Committee, chaired by Martin Dies of Texas, much feared by liberals and the Left but a fairly mild fellow in comparison with the grand inquisitor of a dozen years later, Joe McCarthy. Dies concentrated on Communists and party-liners but also did some investigating of subversives on the Right, including the German-American Bund and the "Silver Shirt Legion" of William Dudley Pelley. I heard the mild-mannered Kansas-born General Secretary of the Communist party, U.S.A., announce at a speech at the University of Virginia: "There is as much chance of Russia and Germany coming together as of Earl Browder being elected president of the United States Chamber of Commerce." Six weeks later, they did come together (Browder never did make it at the chamber), and ten days later, Hitler invaded Poland.

In Washington it was amusing, and disgusting, to watch American Communists and party-liners—who for months had been urging all-out U.S. support for all anti-Nazi forces in Europe—shift to defense of the Soviet-German Non-Aggression Pact as a bulwark against the "imperialist" West. I happened to encounter several young men and women of the Washington Far Left at a Saturday-night party (not originally scheduled for geopolitical reasons) a few hours after the pact was announced. They were in the act of shifting gears, that very evening, and most of the rest of us had a good time making fun of them. Unfortunately, I was no longer in touch with the same people when Germany invaded Russia two years later and Hitler again became the bad guy, and the West, to the extent it aided Russia, again was a good guy.

On Capitol Hill, after the fall of France in June 1940, the familiar domestic controversies of the previous decade were pretty well submerged. Many of the conservative Democrats on the Hill, especially the Southern grandees whose seniority gave them control of key committees, were now Roosevelt's allies in the struggle between "interventionists" and isolationists. And it fell to Hitler to do what had eluded the New Dealers: put an end to the Depression.

One glorious interlude of old-fashioned Democratic vs. Republican politics remained: the presidential campaign of 1940. I had landed a place on the *Post* campaign team courtesy of the *New York Herald Tribune*. The *Herald Trib* had offered me a job at $75 a week.

In an athletic bargaining session with Casey Jones, I worked him up in $5 increments from the $42.50 I was then getting. At $57.50, I sensed I was approaching a zone where he would wish me luck at the *Herald Trib*. I proposed we settle at $60. I felt I would get better assignments at the *Post* than at the bigger and better-staffed *Herald Trib*, and just to nail that down, I asked to go to the nominating conventions. The Republican convention in Philadelphia was a rip-snorter, the kind that actually chose a candidate, as opposed to ratifying the results of a string of primaries: dramatic roll calls, wheeling and dealing right out on the floor, finally Wendell Willkie on the sixth ballot. At Chicago, the press watched more as theater critics: How well would Roosevelt's men stage his unprecedented third-term "draft," how gracefully or otherwise would the losers withdraw, who would FDR choose to replace the disgruntled Jack Garner as VP? (It turned out to be Henry Wallace, himself to be dumped in 1944 in favor of Harry Truman.)

I was the "color" writer on the *Post* team, and I had lovely stuff to work with: the suburban garden-club ladies chanting, "We want Willkie" in the streets and hotel lobbies of Philadelphia, the Cook County machine pols who unmistakably wanted Roosevelt, the crazy vice-presidential boomlets, the outlandish oratory. H. L. Mencken wrote that a nominating convention could be "a show so gaudy and hilarious, so melodramatic and obscene, so preposterous . . . that one lives a gorgeous year within an hour." Imagine then, being twenty-six years old, sitting next to the great Mencken himself, who was holding court in a Baltimore & Ohio club car on our way out to the Democratic convention. After some pungent political talk (Mencken thought FDR was a fraud), he asked the little circle of reporters: "What was the funniest spoken line you ever heard of in your life?" He listened to our entries and then answered his own question: It was Mark Twain saying he would rather sleep with Lillian Russell stark naked than with General Grant in full uniform.

But the war in Europe increasingly dominated Washington and the work of the press. On the *Post* National Desk, still understaffed, everybody got a crack at everything at one time or another. I covered the stream of supplemental appropriations bills for the War and Navy departments, congressional hearings on Roosevelt's destroyers-for-bases deal with Britain, lend-lease aid to Britain, legislation to authorize the president to order the Army Reserve and National Guard into immediate service, Senator Harry Truman's hearings on defense production, the modification and ultimately the repeal of the "Neutrality Act." The administration was indeed becoming more and more unneutral by the month.

I had a close-up look at Roosevelt's supremely skillful dealings with congressional and public opinion. Along the way, he told some lies, possibly necessary. He was more convinced than most of the American public that it was imperative to prevent a German victory. In stages, and with uncanny timing, he marshaled support for the "short-of-war" measures that increasingly committed us to the defeat of Hitler. If he was in front of much of the country, he was grateful to have others publicly in front of him. Among those up front he valued most were some of those unreconstructed Bourbon senators, anti–New Deal but pro-intervention, men of that strong Southern military-patriotic reflex that still (I would argue) is a great American asset. FDR did not stop the Republican warriors he had coopted for the Cabinet—Henry Stimson to the War Department, Frank Knox to Navy—from saying whatever bellicose things they believed. And he was happy to have much of the Eastern press—the *Herald Trib*, the *Times* more cautiously, Henry Luce's incautious *Time, Life, Fortune*, and the *Washington Post*—urging him to go farther and faster. The *Post* had come to a parting of the ways with Felix Morley. He was a Quaker of pacifist tendencies who had been a strong "collective security" supporter in the prewar days, but once the war started, he gravitated toward isolationism. Meyer was a fervent interventionist and, much as he had despised many aspects of the New Deal and FDR, he backed him to the hilt on the war.

The most sensitive of all the administration's defense measures was the draft. "Charges of 'slacker' and 'liar' were traded in the Senate yesterday," I wrote in the *Post* of August 7, 1940, "as the dynamite in the conscription issue exploded in both houses of Congress." Casey Jones soon asked me to stop calling it "conscription"—the word reminded him of "Russian serfs clanking along in chains." So it became "the draft," or, more formally, "selective service," in the dozens of stories I was to write on the subject (in which I also took some personal interest, as a healthy young man with no dependents). I covered the ceremonial drawing of the first draft numbers, in the cavernous Interdepartmental Auditorium on Constitution Avenue. The president spoke, briefly and solemnly, and Secretary Stimson, blindfolded, reached into the glass bowl that had been used for the same purpose in 1917.

Some of Eugene Meyer's grandchildren took over the same auditorium in 1987 for a birthday party in honor of their mother, Katharine Graham, the chairman of the Washington Post Company. I suspected I was the only one among the Grahams' six hundred guests who had been in the room on that earlier occasion (I know Henry Kissinger and George Shultz weren't), but since I was not on the speaking program, I had no chance to assert my claim. President Reagan did speak, in spite of everything the *Post*'s writers and the merciless cartoonist Herblock had done to him, and finished with a jaunty toast to Kay: "Here's looking at you, kid." The equivalent courtesies between Franklin Roosevelt and Eugene Meyer are hard to visualize.

The climactic event in the long-running draft story came on the night of August 12, 1941. I watched the House, in one of the most dramatic roll calls in its history, vote 203 to 202 to extend the service of draftees, reservists and guardsmen—originally set at one year— by another eighteen months. The vote was a fair reflection of the division in national opinion as to whether the country was in serious danger. There were no cliff-hanger roll calls on the huge appropriations for more ships, planes, tanks, guns. These made sense for the same reason the draft extension did, but they also had an interested constituency: labor unions, business, seaports, and scores of other cities—maybe three hundred of the 435 congressional districts. But that was only money; "American boys" were a different matter.

I would have voted that August night with the 203, and I was relieved there were only 202 against us. I don't think my story in the paper the next morning reflected any partisan tone of triumph. The old protocol was, "No cheering in the press box."

When the war started, I had thought America would stay out and certainly should. I preferred, of course, not to be shot at. I also carried a touch of Middle Western isolationism and my college-bred convictions on the folly and futility of the previous war. In June 1940, when I was in Minneapolis for my sister's wedding, France was falling in the paper every day, and my father, who hated "harrowing" war movies or novels—indeed anything bloody or brutal—said he was afraid we might have to "go in." Somehow his quiet comment, in the safe and gentle mid-American house where I had grown up, weighed more with me than any senator's speech up on that Hill, where thunderous warnings and prophecies were so commonplace.

I was in favor of all the defense legislation I covered in 1940–41, but nobody ever complained that it showed in my reporting. Indeed, my being from Minnesota, forgive the *Post*, gave me a kind of safe-conduct pass in the isolationist camp. I had a history student's awe at seeing the legendary Western isolationist senators, whose roots I understood, making their last stand: Gerald Nye of North Dakota, Burton Wheeler of Montana, the great William Borah of Idaho. On the administration side, the most consistently impressive and convincing of all the witnesses who came before the Hill committees was the army chief of staff, General George C. Marshall. Covering many hours of his testimony, I knew then this was a great man.

Late in the summer of 1941, I moved downtown from Capitol Hill to the White House and the State Department, which became my beat for the last few months before Pearl Harbor and the first month or two after. Now I was seeing Roosevelt twice a week at his press conferences, which in those civilized days before TV, drew just forty or fifty correspondents who could stand comfortably in two rows (taller men behind) arcing around the president's desk. We left our forty or fifty hats on a big table in the West Wing reception hall and were glanced at by one Secret Service man as we walked to the Oval Office. I would guess the Secret Service in 1941 was maybe one-fiftieth its present size; one didn't know the numbers then and doesn't now. I am not complaining—we have had Lee Harvey Oswald and the shots at Ford and Reagan, and the whole ghastly proliferation of crazies, foreign and domestic. But "security" burdens the interchange between the president and the country, including the press. Isolation from "out there," always a hazard for presidents, gets more enveloping.

The spectacularly self-confident FDR, as I saw him in those press conferences, clearly thought he knew the American voter backward and forward. He was not far wrong. Even as he cherished and used his bitterest political enemies, he appealed to, and himself deeply believed in, the patriotic values of generally conservative Americans. He knew, too, that some traditionally Democratic voters were against him on the war issue—those Irish who still hated Britain, those Poles who hated the Russians even more than they hated the Germans— and he needed Republican supporters to offset these defections. The numerous isolationists who were not so isolationist about Japan and the Pacific could also be useful to him. Working with all these themes, he played the press conference like an orchestra. He almost never gave an exclusive interview, but the press conferences and frequent speeches were a generally reliable guide to where he wanted to go, and he did not discourage White House staff, congressional allies, the executive departments from elaborating. Quite a lot could be found out.

By November 1941, the administration was heavily preoccupied with the Pacific. Japan sent a special "peace envoy" to Washington, Saburo Kurusu, even as its fleet and troop maneuvers in Southeast Asia became increasingly aggressive. Kurusu and the Japanese ambassador, Admiral Kichisaburo Nomura, saw Roosevelt and Secretary of State Cordell Hull on November 27. The day before, however, I had concluded from conversations in State, the negotiations had already collapsed. I wrote a story saying so, that the United States had refused to recognize Japanese conquests in China and had rejected proposals that would have amounted to "a Pacific Munich." The Associated Press, however, was taking a more hopeful line about the negotiations, and so was *The New York Times* (whose first-edition front page was summarized nightly on the AP wire for editors all over the country). Casey Jones came over to my desk, asked me a few questions about my sources, and said he would go with my story. He could have run the AP story by its experienced diplomatic correspondent. He was taking a big chance on a big story, with a brand-new man on the White House–State beat. This was an act of "loyalty down" that I never forgot.

I covered the Far Eastern news of the next ten days, as seen from the White House and State. My lead story in the *Washington Post* of Sunday morning, December 7, said that President Roosevelt, "in an eleventh-hour attempt to stave off war in the Pacific," had taken the unprecedented step of addressing a personal message to Emperor Hirohito, appealing to that divinity "over the heads" of the militarist cabinet in Tokyo. I wrote of "storm signals flying all across the Far East," as I worked to weave into one story what could be learned in Washington with the cables coming in from the other side of the world.

My story finished, I went home around 2 A.M. to Dorothy, my wife of a few weeks. I was fairly well wound up, and we talked a while about the news. I thought war was now almost certain and would begin with a Japanese attack on Thailand or the Dutch East Indies (oil), or both.

We were still in bed, early the next afternoon, when the symphony concert on our radio was interrupted by the bulletin about Pearl Harbor. I dressed and got right down to the State Department, leaving barely seconds ahead (Dorothy told me later) of a call from a *Wash-*

ington Post operator. Afterward, people were celebrated for having been paged over the public-address system at a Washington Redskins football game. I felt no need to compete in the where-were-you-when-you-heard conversations.

Now that it was "U.S. At War" (the December 8 headline), I entirely agreed with the *Post* authorities that our incomparable Eddie Folliard should take over the White House beat. From there he wrote the paper's lead story for several days, but he and I and two or three other *Post* reporters were soon moving more or less interchangeably between the White House and State, War and Navy. Those were long working days and grim, as we reported at least some of the dimensions of America's initial defeat and of the long effort ahead.

The most cheering sight in that somber season was the mischievous face of Winston Churchill, as he stood on a chair in the Oval Office, a few days before Christmas, to give the V-for-victory sign. (On the night of Pearl Harbor, as he wrote in his war memoirs, he had gone to bed "and slept the sleep of the saved and thankful.")

On my final day at the *Washington Post*, in late January 1942, the paper, thrifty to the last, got two stories out of me: "Americans Serving Allies Urged to Stay" (in the RAF, and so on), and "Roosevelt, Churchill Reached Full Accord on Joint War Operations, White House Says." Well, for a few weeks, anyway.

The girl I went home to the night before Pearl Harbor had been somebody else's date at a Georgetown beer party two years earlier. When I met her, Dorothy Hannon had just finished training at one of the Washington hospitals as a bacteriologist. This was a field in which my interest was minimal, but Dorothy had an enthusiastic curiosity about my work—indeed, about everything and everybody in Washington. She had a quick mind and a sharp sense of humor. We were to do a lot of laughing together over the next thirty-nine years. She was also very attractive—not quite beautiful, perhaps, but close. She had come from Erie, Pennsylvania, where her father had been an accountant and broker. He was badly battered by the Depression, seriously ill for years, and died in his fifties. Dorothy studied at nearby Allegheny College, in Meadville, Pennsylvania, but two years was as long as the family finances would allow her to stay, so she came to Washington to earn her living.

We began to see a good deal of each other, and I delighted in the warmth and speed of her rapport with my *Post* friends, with miscel-

laneous Minnesotans in Washington, visiting Donovans, Rhodes
scholars, and the S Street–Hockley dwellers. Indeed she got on so
well with the latter that no fewer than three of them at one time or
another asked me if it would be all right to phone her for a date.
(Others may have phoned her without my permission.) I said of
course. We each continued to see other people for quite a while after
we had met, then that began to seem a little silly, and we decided to
get married, which we did on October 18, 1941. The wedding was in
Erie's Episcopalian Cathedral of St. Paul (though no Episcopalians
were involved) for the sufficient reason that Dorothy's mother liked
the service there. She herself was a Congregationalist of Connecticut
Yankee stock tracing back to colonial times; her Irish-blooded husband was a fallen-away Catholic; Dorothy had gone to a Presbyterian
Sunday school; and my own Baptist upbringing added a further ecu-
menical detail. Notwithstanding, the legality of the ceremony was
never challenged. I was twenty-seven, Dorothy not quite twenty-
three.

It was just a week or two before I was to be married that I received
a notice from my local draft board—"Greeting!" A board of your
neighbors has selected you . . . to report for induction into the army
a month hence. I knew this summons would arrive sooner or later
because I had been classified 1A in my physical exam and I had no
family or occupational grounds for a deferment. The timing was jolt-
ing, however, because I had a fairly high (i.e., nice) draft number and
the general tempo of the call-ups had been such that I wasn't expecting that greeting for at least another year. I had admired several
low-draft-number friends who might have tried for commissions but
chose instead to let themselves be drafted, took basic training at $21
a month, and then earned a place in officers' training camp. This stoic
course had some appeal to me, but Dorothy had more appeal. I applied for a commission in Naval Intelligence, hoping that the training
might keep me in Washington at least a few months, and, in a period
still officially "peacetime," I might even be stationed there.

The Office of Naval Intelligence, in those pre–Pearl Harbor days,
took its sweet time investigating candidates for a commission. I had
completed all the application formalities by early November 1941
(my draft board then gave me a deferment), and now the ONI investigators went to work on my character, habits, political views, family
background. It took them three months to check me out. I was amazed

they could find so much to investigate in somebody only twenty-seven.

Two questions of political reliability turned out to be the problem. A possibility of subversion from the Left arose when the ONI investigators found my name on the mailing list of one of the many aid-to-Russia groups that flourished in Washington after the Nazi attack on the Soviets. I explained to the gumshoes that reporters accredited to the Capitol and White House press corps were listed by name and address in the *Congressional Directory* and tended to get a lot of mail—from Right, Left, Prohibitionists, Single Taxers, friends of the sugar industry, etc. (I thought it would only confuse the issue to tell them I had gone to a Paul Robeson concert where some prankster in our party put my name on a card requesting further literature from the party-line coalition that sponsored the event.) The ONI people were further comforted by an interview with the staff chief of the House Un-American Activities Committee, who told them I was utterly un-Communist and totally American. Not being a great fan of the Dies Committee or the tactics of its staff, I found this testimonial a little disconcerting, though maybe the moral is, you take your character witnesses where you find them.

I was reminded of my Dies Committee credentials when I learned that Richard Nixon many years later certified me as an upstanding anti-Communist. His good friend and legal client Elmer Bobst of the Warner-Lambert Company was a fellow trustee of mine at New York University (Elmer was very rich and generous, hence Bobst Library). His wife was Lebanese and intensely suspicious of the U.S. media because of their well-known pro-Zionist and pro-Soviet bias. She and Elmer had both missed out on the news that the Soviets and their stooges and satellites were stridently anti-Israel. She and I had some heated dinner-table arguments (late 1960s), which led Elmer to ask Nixon, whom he understood to know everybody in the press, whether I was some sort of pinko. Nixon assured him I was okay.

The other "loyalty" question that ONI looked into arose out of a profile of Viscount Halifax that I wrote for the *Post* when he arrived in Washington as British ambassador. As he was making his courtesy calls, he arrived at the Capitol chambers of the crusty Speaker, Sam Rayburn, and gave his name to a secretary. She, according to an embassy aide I knew, phoned in to the Speaker: "A Mr. Halifax to see you." I printed this in my (generally admiring) profile, and Rayburn was incensed. He thought I had made him and his staff look like yokels and had embarrassed the ambassador. I was called into

Rayburn's office, a woodshed where men much more important than I had often quailed. I "stood by my story," as the saying goes, and months later there was enough lingering resentment in the Speaker's office that somebody there told ONI that I must be anti-British, and possibly pro-German, perhaps because of Irish antecedents. Friends of mine at the British Embassy, including the naval attaché, reassured ONI and even confided that the ambassador rather liked the "Mr. Halifax" story.

The investigative proceedings came to a suitably comic ending. While one branch of ONI was still probing my loyalty and patriotism, another branch asked me to come to work right away as a "civilian agent"—let the commission come through later. So on January 26, 1942, I reported to a section called Op-16-P-4, and within hours was asked to start studying several files of classified documents, some highly sensitive. Fortunately, this threat to national security lasted only a few weeks; in mid-February, the other fellows finally cleared me. I was appointed an ensign in the Naval Reserve and ordered to report for active duty in the office where I was already working.

Op-16-P-4 was putting out confidential publications on enemy naval dispositions; "order of battle" of the Japanese, German, Italian armies; new enemy equipment; economic and political conditions within the Axis countries and their occupied territories. My boss was Navy Commander Vaughn Bailey, and, like so many Annapolis men of his generation, he felt that war with Japan was what his education and training had prepared him for. When it came, he was not entirely pleased to find himself anchored on Constitution Avenue, Washington, D.C., commanding a miscellany of lawyers, journalists, and professors. He was good-natured about it, though, and tolerant of the incorrigibly civilian character of the fake ensigns and lieutenants in his command. (When he made out the annual "fitness reports," he would rate me a perfect 4.0 in courage, alertness, and other martial qualities, and then, to give the report a faint plausibility, would mark me 3.8 in "military bearing.") The commander could be a stickler on some points, however, and this led to a further awkwardness about my commission. By the time I got my ensign's appointment, Bailey had already put me in charge of half a dozen people, including two Lieutenants Junior Grade. He felt it was unseemly for me to be bossing men who outranked me, so he undertook a long bureaucratic struggle to get the authorities to change my commission from Ensign to Lieutenant J.G., one rank higher than customary for reservists in their twenties. So I continued as a civilian agent (sorely trying the patience of my draft board, who thought I should be in uniform by now) until May 1942, when Commander Bailey finally prevailed over the "Bureau of Navigation" and landed me the extra half stripe.

What followed was an utterly unheroic and richly instructive experience. I was eventually supervising the work of about fifteen people, chiefly engaged in publishing the ONI *Weekly*, classified Confidential—halfway between Restricted and Secret. The enemy and his equipment were our chief subjects. We printed about fifteen thousand copies (at the Government Printing Office), and probably had a "readership," as the competitive magazine ads would now say, of at least a hundred thousand officers. We benefited, it must be admitted, from the general shortage of reading matter in the fleet and at overseas bases, and from the relatively high priority we were given in navy mail. When Admiral Thomas Inglis, chief of Naval Intelligence at the end of the war, issued me a Letter of Commendation, he noted that I had put out some four million words of intelligence material without ever compromising security; among other virtues, I had shown "sound judgment in questions requiring the greatest discretion." I think he sincerely believed this quite remarkable in a civilian, a newspaperman at that.

So I was essentially an editor disguised by a uniform, dealing with special kinds of material, surrounded by special ground rules, but working with a staff from out of my own worlds. Some of what I may know about the management of intellectuals (chapter I), I picked up in the navy. Though I was still a journalist of sorts, I was now expected to lead others—very different work from that of the reporter, who is a highly individualistic and competitive character, competitive not just with other publications, but with colleagues in his own organization. The atmosphere in the *Weekly* office was a mix of Ivy League law school, newspaper city room, ad agency, and faculty club. Theoretically, I could issue orders—my writers couldn't threaten to quit—and I suppose I sometimes did, but in general the *Weekly* got written by suggestion and persuasion.

Around 6 P.M., one of my bespectacled lawyer-writers might approach my desk and in great good humor sing out, "Permission to leave the ship, Sir!" Permission granted. And off we would go to queue up for buses on Constitution Avenue. Among the alumni of Op-16-P-4, Peter Frelinghuysen became an eleven-term congressman from New Jersey; Roy Steyer and John Woolsey partners in prestigious New York and Boston law firms; C. Vann Woodward, Sterling Professor of History at Yale; Will T. Jones, a distinguished professor of philosophy at Pomona College; and William Bentinck-Smith, a Harvard administrator and historian of the university.

One lawyer who did not work out well in Op-16-P-4 was James Pike, who had been with the SEC in civilian life. He later became a navy chaplain and rose in the Episcopal Church to become Dean of the Cathedral of St. John the Divine in New York, and then bishop of California. I had not seen him for more than twenty years when I was invited to a lunch by *Time* editors who were interviewing Jim for a cover story. Jim was startled to see me, then startled my colleagues even more by saying he owed his whole career in the Church to me, since it was I who had told him he was not meant to be an intelligence officer. Jim was passionately liberal in social outlook, held increasingly unorthodox doctrinal views, and led a hectic personal life. In the press, "the controversial" became as much a part of his name as Bishop. He eventually resigned his diocese, was censured by the House of Bishops, took up spiritualism, founded his own "Foundation for Religious Transition," and on his honeymoon with his third wife lost his way in the Judean Desert and died there at fifty-six.

I came to respect the professional military whom I had once thought so laughable, when not actually sinister, in my *Minnesota Daily* editorials. (I did happen to be right in my impression that Lieutenant Colonel Lloyd Fredendall, commandant of the Minnesota ROTC, was not terribly smart. Ten years later, Eisenhower had to relieve Major General Fredendall of command of II Corps after his sorry performance in the Tunisia campaign.) But the professional officer corps of the U.S. Navy and U.S. Army, as of early 1942, was a more devoted and generally capable body of guardians than our stingy and semipacifist society understood, or maybe deserved.

I learned, along with the rest of our idealistic and once-isolated country, that the human capacity for evil can create horrors worse than war, that there can be a necessary war, a good war. I had already come to understand this as a reporter in 1940–41, but now there was a pride, which I once might have thought juvenile, in being an officer of the United States Navy in a just war. Out of such emotions and excitement, nations defend themselves—or overreach themselves. But I came to a fuller respect for—in a word—patriotism. And I would tack on, in a Blimpish footnote of the late 1980s, that I do not believe that the "true strength" of the nation lies in the quality of our school-lunch programs or our care for the elderly. Much of it resides, and always has, in the willingness of men to fight for their country.

Encrusted with tradition as it was, intensely bureaucratic in its shore structure, the U.S. Navy did work. Indeed, it showed remarkable adaptability—to a war all over the world, to torrents of billions of dollars, and to three million young men and women pouring in. I saw that there had to be a solid core around which all this could be organized, and the core was the men who had gone to Annapolis ten, twenty, twenty-five years earlier.

That core: I could see in the combat reports that came into Op-16-P-4 how most battles, even the fate of nations, might come down to the bravery and reflexes of a very few men at the crucial point of concentration. This was famously true of the Hurricane and Spitfire fighter pilots in the Battle of Britain. And at Midway, the navy men in fifty-odd dive-bombers started the United States on the long road back against Japan. Even nations with the massive manpower of the United States and the Soviet Union, and the industrial base and geographical isolation of the United States, though they can afford blunders and defeats, are not guaranteed victory. I came to see chance and fate as being at least the equal of any impersonal forces of history. What if Britain had been led by anybody but Churchill in the late summer and fall of 1940? What if Hitler had followed his generals' advice, consolidated his sensational early victories over the Soviets, and let the capture of Moscow await good weather in 1942? For that matter, what if Hitler had been in all other respects the totalitarian aggressor that he was, but not anti-Semitic? What if the Japanese continued their aggressions elsewhere in the Far East but had not attacked the Philippines or Pearl Harbor? What if a few brilliant back-room people in the United States and United Kingdom had not broken some of the Japanese and German codes? Even with that immense advantage, we came close enough to not winning.

I thought I already knew the distinction between emotions about the enemy and facts (or probable facts) about the enemy. ONI was insistent on this point. The *Weekly* was expected to be utterly immune to the propaganda of our own side, the misleading communiqués that could come out of some Allied headquarters, the cheerleading tone, natural enough, in much of the American and British press coverage of the war. From the intelligence materials we received, it was all too clear that the quality of the German soldier and his officers was superb; we would have outraged people who knew this firsthand if we had implied otherwise. Likewise, the fanatic bravery of the Japanese, often squandered by some impossibly rigid plan, but inspiring awe among U.S. Navy, Marines, Army who came up against it.

All this flowed through Op-16-P-4. To put out our Confidential weekly, we had to know some of the Secret material to avoid, and why it was Secret. In late May 1942, Op-16-P-4 was preparing to publish some material on Japanese fleet movements. I was called into the office of the ONI director himself, Rear Admiral Theodore Wilkinson. He told me, "You can't use that." (No suggesting or persuading nonsense.) I offered the layman's usual response: Surely the Japanese know where their own ships are? The admiral was patient. "The Japanese don't know that we know," he told me, and he told me how we knew. Only a few days later, the United States won the Battle of Midway; the cryptographers could share the glory with the dive-bomber pilots. I was not to tell my staff about the code—just to make sure that nothing that could have been derived only from crypt-analysis ever got printed with a mere Confidential classification—in case of doubt, check with the director's office.

Confidential was indeed an ambiguous classification. It meant, approximately, that there would be no grave damage to the national interest if this piece of paper fell into enemy hands, but we certainly preferred that it didn't. For the *Weekly*, with its print order of fifteen thousand copies, and a much wider circulation, Confidential was a very liberal charter. (Absurdly so, a few old Regulars thought; for anything to be *printed* and call itself Confidential was to them a contradiction in terms.)

The P-4 staff needed to be fully aware of everything that was already in this morning's utterly unclassified *New York Times*. The latter necessity led to a terrifying moment for Commander Bailey, because our section for a time was lodged right outside the Top Secret Chart Room (whence we derived some of our raw material) to which the ferocious Admiral Ernest King came at 0815 for his daily briefing. King was commander-in-chief of the U.S. Fleet, though President Roosevelt hadn't been too keen on having another commander-in-chief around. But he needed King, and COMINCH was what King wanted (instead of the customary CNO, Chief of Naval Operations). An eager new flag lieutenant is said to have told Admiral King, "Sir, your every wish is my command," and the admiral is said—I hope this story is true—to have replied, "You're goddamn right it is." In P-4, our odd little flotilla came to work at 0800, and then started reading the *Times*. King had to walk through our office to reach The Room; when he approached, attended by lesser admirals and captains, we put down the *Times* and stood to attention. After a few days of this, King asked some aide to find out why all these healthy-looking young men, supposedly officers "of the line," were sitting in Washington reading newspapers. Bailey told a captain, who told a rear admiral, who told King why these healthy young men were reading the papers. I don't know whether he was persuaded, but we were soon moved from that sensitive region to a newly slapped-together "tempo" alongside the Lincoln Memorial Reflecting Pool. This was an un-air-conditioned plywood and plasterboard affair. Summer in our second-"deck" office, right under the flat roof, was an inferno.

Admiral King had a point. Though most of the young officers of P-4 had such bad eyesight they could not have qualified for sea duty, two of us could have. The other was the son of an admiral, and he eventually wangled himself out of Washington and to the Pacific. I kept applying for sea duty, but ONI insisted I was more useful at what I was doing. Finally, in June 1945, my boss agreed to let me transfer in September to a training school that sent combat intelligence officers out to the fleet. But until I took the course in "Navy Regulations and Customs," I wouldn't be admitted to the Combat Intelligence School. "Regs" was a charming sort of primer, much of it laid down in the nineteenth century, for all newly commissioned officers. I had somehow served three years in the navy without doing the course. So, in the summer of 1945, after a day of editing the *Weekly*, I would stay late at the office to study such matters as:

- The personnel of the Navy are not required to respect religious institutions and customs of pagan countries. (False)

- The proper salute for the Secretary of the Navy. (19 guns)

- What governs the size of the shore patrol landed in liberty ports? (The shore patrol should be large enough to maintain order and suppress any unseemly conduct in the liberty party. Other considerations would include degree of cooperation to be expected from the local police and length of time since the last liberty.)

I was getting good marks in Regs, usually 3.85 or 3.9 out of the possible 4.0. I completed my seventh assignment—there were fourteen in all—a few days early; it was due on the date that turned out to be V-J Day. I'm afraid I never did finish Regs. Had I done eight through fourteen, and had there been an invasion of the Japanese home islands in the spring of 1946, I might have been along.

. . . .

Up to a point, ONI did understand the restlessness of its desk-bound officers. Somebody worked out a kind of Fresh Air program for deserving young men who had served eighteen months or more in Washington; they could apply for courier duty and carry the classified mail pouches that had to be escorted by an armed intelligence officer to destinations overseas. So, in the winter of 1944, I was awarded one of these six-week scholarships. I took a revolver marksmanship course in a basement shooting range under the National Art Gallery, of all places. The .45 was in case anybody tried to steal my pouches. I also received a distasteful medical briefing in a bleak hangar at the Washington National Airport, where an army doctor advised me by no means to touch or even kick any dead rat at "the next place you are going." I went, in fact, to LaGuardia Airport (which was not where he had in mind), Newfoundland, the Azores, Casablanca, and then Algiers, where the plague that Albert Camus later wrote about was still considered a military secret, because of its effect on the Allied bases. I never saw any rats. I got an intelligence officer in Algiers to write me orders to Naples, where I could hitch a ride to the Anzio beachhead, where I thought I might find an article for the *Weekly*; then a higher-ranking officer told me I had to move my mail along. So I proceeded to Cairo, Alexandria, Karachi, and New Delhi, where I unloaded the last of my pouches. Back to Washington with more mail, via Aden, Khartoum, Accra, Ascension Island, the bulge of Brazil, Puerto Rico, and Miami. Everything was new to me; flying across the ocean, North Africa, Egypt, India, even Florida. It was a great adventure, even the long hours in those noble old DC-4s and DC-3s of the Army Air Transport Command.

I had a sinfully easy life during the war. Dorothy and I found a pleasant little apartment on Summit Place, above Rock Creek Park and the zoo, so close that at night we could sometimes hear the creatures down there shrieking and bellowing—all entertaining, of course, to a young couple much in love. My old S Street bachelor household was always full; people went off to all the fronts and services, others came in, and the place remained a kind of club for us. Dorothy was the leading spirit of the Ladies' Auxiliary. She kept her medical job for about three years, until our son Peter was about to be born. With two paychecks and the wartime limitations on what you could buy, we had, oddly enough, as much money as we knew what to do with. We came out of World War II with a net worth of $2,000 in U.S. Savings Bonds.

I'm not sure the bonds had anything to do with it, but I moved during those years from somewhat liberal to somewhat conservative. (I am not a very fiery fellow.) The war and the navy and its values certainly influenced me. So did getting married and signing my first will—two standard sentences supplied by the navy—before I set out on my courier trip. Becoming a father had something to do with it. Also, having a widowed mother-in-law turn to me as "the man in the family" to handle her pitifully small investment portfolio (utterly innocent as I was about the stock market). "Widows and orphans" as stockholders were figures of fun in New Deal mythology; they seemed less funny now.

I liked ONI so much I even considered staying in after the war. Briefly. I did keep up active status in the Naval Reserve for several years, and voyaged by subway to the Brooklyn Navy Yard for monthly classes and briefings. These meetings began to be hard to fit in with the rest of my life, and I eventually applied for transfer to the Inactive Status list. When I was notified of my transfer, the message from Admiral J. L. Holloway, Jr., stated:

> During your career you have witnessed the growth of our Navy into the world's mightiest. You have contributed materially to that tremendous growth. . . . Please acknowledge receipt of this letter.

V

Fortune University

A week or two after V-J Day, I paid a call on Casey Jones at the *Washington Post*. He said he would be delighted to have me back on his staff. He was in fact compelled by act of Congress to be delighted; returning veterans were legally entitled to their old jobs. But I knew he would be genuinely pleased to have me back, in part because he urged me to look elsewhere. He was against my exploring Minneapolis (which we both liked as a place to live). "In our work," Casey said, "you should be in New York." This was wise and generous advice—mildly disadvantageous for the *Washington Post*, which would be losing a useful and inexpensive reporter, good for Hedley Donovan. So in the autumn of 1945, I relished the once-in-a-lifetime situation of being on one payroll (the U.S. Navy for a month or so longer), having a solid backup offer from another employer (the *Post*), and enjoying the encouragement of both bosses to look for the best other job I could find. It was a situation in which a young man could go into job interviews with a certain confidence and no sense of disloyalty to his present place of business.

And it was a zestful time to be job hunting in journalism. Almost everybody I interviewed was interested, a happy contrast with the bleak Depression days when I had previously made the rounds. Most publishers had prospered during the war; people had been hungry for things to read, about the war of course, but also about everything else; and the excess-profits tax meant that big national advertisers were getting their ad pages for fourteen-cent dollars. Publishers were full of expansion plans—new publications, new editions, bigger staffs.

In New York, I approached just about everybody I could think of in what we didn't then call the media: *The New York Times*, *Herald Tribune*, *Daily News*, Associated Press, *Newsweek*, *Reader's Digest*, CBS News, NBC News, Time Inc. A Minnesota fraternity brother, Carl Burkland, arranged a CBS radio recording test and said of my platter that I sounded like "the voice of doom—slow doom." Carl himself was an experienced announcer with a mellifluous baritone, and he suggested print would be better for me. I'm sure he was right (though I catch the occasional TV commercial these days where I think I could handle the old-codger role better than the fellow they seem to be stuck with).

At Time Inc., I was interviewed by Eric Hodgins, a former publisher and managing editor of *Fortune* (it was Hodgins the drunken writer had threatened to kill), now a corporate vice president assigned to a postwar talent-recruiting program. His office was on the topmost floor of the "old" Time and Life Building, later the General Dynamics Building, on Rockefeller Plaza. Our appointment was on one of those electric October evenings when Manhattan did indeed seem a magic island, and perhaps not quite impregnable. I had allowed forty-five minutes, and as an outlander was pleased I hit it just right, to walk from the neighborhood of 72nd and York, where I was staying with friends.* I had drunk in the glorious views of the skyline all the way down Fifth, as the smoky-red sunset faded and the lights came up in the skyscrapers of Central Park South and West. (I still can't bring myself to say "high-rise.") Mr. Hodgins offered me a cigarette and, as his secretary was closing the door, said, "Oh, Miss ———, please hold my calls for the next half hour." What class! Years later, I still hadn't got the hang of telling my secretary to hold my calls. Eric eventually would give up the executive life, becoming justly famous and rewarded as the author of *Mr. Blandings Builds His Dream House*. And when I was managing editor of *Fortune*, he and I enjoyed an affec-

---

*William Baring-Gould and his wife. Bill was an established writer in the *Time* Promotion Department, but I knew him as "Billy Boy," because he had lived next door in Minneapolis, where his mother more than once predicted that my brother David and I, because of various hoaxes we engineered, could well end up in the state penitentiary (especially David). Bill, a grandson of the Anglican rector who wrote "Onward, Christian Soldiers," became a Baker Street buff and published a "biography" of Sherlock Holmes. Bill was also a world-class collector of limericks and gathered some of his favorites into an anthology, *The Lure of the Limerick*, not all the verses suitable to the rectory.

tionate and peppery relationship in which he was one of my best and most maddening (which is saying a lot) writers.

But that evening in October 1945, Hodgins was charmed by what he chose to regard as an incredible coincidence: that I had sought a job interview with Time Inc. even as he, in his recruiting-sergeant role, had been trying to locate me. He was hunting for, among several species, Rhodes scholars who had gone into journalism, then into the war, and might now be receptive to a new employer. He had sent notice of his mission to the Time Inc. staff, and the memo reached my sister, Elizabeth Edmonds, in Minneapolis, where she was the Time Inc. "reader relations rep." These reps were bright and personable young men and women who made soothing visits to important people offended by some *Time* article, helped teachers get educational materials from *Time* and *Life* for their classrooms, and so on. She responded to Hodgins's memo by suggesting that her brother Hedley might be worth an interview.

Hodgins thought I was for *Fortune*. The possibility dazzled. I had been admiring *Fortune* since it first appeared in 1930. I had marveled, as everyone was meant to, at the audacity, in the depths of the Depression, of charging a dollar for a magazine. So I read it on other people's dollars and thought they were really getting their money's worth. I read it in the houses of families more prosperous than mine, in the University of Minnesota library, the *Washington Post* morgue, and then on a special cut-rate subscription for servicemen that my sister gave me during the war.

Fortune seemed to come from a realm of journalism unbelievably distant from the *Minnesota Daily* and *Minneapolis Journal*, the United Press and the *Washington Post*, places I had "been published." In the 1930s, it was the most handsome magazine that had ever been published in this country: elegant typography, stock so thick it would bankrupt you today, hand-sewn binding, and superb illustrations. *Fortune* published contemporary artists—Charles Burchfield and Reginald Marsh, among others; the pioneering industrial photography of Margaret Bourke-White; the head-on realism of Walker Evans; the "candid camera" insights of the German Jewish refugee Erich Salomon (an important prenatal influence on *Life*); and the mind-disturbing maps of Richard Edes Harrison. Ricky Harrison would stand continents on their head to make you pay attention (leading to the geopolitical *mot*, alas not mine, I forget whose, that "Argentina is a dagger pointed at the heart of Antarctica"). But the centerpiece of that great magazine of the 1930s was the long articles—some very long indeed—that "discovered" American business and how it worked, especially such dramatic industries as steel and chemicals and meat packing, and treated them as subjects worthy of a serious journalistic literature. And all through the 1930s, I could see in *Fortune* perceptive reporting and analysis of the impact of the New Deal on business (far deeper than what was appearing in newspapers). From time to time in those Depression years, *Fortune*'s editors would also come up with a brisk Bourbon-style decree that the reader this month should be told all about the economics of, for instance, running his own racing stable.

The research that went into all these pieces was meticulous, and much of the writing truly distinguished. Henry Luce had done some imaginative hiring. Asked once why, as a good Republican, he employed so many Democrats on his magazines, he said, "Goddam Republicans can't write." He also liked to say it was easier to turn poets into business journalists than to make poets out of accountants. I would argue that the *Fortune* of the late 1930s—Archibald MacLeish, James Agee before he went to *Time*, Wilder Hobson, James Gould Cozzens, John Chamberlain, among others at bat—was the best-written magazine the United States has produced. I would not make a rival claim for the *Fortune* I edited in the 1950s, much as I would like to.

So this legendary magazine might maybe find a place on its payroll for LCDR, about to be Ret., HW Donovan. Hodgins set up an interview with Ralph Delahaye Paine, Jr., the managing editor. I learned later that an overemphatic recommendation from Hodgins to Paine could be the kiss of death for a candidate, since Paine was a very independent character who liked to do his own appraising. I survived a long memo (given me as a souvenir some years after) in which Hodgins not only found me equipped with "a level gaze and deep voice," but told Paine that hiring me "at around $6,500 to $7,500 a year on a three to six month trial basis would be a very good gamble indeed." Paine was willing to play. When asked what sort of money I was looking for, I said, "Whatever the traffic will bear." This apparently convinced Paine that, however meager my experience in business journalism, I had a certain basic feel for *Fortune*'s subject matter. He started me at $10,000.

My bargaining position may have been stronger than I realized, because the Time Inc. management in those days was privately considering conversion of *Fortune* from a monthly to a fortnightly, and Paine felt he would need a dozen additional writers to handle this. He got his dozen. The fortnightly idea was soon dropped, but some of the new recruits hung on. When the magazine did go fortnightly thirty-one years later, with my approval as editor-in-chief, it occurred to me that I might be repaying an old debt.

When I told Casey Jones at the *Washington Post* of the *Fortune* offer, and my snapping it up, he was touchingly pleased for me. He spoke those warming words, older man to younger man, somewhere west or south of the Hudson, that now seem like something out of an old movie: "You're going to the big leagues now."

I was hired as of December 1, 1945, and though that date fell on a Saturday, I thought I should show up for work. A building guard eventually persuaded me that nobody would be around the place until Monday, and on Monday, by the way—none of his business, of course—but if it was him, he wouldn't knock himself out to get there before 10 or 10:30 because there might not be anybody to talk to, get what I mean?

Well, not everybody, as I have said, can be from Minnesota, and the next Monday, I couldn't refrain from reporting for work about 9:30. I did find someone to talk to, a lovely woman named Harriet Hughes, the managing editor's secretary. She gave me some pencils and paper and a little cell on the south side of the fiftieth floor of the Empire State Building (*Fortune* had been crowded out of the Time and Life Building), with a sensational view down to Wall Street, the harbor, the Statue of Liberty, Staten Island. That was pretty much all that happened my first day at *Fortune*.

The second day (don't panic: this will not be a day-to-day narrative), still not having done a stroke of work, I was amazed to receive a check for eight hundred and a few dollars, my $10,000 salary divided by twelve minus a deduction or two. What if I just walked off that afternoon and never came back? What if the boss decided next week I wasn't going to work out? I mentioned to somebody at lunch my astonishment at getting a month's pay as soon as I took my hat off, and was embarrassed to learn I had inadvertently revealed myself as a member of the privileged classes. People getting $10,000 (good money in those distant days) and up were paid in advance by the month. Those getting less—most of the staff—were paid by the week.

In a few days, however, I was working harder than I had ever worked in my life, or ever would again. For five years, I wrote *Fortune* "middle-of-the-book" stories, those big, solid reportorial and analytical pieces that were the guts of the magazine.

The difference between a *Fortune* article and a *Washington Post* story was profound. A story for a morning newspaper (unless it was a "feature") usually revolved around something that happened yesterday. So the lead paragraph organized itself. It could begin, "President Roosevelt yesterday said . . . ," or "The Senate last night defied the Administration by . . ." A degree of art and judgment went into choosing which details to put in and which to leave out. An ear for a good quote certainly helped, and an eye for descriptive color. You related details in descending order of importance, so the copy desk could cut from the bottom up as it fitted the story to space that might change all through the evening. There was no point in concocting some snappy punch line; there was an excellent chance it wouldn't get into the paper. If the story demanded some element of interpretation or prediction—"Observers [i.e., two congressmen and the reporter] doubted the veto would be overridden"—it was obviously desirable to be right more often than not. And factual accuracy of course mattered, though even on a good paper, which the *Post* was getting to be, there was a charitable attitude toward the little slips, and even middle-size mistakes, that could creep into copy written at high speed against unyielding deadlines. So I learned to rattle off one or two thousand printable words in two or three hours.

But *Fortune*! *Fortune* articles could be six, eight, ten thousand words long. These monsters required a *structure*. They were more like a miniature book than a long newspaper story. They required an ending as well as a middle and a beginning, and they most definitely did not "write themselves." The beginning—the "lead"—was crucial, because *Fortune* was coming along once a month, not telling you something that happened yesterday or even last week, but telling you about some situation that you could just as well hear about next month, or last month, or perhaps needn't hear about at all. So the writer had to build into his lead every conceivable inducement to get the reader to read this article instead of doing all the other things he might do—some doubtless more diverting than curling up with *Fortune*. The lead had to foreshadow the principal themes of the story without giving it all away. The lead might run to five hundred words or more; it was an art form in itself, and writers could spend days struggling with it.

The amount of time allowed a writer in those days—seldom less than six weeks for a major article, sometimes up to three months—

far from lightening the work, was daunting to an ex–newspaper reporter. It meant the story came home with you nights, weekends;
there was always more stuff that might be read, more people who
might be interviewed.

It was a delight, after working on a chintzy newspaper in the
Depression, to partake of the expense-account liberality of Time Inc.
It was also a burden. If you thought you should leave home Sunday
for one more trip to Dallas that might be productive for your story,
nobody from the business office was going to question the expense.
It was up to you. I could remember arguing with some deputy comp-
troller at the *Washington Post* about a $1.50 dry-cleaning charge I
had submitted after wading around various flooded intersections in
a flash-storm assignment. I think he finally gave in.

Another culture shock for an ex–newspaper man was the *Fortune*
researcher. She (they were almost all women in those wicked old
days, and almost all the writers were men) would join the writer on
the road, take notes on the interviews, and check the finished draft
for factual accuracy. She was free to argue with the writer on points
of interpretation, and sometimes could change his mind. It all seemed
very odd to me at first. As a *Post* reporter, I had considered myself
responsible for the accuracy of what I wrote and quite capable of going out all by myself to interview senators, ambassadors, and such.
I gradually began to see some advantages in the researcher system,
including the seductive TK—To Kum. Those blessed letters allowed
the hard-pressed writer to pound ahead with his story without stopping to nail down every name and number. "In Year TK, at a time
when his company was producing only TK widgets a year, he bought
up the patents held by Name TK of Toledo, and was now on his way."
TK could be abused; the researcher would tidy up. But for the best
use of the researcher's time, I always thought she and the writer
should divide up the reporting and reading, perhaps doing only a few
key interviews together. As time went by, I learned that the researchers considered me generally dependable on facts, hopelessly stubborn
in the opinion department. I found them generally very bright, only
occasionally pedantic; most were excellent reporters out on their own,
and when we were together out of town, they were good company,
well stocked with Time Inc. lore and gossip.

Most of the researchers were stout supporters of the American
Newspaper Guild. The New York Guild chapter was then allied with
the small Stalinist wing of the CIO. The two or three *Fortune* researchers who were militant party-liners were also among the best

on the staff at reading financial statements. One of these furies actually liked to knit during meetings, and to the counterrevolutionaries she was known, of course, as Madame Defarge.

I had been a Guild member in my *Washington Post* days, and, like all members in military service, was carried on the Guild rolls during the war. I had expected to resume paying dues when I came to *Fortune*, but was stupefied in my first weeks there to find the Time Inc. unit seriously considering a strike over issues that seemed to me ridiculously unimportant compared with the indisputable superiority of Time Inc. pay scales and benefits over those at the other places where I had just been job hunting. I couldn't help thinking that the Guild rank and file, more or less "liberal" but certainly not leftist, was being manipulated by the New York leadership for purposes more political than bread and butter. I never resumed my Guild membership. All this made for spirited disputation when a researcher found herself marooned with me in some hotel dining room in Chicago.

I would usually allow myself and the researcher about a month for the traveling, interviewing, reading. Then I gave myself about a week to write the thing. One day to stare out the window, write leads I didn't like, crumple them up, and throw them around my study. Down to business the next day, then up later and later each night, finally churning out most of the wordage in the last forty-eight hours before the deadline, usually with no sleep the final night (one source of my theory about nerves, digestion, and stamina as aspects of success).

It was physically punishing work and enormously instructive and stimulating. Some of the punishment derived from my intent to turn in my stories on the posted due date—and I always did. Even after learning that this performance was considered eccentric—the due date was supposed to be the opening bargaining position between writer and editor—I could not seem to break the habit. It became a kind of athletic event, and I suppose a touch of literal-mindedness, or pigheadedness, was involved.

Nobody cared whether you wrote at home or at the office, provided you wrote. I usually wrote at home. Dorothy was a wonderfully sympathetic audience. She would smile loyally when I reported at breakfast, "Once again it failed last night to write itself."

Under this rugged regime I was discovering a fascinating new world. In college I had taken just one introductory course in economics. Very little of my *Washington Post* reporting had been concerned with economic policy. What I knew about American business (in addition to certain things I knew that weren't so) was mainly what I had picked up from reading that awesome magazine *Fortune*. Now here I was writing those articles myself!

The opportunity to dig deep—very deep by normal journalistic standards—was enormously satisfying. At the end of those six or so weeks, a writer could feel, along with all the fatigue, a certain sense of intellectual victory.

And I was lucky in my bosses. Ralph D. Paine, Jr. ("Del" after you had been there a little while) was a great managing editor. Anecdotes collected about him like magnetic filings. In my lifelong run of good bosses, I had already worked for some colorful and gifted teachers at the *Washington Post* and in the navy. But working for Del Paine gave me my first real insight that a boss, whatever else he needs, should also be *interesting*. I mean interesting for his staff to talk about.

Paine was ideal. He is a New Hampshire man, famously taciturn, and his frugal approach to conversation was further protected by an almost impenetrable mumble. Hence the story that "Old Lockjaw" found himself in the men's room one day standing at the next urinal to a writer he had long been intending to fire. So then and there he did tell the man he was fired, and it came as a surprise some weeks later when he ran into the fellow in the corridor. Paine asked one of his deputies to look into it, and this editor reported back that the writer had simply had no idea what the conversation in the men's room had been about. It would be heartwarming to relate that the writer was then given a reprieve and went on to a fine career with *Fortune*, but alas, he was fired a second time, by a more articulate editor.

If a writer went into Paine's office in those primitive days before employees were entitled to a formal job evaluation every fifteen minutes or so, and wanted to know how he was doing, it could be very heavy going. Some were sufficiently driven, by ambition or anxiety or plain curiosity, to press Paine too hard, and then there was the possibility of a dangerously comprehensible answer: "Maybe you *should* look somewhere else." Once, as a quite junior writer, a little officiously, I suppose, I mentioned to Paine a writer who, it seemed to me, needed some reassurance about his work. "Well," said Paine, "he's still on the payroll, isn't he?"

I had a chance some years later to be a little officious in behalf of Paine himself. I was the new managing editor of *Fortune* and he was the new publisher. We were now peers. We were having lunch with Harry Luce on the subject of *Fortune* "art"—covers, photographic portfolios, layout, and so on—and Paine chose to interpret Luce's comments as criticism of the looks of *Fortune* during the latter years of his regime as M.E. His interpretation was correct. They both got angry and fairly foolish. *Fortune* covers, for some reason, could provoke extravagantly emotional scenes. I once saw Paine, in one of those bookish private dining rooms in the gentle old Century Club, come close to blows with a colleague who thought one *Fortune* cover Paine especially admired was "simply crap." But in the Luce-Paine argument, I thought Luce was more at fault, because the top boss after all has an obligation to stay sensible longer. I didn't formulate it just that way when I went to Luce afterward, but I told him he had been rude to Paine and had some amends to make. A few days later, Del told me of a lunch with Luce where "Harry couldn't have been nicer."

Paine was Yale '29 and Skull and Bones, which did him no harm with Luce, '20 and ditto. It is possibly true that Time Inc. in its first twenty years or so was employing more Yale graduates than a strictly scientific sample of the U.S. population would have dictated. By the mid-1950s, however, Luce could delight in telling a business audience in Chicago, where Time Inc. was still thought suspiciously "East Coast," that the managing editor of *Time* was from St. Louis, the managing editor of *Life* from North Dakota, the managing editor of *Sports Illustrated* from St. Louis, and the managing editor of *Fortune* from Minneapolis.

But Del Paine, New Hampshire, Yale, lockjaw, and all, was a marvelously creative journalist. He could see when somebody's seemingly exotic story idea—on trout flies, for instance, or on poker—could give a lift to a magazine that had its forbidding aspects, and how the lift could be made to seem legitimate, not utterly ungermane to *Fortune*'s basic franchise. Del could pick up on a casual social conversation—a hilarious recitation by Eric Hodgins, for example, on the travails of building his Connecticut house—and say, "Hey, why don't you write it for *Fortune*? Just that way." This became *Mr. Blandings*. (*Blandings* included the deathless insight, which I confirmed firsthand many years later, that a $6,000 "extra" that you had added to a structure somehow is worth only $1,200 when, in a frantic final effort to "bring this thing under control," you offer to do without it.)

Paine could steer writers toward rich new regions for business journalism. He put Perrin Stryker, a dogged and thoughtful writer, on the "management problem" story—how to recruit, promote, pay executives; relations with the board of directors; when to ignore organization charts; how many vice presidents is too many. All very obvious, even overworked, subjects in business journalism now, but not forty years ago. Del helped give journalistic shape to the enthusiasms of William H. Whyte, Jr., who became a wonderfully perceptive and witty observer in the field that *Fortune*, thanks to Whyte and Paine, pretty much owned for a decade. Business sociology: *The Organization Man* and *Corporate Wives* were Whyte classics—again, something everybody does now, but it was brand-new in the 1950s, and indeed has never been done better than when Holly Whyte did it. ("Holly" from his stately middle name, Hollingsworth.)

In editing copy, Paine was a big-stroke man. Back around pages 18 and 19 of your first draft, you might find in the margin heavy vertical lines and the message: "Wow! This is your lead." And perhaps parenthetically, gently: "I'm not sure you really need your present pp. 1–6." Those pp., of course, had cost you only thirty-six hours of agony.

Albert L. Furth, executive editor, was Paine's perfect partner. Bill Furth was a superb close-in editor; Paine perhaps could have been but didn't have to exercise that craft because Bill was there. A fairly innocuous cliché would draw from Bill a marginal "Oh dear" or "Must we?" A flagrant cliché provoked Bill's dread "Oooh" or "Ouch" or "Ugh." A point proved too many times over could bring a mock-prim note: "Too much of your research is showing." Wordiness could not get past him. If the writer, on due notice, couldn't compress, Bill could cut so skillfully the writer hardly felt the knife. He could de-muddle very bad stuff, if necessary, but only after giving the writer a chance to do it himself. He had a strong feel for narrative pace and the internal logic of a story. When Bill had to do a touch of rewriting, he was scrupulously attentive to what the writer lovingly thought of as his own style.

In people management, Furth was as unmysterious as Paine was opaque. Writers would talk to Furth about things they wouldn't quite want to take up with Paine. Working for them both, I saw what is now so often labeled "the Good Cop/Bad Cop" technique. (An "Ugh," I know. Sorry, Bill.) But it was not a calculated thing at all. Del and Bill were simply doing what they did best, and each respected what the other did better.

Furth and Paine taught me a lot about writing, and—though I wasn't consciously studying the subject—about editing. And about managing. Including the essential wisdom that the boss can't do everything, and furthermore isn't qualified to, and if he has the luck to find or inherit a deputy who has gifts he doesn't, he should use them.

Bill Furth continued as executive editor of *Fortune* when I became managing editor in 1953, left a few years later to become executive assistant to Luce, who then shared Bill's services with me when I moved "upstairs" as editorial director in 1959. Until Bill died in 1962, he was my closest friend in Time Inc.—a warm and funny man I still miss.

Bill was the first Jew I knew well who discussed Jews and Jewishness in a perfectly easy, natural way. He was a member of the editorial advisory board of the American Jewish Committee, which sponsored *Commentary*, a distinguished liberal monthly then, a distinguished conservative journal now. In the late 1940s and 1950s, *Commentary* was publishing a lot of fascinating sociology about American Jewish life—including some wickedly funny stuff about Jewish suburbia. *Commentary*, along with Bill Furth and other Jewish colleagues at *Fortune*, had a liberating effect on me. I was being liberated from the virtuous Christian reaction to Hitler that one must not "generalize" about Jews lest anti-Semitism ensue. So it was not permissible to think, for instance, "Jews are smart." The morally correct view was, "Yes, some Jews are smart, some are not smart, just like with the Methodists." Breaking away from that cant enhanced enormously my enjoyment and perception of the city where I have lived most of my adult life. How stultifying it would be to spend forty years in New York and not be allowed to notice that there is anything Jewish about this fabulously creative and energetic urban civilization. It would also be absurd to spend a lifetime in journalism without being allowed to admire the success of Jews, who surely occupy more than 3 percent (ratio of Jews to U.S. population) of the top jobs in newspapers, magazines, and network news. Thanks, then, to *Commentary*, Furth, and some other talented Jews in journalism, I believe I am able to think honestly, and above all gratefully, about *A Certain People*. That is the title of a fine book about Jews in America by my former *Fortune* colleague Charles Silberman.

I also generalize with abandon about Italians, Germans, Russians, Chinese. And I am very clear in my own mind about the attributes of another "certain people," the Scots-Irish.

. . . .

Before Furth and Paine did the heavy lifting, various senior editors might do preliminary critiques of *Fortune* story drafts. One of those advisory editors, William B. Harris, read drafts of corporation stories for "business sense," something many of the writers needed more of. I was among the neediest, and Bill nursed me along from freshman to sophomore in business journalism. He gave a seminar for new writers and researchers on how to read a balance sheet, how to interview a VP for finance, how to question a company president. Bill told the class, with a meaningful glance at me, that we were taking on something much tougher than Washington reporting; in interesting business situations, it is often in nobody's interest to talk, unlike most political stories, where the hotter and more controversial the situation, the more urgent somebody's motive to talk. Bill noted that American businessmen generally like the sound of their own voices, and also abhor any socially awkward silence, so if you've asked a tough question and received only half an answer, don't rush in right away with another question. Just sit there and stare at your man and chances are he can't help saying more.

Bill was a dressy, fast-talking fellow who had worked in Wall Street in the legendary era just before the Great Crash of 1929; it was easy to imagine him selling stock, possibly to widows. He was talking about the Crash one day at a *Fortune* "ways and mean" (story scheduling) meeting, when the phone rang for Wilder Hobson. Wilder was a versatile writer (and a first-class trombonist) who graduated from Yale in time for the Depression. He was also something of a prankster. He listened to the phone in silence, hung up, looked stoically at us all, especially Bill, and said, "Ruined."

I saw Harris nonplussed only once. He was telling his seminar that in the Crash, "Everybody wanted to sell, there simply weren't any buyers." A sweet freshman researcher caught him up: "But anything that got sold—didn't there have to be a buyer?"

I also cherish a piece of literary advice Bill Harris gave me. *Fortune* writing was much less stylized than newspaper writing and far more idiomatic, to say the least, than U.S. Navy prose. Amid the artful passages that had taken a lot of writing, it was perfectly legal— indeed a writer was encouraged—to break in with a relaxed sentence or two in a conversational tone of voice. In one manuscript, carried away by the new freedom, I was starting sentences right and left with "Well" and "But." Bill finally wrote in the margin, "You're spending your Buts too fast, and you've been to the Well too often." I've tried to watch those tendencies ever since.

Another of my *Fortune* professors was John Davenport, who has left a lasting imprint on my notions of economics. John was a devout believer in the free market and an implacable foe of "statism." It was not just that the market—i.e., the free opinions of buyers and sellers— was the best director and allocator of resources, but it was also one of the underpinnings of a free society. His polar opponent among *Fortune* senior editors of that day was Ken Galbraith, New Deal economist and a wartime price administrator. He would refer to Davenport's office, with amused indulgence, as "the Adam Smith corner." Davenport, as an advisory reader of first drafts of several of my pieces and frequent lunchtime sparring partner, gave me my first full exposure to the rigors and comforts of the free-market philosophy. Comforts because, as in the Catholic Church (at least before Vatican II) or in the Communist party, you were enrolled in a faith that told you more or less automatically what to think about a great many questions that might vex other people. But a rigorous faith, laissez-faire, because it can seem uncaring about the unfortunate (though true believers say any such impression is simply sloppy thinking); and a rigorous faith because it was so much ridiculed in circles where journalists especially like to be liked—i.e., among other journalists and in academia.

I came to admire the Adam Smith–John Davenport answers, and increasingly mistrust the Ken Galbraith answers. I was less a purist than Davenport, however, and rather more respectful of public opinion, including when it was being foolish. I once suggested to John that he try an essay on the concept of consent in economic policy. In our fully enfranchised society, economic policy must of course be supported by political majorities; some majority views will be wrongheaded; but which are really worth fighting to reverse and which might as well be put up with? John said, "Why don't you write it?" Neither of us did. But I will still go along with some logically "bad" economics, up to a point. This is not cynicism but a willingness to pay a certain tax for living in a democracy.

John Davenport's father had been an executive of Bethlehem Steel. A *Fortune* writer sometime in the late 1940s was interviewing Eugene Grace, chairman of Bethlehem, a formidable man from those days when steel was steel. Grace asked what ever happened to the Davenport boys. John's brother, Russell, had been managing editor of *Fortune* for a time, impresario of the Wendell Willkie run for the presidency in 1939–40, a versatile and somewhat theatrical editor-writer-poet. "Well," said the *Fortune* writer with enthusiasm, "Russell is writing poetry and John of course is writing for *Fortune.*" "Mmm," said Mr. Grace, "I knew their father very well. A fine man. I always wondered why those boys never went to work."

In 1949, John Davenport became editor of *Barron's,* which he hoped to transform into an American equivalent of *The Economist* of London. And it was from that position that he gave a useful kick to my career, offering me a job as one of his top editors. John was not going to pay much more than carfare above my *Fortune* salary, but he was offering more responsibility and authority, within a smaller world—a choice many ambitious young people have wrestled with. In my case, a couple of other outside job feelers, from *Business Week* and *Newsweek,* happened to arrive at about the same time as John's. I was emboldened to enter into a fairly hard-boiled conversation with my laconic friend Del Paine. He blinked first. I stayed at *Fortune.*

But back in the winter of 1945–46, struggling with my first assignment, I hadn't been all that sure I could stick it out on *Fortune.* In my fourth draft of the lead story for a special issue on housing, I finally came up with an opening sentence that satisfied my editor: "In the first postwar spring, the masters of atomic energy are short of an absurdly commonplace commodity, the house." Looking back now on that sentence, I am embarrassed to see only a precocious variant on a great cliché of the 1960s: If-we-can-send-a-man-to-the-moon-why-can't-we-cure-cancer? (The answer, of course, being that it is much harder to cure cancer. And it is hard even for a very vigorous economy to provide enough decent housing at affordable prices.) By the time I had come up with my atomic insight, the editor and I were both very tired of my housing article. The whole six thousand words had been chewed up and pushed around unmercifully, over and over.

I was operating on two and three hours of sleep a night, inhaling Camels and black coffee. I had in fact spent some of the time between the third and fourth drafts wondering whether I wanted to stay at *Fortune.* The decision to hang in at least a little longer had a belligerent and slightly punch-drunk quality to it; I was getting curious to see who was tougher, *Fortune* or me.

One of those awful nights, in my excess of Protestant work ethic, I was slogging away at the *Fortune* office at 4 A.M. Out in the hall, I came across a disheveled fellow who looked as if he had not been outdoors for several days. But in fact he had just been out for coffee, and while he was gone, the cleaning lady had got at his office. So he had now overturned a couple of trash bins in the corridor and was rummaging through the stuff: "She's thrown away three pages!"

We introduced ourselves. He was John McDonald, and I helped him rummage. The precious pages were never found, even when John went down to the very bowels of the Empire State Building, five levels below the street, and bribed some janitors to spread out bales of the night's trash. Final copy, as I was beginning to learn myself, was almost a part of the writer's body. McDonald went on to become one of the first journalistic discoverers and expositors of "game theory," as developed by the great John von Neumann, Einstein's protégé at Princeton, and Oskar Morgenstern of MIT. McDonald wrote some *Fortune* articles that became a little book of mathematical elegance, *Winning Strategy at Poker, Business and War*. The articles gave John excellent entrée to several entrepreneurs of editorial interest to *Fortune*, among them William Zeckendorf, Sr., and Roger Stevens, and ultimately to Alfred P. Sloan, Sr., the retired chairman of General Motors, who wanted to write his memoirs "with" McDonald. This labor of five years became one of the classics on American corporate management, still required reading at many business schools.* John still goes to bed at dawn and gets up around noon, still writes, still plays poker, and claims to be slightly ahead, lifetime.

A few months after my housing story, assigned to the leadoff for a special issue on U.S. labor, I got my opening sentence on the second try: "Labor, the basic ingredient, was scarce, expensive, rebellious." My researcher, earnest, mildly socialist: "But labor and the unions have fought for years for the dignity of *not* being considered a commodity." HD: "Oh, come on."

The writing continued in general to be torture, but there began to be moments when something felt just right. My first corporation story was on Raytheon, whose president, Laurence Marshall, "looks like a friendly and uncommonly intelligent wrestler." The company name had been dreamed up by somebody who thought it sounded good over the telephone, "though some of the company's newer em-

*But John's books are less famous, he complains, than an article he wrote for *New York* magazine telling how he inadvertently locked himself out of his apartment one hot summer night and had to lurk about the streets of Greenwich Village for a couple of hours stark naked.

ployees are under the harmless delusion that Raytheon is Greek for 'God of Life.' "

I began to have longer intervals of fun. An article on rent control: "Of all the contractual relationships devised by man, few have chafed so consistently as the contract between owner and renter. The literature and legend of many peoples testify to the possibility that a merchant may be honest, an employer kindly, a servant faithful. Favorable mention of the landlord is exceedingly rare. It must be noted that the National Association of Real Estate Boards has done little to make the landlord more lovable."

Between assignments, the writer might enjoy a couple of slow days—time to get a haircut ("grows on company time, cut on company time"), answer the mail, even go home early. Once in a while, a "junket" might be handed out. Today, reputable publications won't accept trips paid for by some publicity-eager company. In the naughtier time when I was a *Fortune* writer, the magazine might send someone on a junket so he could have a change of scenery at the expense of the host company or government, but there was no presumption he would write about them. On a TWA junket, our planeload, mainly Catholic newspapermen, had an audience with Pope Pius XII. Most of my fellow travelers of course knelt and kissed his ring. As a Protestant, I decided a manly handshake would be more appropriate. "Blessings on your work" was the Pontiff's gracious response. I reported this to Paine and Furth in a little memo on my return, cautioning them that from now on, they had better take it easy with my copy. On a Bank of America press junket around California, the host was Clark Beise, then president of the bank—a nephew, as it happened, of my father's friend Dr. Rudolph Beise of Brainerd, Minnesota. When it came my turn to respond to a toast at some civic meal, I bragged that I was the only member of the tour who had been delivered by an uncle of the president of the bank. I was never contradicted.

Sometimes the editors might not notice for three or four days that a writer had no assignment. I was hoping to stretch one such lull to a full week when Paine phoned: "What are you doing?" "I'm reading *The Red and the Black*." "You have good taste, but I have a different story for you."

I was to do a profile of the eighty-year-old "judge" John Haussermann, of Cincinnati, who had made a pile of money in gold mining in the Philippines. I liked the judge, and I enjoyed writing about him:

He is a full-blown gilt-edged capitalist out of the time of Taft Père,*
whom he still regards as the greatest statesman of the century. . . . If
Irving Olds [then the chairman of U.S. Steel] were to appear before
the Homestead local of the United Steelworkers and announce that
he regarded all those present as members of his family, that he would
reward those who served him well but would be obliged to punish
the disobedient, he would doubtless require police escort to get out
of the hall. But a whole generation of Benguet miners [in Luzon]
listened with apparent satisfaction to speeches in which Judge Haussermann embroidered on this paternal theme. He sometimes opened
his remarks at company rallies with the simple affirmation, "I am
your father."

From a story on Nabisco, I carried home a lot of free cookies and
a nice compliment from the CEO, George Coppers, who asked, just
before I started to write, what were my impressions of the management. I mentioned senior executives who had impressed me and omit-
ted to mention those who had not. I said my story would put some
emphasis on obsolescent plant and materials handling, and the company's complacent merchandising. Coppers, a lawyer and a CPA, said
this was very interesting, because he had just paid $180,000 to a
management consulting firm for some of the same critique. In *Fortune*, for $1 a copy, I began:

In the tough old Chelsea quarter of Manhattan the presence of the
home office and senior bakery of the National Biscuit Co. strikes an
unmistakably reproachful note. The effect is not unlike that of the
placard on the mission flophouse wall, "How long since you wrote
home?" When the wind is right, seamen and stevedores coming off
the North River docks are overwhelmed by the bouquet of Marsh-
mallow Fancies and Vanilla Wafers; on other days the aroma of
animal crackers and Fig Newtons rebukes the tavern keepers of
Ninth Avenue. But if an air of innocence clings to the National Biscuit
Co., as it must to any business where grown men concern themselves
with a gingersnap named Zu Zu . . .

For a reporter who had known nothing of business, it was heady
stuff to visit a corporation for a few weeks and come away thinking
I had perceived the inner workings of a company. And often I had,
thanks in good part to the business sophistication and the tireless

*Some wretched editor changed this to "Papa Taft."

digging of my researcher-collaborators. In the actual writing, however, I looked on the delivery of the financial analysis as license to work at something that interested me still more: trying to convey the feel of places and the flavor of personalities.

From "The Awkward Case of Eastern Airlines," a 1948 story that made nostalgic reading forty years later:

> A gullible visitor at the last general [management] meeting of Eastern Airlines, held in Miami in late November, might have supposed that the company was fighting desperately to stave off receivership . . . outdoors, a medium-size hurricane was ripping down the palm fronds and bouncing coconuts off the sidewalks along Biscayne Bay. Seventy-five-mile winds broke against the boarded windows of the waterfront buildings, and a slight sway was noticeable in the seventeenth-floor ballroom of the Columbus Hotel, where Captain [Eddie] Rickenbacker [president of Eastern] was outshouting the storm. "My God," he cried, on one of the several hundred occasions when his patience was taxed beyond endurance, "Let's not give away the airline!"
>
> So far from giving away the airline, of course, the fanatical Captain and his hard-driven help have made Eastern the one consistently profitable company in a money-losing industry. . . .

From "Big Money in Boston" (1949):

> Last summer, after twenty-five years of blameless business life, the Massachusetts Investors Trust abandoned its discreet Victorian chambers on Boston's Congress Street, and moved straight to the top of the newest and tallest office building in town. . . . Walls, drapes and carpeting are of the pastel tints recommended by a New York decorator. A curved-around-the-corner sofa, upholstered in dashing fabric, is installed in the reception room. The Massachusetts Investors Trust, in short, has grown so large and respectable that it can afford not to look like a Massachusetts investors trust.

Working on a story on the trucking industry, I once took a seventeen-hour ride from Winston-Salem, North Carolina, to Jersey City, in a McLean Company rig carrying television cabinets. The driver was a cordial man from Charleston, South Carolina, with an accent that took me a hundred miles to decipher.

As we were approaching Danville, Virginia, the driver told me we were going to stop for supper at a place that had wonderful food and lots of real good-looking waitresses. It was run by this very nice lady who would trust you for the supper check, if you were low on cash, until the next time you came through. "You know," the driver confided, "it was quite a time before I realized the place is a ho-house."

Sure enough, the sandwiches were good, and the proprietor was most hospitable. When the driver proudly introduced me as coming from "*Fo-tune* magazine," she gathered some of the waitresses around (there were a good many more than the supper trade would have required) to meet me. She said she didn't know about "this *Fo-tune* magazine." I explained it was put out by the same company that put out *Time* and *Life*. She and the girls brightened. "Oh, I know about *Time*," she said, "but that *Life* magazine! I could look at it and look at it." In later years, in speeches at *Life* sales conventions, I had a good many successes in recounting this testimonial. If that friendly soul is still in business on the outskirts of Danville, I would like to think she now looks and looks at *People* as well as *Life*, and if her enterprise has truly prospered, perhaps she now takes *Money* and *Fo-tune*, too.

From Winston-Salem to Boston, from Captain Eddie's rich route system to "The Undiscovered City" (industrial Los Angeles), most of my assignments dealt with business successes. The *Fortune* table of contents generally reflected a sense that those late 1940s were good years for America. Meat and automobiles had reappeared, houses were getting built, and the money was there to pay for them. We were enjoying the first peacetime prosperity since the great boom times of the 1920s, now surpassed in all the statistics *Fortune* was full of, but there was still a precarious-seeming novelty about it. Nobody was taking the future for granted.

Looking outward, *Fortune* articles and editorials also reflected a certain wariness. As a nation, we were still glorying in the righteousness and success of our effort in World War II. Now we were helping our recent enemies to their feet and offering aid programs to much of the world. With almost unanimous public support, the country was embarking on a crusade to "contain" Stalinist communism. World War III did not seem utterly impossible, but in those years of our atomic monopoly, it did not look like the apocalypse. When we talked about it at *Fortune*, we thought the Soviets, still staggering from the last war, would be crazy to start a new one, and we knew we weren't going to.

After I had been writing *Fortune* stories for four or five years, I was promoted to the Board of Editors. This was a body of seven or eight, some of them very senior writers, others engaged in some editing as well as writing. From my own 1945 "class" of writers, John McDonald had already made the board—it was a little like making partner in a law firm. When Bill Furth once invited me to muse about my future, in my early days at *Fortune*, I said I seemed to be running on a certain rhythm—four years at the University of Minnesota, three at Oxford, four plus at the *Washington Post*, four in the navy. So around 1949 or 1950, I would want to decide whether to stay at *Fortune* or move along. It would probably depend—though I didn't say so to Furth—on whether I had been put on the board. Bill may have made a notation in a tickler file.

Much as I liked journalism, I was subject to almost studentlike wanderings of attention. If I had had any money, it could have been great fun, as Dorothy and I agreed, to go into real-estate speculation. Certain areas of Washington, D.C., and the West Side of Manhattan attracted me especially. I had not yet grasped how much could be done with other people's money, especially the taxpayers'—an innocence that doubtless disqualified me from that line of business. I still thought of the law once in a while, also architecture, but I didn't really want to go back to school. I would have loved to have a shot at politics, but there was no way that could have worked. I was too reserved to be any good at campaigning. But, even more disabling, I couldn't have enrolled in either major party; there was just too much that bothered me in each of them. I did like to think that if some series of electoral flukes put me into the House or the Senate, or possibly even loftier precincts, I would be good at the work.

So I ascended happily to *Fortune*'s Board of Editors. I continued writing but also began getting some editing assignments. I helped convert the "Business Roundup" from a summary of the month's business news into an economic forecast, and was rewarded with the job of editing Sanford Parker, a brilliant and eccentric economist whose monthly insights I would translate into English over two twenty-hour days. Sandy's working habits were chaos; among other neuroses, he had an acute fear of heights. This was awkward because *Fortune*'s offices now were on the twenty-first floor of the old Time and Life Building (we had moved from the Empire State), and some of our working lunches were held in private dining rooms on the sixty-fourth floor of the RCA Building. One stern Time Inc. doctor told me I was pampering Sandy by allowing him to stay home days at a time and by scheduling my own lunches with him at La Reine, a comfortable little bistro near his apartment. But Parker was a great asset to *Fortune*. I couldn't get mad at him. This lovable man once told me I could have been a good economist myself, and on another occasion, in what he regarded as an equal tribute, he told some interviewer I should be president.

I also edited a section of brief (by *Fortune* standards—i.e., one thousand to two thousand words) articles with strong public-policy content. These pieces usually occupied about a fifth of the magazine's "middle-of-the-book" space and were a kind of extended editorial page. Many of the articles dealt with U.S. foreign policy and defense policy in the light of the Korean war. I wrote a good many of these myself. Each month, I spent about a week in Harry Truman's Washington. Watching him at press conferences, now in his fifth year as president, I could admire this classic case of "growing in office." The gray, meek-looking Missouri senator I had known when I was a *Post* reporter covering the "Truman Committee" hearings had even come to look like the president of the United States. I interviewed people in Congress, State, Defense, Treasury, and the various "mobilization" agencies of that odd era when the country, fresh from total victory in a total war, halfway fought another war—precursor of a much more troubling halfway war, a decade later, on the same overwhelming continent.

In July 1951, I was promoted to associate managing editor, a newly minted title, number 3 on the masthead, specifically responsible for "national policy" articles. I presided over a special issue, a hundred thousand words or so, on the U.S. government, which appeared in February 1952. This was a fascinating exercise in journalistic architecture and in the management of a sizable journalistic task force—some three dozen writers, researchers, photographers, artists, fellow editors. A year later, I edited a special half-issue on the Soviet Union. Stalin was still alive, Eisenhower had just been inaugurated, and I wrote in the preface: "The central problem of the new

Administration in Washington is how to deal with the old Administration in Moscow."

The new administration in Washington did a thoughtful thing for me. President Eisenhower appointed C. D. Jackson, who had been publisher of *Fortune*, as a special assistant. In February 1953, Del Paine was appointed publisher, and I his successor as managing editor.

VI
Running a Magazine

The first few weeks I sat behind the managing editor's desk at *Fortune*, I had the occasional tremor that I was impersonating an officer. I was supposed to boss around a staff of eighty or ninety people, which included many older than I (then thirty-eight) and at least a few who had recently bossed me around. Was I really as good as people seemed to think? There was a passage in an Eric Hodgins sequel to *Blandings* that had a certain resonance for me: Some up-and-coming advertising man is commuting from his Connecticut suburb, and one morning the clickety-click of the rails seems to be saying, "This is the day they'll find you out, find you out."

Del Paine was a stout ally. He had not been all that pleased about becoming publisher of *Fortune*, which translated in Time Inc. terms to manager of the magazine as a business. Del thought of himself as an editor, not a businessman, and certainly not a high-powered salesman, which the publisher must spend some of his time trying to be. Even though he had been managing editor for twelve years—too long, he freely said—he didn't really like stopping. His office was just one floor away from mine, closer than if he had been transferred to some totally different region of Time Inc. But Del found his own ways to let everybody know I was indeed in charge of the editorial side of the magazine—and, teeth clenched, that he thought I was doing very well at it.

Bill Furth was older brother—a protective brother who for some reason thought younger had a better shot at things. At times self-effacing but never obsequious, he pretended that I was even more taciturn than Paine, and thought the subarctic winters in Minnesota and New Hampshire must have something to do with it. (Bill was from California.) He told the Time Inc. house organ *f.y.i.* (for your information), "Beside Donovan, Paine sounds like a chatterbox."

When Paine had first broached the managing editor appointment to me, I said it surely should go to Furth. Paine said No, Furth thought it should be me, and if I didn't believe that, I should have lunch with him. (Readers will have grasped by now that a lot of Time Inc. business was transacted at lunch.) Bill and I did have lunch. Bill claimed I was better qualified, and also said he was in general more comfortable with a number 2 role than number 1. I don't know how much of this was Bill's generosity and how much was a preference that someone else should take the final responsibility. Perhaps some of each. In any case, Bill's visible enthusiasm about my appointment gave my regime more or less instant legitimacy with a staff that ardently admired him.

One evening in May 1953, two months after I took office, I had to outline my plans for *Fortune* to a difficult audience—some seventy-five men who had been exposed to Florida sun all day, then exposed to a long cocktail hour and large dinner. This was my inaugural, the first of hundreds of speeches, as it turned out, that I eventually unloaded on Time Inc. audiences, but I didn't know then how much practice I was to get. I spoke from a very dry mouth. The occasion was the annual ritual of the *Fortune* sales convention, usually held in those years at Ponte Vedra, a comfortable oceanside golf resort down the beach from Jacksonville. The meeting was attended by the advertising space salesmen as well as the circulation, production, and financial people—the whole "business side" of the magazine plus a few of the top Time Inc. brass. It can be disconcerting to rise to address these people at 10 P.M. Many are impatient to get to the poker table, some wish they were asleep, and indeed a few may be. After informing the salesmen at some length about the magazine's editorial schedules for 1953, I moved on to 1954, admitting that it might be a little presumptuous—not to say foolhardy—for a brand-new managing editor to talk about what he is going to do *next* year. They laughed at all the right places and assured me I would be back at Ponte Vedra the next year. And so I was.

The managing editor can't stay sweet and modest too long. He needs a good opinion of himself just to go to the office in the morning, because he is going to be passing judgment dozens of times a day on the work and ideas of highly gifted people. It also takes a certain lack of humility to make the final decision that, yes, *Fortune* will publish Controversial Opinion A on Sensitive Subject B. After I had put out half a dozen issues of the magazine to generally good notices from the Time Inc. authorities, and without any libel suit, federal injunctions, or blank pages, I decided I had some tolerance, even appetite, for these decisions. From "This-is-the-day-they'll-find-me-out," it didn't take too long to move to: "Okay, this is as much as they get out of me today; they're getting their money's worth."

I was growing very fond of this club-conspiracy-college disguised as a magazine. The staff, no two alike, continued to educate and entertain me. Though to them I had become a "they," there was still the comradeship of fellow toilers in a difficult calling. I think it helped that I was seen to work hard and care strenuously, and in some detail, about quality.

I put in many marathon editing sessions, but on the whole it was a little less arduous being boss than being a *Fortune* writer. I was a fairly heavy-editing editor and saw a good bit of my own prose in print in other people's articles. Professor Gilbert Cranberg, of the University of Iowa, writing in the *Columbia Journalism Review* of March–April 1987, tells of a sign on a newspaper reporter's desk: "The strongest desire is neither love nor hate. It is one person's need to change another person's copy." Just so.

Editing the copy of Henry Luce was a different exercise. For *Fortune*'s twenty-fifth anniversary year, 1955, I was publishing a series of speculative articles about 1955–80 by such eminences as Chief Justice Earl Warren, Adlai Stevenson, John von Neumann. I told my staff and the distinguished contributors that our stance was not "after twenty-five years" but "midpoint in fifty years." I asked my editor-in-chief for the final article of the series, "to deal with the most speculative topic of all" (as I wrote in a preface), "the measureless future of a measureless force: the human spirit." Luce wrestled with his impossible subject in masterly style, in a somehow lively and witty article rich in historical, philosophical, and theological argument. I think it is fair to say that I edited his piece less heavily than I edited most *Fortune* writers. It is also fair to say that he was a much better writer than most of my staff.

One night, when I had been rewriting some story until 3 A.M., Mary Grace, the wonderfully serene and wise woman who ran *Fortune*'s copy desk, said, "Hedley, do you *like* to write?" I said, "I like to have written." Mary, and here and there around the floor a few writers and researchers, might have to stay as late as I—because of me, or because of the original sin in writers. But I never fancied the spectacle of troops or underlings waiting until all hours to get the editor's word. I tried—and it could be a struggle—not to tinker so long with some absorbing detail that a lot of people would be home late for dinner.

If I no longer had pride of authorship in a particular article, I knew the creative satisfaction of "composing" a whole issue of *Fortune*. There were half a dozen standing departments breaking up the ad pages in the front and back of the magazine. But the "middle of the book," the eight or ten big articles of the month, had to be thought up issue by issue. The planning of future issues of the magazine was in fact the biggest responsibility of the managing editor. There were always two issues of *Fortune* in real production and sometimes parts of a third and fourth; there were at least two or more issues in a state of serious planning, and some projects might be in the works as much as a year in advance. This led to a daylong Ping-Pong movement between different issues and different problems and different sets of people, and I found these abrupt shifts of focus stimulating. If, back in Oxford days, I ever had any scholarly bent for the pursuit of one subject for months on end, I was fully unfit for it by now.

The inventing of *Fortune* month by month was very different from the planning of an issue of *Time* or *Newsweek* or *Sports Illustrated*, for whom, as Harry Luce observed, "God provides," meaning the week's events would tell the editors at least some of the subjects that must be in the next issue. For *Fortune*, however, there was nothing on the front page of the newspapers that dictated the table of contents. In making assignments during, say, December, the editors had to gamble on topics that might seem interesting and important to readers picking up the issue in March. This was exciting guesswork.

Being a Time Inc. managing editor was almost like owning your own magazine—without the proprietary headaches. The publisher attended to advertising sales, circulation, physical production. The managing editor had very broad autonomy—assuming his magazine was doing well—and ran his own show subject to agreement with the publisher on the budget and general oversight of his editorial stewardship by the editor-in-chief.

Tensions could arise, of course, between the editorial side's pursuit of truth—to use a priggish formulation—and the business side's pursuit of ad-page orders. Mock-priggish, I once assured a gathering of our ad salesmen that it was not true that the editors "actually go out of our way to insult companies just because they advertise in *Fortune*." There was no presumption that a company could get itself written about by advertising in *Fortune*; or keep itself from being written about—which at least a few preferred—by advertising; or influence what was written by threatening to stop advertising. A bit of puffery did occasionally slip into *Fortune*, but it was not venal. Writers, researchers, editors might be more impressed by some company or businessman than subsequent events justified, but this was simple fallibility. *Fortune*'s ad salesmen understood very well that the magazine's editorial independence and integrity—its utter un-buyability—were priceless general assets, however blighting to some particular sales prospect.

This independence of the editors, and the genuine respect the business side accorded it, came in good part from the attitudes of the principal owner, Henry Luce. But I give at least equal credit to his closest business partner, Roy Larsen, president of the company, ab-solutely unshakably pro-editor when some advertiser, angry ex-ad-vertiser, or potential big advertiser was trying to lean on *Fortune*.* The chief executives of many of the big corporations and banks were first-name friends of Luce and Larsen. But Luce was not exactly a jolly locker-room type; most of the CEOs felt more comfortable with Larsen. I think it fell to him more often than Luce to say, "Sorry, call the editor." A friend of the boss could certainly get a hearing more easily than someone calling in cold, but that was about it.

For *Fortune* especially, given that virtually every article dealt with advertisers or potential advertisers—the separation of editorial-side and business-side considerations was imperative. Luce and Lar-sen were rock-solid on this point, which did not spare me from dealing with a few awkward matters they quite correctly bucked along to me.†

Fortune customarily showed first drafts to corporations or individuals who had been cooperative in interviews. They were welcome to argue on points of interpretation, and more than welcome to correct factual errors. Their comments could be useful, but the practice could permit laxity on the part of our reporters, and it also led to the understandable, if completely erroneous, allegation that *Fortune* allowed companies to edit stories about themselves. I should have stopped the practice but didn't; one of my successors, Louis Banks, did.

†I sometimes had to restrain Luce's crusading impulses. While the present Time and Life Building was going up, in the late 1950s, Harry was getting his first firsthand exposure to the extortionist grip of the building-trades unions on Manhattan construc-tion. He wanted me to do an exposé. "In some of these hair-raising episodes," I wrote him, "the contractors would not come out looking much prettier than the unions. I'm

Fortune's publisher and advertising director, closer than the top Time Inc. brass to the heart of the marketplace, could plead most touchingly with the managing editor—Couldn't we maybe postpone our story about XYZ Corporation for just a month or two? Couldn't the writer of such-and-such a story be most respectfully requested to go back and listen once more to Mr. R.'s reason for shifting his company's outside accounting to a different firm—Mr. R. wasn't sure the writer (bright young fellow, R. sure wished he worked for him) had fully understood, and no question it was complicated stuff—R. wasn't sure he himself always had it straight! Or, more challenging (because in the case of R. we knew damned well he had it straight), would the managing editor himself receive a fiery delegation from the ZYX industry, most of them advertisers in *Fortune*—perhaps about to be former advertisers—who felt they had been mortally insulted in the last issue of the magazine? The answer to that was Yes, of course. I thought it was perfectly possible that *Fortune* and I would learn something we should know about the ZYX industry. I was also glad to receive the industry because I have suffered from a deplorable lifelong love of arguing. (I can still hear my father's plaintive call to my brother and me, after bedtime in Minneapolis: "Boys, stop *arguing*!") The managing editor and the publisher did not want to be running to Teacher (Luce and Larsen) to arbitrate routine boundary disputes. You prided yourself on settling that stuff without bothering anybody upstairs—and without giving away anything. L. L. Callaway, ad director of *Fortune* in my day (later publisher of *Sports Illustrated*, then publisher of *Newsweek*), told me I had the coldest eyes he had ever seen. In the context, I took it as a compliment.

Callaway's staff tended to be better dressed and better mannered, per capita, than the editorial staff. They were, of course, in the business of being ingratiating, but they were genuinely good company. At the sales conventions, they beat up on me at golf; I came out all right at tennis; and I won more often than I lost at bridge. We would sometimes play bridge all night, take a swim before breakfast, and try to sneak a nap after lunch. Publisher Paine, the somewhat reluctant host of record at these gatherings, confronted me one evening: "Donovan, I think you actually like these things." I did.

Fortune circulation advanced from about 250,000 to 325,000 dur-

---

not sure just how many major industries ought to be mad at *Fortune* at any one time, and we've had our hands fairly full lately. Maybe the troops (including editors) will be better rested by Summer."

ing the six years I was managing editor, and the magazine showed respectable profits. Time Inc. management had the pleasant habit of treating all the managing editors pretty much as equals, even though the weeklies—*Life* with about seven million circulation, *Time* then around two million—were vastly bigger enterprises than my modest monthly.

My editorial budget was generous by standards of that era (about $2 million a year), but there was no throwaway margin. I published about 650 middle-of-the-book articles during my tenure as managing editor. I threw away not more than five or six. Some fairly dreadful first drafts were rendered printable, even good, in endless new drafts by the writer, worked over by his editor.

I once expressed some irritation at the brilliant Daniel Bell, our labor editor—subsequently a distinguished sociologist at Columbia and Harvard, and such a virtuoso of the intellect that I told one interviewer, "If Dan were a corporation, the Anti-Trust Division would break him up." I had come across a beautifully written article of his in one of the scholarly quarterlies. I knew the quarterly did no serious editing, and I asked Dan why didn't he write that well for me. He took no offense: "Because I know you'll fix things."

So I did; so did Bill Furth, and so did four indispensable men who served as assistant managing editors at one time or another during my tenure as managing editor. One was Edgar Smith, a plain-spoken commonsense fellow with a strong instinct for story organization and a good grasp of finance and marketing. (It was Smith who came up with the inspiration that the list of the five hundred biggest corporations, which for a couple of years had been compiled for internal use at our office, should be published as an annual supplement. "Fortune 500" passed into the language. For years afterward, I thought the 500 had been my idea, but dependable witnesses eventually persuaded me it was Edgar's.) When Smith left *Fortune* in 1957 to become managing editor of *Architectural Forum*, I appointed in his stead John Davenport, who had recently returned to us from *Barron's*, where he found the owners, Dow-Jones, unwilling to fund the kind of magazine he had in mind.

Another assistant managing editor was Duncan Norton-Taylor, once a pulp-fiction writer, then a polished and prolific performer for *Time*, who eventually tired of the pace there (in his day he held the record for most cover stories—sixty, or some such). Dunc was a Taft Republican and devout Episcopalian. He was a small, graceful man of dignified presence. A *Time* interview Dunc once conducted with the elegant secretary of state, Dean Acheson, had gone badly from the beginning: In an opening pleasantry, Dunc had commented favorably on the fact that Acheson's father had been an Episcopalian bishop in Connecticut. As one Anglophile to another, Dunc inquired when the Achesons had come over from England. It developed that the secretary's father as a young man had served as a sergeant in the Queen's Own Rifles in Canada. It further developed that Norton-Taylor's grandfather had come to Canada, tactlessly, as a colonel in the same regiment.

Dunc had a kind of medieval-scholastic view of capitalism. He had no consuming interest in business and scant regard for businessmen, and he wrote some very entertaining *Fortune* articles. I talked him into editing. His great storytelling skills (and masterly cutting techniques) rescued some very dismal manuscripts. He was also a careful and tactful administrator.

My other assistant managing editor, Holly Whyte of *The Organization Man*, was deeply disappointed with a decision I made in 1958. Whyte had continued some writing of his own while helping out with the editing load. The assistant M.E.s would take turns as "acting managing editor" when I was away. This rotation had its awkward aspects, and I decided a couple of years after Furth had left for Luce's staff that I must again have an "executive editor," a clear number 2. I chose Norton-Taylor and, in a painful conversation with Whyte, failed utterly to persuade him he would have more fun, and do the magazine more good, with an editing and writing portfolio than as executive editor. Holly thought this locked in Dunc as the next managing editor. When Henry Luce did indeed appoint Norton-Taylor as my successor, I couldn't talk Whyte into staying on.*

"I aspire not to be the editor of first resort on any stories," I told the assistant M.E.s in one memo. I would give the story editor my comments on a first draft, and not weigh in again, unless asked, until the article appeared in proof. I wanted to spend less of my time on the next issue of the magazine and more on the issues after that. But I could never quite rise above my fascination with journalistic detail. There were, in my judgment, no *Fortune* writers so skillful—and so vigilant about details—that they should be left to send sideheads, new captions, one-paragraph inserts, and substantive text revisions

---

*Holly went on to brilliant observations and advocacies, in film and books, on the dynamics of the city, particularly the ways that people—as opposed to architects and urban planners—actually use cities.

directly to the proofroom without an intervening look by an editor. "Those tedious final-final looks are part of what we're being paid for."

The copy desk kept a posted list, periodically updated, of my abominations: "Sports-page journalese—boost, hike, slash, dub. . . . The fact that cries out for another fact—so-and-so is probably the second richest man in France . . . The unmoored statistic—300 million barrels of oil. Is that a lot?" Etc.

Besides Holly Whyte's resignation, there was one other angry departure from *Fortune* while I was managing editor. (There were two or three happy departures to better jobs and two or three firings I had to carry out. The first man I fired did his best to put me at ease; he said he was surprised I hadn't done it sooner.) Lawrence Lessing, our senior science and technology writer, was indignant at what he felt to be the reactionary and militaristic stance of the articles I was publishing on defense and foreign policy. Many of these were written by Charles J. V. Murphy, who had excellent sources in the military and the CIA. Lessing thought I was permitting *Fortune* to become a mouthpiece for the Pentagon. He was a writer of great distinction, and I was sorry to lose him. A younger writer, Francis Bello—who for a time had been *Fortune*'s only male researcher—soon became as distinguished in the field as Lessing had been. My own grip on science and technology was very tenuous and has remained so; much that Lessing and Bello wrote was beyond me, and I was convinced that this was as it should be. It would have spoiled the articles to pitch them at my level. Lessing returned to *Fortune* in 1960; my satisfaction was tinged with a little amusement, because the managing editor by then was Norton-Taylor, also an admirer of Murphy's work and a man considerably more conservative than I.

I once threatened to quit myself. Charlie Murphy, in a 1956 article on the Eisenhower administration, had told how the president had used the National Security Council three years earlier in his shaping of a new defense policy. The article was on the presses when Murphy, as a courtesy to people he had interviewed, sent it to the White House. The piece was generally admiring of Eisenhower and his defense policy, and Murphy and I were amazed when Ike's men threw a fit about it. C. D. Jackson, back from his Washington service and now a vice president at Time Inc., became the envoy of the concerns of

White House Chief of Staff Sherman Adams, Press Secretary Jim Hagerty, and Treasury Secretary George Humphrey (Ike was quail-shooting with him in Georgia). They said "the old man" would be incensed if the reference to the NSC were published. Apparently he considered any discussion of his decision-making process and apparatus extremely sensitive. In a phone conversation with Humphrey, Harry Luce, I am sorry to say, gave in. He and Jackson instructed Del Paine as publisher to "pull" the article for excision of the offending material. The cost, as I recall, was about $20,000 in scrapped paper and printers' overtime.

The cost to me was considerable. I recognized the constitutional right of the editor-in-chief of *Fortune* to enter into an agreement with the secretary of the treasury, but I thought the managing editor of *Fortune* should have been allowed one more chance to say what a ridiculous agreement it was. I sent a stern memo to Luce and Jackson (copy to the sympathetic Paine), making it clear I would leave if anything like this ever happened again. Luce replied that he might well have been wrong in his decision, though it was always hard to turn down someone "speaking for the President" when he invokes national security. He couldn't imagine anything similar coming up again. Nothing did. I had made my point, but for months afterward I wondered whether I should simply have quit instead of threatening that I would.

I was restrained in part by a sense that the immediate point— *Fortune* being forced to change "The President decided" to "It was decided"—was so laughable that the larger principle could get lost. To be sure, I also liked my job. But I also believed that to be fully independent, you must always be prepared to leave. In fact, I went through a kind of drill with myself every time I got a promotion: Okay, what would it be like to give this up—the money, the recognition—where would I start job hunting, where would we cut the family budget, etc. ("Always edit with your hat on," said Russell Wiggins, who succeeded Casey Jones as M.E. of the *Washington Post*.) But I had a deep distaste for conversational or theatrical threats to resign. Don't say it unless you mean it.

The whole episode was also a glimpse into an unhealthy aspect of the American political system: the power of the presidency to terrify. Respect for the office is fine, but it can go too far. I had seen a bit of this, as a young reporter for the *Washington Post*, in the sycophancy of some of the people around Franklin Roosevelt. Now I was seeing mature and thoughtful men, powers in their own right, like

Luce and Humphrey, absurdly fearful of angering a president. In a later chapter of my life, I saw even the mild-mannered Jimmy Carter intimidate people quite without meaning to, people who should have argued with him. And in 1986–87, in the Iranian arms affair, we saw an abject failure of intelligent men—e.g., Secretaries Shultz and Weinberger—to fight vigorously against a presidential fixation that they considered folly. Larger matters, admittedly, than a long-ago story in *Fortune*.

The excessive intimacy between Time Inc. and the Eisenhower administration did have its uses. When *Fortune* was about to observe its twenty-fifth anniversary, I thought it would be nice if the president would send us a congratulatory letter. C. D. Jackson suggested I write the letter, and it duly appeared in the magazine over the president's signature. I thought it would be unseemly if I/Ike praised *Fortune* at length, but I did get off a pretty good little presidential sermon on U.S. enterprise and its role in the world:

> The American standard of living, high as it is, can be raised higher. Our needs for new highways, schools and hospitals are enormous. Our slums are a disgrace to America. Many of our citizens still lack adequate medical care and adequate security for their later years. American Business has an important role to play in the attack on all these problems. And businessmen, like any other citizens, have an obligation to strive toward an America in which spiritual and cultural values will match the growing richness of our material life.
>
> Beyond the great challenge of a better America, there is the even greater challenge of a better world. In the long run, America cannot live as an island of safety in a world of danger.

Eisenhower did not become the great president I had thought he might be, but I believed he was a very good one. This was my opinion while he was in office, so I did not have to become a "revisionist" in later years.

I did not see the Age of Eisenhower as a time of national torpor. The country was very busy, the Donovans were very busy. It is an odd intellectual provincialism that can see in all the exertions of the 1950s, individual and corporate, only an era of "apathy." Dorothy and I were drawn to people who were also energetic and ambitious; a few of our friends were rich, but none were idle rich (who would not have liked us, either). Our friends were hardworking Wall Street lawyers (longest hours of all), journalists, academics, stockbrokers, bankers, engineers, marketing men, and their equally purposeful wives. Even in suburbia, enriching our mix, we knew some artists and musicians, and in Manhattan, old connections from Pennsylvania, Minnesota, Oxford, Washington days, and newer connections from my job at *Fortune*, gave us as lively a calendar as we could handle.

Boarding the train one evening in the dingy Long Island Railroad terminal at Penn Station, I saw a man in a business suit storming up and down the platform shouting at his fellow commuters, "Sheep!" A gallant protest, or maybe just two or three too many at some bar. But the great "conformity" menace, it seemed to me, had considerably receded. I thought *Fortune*, through Holly Whyte's brilliant dissection of the organization man, had given a valuable warning to the big corporation. Likewise the Harvard sociologist David Riesman, with his insight into the inner-directed and outer-directed individual, in *The Lonely Crowd*. By the end of the Age of Eisenhower, I had come to think the inner-directed man had it pretty good in America, even in business—perhaps especially in business. Corporations had become very sensitive about conformity, and large, rich organizations could do a lot to nurture individualism. And in the jobs and goods out in the marketplace, there was more than ever before to be individualistic about. I also thought—with due deference to holy men out in the desert—that most of us establish our individuality only in relation to other people. People, as one of my least favorite voices has sung, need people.

By the 1970s, many scholars and journalists who had once scorned Eisenhower concluded that eight years of peace and virtually inflation-free prosperity was a pretty good record for any president. Inflation in fact averaged 1.4 percent a year during the Eisenhower presidency, and *Fortune* thought this was barely tolerable. The editors were hard-money men, very hard. We once got into an argument with the Harvard economist Sumner Schlichter, who was advocating that federal fiscal and monetary policy should encourage an inflation rate of 1.5 to 2 percent to "lubricate" the economy. We pointed out that even an administration like Ike's, which was striving for zero inflation, couldn't seem to prevent some upcreep. If the administration actually aimed at 1.5 to 2 percent, it would inevitably end up—horrors—with 3 to 4! Numbers that seemed quite wonderful to all of us in the mid-1980s, after painful experience in double digits.

As a partisan of the business system, *Fortune* did a fair bit of preaching at the businessman. It pleased me that a good many academics, government officials, and labor leaders followed *Fortune*, listening in, so to speak, on what we were telling the businessman. When the labor press quoted *Fortune* favorably (as it did from time to time), the reference usually began, "Even *Fortune*, the $1.25 Bible of Big Business, says . . ." (The price had gone up a quarter in 1948.) On the other hand, there were some circles, or at least pockets, of industrial opinion where *Fortune* was regarded as "pinkish," if not actually Communist. In certain cases, this sentiment could be traced back to a critical comment in *Fortune* about a particular corporation or industry or business practice; in other cases, it reflected the rather exotic opinion that Time Inc. as a whole—being "Eastern," "internationalist," "anti-segregationist"—was accordingly a hotbed of leftism.

Fortune did not purport to be "impartial." We had a deep respect for facts and went to as much trouble as any nontechnical journal in the world to establish facts. But we presented the facts from a point of view (as did the most "objective" newspapers—despite many claims to the contrary), and we indulged ourselves very freely in "editorial opinion" about the facts. Sometimes we went so far as to print, within a single sentence, (1) a fact and (2) an opinion, and we believed our readers were old enough to tell which was which.

The main body of fact that *Fortune* was exploring was the American economy, and here our main opinion was that the American profit system had evolved into a marvelously proficient producer and distributor of goods. We believed this system had been strengthened by many of the government "interventions" of the previous twenty-five years, but we suspected the intervention had gone about as far as it should (much too far in some places—e.g., farm policy) if the general character of a free economy and free society were to be maintained.

Our general prejudice in behalf of a free-market system led us to criticize businessmen about as often as we criticized politicians. For businessmen themselves—with their use of such price-rigging devices as the "fair trade" laws, demands for tariff protection, grasping for government subsidies—were frequent sinners against the basic principles of the economic system that had served America so handsomely. We also found occasion and necessity to criticize businesses or businessmen whom we believed negligent in the broad political, social, and cultural responsibilities that go with economic power.

I had some trouble holding our editorial "line" just where I wanted it, almost never because of Luce interventions, but often because of the intellectual obstreperousness of my dear friend and economics tutor John Davenport. After his return to *Fortune*, I had bravely put John in charge of our editorials. Though John and I were in broad agreement on economic philosophy, we argued strenuously on journalistic questions of tone of voice, rules of debate, and what's on people's minds.

John frequently complained about my insistence that a good editorial should give a fair accounting of the opposing argument before we batted it down. "Base-covering," John called this, and the ruin of a strong editorial. I said base-covering makes strong editorials stronger, maybe not in decibels, but in the all-important sense of being more convincing. "What is stronger," I asked John in one of our numerous memo barrages, "than an editorial that shows awareness of the best arguments against its thesis and deals with them successfully? I hope none of this sounds like a fatuous hankering for editorials that everybody can agree on."

In the passionate intensity of his views, John made spectacular scenes around the office. He could be charmingly contrite after insulting somebody, do it all over again in a day or two, and then apologize once more. But in print, John's style was beautifully clear and direct, and, after editing ministrations, he came out in the magazine sounding almost calm.

The "policy" role of *Fortune* probably interested me, and several of our editors and writers (not just Davenport), more than our straight reportorial role. But it was *Fortune*'s reporting that licensed us to sound off more spaciously on issues, and those of us who had done footwork out on the factory floor had a sense of having earned our opinions.

We didn't think of ourselves primarily as preachers, however; we were still reporters. We interpreted our "beat" broadly: not just the American economy, but the interplay between the economy and the society and the political order around it, and the interplay between the American economy and all those interesting, promising, dangerous places beyond our own shores. We interpreted "reporting" broadly, too: We did a lot of heavily documented, nuts-and-bolts reporting, but we also did a lot of impressionistic reporting, in which everything rested on the practiced eye and ear and judgment of one good journalist; and we did a lot of predicting and speculating—of an informed, imaginative kind, we hoped.

The most important news about the America of the 1950s was something that didn't happen: There was no Depression. Few Americans would have predicted that momentous nonevent. On Eisenhower's first Inauguration Day, January 20, 1953, there were no Americans under forty-five with any adult experience of prosperity in a more or less normal peacetime economy. The country had gone through the Depression decade of the 1930s; then five years of a war-time economy; then the distortions of the early postwar era, including waves of strikes, surging inflation, and large "catch-up" demand; then the semimobilization of the Korean war years. Looking ahead, economists of the Galbraith school saw a big bust coming unless massive government spending propped up the economy. Many conservative bankers and businessmen also foresaw a Depression; after all, we had always had them.

Instead, the U.S. economy took off. It is hard to remember, now that we have had so much of it for decades, what a big story prosperity was. The country's prosperity was meat and drink—and circulation and advertising—to *Fortune*. (The resurgence of the Western European and Japanese economies also made for exciting copy, and interesting trips for *Fortune* people. We tried to run a major foreign story in every issue.) We analyzed and celebrated the American boom—in prose, photography, paintings even, and of course in tables and diagrams and charts. The charts! The editors struggled to keep them comprehensible to ordinary businessmen (and editors). Also, oddly enough, we had to stay on the alert for charts that were *too* simple—I didn't want a chart burning up half a page of *Fortune's* valuable white space to say something that could be told in two sentences. I sometimes had my way.

There were hazards for *Fortune* in the sheer exuberance of the American economy and the spectacular performance of so many of the companies and people we wrote about. All that success could get boring. So we developed a kind of Bad News Department. We hunted hard for failure and scandal stories. God, as Luce had said in a different context, did provide.

One of the masters of the scandal/failure genre was Herbert Solow. Herb often affirmed his own personal "will to fail"; he was prey to sieges of deep melancholy. I once extracted a memo from him saying, "You were right and I was wrong. The Greek shipping story [one he had gloomed over for weeks] is quite printable." I had this framed and kept it on my office wall along with a signed confession from Norton-Taylor: "Everyone needs an editor—even me."

Solow was implacable in journalistic pursuit of the wicked. Herb was a former Trotskyite (he had even known Trotsky, in Mexico), and he savored all the rich and catty factionalism of the New York literary-leftist world. Solow had been "a catalyst," according to one study of that world in the 1930s, in "leading an important layer of intellectuals away from Stalinism." It was Solow whom Whittaker Chambers first approached when he wanted to break with the Party. I remember my astonishment when Solow related to me the precautions he had very seriously advised Chambers to take against abduction or murder. Herb approached *Fortune*'s seemingly less melodramatic subject matter with a keen nose for conspiracy and a love of plot lines so intricate that many people could simply not keep them straight. The editor, aware that some of his subscribers were among those many people, tried to defend their interests.

One of Solow's best *Fortune* stories was an exposé of improper political influence and general shenanigans in Eisenhower's General Services Administration. It was scarcely a scandal of Watergate dimensions (I grieved that Herb was not alive to enjoy those intricacies) or Iran/*Contra*, but by the standards of Washington in the 1950s, it was a pretty good scandal. Here again, C. D. Jackson tried to get us to go easy, but we didn't.

Solow could be a headache to edit, but he was unfailing fun to be with. He was a master parodist, and some of his lines had a Groucho Marx quality that went well with his mustache and soulful brown eyes. He confided one day to me and his wife and mine how much he admired one particularly delectable *Fortune* office girl, age nineteen or so. "When she walks by my office," Herb said, "I could be put in jail for what I'm thinking."

Richard Austin Smith was another relentless investigative reporter. He poked around the movie business in "RKO: It's Only Money," subtitle: "A Hollywood failure story starring Howard Hughes." He laid out the electrical industry's price-fixing conspiracy in a series rich in fresh dirt. He took apart the cultural standards of the TV industry in "The Light That Failed." The imperious "General" David Sarnoff of RCA, a good friend of Luce and Larsen's, was infuriated by Smith's TV article. In *Writing for Fortune*, a reminiscence by nineteen writers that Time Inc. published in 1980, Smith recalls: "Donovan had long ago decided to provide Luce and Larsen with shelter when the storm broke. He just never sent them any drafts of my story." When the broadcasters were demanding to know why their friends at Time Inc. had condoned such an attack on the industry, they could say truthfully they hadn't known about it. Sarnoff asked Larsen what he was going to do about the story. "Nothing," replied Larsen. "We wouldn't have all these fine people working for us if we could tell them what not to write."

"It was typical of Larsen," Smith wrote, "and it was a very gutsy if typical thing for Donovan to handle things the way he did. At that time Luce was considering appointing him . . . editorial director of all Time Inc. publications and, obviously, his heir apparent. Lesser men would have considered it no time to take sole responsibility for a fire storm. There were, however, no retractions, despite the networks' memo bombardments. . . ." (Bill Paley of CBS, another friend of Luce and Larsen's, had also weighed in.)

Dick Smith had a fine muscular prose style and a powerful allergy to being edited. He was given to huge, five-hundred-word lead paragraphs that could be visually forbidding to the reader. All sentences were devilishly interlocked, and the editor needed a crowbar to pry one of these babies apart. Once, when Dick and I were passing a pile of furniture stacked outside a departing writer's office, I said, "Paragraphs too long." It became one of Dick's favorite anecdotes, but it had no visible effect on his style.

Apart from the failure and scandal stories, we had to sharpen the focus in our abundant success stories. The stately corporation stories of the early *Fortune* were a great Luce invention. When *Fortune* first "did" General Motors in the 1930s, it could invite the reader to marvel at the workings of the assembly line, relish the colorful history of the predecessor companies in the 1910s and early 1920s, and even learn the salaries of the top executives. (*Fortune* and *Time* were the first publications to grasp the titillation potential in the new SEC salary-disclosure requirements; newspapers were slow to notice.) Twenty years later, that was old stuff. When *Fortune* was doing General Motors in the 1950s, for the tenth time or so, we had to locate a *story*, something important and interesting, preferably different from what the reader thought he knew, something happening at G.M. right now or, ideally, *about* to happen. "*Fortune* has learned that . . ." The corporation story continued, recast, as a *Fortune* staple.

I thought every issue of *Fortune* should run at least as many names as appear in a good country weekly. *Fortune* was dealing with such formidable movements in the economy, science and technology, national and world politics, that I wanted us to assert, wherever we could, the role of individual people with names and faces. Individual men and women thought up, or executed, or botched up, or reacted to the "forces" we were reporting. I once assigned Charles Silberman to a story on the woes of U.S. shipbuilding. Silberman was a bright young Columbia economics instructor I had hired; he was now about halfway through his progress (descent?) from academia to journalism. His first draft was an utterly convincing but bloodless analysis of the weak competitive situation of the domestic shipbuilders. In later years, he was kind enough to remember that I had told him to go back and listen to what they were saying in the bars at Newport News (not his normal sort of habitat), and that the trip did improve his story.

We ran more "profiles" than *Fortune* ever had before—to get more people into the magazine and because we had a remarkable number of writers who were good at these pieces. One of the best was Freeman Lincoln, who pretty much discovered the "new rich" of Texas—the Hunts, Murchisons, Sid Richardson, and other freshly arrived tycoons, raiders, and rascals all over the postwar business landscape. (Bill Furth, hearing of a trip I was about to take to Dallas with Lincoln as my guide, said, "It will be like walking through the Forum with Caesar.")

Lincoln suffered frightfully from writer's block—he had been known to spend a week without achieving one sentence he liked—but the stuff was great when it began to flow. He was a salty and irascible man, son of the Cape Cod writer Joseph Lincoln. Freeman took me out once on the infamous Eastward Ho! golf course on Cape Cod, a links in the British seaside style. He was a good golfer, usually shooting in the low eighties. I was spraying balls all over the hopeless rough, and as Freeman helped me look for them—torn between his courtesy as host and his increasingly apoplectic reaction to my game—he began to lose his rhythm, and soon was playing as badly as I. When we finished, each somewhere around 105, possibly worse— I perhaps slightly less awful than Freeman—he announced that he would never play again. He never did.

I spent a good many BTUs (the British thermal unit is one of the few bits of technological lore I have mastered, and I use it whenever possible) in the development of ambitious series of six, eight, twelve articles projecting the dimensions of the economy and all its industries for some years ahead. We bragged—truthfully, I believe—that

Fortune was the first general-interest magazine to publish in readable English original economic research that met the most rigorous standards of professional economists and statisticians. The other business magazines of that era (and the business sections of the newspapers) printed the ideas of economists and businessmen about the economy; we were trying to be one of the sources of the ideas. My method, essentially, was to take Sandy Parker and others of our economic staff, and some of our best journalistic translators of economists, and lock them up together for some months at a time.

Charles Silberman thinks that I got a lot of work out of the economics squad. In *Writing for Fortune*, he recalls:

> Month after month, Hedley would suggest a subject for investigation, and I would reply that there was no way to do that kind of story, at least by academic standards, in the time available. Hedley would smile and explain that he knew I could not do the kind of story I really wanted to do, but might I not be able to do something, say, in between a *Wall Street Journal* article and the piece I would write if I had all the time I needed? Sandy Parker and I would end up doing what Hedley undoubtedly had assumed we would do; we would work every night and every weekend and end up with the article we had said we could not produce. (Hedley always seemed pleasantly surprised; and when the article had gone to press, he would express concern at the pace I had been keeping, suggesting that I actually take a weekend off before starting the next story.)

The most prolific of our interpreters of the economists was Gilbert Burck. He excited our economists, and they excited him. On a staff rich in eccentrics, Gil stood out. His eccentricity was his sheer love of writing for *Fortune*. He turned out twice as many publishable words per annum as any other writer. He teemed with enthusiasm and ideas. In the course of a fairly heavy-footed series on the capital goods markets, Burck proposed a portfolio on "The Greatest Capital Goods Salesman of Them All"—i.e., Diamond Jim Brady, who was in railway cars. To go along with the old photos of Brady, Jim Hill, Lillian Russell, *et al.*, Gil wrote a charming essay on Brady's fabulous appetite (four dozen oysters, two or three lobsters, several pounds of steak at a sitting) and his dinner parties for men in a position to buy rolling stock. The dinners ended with " 'dessert courses' served by comely females innocent only of raiment." Diamond Jim neither smoked nor drank, as Gil scrupulously noted.

Some of my other favorites from those years: "How to Fire an Executive," "A Slight Case of Overcommunication" (I enjoyed thinking up titles), "This is a Bureaucrat" (profile of a capable and devoted man in the federal Bureau of the Budget), "Norton Simon—Like Him or Not" (and, thirty-four years later, like him or not, he bequeathed his 750-million-dollar art collection to UCLA), "Would You Hire Your Son?" (a medium-touchy topic in Time Inc., where several sons of the brass were employed), "The Executive Ulcer" (Robert Osborn cartoons), "How Are We Fixed for Water?," "How Seven Employees Can Be Made to Do the Work of One," "The Good Uses of $750 Billion" (the gross national product in 1959), "Women as Bosses" (novel subject in the 1950s), "The Executive Crackup," "What's Eating the Airline Pilots?," "The Magnificent Decline of U.S. Farming" (a Gil Burck celebration of the spectacular rise of agricultural productivity and hence decline in number of farms and farmers), "Okay, How Would *You* Run the Post Office?" (another touchy one in Time Inc., which was constantly embroiled in arguments about second-class and fourth-class rates).

Then there was "The Problem of Howard Hughes." Charles Murphy, who knew aviation well, and Tom Wise, a shrewd financial reporter I had hired away from the *Wall Street Journal*, had pieced together more information on Hughes's private fiefdoms—Hughes Tool and Hughes Aircraft—along with his 78 percent of TWA, than had ever before been published. They had figured out the financial squeeze that was threatening this nomadic capitalist's control of TWA. From one of his Nevada hangouts, Hughes phoned Luce, whom he knew slightly from Clare's connection with Hollywood and his own RKO days, to beg for postponement of the story. Luce told him to call me. There ensued a colorful conversation in which Hughes wheedled, cried several times, threatened to come to New York and take a poke at me (I told him my business address, room number, and office hours), and wheedled again. We could have a hell of a party in Las Vegas—did I like blondes, brunettes, or redheads? I had often confessed to my brunette wife my aesthetic appreciation of redheads, but I did not confide this to Hughes. I did, however, respond to one plea he made: If you say an airline is in financial difficulties, some readers will assume it's scrimping on maintenance and is unsafe. That was not the case with TWA. After checking with our reporters, I stuck into our article, close to the lead: The airline has an "excellent reputation for service and flight operations." Otherwise, I gave nothing, and rejected Hughes's frequent suggestions that if I would just put off this article for a few months, he would tell us everything.

A couple of years later, Tom Wise was again pursuing Hughes; this time, finally, he was losing control of TWA. Executives of the financial institutions that were negotiating with Hughes never saw the man himself; he was occasionally heard over the phone. The *Fortune* story was to be called "The Bankers and the Spook." Hughes got wind of the title and one of his lawyers made threatening noises about the use of "spook." Hughes called Luce, and Luce again told him to call me. We were becoming regular phone pals. Tom Wise, in *Writing for Fortune*, had this call running from 4:30 to 10:30 P.M., with Donovan "patient and courteous . . . but he held his ground." I hope Tom's heroic version is correct, though I could worry as to when I got my supper. "Spook" did stay in the title. Ten years later, Hughes got even with me, and then some. I knew so much about his weird ways that I was prepared to believe an otherwise-preposterous account of how his "autobiography" (see chapter X) came to be available to *Life*.

One of our most polished writers was Robert Sheehan. He did *Fortune*'s first drama criticism, a delightful essay on a comedy of the mid-1950s, *The Solid Gold Cadillac*, with the indomitable Josephine Hull as a small stockholder who parlays a few guileless questions into a senior management job in General Products Corporation. In the final scene, Josephine squelches another woman stockholder trying to ask a question at the annual meeting: "Oh, no. That's how I got *my* job." This piece was by way of a holiday for Sheehan, who wrote remarkably gracefully about some rather unromantic subjects, including the insurance industry.

Another skilled stylist was the suave and handsome Emmet Hughes, who had been a Time-Life correspondent in Europe in the early postwar years. He was a great favorite of the Luces, Clare as well as Harry, and among his colleagues in the Time-Life News Service, he was considered something of a courtier; their code name for him was "the Florentine." Luce loaned Hughes (along with C. D. Jackson) to the Eisenhower campaign in 1952; Emmet stayed on as a White House speechwriter for two years. He had a weakness for deep-purple prose, and I often marveled that Ike was willing to speak some of the lines Hughes wrote for him, so outlandishly unlike the man. Bryce Harlow, also a White House assistant in that era, told me years later that Ike certainly knew one literary style from another and knew perfectly well what he was doing. Ike thought Emmet's style was appropriate for certain presidential occasions, and nobody was being asked to think that he (or even Emmet) talked that way in ordinary life.*

When Emmet left the White House, Luce asked me to take him on the *Fortune* staff. He thought it would be good for Hughes "to know something about business." Furth and Paine, mindful of Emmet's reputation for intrigue, were wary on my behalf, but I saw no difficulty and told Luce, "Everybody should know something about business." If Hughes ever plotted a coup d'état, I was too dense to know about it. We got on very well, and he wrote some excellent *Fortune* articles, duly de-purpled by me and my deputies. Emmet went on to become a political adviser to Nelson Rockefeller, helped to sell him on a foolishly Byzantine (or Florentine?) approach to the 1968 campaign, and then became a Rutgers University professor and respected scholar of the presidency.

As managing editor, I milled around a lot because I liked the *Fortune* people so much and liked what they were working on (which, indeed, I had asked them to work on). I was viscerally incapable of pounding the furniture or yelling at people. "A writer who was a week late delivering a manuscript, and who chanced to encounter the M.E. on the elevator, could count on two things," according to an article in *f.y.i.* "Donovan would know exactly how late the manuscript was, and he would wait for the writer to raise the subject himself. Once another editor asked him why he didn't simply give fictitious deadlines to the writers who were always late. Donovan's answer was that reporters who were smart enough to find out everything that goes into a *Fortune* corporation story were smart enough to find out when *Fortune* magazine goes to press; why kid them?" It was only some years after I had left the M.E.'s chair that Mary Grace confessed she sometimes fibbed even to *me* as to when an article really, finally, irrevocably had to go to press.

*A sensitive perception by a president not always thought of as a student of literary conventions. I have always been fascinated by the tone-of-voice differences between a speech (in my own case, unlike Ike's, always written by me), a journalistic piece, a memo, a letter, and everyday conversation. If you pride yourself (as I do) on being unaffected, it can be a little disconcerting to notice how many different prose personae you maintain.

. . . .

After hours, my colleagues and I talked a lot of shop—on the street, on the subways and commuter railroads, in one another's apartments and houses, and at the endless office parties that impregnated (occasionally literally, or so it was said) Time Inc. Somebody was promoted, somebody was retiring, somebody had been there twenty-five years; let's have a party!

The only thing stingy about *Fortune* was its by-line policy. I was concerned that this could cost us valuable people, the hunger for recognition being so powerful in writers. Traditional *Fortune* doctrine was "Fortune says," not some writer says; the full weight of the magazine was behind every article, and if the writer wanted recognition, he could look up his name on the masthead. When I was a writer, by-lines were awarded only for pieces the managing editor considered exceptionally distinguished (I had one by-line in five years) or so polemical that the magazine wanted to lay off the responsibility onto the writer. The policy had loosened up a little by the time I became M.E. I loosened it altogether. Apart from individual ego gratification, I thought that as our better writers became known in their various skills and specialties, their by-lines enlarged the audience for their pieces. So everything got a by-line except stuff that had been so bad that some editor had to rewrite it almost *in toto*.

The senior writers belonged to that pleasant little club within the club, the Board of Editors, whose principal function, as with so many clubs, was to decide who to let in and who to keep out. When I first became M.E., I was told by some of the elders that there was a serious question whether the M.E., though he might once have belonged to the Board of Editors, was any longer a member. There was a school of thought that held he was the board's servant. There were dark legends that the board had sometimes met without his being present and even unbeknownst to him.

Legends aside, the form was that I would give a lunch or dinner for the board once or twice a year, and at these gatherings propose any people I wanted to promote from associate editor. A move up to the Board of Editors brought no more money or responsibility; it was strictly glory on the masthead, and greatly prized. The board once proposed a writer sooner than I would have elevated him, and there followed a lively mock-solemn debate as to whether the M.E. could constitutionally veto their selection. I deferred to the board that time, as I did at least once when they wanted one of my nominations held over for a year. I believe in preserving dignified old institutions that do no actual harm, perhaps a legacy from my years in England.

A seductive fringe benefit of the M.E.'s job was the right to be amateur art director of *Fortune*. The magazine had to have a real art director, of course. This was Leo Lionni, a spectacularly versatile man whom my predecessor Del Paine had discovered. Lionni was probably Paine's most brilliant stroke of hiring. For "word men" like Paine (or me), the judging of other word men—though speculative enough, God knows—is not so mysterious as the sizing-up of a fellow who might or might not work out or fit in, especially with you, the managing editor, as art director.

Lionni was born in Amsterdam, studied in Switzerland and Italy, and came to America in 1939. He went to work for the N. W. Ayer advertising agency in Philadelphia, where he designed, among many other ad campaigns, the famous "Never underestimate the power of a woman" series (for *Ladies Home Journal*). Lionni is a graphic designer, industrial designer, sculptor, mosaicist, painter, photographer, prolific author and illustrator of best-selling children's books, and, perhaps not incongruously, holds a doctorate in economics (University of Genoa). He is a man of infectious curiosity and enthusiasm who can stop you five times a block, walking along a street in Ahmedabad or Verona or Manhattan, to notice something unexpectedly beautiful or unintentionally funny.

A Time Inc. managing editor was not to delude himself that he could be "his own art director." Still, he could hire and fire real art directors, and he was bound to have some notions of how he wanted his magazine to look. I was strongly attracted to the visual dimensions of *Fortune*. Leo welcomed this, and let me win an occasional argument. I let him win more, which was as it should be.

My assistant M.E.s, good as they were with words and ideas, were not always as fertile in layout. I once had to deliver a little lecture: "With almost all of our writers, 'the story,' naturally enough, is the thing, and 'the art' is something separate, a sort of afterthought or irritation. The Art Department, also naturally enough, tends to see rather than read *Fortune*, often with brilliant results. Editors are the only people with equal responsibility for the words and the looks. The responsibility goes much beyond a veto power over a layout you don't like; it carries a definite obligation to come up with fresh and imaginative ideas for illustrating the stories in your care."

When it came to *Fortune* covers, Lionni and I had a simple rule: We both had to like them. They no longer stirred shouting matches around the office, though subscribers could still be baffled and antagonized. My ophthalmologist, Dr. Maynard Wheeler, was once looking into my eyes with that gadget that seems to beam straight through your skull and on into Central Park, when he asked, "Mr. Donovan, who chooses those . . . ah . . . unusual . . . *Fortune* covers?" I admitted that I helped. Lionni once let me design one—a sequence of large numbers, 1930–1955–1980, for our twenty-fifth anniversary. A work of deceptive simplicity, I told jealous colleagues.

There was more than enough art that Leo and I both admired. We published Ben Shahn, Saul Steinberg, Rufino Tamayo; cartoons by William Steig, Robert Osborn, George Price, Alan Dunn; photography by Ansel Adams, Dan Weiner, William Garnett—discoverer of the American landscape from three hundred feet up in a helicopter— and our own Leo. (And I once snuck into the magazine a photograph of Soviet workers on a footbridge over the Volga, taken by Hedley Donovan.)

We persuaded Margaret Bourke-White, who had done a memorable black-and-white portfolio on Great Lakes shipping for *Fortune*'s first issue, to return to the subject for *Fortune*'s twenty-fifth anniversary. This time, she showed the grain and ore boats and the locks and mills and docks in color from the air. The portfolio celebrated the approaching opening of the St. Lawrence Seaway, which could even enhance the splendid lakes, "a majestic and economical system of transportation for the rich bulk product of the midland." The hateful notion of a "rust belt" was still some years in the future.

Fortune's only staff photographer was the great Walker Evans, though he preferred his modest masthead billing as "Associate Editor," which was our general label for a writer. Walker, in fact, wrote beautifully—and infinitely slowly. Chipping away at the introductory "text block" for one of his photographic portfolios, he counted it a good day—and I did, too—if he carved out an acceptable sentence or two. His photographic approach in the 1950s was still the direct and unblinking focus he had applied in the 1930s to the rural Southern poor, in the classic *Let Us Now Praise Famous Men* (with James Agee). Walker had a kind of faded-aristocrat air; he was something of a dandy. Whether he had been angry at what he saw in the South, I could never tell; he was reporting it with his camera. But now he was attracted to a kind of elegiac view of a vanishing America: small-town railroad depots, steam locomotives, gently decaying downtowns, the "Dark Satanic Mills" of nineteenth-century New England, mellowed into beautiful relics in the mid-twentieth. I reveled in this nostalgia. It was probably just as well that Walker's work tempo (and a severe neurosis about travel) held him down to about two portfolios a year.

But we lived in the present tense, of course, in our big photographic essays on industrial America: "The Houston Complex," "Chicago Industry by Night," "Beauty in Chemical Crystals," "The Building of the Connecticut Turnpike," "The New Minnesota Taconite Plants." Leafing through those essays thirty years later, I think they still have great vitality, even as the pictures take on their own appeal to nostalgia.

It is always hazardous for me to start hunting up some particular point in "my" *Fortune*s of the 1950s. I can emerge, point unfound, after an hour of truant browsing amid the costumes and faces, male and female, of the Age of Eisenhower; the automobiles; the look of city streets; the decor of office and home; the quaint old airplanes. And the cigarettes: Middle-aged executives not only smoked them but were pleased to be photographed doing just that. And, oh, the prices: A Rolls-Royce Silver Wraith cost $21,000. In a gorgeous two-part article on the art market by Eric Hodgins, we learn (1955) that Van Eyck's *Virgin and Child* went to the Frick Collection for "a reported $750,000," an El Greco *Pietà* to the Greek shipping tycoon Stavros Niarchos for "a reported $300,000," and a Modigliani *Reclining Nude* that the Museum of Modern Art bought in 1949 for $12,500 is "now worth better than $50,000!"

I think my colleagues and I made *Fortune* more topical during the 1950s, more "journalistic," more talked about—and kept it as handsome as it already was. I hoped on just about every page of *Fortune* we could make the reader say, "That's something I better watch." And now and then it was nice if he said, "By God, that's what I've been trying to tell people!" I tried to keep in mind that there does come a moment—after all the best efforts of the most gifted art director, after all the lively titles and typographical enticements you can think of—when the reader is left alone with the reading matter. And at the moment, if he didn't read, we didn't have a magazine. He did read, not every article, of course—we never aspired to that—but enough to feel he was getting his money's worth. Various surveys suggested the mythical "median" subscriber spent two to three hours, in two sittings, with the magazine. (It could take five to six hours to read every editorial word.)

We missed some tricks. After getting Dick Smith in 1957 to do a systematic study of the richest people in America, the names and numbers, I let the subject lapse. I should have staked it out as an annual *Fortune* entertainment (vulgar as it might be), which might have foreclosed *Forbes*'s annual directory of the "400 Richest," started many years later—a feature prolific in free publicity for *Forbes*. For the occasional "outside" piece, we could have worked harder at getting just the right businessman to sound off on just the right subject. Granted that most businessmen wouldn't or couldn't write. One of my favorite unrealized businessman-by-line pieces was "Why I No Longer Like Ike" (though I myself still did).

But story length was the most stubborn problem. As I worked down the length of major pieces from an average of six thousand words to perhaps five thousand, over half a dozen years, I sometimes felt I was trying to program the receding of a glacier. But it was not just writer habit that was involved; there was a real tension between *Fortune*'s traditional thoroughness—"authority"—and readability. I don't think I resolved it.

I concluded in my years as M.E. that an established magazine like *Fortune* had only two alternatives—to improve, or presently to get out of business. The general art of magazine-making was advancing; the customers were getting harder to please; and the competition, especially in *Fortune*'s field, was steadily improving. And, as I noticed, you had to spend money; editors got approximately what they paid for.

I acknowledged that advertising performed an admirable social service in helping pay my salary, but I also saw that ad pages could be very tough competitors, visually, with editorial pages. The art departments of ad agencies and corporate advertising departments had learned a lot in the 1930s and 1940s from magazine journalism, including *Life* and *Fortune* itself (not much from *Time* in those days). *Fortune* ad pages were sometimes more compelling, to my distress, than "my" pages. I envied the *New Yorker*, where, as it seemed, some subscribers were actually attracted at least as much by the ads as by the editorial matter (some of it quite hostile to the world whence the ads came). Strong newspapers, as I knew, had the same lovely formula: The advertising was an indispensable service to the reader, and reader and advertiser both paid the carrier.

I saw all around me the ways that news breeds not only more

news, but also the appetite for more news. This was especially striking in the business journalism of the 1950s, as the U.S. and world economies expanded, as capitalism became demonstrably successful in so many places, from Taiwan to Milan, as the underlying technologies threw off their amazing progeny. There was more than enough subject matter to go around for *Fortune, Business Week, Forbes, Barron's*, the *Wall Street Journal*, the trade press, and the slowly improving business sections of *The New York Times* and a few other newspapers. We each built and enlarged the audience that we all shared—and fought over. The audience had its various layers and segments, of course, and *Fortune* was especially strong in "the boardroom." The *Wall Street Journal* was probably the biggest business journalistic success of those years, well on its way from the obscure stock-market sheet of the prewar era to the great national institution (and money-maker) it became in the 1960s and 1970s. (Once in the mid-1950s I tried to hire Vermont Royster, whose *Journal* editorials I greatly admired, to come write the same kinds of editorials for *Fortune*. He was slightly tempted, but I think the main result of my sally—perhaps in the long run best for the national interest—was a firming-up of his prospect of becoming editor of the *Journal*.)

I thought often about "institutional memory" in *Fortune*. Editors and staff felt they were in competition with all the good things the magazine had done in the past. This was up to a point salutary—but the danger was somebody saying, "But we did that! Don't you remember?" The M.E. had to keep in mind in 1955 that at least half his audience had not been subscribing to the magazine five years earlier, and the half who were could not necessarily stand an examination on what they had read in 1950.

I was to have six and a half years—eighty issues of the magazine, eight million words, give or take a few paragraphs—as managing editor of *Fortune*. I carried away from the experience, along with whatever I had learned about magazine-making and the management of intellectuals, a kind of exasperated admiration for *Fortune*'s reader and protagonist, the American businessman. The fellow was a very considerable force in the world. He was a constructive radical, in his willingness to reexamine all products, all ways of manufacturing, selling, managing, financing. He was a democrat—at least by comparison with most of the business Direktors and dignitaries of other nations—receptive to the rise of fresh men and fresh ideas from below.

He also thought business was an honorable calling—not the attitude in many European and Asian cultures—and thus in his business life he professed, and often observed, the same ethical standards expected in private life. He was a very hard worker despite silly arguments that high taxes were depriving him of all incentive. He had a weakness for ritualistic oratory, as speaker and as audience, that sounded as though American business were fighting a desperate last stand against armies of agitators, statists, and Socialists, while an economically ignorant public turned its back on the fearful struggle. In fact, a generally admiring society was willing to offer the businessman leadership responsibilities in the community and the country, but he was often ill-equipped by temperament and education to run anything except his own business.

These were views I often pursued in exchanges with Harry Luce. The American Businessman (the "B" always uppercase in a Luce memo) was one of his favorite subjects, and *Fortune* was either his favorite magazine or second most favorite, or perhaps tied (with *Time*) for first. It was in that sixth year of my *Fortune* tenure that he invited me into the management of his other magazines.

VII

The Proprietor

Henry Luce has already appeared in these pages—he could hardly be kept out—but now I want to attempt a fuller portrait. He is rich subject matter—and difficult to get just right. I think he would agree.

When I first met Luce, in 1946 at a *Fortune* lunch in a rather drab room in the Empire State Building, I was prepared not to like him. I was curious, as a journalist should be, about a famous and powerful man. I was curious, as a journalist should certainly be, about a man who had invented or coinvented not merely three magazines but three new *kinds* of magazines. I was thirty-two as I sat at the lunch table; Luce and his partner, Briton Hadden, were twenty-four when they launched *Time*; Luce was thirty-one when he launched *Fortune*. He was only thirty-eight when (with various coclaimants, including Clare Luce) he created *Life*. This was enough to make you feel a little retarded. I came to be still more impressed by these marvelous strokes of imagination in later years when I had myself grappled with the challenge of conceiving a new national magazine. As reader/looker, I had lapped up the *Life* of 1936–46 in its glorious pre-TV days, and I had always been awed by the depth and elegance of *Fortune*.

But alongside Luce the inspired inventor, there was also an editor who apparently encouraged, or at least permitted, the cruelty and glibness (as I saw it) that often disfigured *Time*. I suppose I also had lingering recollections of Wolcott Gibbs's famous *New Yorker* profile (1936), a parody that for years stood as the only major piece of journalism about *Time* and Luce. And even as new to the company as I was, I had already heard the anecdotes about Luce the boor, a rude and domineering figure who could devastate his editors and writers, usually without knowing it. He could avoid looking at people he knew perfectly well, I was told, or stare through them in elevators, in corridors, at meetings. He could crush somebody's well-meant try at small talk with a change of subject so swift and total that, as one of the walking wounded put it, "You felt inexpressibly stupid." A few years later, a fairly senior Time Inc. executive, congratulating me on a midlevel promotion at *Fortune*, said, "The work here is interesting, the pay is good. The only problem about doing well here is that you will be seeing more of Luce. And if you do very well here, you will be seeing a lot of Luce."

Then there was Luce's wife, as famous in her own right as he— congresswoman, editor, playwright, recently converted to Catholicism by Fulton Sheen. I was not a great admirer of the "radio priest," who seemed to specialize in celebrity converts.* And I disliked the stridently partisan, hard-edged quality of Clare Luce's Republicanism. It wasn't fair to tax the husband with his wife's views, but each did reinforce the other's fame, and there was a kind of entity—a glittering entity—"the Luces."

He was said to have dividend income approaching $1 million a year from Time Inc. stock by the time he was forty. (This in hard prewar dollars, barely taxed.) He enjoyed some of what money can buy (an elegant Manhattan apartment and a place or two away from New York—though he didn't want real estate all over the map) and was indifferent to much else (gourmet dining, racehorses, fleets of grand cars, yachts—though he enjoyed being a guest on somebody else's). He came rather late and cautiously to art collecting, and his approach was more dutiful than acquisitive: the editor-in-chief of *Time*, *Life*, and *Fortune* should know something about art. The biggest single improvement in anyone's living standard, he said, was when you could first afford to hire a maid. I think his money mattered to him mainly as a sign that Time Inc. and Henry Luce were performing useful work in this world. His political outlook was far more liberal than that of many self-made rich men, and his own Republicanism was of the "Eastern progressive" school.

---

*An anticlerical friend in Washington, knowing I had just come to work for Time Inc., sent me a telegram: "You're next. SHEEN." I wired him back: "Very satisfactory conversation with Donovan. Am converting to Congregationalist. Best. SHEEN."

He had been a boss pretty much all his adult life. He was a cub reporter, in Chicago, then Baltimore, less than two years before he and Hadden launched *Time*, in 1923. They were not especially congenial personally—the wisecracking, cynical Hadden seemed almost frivolous alongside the solemn young Luce—but they were effective partners. After Hadden's death in 1929, Luce ran Time Inc. He was forty-six when I met him, the unchallenged proprietor of this young and cocksure company that had prospered all through the Depression and war. His senior publishing and editorial executives were around his age or younger; the few Time Inc. people over fifty tended to be in rather modest positions.

The Fortune editors and half a dozen writers had been summoned to lunch with Luce that day in 1946 to review the plans for their special issue on labor. The country was besieged by strikes in the first postwar year, and stunned by the militancy of the unions. Since I was writing the "roundup" piece that would lead off the issue, Luce directed much of his machine-gun-tempo questioning at me. "You remember what Samuel Gompers said when somebody asked him what labor wanted. Well, has anyone improved on that?" I knew who Gompers was, all right (founder of the American Federation of Labor), but not what he had said. It was the first time—but far from the last—that I had to confess not knowing something Luce thought every schoolboy must know. But he took it calmly, and for my part, as I remembered the episode, I managed to work Gompers's answer—"More"—into my story. Yet on rereading the story now, I can't find that "More." Had I been too stubborn to put it in? Ten years later, I did accommodate Luce. I was now managing editor, and I signed up George Meany, then chief of the AFL, to write an article. I gave it the title "What Labor Means By 'More.'"

That lunch was my first glimpse of Luce's extraordinary ability to move in on a subject that some of his staff had been immersed in for weeks or months, and in two or three hours thoroughly shake them up—constructively. Wasn't a profile of so-and-so (the secretary of labor, I think) kind of a tired idea—does anybody really want to know more about him or are we just being "dutiful" (a journalistic sin to this deeply duty-driven man)? Were we paying enough attention to such-and-such, what about combining this piece here (shuffling the rough mock-ups) and the one back there to open up space for a real look at some of these lesser-known union leaders? It was an impressive intellectual feat, and the next day he was going to do the same thing with some *Time* or *Life* editors who had been totally absorbed in some other subject. At least equally impressive to me was the fact that Paine and Furth, going back to the drawing board, could utterly disregard some of Luce's ideas. It was another important first glimpse: This bristling boss, for all his scariness, was creating an atmosphere in which people could disagree with him or—happier outcome—take a suggestion of his and turn it into something much better.

As a *Fortune* writer, I would see Luce perhaps four or five times a year, at a lunch or some planning session in the office. There was a burst of such meetings in 1948 when Luce emerged from a portentous retreat of several weeks in which he was "re-thinking" *Fortune*. The magazine was beginning to lose money after its wartime circulation and ad bulge wore off, and Luce the businessman felt "the box office" must be telling something to Luce the editor. Indeed the message mattered more than the money, but just what was the message? Luce came up with a "Directive" for *Fortune* and an embarrassingly didactic set of "Basic Propositions": *Mission, Goal, Sanction, Dedication, Journalistic Modes*. When he got past those sonorous pronouncements, he had some perceptive critiques of *Fortune* and a long laundry list of journalistic ideas, some excellent. Paine and Furth winnowed them and began putting out the "new" *Fortune* a few months later. It was a year or two before the new magazine took. Some of the surviving Luce ideas had helped, and so did the ideas he prodded and bullied and frightened his editors into producing. The moral: If you don't want Harry reinventing your magazine, you better keep doing it yourself.

I had, somewhere in there, begun calling him "Harry," at a suitable interval after he began calling me "Hedley." But junior writers didn't exactly relax in his presence. Nor senior editors. I saw some of the legendary brusqueness in the closing-off of a meeting or the closing-down of a conversation that didn't interest him. I recall a lunch Luce gave at his apartment for some Iranian dignitary; before coffee, he led the guest of honor to his study, saying nothing to the six or eight of us left sitting at the table. After ten minutes or so, a Time Inc. vice president spoke up: "Gentlemen, I believe we are dismissed." Loudon Wainwright of *Life*, in his book *The Great American Magazine*, quotes a woman who said Luce had "the worst natural bad manners" of any man she had ever met.

The Luce style in a working conversation could indeed be unnerving. A touch of early deafness, more than a touch of early power

and money, and an enormous intentness went into his habit of paus-
ing a few seconds to marshal the next material in his argument, then
cutting straight through some hapless employee (or even guest from
the outside world) who thought a few seconds of silence meant that
Luce had made his point and the floor was now open. Everybody
present cringed for the victim and felt at least a little demeaned to
witness such bad manners. By the time I got to know Luce well enough
that I might have told him this, his conversational style had become
somewhat more civilized. And in our one-on-one conversations, being
a fairly competitive type, I had begun occasionally to trample on *his*
lines.

He could be beautifully dry when somebody began to belabor
the obvious. *Fortune* editor trying to sell an automobile-industry story
at the time of a much-publicized boom: "Detroit is really having a
tremendous year." Luce, after staring several cold seconds at the
advocate: "So I have heard." But he could glow with excitement when
somebody came up with a fact or idea that was new to him. He
relished argument, and you could disagree with him with impunity—
if you knew what you were talking about and had some conviction
about it. He seemed to smell out yes-men agreeing with him to curry
favor; they might have their uses, but these were limited. His hospitality to argument was such that it could even take a certain amount
of intellectual courage to agree with him when he was right.

As a junior *Fortune* writer, I once startled some other junior
Fortune writers by announcing over lunch a thesis that one's employer
is not always wrong. When I later became an employer myself, I was
glad I had previously put that statement on the record. After I had
become editor-in-chief, Luce once asked me how often I expected to
win in lunch-table arguments with the editors. I said at least two out
of three. He claimed he would settle for fifty-fifty.

I also had a few glimpses in my early *Fortune* years of a thoughtful
and even affectionate boss. I remember being charmed, as a junior
writer, having been asked for some reason to accompany Luce to a
lunch with a group of foreign bankers, to hear him say to the visitors,
"Now these magazines that Hedley and I work for . . . " There were
many more of these graceful and flattering touches after I became a
Fortune editor in 1950.

But higher rank also carried an admission ticket to some angry
debate. The day after President Truman fired General MacArthur, in
April 1951, I found myself, during a painful lunch with Luce and eight
or ten Time Inc. editors, the only one defending the firing. One thing

led to another, and I was also moved to question the need for MacArthur's bloody reconquest of Luzon in 1945, arguing that the liberation of the Philippines could have awaited the resolution of the war elsewhere. My views were near-blasphemy to Luce, but he never referred to that argument again, and in fact only a few weeks later approved Paine's plan to promote me to associate managing editor of *Fortune*, responsible for "national policy" articles, which could indeed embrace such questions as when can a mortal president dismiss a five-star deity.

When he moved me up to *Fortune* managing editor in 1953, Luce, in an odd lapse of protocol, failed to inform me personally. He left it to the outgoing managing editor to tell me. Del Paine, who was becoming publisher, was suitably entertained when I said, "I hope Harry knows about this." "I think he thinks it was his idea," said Paine. "I suspect he thinks he conveyed it to you in the last few weeks." If so, the message had been too subtle for me.

John Shaw Billings, Luce's deputy, said he was sorry he hadn't been the first to congratulate me on my becoming managing editor because he would have to be the first, when the time came, "to tell you you are through."* This pleasantry was a reference to Luce's well-known distaste for firing a man face-to-face. With great reluctance, Luce could steel himself to tell somebody else to fire the fellow. "I can find a new managing editor," he once told me, "easier than he can find a new editor-in-chief." In fairness, it should also be noted that Luce found it embarrassing to tell anybody about a raise, a bonus, or stock options, and he also managed to have somebody else relay such tidings. When I was editor-in-chief, some hair-shirt notion of duty made me convey bad news directly. In compensation, I also conveyed good news directly, and, as I was doing it, I had the decency to be, very slightly, embarrassed.

---

*Billings was a versatile journalist who had been managing editor of *Time* and the first managing editor of *Life*. He was editorial director of the company from 1944 until he resigned in 1955; if Luce had died during those years, Billings might well have succeeded him. But Billings and his wife had come to detest New York living, and they retired to his family plantation in South Carolina. Luce had a great respect and fondness for Billings, but Billings, in diaries and papers that came to light after his death in 1975, discloses a deep dislike of Luce: "He seemed hard and impersonal and some of his remarks were cuttingly critical. I despise him in such moods when he seems contemptuous of me and my views . . . never listens to what I say . . . I suppose has no idea how much I dislike him personally." (However, Luce was "damned smart," and from time to time there was a "pleasant" or "nice" lunch.) Billings, for all his talent, was tortured by self-doubt. There came a "dismal sense that Luce is trying to squeeze me out." Luce would send him away "like a beaten dog."

. . . .

In time I came to see Harry Luce as a great man. This was not because he had (apparently) appointed me managing editor of *Fortune*, but because in that role I was now fully exposed to the force of that extraordinary mind. He did take some getting used to. (Doubtless I did, too.)

Luce would arrive at the office with his pockets stuffed with odds and ends he had torn out of the morning papers. Working from these and other things he had been reading at home, and scraps of this and that he had heard at a dinner the night before, he would fire off memos to his editors and business-side people. He could write at high speed, at least a thousand words an hour—vivid, vigorous, idiomatic prose, very tightly packed. The Luce memos were an art form. They covered as vast a variety of subjects as the pages of *Time* and *Life* (and *Fortune*, and a bit of *Sports Illustrated*). He was also an excellent audience for memos, though I was nowhere near so prolific as he. When I became editor-in-chief, I was more inclined to do business by phone and face-to-face.

Luce did plenty of face-to-face, too. I was now seeing him more or less continuously at lunches, dinners, meetings in the office. (The power breakfast was still, mercifully, uninvented.) Luce liked to place his own phone calls inside the Time and Life Building and barely tolerated the tendency of his editors to have a secretary answer. When he was put through (promptly), his invitation to come up to his office consisted of: "Busy?" Usually you were not.

In all our thousands of hours of dialogue, I saw the workings of his nonstop curiosity and his almost infallible instinct for converting his own intellectual itchiness into effective journalism. The same kind of originality that went into the creation of new forms of journalism and into the most casual suggestion that "there might be a story" in this or that could also animate his meditations on the largest questions of national and human destiny. He could be superficial, in his haste to know everything. He was susceptible, as many journalists are, to the "mother-in-law sample"—a relative or friend told him such-and-such the other day, or Clare's hairdresser had told her such-and-such—and if people are feeling that way, it could be a hell of a story. He could be talked out of such notions, but sometimes you found out he was onto something. He had a great instinct for the big, simple, about-to-be-obvious thing that was suddenly journalistically ripe. Sooner than any other journalist I knew, he sensed, for instance, the momentous shift in the national temper brought about by Vietnam, the civil rights movement, all the forces that came later to be called the "counterculture." His word for it was different—the country's mood had turned "sour," he was telling me as early as 1965.

His mind was truly profound—and well stocked. He had learned a lot to begin with, from his missionary parents in China and from Hotchkiss and Yale; he kept on reading and learning, and he remembered what he had learned. In his full maturity he was a semipro theologian, a hungry student in a dozen fields, an astute businessman with a better feel for "the bottom line" than many of the Philistines, and, in journalism, a restless, compulsive innovator. To be original on the Harry Luce scale, one needed, of course, a searching skepticism about received wisdom in many fields—the ability to question all the good reasons, for instance, why a national sports magazine could never work, or the ability to notice that many revered churchmen pronouncing on political issues were full of hot air. He had guts—entrepreneurial guts and a healthy dose of pride went into the semiannual decisions in the middle and late 1950s to keep *Sports Illustrated* going despite daunting losses.

Though his skepticisms could be expressed in withering terms, Luce was in no way a cynic. He had a steadfast devotion to Christianity and country, and a deep belief in the possibility of human progress. He was certain that Henry Luce and the United States of America were here for a purpose. Yet he could also listen with absorption to anybody questioning his most dearly held principles—provided the argument was interesting. As he grew older, he became still more open to argument. He could change his mind. The salutes to younger colleagues became more frequent and graceful. Many still found him intimidating and he was in no imminent danger of becoming Mr. Chips. But he had unmistakably mellowed.

His employees loved to tell stories about him, many of them true. I have always thought the generation of anecdotes is one of the attributes of leadership. How dull to have a boss nobody wants to talk about! In the in-house stories he was "Luce" or "Harry" or often "the Proprietor," but seldom "the Boss" or "the Old Man." On paper, in the third person, he was usually H.R.L., never a tycoonish H. R. As he did mellow, and as a genuine affection grew between him and many senior colleagues, and younger staff as well, the chosen anecdotes tended to be more affectionate, and the old horror stories of the rude, brash Luce tended to be retired.

I suspect some of the harshest things said and written about Luce while he was in his thirties and forties were at least partway true at the time. I think they became less and less true of the man I came to know so well in his fifties and sixties.*

I never heard Luce complain in personal terms about the literary and journalistic savagings he had taken—I suspect he thought some were an honor—though these almost invariably became attacks on his magazines as well, primarily *Time*, and that did wound. I think he suffered more, however, when one of the magazines angered one of his friends. I was in his office once discussing some bit of *Fortune* business when he fielded a phone call from his fellow liberal Republican Helen Reid, publisher of the *New York Herald Tribune*, who was indignant about some *Time* story. Harry wilted visibly during the conversation, blew out all his breath when it was over, and looked sadly fatigued and furrowed for a man only in his early fifties. He said, "Some of this gets hard to take." I felt like an unwilling eavesdropper.

Some of Luce's mellowing came, I think, from a recognition, slightly rueful, that he was not cut out for political office, that he could settle for the influence Time Inc. gave him. He had been intermittently tempted by politics, as rich and powerful publishers often

---

*Luce is skewered in various novels of thirty and forty years ago, including *The Big Clock*, *The Great Ones*, *The Big Wheel*, and *Death of Kings*. A first-class biography remains to be written. Authors have generally been reluctant to allow the man to mature.

John Kobler expanded a rather friendly *Saturday Evening Post* profile into a rather thin book, *Luce* (Doubleday, 1968). I gave John two or three hours of my time and, as I thought, some valuable insights into Luce. He used none of them in his book, and I found myself described, for my pains, as "taciturn."

W. A. Swanberg, biographer of Hearst and Pulitzer, put a prodigious amount of research into *Luce and His Empire* (Charles Scribner's Sons, 1971). The result is disappointing. Swanberg has claimed that he set out to write an "objective" biography, but says he abandoned that idea early in his research because he became persuaded that Luce had been a thoroughly sinister force in American opinion and policy. That, indeed, is the thesis of his book, which includes lurid exaggeration of the influence of Luce and Time Inc., considerable though they were.

A much more sober view of the influence of Luce and Time Inc. can be found in *Henry R. Luce and the Rise of the American News Media* (Twayne Publishers, 1987), by James L. Baughman of the University of Wisconsin School of Journalism. This somewhat pedantic work does not purport to be a full-dress biography of Luce, and has little feel for the flavor of the man.

Wilfrid Sheed, in *Clare Boothe Luce* (Dutton, 1982), is lively and sympathetic about his principal subject but unperceptive about her husband, his impressions dating mainly to a summer-long visit with the Luces in 1949, Sheed then eighteen.

Probably the best published portrait of Luce is the one scattered through the three thick volumes of *The World of Time Inc.: The Intimate History of a Publishing Enterprise*: Vols. I and II by Robert T. Elson; Vol. III by Curtis Prendergast and Geoffrey Colvin (Atheneum, 1968, 1973, 1986). Though this is an "official" company history, the writers, researchers, and editors went at their work in a forthright way. The approach to Luce is admiring but by no means sycophantic.

are, and in 1950 some Connecticut Republican pols considered him for a run at a Senate seat. But he wasn't sure he would have liked being a senator, even if it were handed to him (president yes, as he once told me). He suspected he would not enjoy *running* for senator, or be good at that, which was correct. The only appointive office that would have appealed to him was secretary of state, but he thought, again correctly, he would not have been diplomatic with jackasses in Congress or with some foreign governments that were prone to preach sermons at the United States. If sermons were to be preached at the United States, they should come from the likes of Walter Lippmann or Reinhold Niebuhr or Henry Luce. After Eisenhower won in 1952, Harry dropped in my office on his way to a visit with the president-elect; he thought he would be asked, in effect, what he wanted. He could truthfully say there was nothing; he knew his good friend and fellow Presbyterian John Foster Dulles was in line for State, and Luce thought this was an excellent choice.

He was also delighted with Eisenhower's choice for ambassador to Italy: Clare Luce. Friends who knew the intellectual competitiveness of the Luces, their powerful egos, the fierce dinner-table debates—conducted in her cool and mannered diction and his excitable staccato—found it difficult to visualize Harry meekly settling into the consort's role. He had always held Clare at a certain remove from the vitals of Time Inc. Some of her ideas had influenced the starting formula of *Life* (it was also her inspiration that Luce should buy the name of the old humor magazine), and during World War II she did some vivid reporting for *Life* from the Middle East and the Italian Front. In my hearing Luce would occasionally identify one of his story suggestions as coming originally from Clare, but if she had any larger influence on the magazines, it was decidedly indirect. I never heard him cite her as support for any of his general views on public policy, and I never heard of her attempting to intervene with any of the editors about anything. Having kept Clare out of Time Inc.'s corporate antechambers, how would Harry adjust to a place where his wife embodied the United States itself? When the brandy and cigars came, would he retire with the ladies?

The jokes did not continue very long. Harry adapted beautifully. He took tremendous pride in Clare's notable success in Rome, played the unobtrusive consort when protocol indicated, and circulated energetically among politicians, businessmen, and intellectuals (seeing more of some people than would have been politic for Clare), reporting his findings to the U.S. ambassador as well as his Time Inc. editors.

Important Italians did not mistake him for a homebody from the American suburbs. But Harry in Rome also kept the greatest journalistic gift—he was never jaded. Italy might not be as important in the 1950s as Classic Rome in its world, but by God, it was *interesting* (emphasis on the third syllable, as opposed to the effete English collapsing of the second and third), and so, of course, was the Forum and all that history Harry knew so much better than most American journalists. A common precaution among Time Inc. people traveling through Italy in Harry's Roman years was a fast brushup on five or six centuries B.C. and A.D., and just pray Harry would only offer his $2 tour of the Eternal City, as opposed to the $5 tour, from which you could not come away all A's. I didn't happen to visit Rome in those years, but I received plenty of *Fortune* story suggestions from there. I had to decline most of them. Harry took this amicably and confessed he might be suffering from the Foreign Service sin of "localitis." In fact, he spent only about half his time in Rome during the four years Clare was ambassador, and, "on home leave," as he put it, was a very active editor.

In those years, Luce could be considered the most influential private citizen in the United States. It was hard to think of any American who had been a continually important man for so long. Luce had become a major national figure by the middle 1930s, when Eisenhower was an unknown major, Kennedy a schoolboy, and Johnson a minor bureaucrat in a New Deal agency. This never led him to "pull seniority" on the more recently famous; he remained intensely curious about all the newsmakers—and the newer and younger, the better.

He was in demand as a public speaker, and he had got very good at it. His range was very broad: journalism (of course), responsibilities of the businessman, Christianity, the rule of law (a favorite theme), East and West, architecture, the meaning of America. He would have scorned a ghost writer. He might ask a colleague to criticize a speech draft, though he was not easily budged from something he wanted to say.*

---

*I did talk him out of an occasional foolish idea. One was an easily misunderstood thing he proposed to say in a lecture at Columbia: that businessmen because of the money they invest in advertising have a special responsibility to be thoughtful critics of the press. My argument: "Along with all the wonderful busyness of everybody about everything, in our kind of society, we badly need some compensating disciplines—and one of them is certainly the principle of concentration, i.e., people should mainly do the things they do best. If there are some qualified businessmen who do indeed have the time and energy to look into the shortcomings of the U.S. press, it should precisely

He had overcome an early stammer, and his somewhat harsh, blaring voice held his listeners' attention. They needed to keep their wits about them, because his prepared speeches were demanding, dense with facts and ideas. He could be moving—and witty—but he offered an audience no "air."*

People were curious to see him and meet him, and he did not disappoint. Though he was utterly without pretense or affectation of any kind, he had some of the "star quality" that is attributed to successful actors and politicians. He carried quite a charge of electricity into any room he entered. He "looked like somebody"—a trim man of a bit more than average height, erect in bearing, with a strong, proud face dominated by deep-set eyes and vast brows. (The sculptor Jo Davidson did a noble Roman head of Luce.) He was conservatively and carefully dressed, except for disgracefully dirty eyeglasses. The only Christmas present I ever gave him was one of those 25-cent packets of lens-cleaning tissues, but I never could see any evidence that he used them.

For the last eight years of his life, I was Luce's closest professional associate. It was in January 1959 that he asked me to succeed him some day as editor-in-chief of Time Inc. I had been invited to dine with him on a Sunday evening at his triplex apartment on 52nd Street, overlooking the East River. (I was shocked the first time I noticed in the beautifully paneled library that the book spines were fake. There were real books elsewhere in the apartment, of course, and at the Luces' country place in Ridgefield, Connecticut.) He had phoned only the day before, but I was used to these rather regal short-notice invitations. They might be issued half a dozen times a year; Clare was out of town, he wanted somebody to talk with, and he tended to call one of his editors. (Another two or three times a year,

---

not be because of those advertising dollars which [you say] link them indissolubly to the Fourth Estate. It's one of the great triumphs of our system—a tribute to the integrity of the publisher-editors and the wisdom and restraint of the businessmen—that advertising dollars do not give a businessman any special privileges as critics of the press. The line between privileges and responsibilities would be terribly difficult to draw. The present no-privilege position is so satisfactory—both for us editors and for the U.S.—that I hate to see any monkeying around with it, even though in theory it might be improved or refined."

*Without a prepared text, he could sometimes offer too much air. If a Time Inc. audience saw him stand up after dinner to talk extemporaneously, sporting men at various tables would form pools, $5 to play, as to how long he would go on. Pay dirt was in the forty-five- to seventy-minute zone.

you might be invited to a proper dinner party, with wives and other guests from outside Time Inc.) I had a policy that I would decline these last-minute summonses if Dorothy and I had an engagement; otherwise, I would report for cocktails with Harry at 7 P.M.

Dorothy didn't begrudge me these disappearances. She was fascinated by Harry, and fond of him, and a little scared of him, but only a little; she didn't scare easily. She thought it was sad that this important man should have to spend a lonely day in his own city, and was glad her husband could help keep him company. With Dorothy, Harry was invariably gallant, as he could be, and unintimidating, as best as he could be. She modestly claimed that all this was because of his regard for me. I told her, No, Luce had to admire her intellectual liveliness and curiosity (as I did)—to say nothing, since he was not blind in these matters, of her good looks.

Anyway, Dorothy and I that winter day in 1959 went to the Seventh Regiment Armory on Park Avenue for the Antiques Show, chiefly memorable to me because I couldn't get up the nerve to pay $2,000 for a glorious little Bierstadt, maybe eight inches by twenty inches— much more than we had ever spent on a picture. Probably worth $200,000 today. Oh, well, I can go look at Bierstadt in the Metropolitan Museum.

Then I went alone to cocktails with Harry. Two apiece (his tended to be syrupy-looking old-fashioneds), and in to dinner not later than 7:30. Luce despised long cocktail hours, especially of the stand-up variety.* He served good, sturdy American food—maybe a slightly fancy appetizer like a salmon or lobster mousse, but then a steak or roast or chops, and often pie (his favorite dish).

I was expecting a painful evening. I had been in a running row with one of Harry's closest friends and most senior colleagues in Time Inc. management, Executive Vice President Charles Stillman, a brilliant financial man. Luce had asked Stillman to read the drafts of a *Fortune* series on tax reform that I was about to publish. Stillman had many criticisms, some useful, but he went on to suggest that the writer of these articles must be "pretty damn pink." The writer was

---

*I was surprised that such an imperious man would endure the marathon cocktail parties, dinners, and sales conventions in the hard-drinking Time Inc. "culture" of the 1940s and 1950s. Many of the editorial people had started out in the convivial newspaper city rooms of the 1930s, and "the business side" was awash with genial nineteenth-hole types. At least two senior publishing executives had their careers derailed by drink. I had to caution one senior editorial executive, after an especially egregious public display, that once more and he was out. Time Inc. is a much more temperate place today.

Robert Lubar, whom I later appointed managing editor of *Fortune*. I was outraged, and had told Luce that I wanted Stillman to withdraw the personal innuendo and only then would I deal with the substantive criticisms on their merits. This put Luce in an uncomfortable spot, and I was expecting that the Stillman-Donovan problem would be the principal item on our dinner agenda.

So Harry began talking with me about the bad state of the modern novel, and the politics of America, Asia, and Europe, and a couple of good movies he had seen lately, and the theories of a certain theologian he was distressed I hadn't heard of. I ventured to bring up the *Fortune* tax-reform series, but he brushed that aside: "Let's talk about that in the office." It was as though I was being a touch gauche to try to talk shop on a Sunday evening in his apartment—though this did not inhibit him from questioning me about a dozen other projects and problems at *Fortune*.

My one-on-one dinners with Luce usually ended right around 10 P.M. (More sparkling editor-conversationalists than I may have kept him up later.) He would stop talking, slap his hands down on his knees, peer at me pleasantly from under the massive eyebrow-thatch, and if necessary haul out his vest-pocket watch. If you still didn't get the idea, he might say, "Well, I mustn't keep you."

That evening, however, at my usual leave-taking hour, Harry said in a somewhat apologetic way that he had to bring up something "rather personal." He wondered if I would be interested, "not right away, in a few years or so," in being the next editor-in-chief of Time Inc. I told him I was honored. I was in fact astounded as I began to focus on what Luce had said. I said I didn't think he should commit himself just then. In a few years, someone else could emerge who would look like a better choice. "You'll do," he said in a not-unfriendly way. He added that he had of course considered "just leaving it up for grabs . . . you know, blood running in the streets," but he preferred to have it settled.

My own thinking in any halfway comparable executive situation would have been: Why tie yourself down with a choice you don't have to make just yet? I also told Luce I wasn't entirely sure I would like the job, or be any good at it, so we should both think about it some more. At the end of the evening (no later than 10:15), with a touch of the ceremoniousness that could be both warm and ironic, he summed up: "Well, it is left, then, that you are complimented by my suggestion and will at least think about it, and I am complimented by your suggestion that the present editor-in-chief is good at his job."

When I saw Dorothy afterward, she was thinking of the Stillman business, and asked, "Did you get fired?" I said, "No, he wants me to be him." I had never imagined I would be fired because of the tax articles, but I did think it was possible Luce would feel he must stand by Stillman, his old and valued colleague. And if Stillman wouldn't retract his slander of my writer, I would quit, as Dorothy knew, so her question was a kind of shorthand summary of a tense situation. Charlie and I, little boys perhaps, glaring at each other in a school-yard. I suppose I had never quite got over my brief domination of the playground at Douglas School, Franklin and Dupont Avenues, Minneapolis.

A day or two later Luce asked me to go see Stillman, or Stillman to go see me—I forget which—and we composed our dispute directly. Over the years, we became good friends. I doubt if Luce told Stillman he'd better be friends with me because I was going to be editor-in-chief some day. He didn't tell me whether he had discussed his plans for me with anybody else, though I believe he had done so with Roy Larsen, Maurice T. Moore (chairman of the Time Inc. board and Luce's brother-in-law), and Clare.

The previous February—though I did not learn this until several years later—Luce had suffered a serious heart attack at the winter home he and Clare had bought in Phoenix. What I and all but a very few intimates were told at the time was that he had been laid up a week or so with pneumonia. But the heart attack must have set him to thinking about his successor with a little more urgency than a fifty-nine-year-old proprietor might normally feel. He now had been told he should spend most of the winter months in Phoenix. This could be explained by his susceptibility, well known to staff and friends, to the common cold. Since he also enjoyed travel, foreign and domestic, he was going to be away from New York up to half the year.

But Harry Luce wasn't ready to let go, either. The secrecy about the heart attack, as I later realized, was to make sure nobody imagined he *had* to take it easy. At the same time, he and Larsen and Moore began to shape up a succession timetable.

After our conversation that January night, Luce did not mention the succession again for some months. In our private conversations, he did begin inviting my views on various problems at *Time*, *Life*, and *Sports Illustrated*. That would not have happened when I was wearing only the *Fortune* hat. Luce was punctilious in never putting one managing editor in the position of commenting on another managing editor's magazine, but now I was putatively something more than the M.E. of just one magazine.

Then in June of 1959, one evening in the Union Club (that large and solemn dining room is utterly secure on a summer night), Luce asked me to become editorial director, his deputy. He said he was "prepared to accept a ninth term" as editor-in-chief, but meanwhile he thought there was more than enough work for both of us in the editorial management of the company. The editorial director's position had been vacant since Billings retired, though Luce had assigned to C. D. Jackson, after his return from Washington, some of the duties of an editorial deputy. The charming C. D., one of my favorite people in Time Inc., was not successful in the role; he was not accepted by the editors as a legitimate boss of editors. C. D. was from "the business side"—but the coolness of the M.E.s was more than simple clannishness. They thought Jackson tended to agree too quickly with Luce, and they had found him overresponsive to complaints from advertisers or (as in my disputes with him) from the Eisenhower administration. C. D., in indignant letters and memos to Luce, would refer to the managing editors as "Their Lordships."

I was wary of Luce's invitation. My elevation to editorial director would seem to signal to the company his longer-range plan, which I had thought we should both stay flexible about. I was also concerned about trying to become the deputy boss—ambiguous role—of the managing editors of *Time*, *Life*, and *Sports Illustrated*, all senior to me in age and in Time Inc. service stripes—and, in the case of *Time* and *Life*, editors of vastly larger and more important magazines than mine.

I asked Harry if he had checked out this idea with the M.E.s. He bristled. "Can't I ever just *do* something?" he said. I persisted. He checked. He reported later that Roy Alexander, the M.E. of *Time*, thought it was a fine idea. Edward Thompson, the M.E. of *Life*, was not sure the job was necessary, but if it was, I would be a good choice. Luce did not report from the *Sports Illustrated* precinct, but the magazine being so new, and still so unpleasantly unprofitable, perhaps he felt *S.I.* was not entitled to vote.

I accepted, but vexed Luce once more, I fear, by insisting that I stay at *Fortune* two more months to edit some articles I was especially interested in. Looking back, years later, I marvel at the patience of Henry Luce, a notoriously impatient man, at my various diffidences, demurrals, modesties. He never said, Oh, come off it. It's not a bad job, you know. He did sound a strangely defiant note in an interview with *The New York Times*, baffling to everyone in Time Inc. but me, that he had made the appointment "without consulting anybody." It had been generally assumed at Time Inc. and elsewhere that Henry Luce could do that sort of thing without consulting anybody.

My original surprise that Luce should have lighted on me as his successor, and then should have wanted the matter locked in place so early, did not come from false-modest self-deprecation. But I had a very high regard for the managing editors who were senior to me, particularly Thompson and Alexander. I also admired several of their deputies and in general thought the company very rich in thirty-five- to forty-five-year-old editorial talent.

As to why Luce chose me instead of somebody else, he never told me anything beyond that unforgettable "You'll do." I think he would have considered it embarrassing and unnecessary to say more, and I was content to leave it there. When his partner, Roy Larsen, was congratulating me, he simply said, "It was inevitable."

Second and third hand, I did gradually hear how I got to be inevitable. Luce never considered "going outside" for a successor; he thought that would be bad for morale, but, more serious, a reflection on Time Inc. and indeed on his own eye for young and middle-rank talent within the company. He thought Time Inc. was a special place with its own way of doing things, and he was never keen on outside hirings anywhere in the upper levels of the editorial staffs, though he would make an exception for exotic creatures like economists or art directors.

In fact, nobody but a Time Inc. managing editor, or former managing editor, would be considered by Luce as a successor. He saw the M.E.s as his line officers, men who had put out a national magazine under deadlines and all the rest of the pressures from inside and outside the Time and Life Building, including those he generated. It took an M.E. to boss around other M.E.s. This eliminated two people from the Time-Life News Service, outstanding journalists, both greatly admired by Luce: James Shepley, later to be president of Time Inc., and my sometime *Fortune* colleague Emmet Hughes. There may have been some connection between my appointment as editorial director and Hughes's decision shortly afterward to leave Time Inc.; to be sure, he left for a great job—as a senior adviser to a man who had a chance to be president, Nelson Rockefeller.

Of the four managing editors of 1959, I think I learned why two were eliminated. Sid James of *Sports Illustrated* was running a new magazine that hadn't yet succeeded and thus didn't quite qualify as a full-fledged M.E. Roy Alexander of *Time*, however, held the job Luce considered second only to his own. Roy was the consummate old pro, an easygoing man who got along with everybody, including Luce. His disability was that he was only a year younger than Luce. Harry, after his heart attack, did consider designating Roy his deputy, but then, as an increasingly optimistic convalescent, he decided he had time to arrange things for the longer term. But I am not entirely sure why Luce preferred me over Ed Thompson of *Life*. It could have been age, again. I was seventeen years younger than Harry, Ed seven. Not the ideal distance, but it could have been enough for a solid successor administration. Ed's *Life* had been prodigiously successful, and it was more particularly Ed's magazine than *Time*, with its long-running and powerful formula, was Roy Alexander's magazine. That may have been part of the difficulty for Luce in contemplating Ed in editor-in-chief clothes. Luce was never totally comfortable about *Life*—even or perhaps especially when it was being sensationally profitable. There was something going on here he didn't totally grasp. He understood *Time* and *Fortune* much better—hence, perhaps, their managing editors. And he was happier with my *Fortune* (so he told others, not me) than with any of its predecessors.

Luce had also been impressed with some individual journalism I had rattled off during the year that turned out, fortuitously, to be the year he was deciding about a successor. Some of this journalism had to do with the Soviet Union, some with the quality of life in America—both subjects that Luce thought serious editors should be wise about.

In February 1958, the State Department appointed me one of three official observers of the "election" of the Supreme Soviet, the figurehead parliament. The Soviets were reciprocating for the visit of a Soviet delegation, which had included one editor, to observe our presidential election of 1956. My fellow election-watchers were Professor Cyril Black of Princeton, a scholar in Slavic studies, and my old Minnesota confederate Dick Scammon, now an international authority on elections. Dick was chairman of our little delegation, and it was no coincidence, as Marxist dialecticians would say, that I was invited along. We lived months in a fortnight of fantastically full days, spread over ten thousand miles: out into the cold winter dawn to board the black limousines acrid with kerosene and disinfectant; on to eight, ten, twelve meetings, interviews, inspections of schools, collective farms, factories, election headquarters; endlessly talked at, talking back; trying to restrain scorn or sarcasm about the travesty of the "campaign" we were watching, but letting no anti-American polemic go unchallenged. The days usually ended with a six- or seven-course, ten-to-twelve-toast banquet. It was crucial to watch for the moment when the Soviet hosts, while still urging vodka upon the Americans, unobtrusively shifted to Georgian white wine or even mineral water. It was also useful to remember that you were going to stick up for the United States of America when the time came for responses to the inevitable Slavic toasts; this could help keep you awake and focused. Back in my hotel room around midnight, I would stay up until 3 A.M. or so writing down everything that had happened during the day. From Warsaw, on the way out, I filed a story for *Time* on a ninety-minute interview Khrushchev gave us. I did an article for *Life* on the mechanics of the election and the interesting and somehow touching reasons the Soviets went to all the trouble—a monstrously long article by *Life* standards, and Ed Thompson gamely jammed it all in. For *Fortune*, I wrote general impressions of the country and people and system. "You saved your best stuff for your own magazine," Luce said, not reproachfully. Embarrassed as he sometimes was to deliver a compliment, he turned somewhat formal: "If I may say so, I don't know how you did all this."

I was thankful I had resisted a temptation to crank out a short piece for *Sports Illustrated* on the Soviet ice-hockey menace. I had gone to a couple of games in Moscow, and as a patriotic Minnesotan, I felt threatened by the obvious Soviet intent to get as good at the sport as they have since become. But producing articles for all four of the Time Inc. magazines, all from a two-week trip, would have been quota-busting, well regarded in the USSR in the cult of the Stakhanovites, less so in the United States. My fellow managing editors would have been less than enraptured; even Luce might have thought enough is enough.

Harry was happy, however, for me to take on John Kenneth Galbraith. In late 1958, Ken, long since gone from *Fortune* and now a renowned Harvard professor, brought out his book *The Affluent Society* (Houghton Mifflin). Harry liked Galbraith, despite his far-liberal views, and was proud that Ken had worked for a few years for *Fortune*.

At least part of the thesis of *The Affluent Society* was congenial to Luce: that this rich American society was tolerating much shoddiness and ugliness. Ken thought the solution was a greatly enlarged role for government, which in its fatherly way would subsidize the desirable services and amenities the affluent society was too crass to create voluntarily. The requisite tax increases would cut down on consumers' ability to buy unnecessary or harmful things that an immoral advertising industry had taught them to want. (Ken came from the same Calvinist stock that Luce did.)

As managing editor of *Fortune*, I had set up a small lunch where Luce and I and a few colleagues would discuss the Galbraith book and what *Fortune* might say about it. Because of a sudden flu attack, I had to miss my own lunch. I sent in a long memo to represent me. I pointed out that for some twenty years Galbraith and his school had been attacking the free-market economy because it couldn't deliver the goods—or, if it could deliver some goods, it couldn't deliver the purchasing power to enable the American people to buy them. But now, in the mid-1950s, the free economy was delivering the goods in profusion and the purchasing power, too. So Galbraith is already bored. He says, "Aw, that's nothing; even American businessmen can do that."

Luce thought my memo was the definitive demolition job on Ken's book—he told my deputies to be sure I would publish it in the magazine just as it stood—and he felt the sickbed provenance of the memo made it an intellectual tour de force. I didn't follow Luce's fiat that my memo be published verbatim, but instead turned it over to my colleague Gilbert Burck, who melded it with some powerful argumentation of his own. In print the result was a two-thousand-word assault on Galbraith's book. Shortly after it appeared, I was having lunch with friends at the University Club when across the stately McKim, Mead and White dining hall I saw Galbraith loom up, all six feet seven inches of him, and head for my table. I thought, "Uh-oh." Ken shook hands most affably. "By the way," he said, "thanks for the mention."

Whatever literary or analytical talents had gone into those 1958–59 articles of mine, they did demonstrate physical endurance, a necessary quality in the editor-in-chief. Beyond that, given Luce's age and my own, I was clearly a classic case of being in the right place at the right time. And it didn't hurt, scandalous though this may be, that the business side of Time Inc., starting from those long nights at Ponte Vedra, Florida, liked me.

So Henry Luce had begun to disengage from the extraordinary institution he had created and from the extraordinary power he had relished. The process was to be very gradual, but gradual though it was, it still represented a decision that many of his friends and colleagues had doubted he could ever face. Still more amazing to them, he was soon heard saying he felt just wonderful about it.

VIII

Apprentice Luce

So I went to work, on September 8, 1959, as apprentice Henry Luce. I received a three-word letter of congratulations from *Fortune*'s famous photographer. "What in *hell*," Walker Evans wrote. I could only reply, "It's true." It was a strange job I had stepped into, slippery to define, and enormously absorbing. The hours were shorter than at *Fortune*, but the work was harder. For at least the first months, I went to the office in a state of some tension.

My relationship with Luce was now ratcheted up two or three notches from the *Fortune* M.E. level. Much as I had come to enjoy and admire my editor-in-chief from that perspective, this was a new intensity of exposure to a not entirely restful personality. At the same time, as editorial director of the company, I was now dealing with some formidable potentates and rivalries on the other magazines. I had grappled with some difficult people when I was M.E. of *Fortune*, but they and I knew I was their boss. Now I was trying, very tentatively—very tactfully, I hoped—to give suggestions, nudges, never quite orders, to men who knew I was not finally their boss—Luce still was. I can remember one morning, a month into the new job, cranking up my nerve to ask Roy Alexander to come up to my office. Time Inc. was a very informal place where people, starting with Luce, dropped in on other people with no concern about protocol, the junior a little flattered the senior had stopped by, but it was also clear who could ask whom, when it came to that, to whose office. Roy arrived at my office with such a relaxed and matter-of-fact air about him—as if he had been doing this for years—that I was emboldened a few days later to ask if Ed Thompson could "come up." He did—not as though he'd been doing it for years.

Somewhere in those first months of my Apprentice Luce role, I experienced a touch of insurrection in the digestive system I bragged about earlier in this book. My doctor said I was developing a "pre-ulcer" condition. As I grew more comfortable in my new job, the condition, whatever it was, went away. Within a year, I must confess, I had overcome my surprise that Luce had chosen me. I decided he had picked a good man for this strange job, and that the ambiguities could be lived with—even, now and then, exploited. By May 1960, I was writing Philip Graham—an old friend of S Street–Hockley days, now publisher of the *Washington Post*—who had complained about something *Time* said: "I am sort of responsible for various things, but not exactly responsible either. Thank you for this opportunity to explain."

For my increasing sense of ease as editorial director, I was again in the debt of Bill Furth. Just as he had smoothed my way as the new M.E. of *Fortune*, he now warmly welcomed me "upstairs," even though my arrival meant he was acquiring an additional boss in his role as executive assistant to Luce. Bill had spotted an item on my appointment in the *Gallagher Report*, a media newsletter of feverish insider tone. Gallagher had named the two of us first on a list of half a dozen "Big Time-Men of the Future." But "Big question: will they carve out their own programs for successful publishing? Or will they second-guess Luce and Larsen? Time will tell." Bill's covering note said, "Next meeting—Thursday midnight—the *usual place*. (Bring gingersnaps.)" Bill was the indispensable colleague to whom you can tell anything and count on a wise and utterly honest reaction. He was an acute and affectionate student of the personality of Harry Luce, and over many a long lunch (martinis more common than gingersnaps), Bill and I shared our war stories.

I now held some vague degree of authority—or at least influence—over editorial staffs totaling about twelve hundred people. *Fortune*'s ninety seemed almost like family as I set about matching names and faces, and sizing up talents and temperaments, in all these new principalities. Each of the magazines had its distinct personality in print, of course, but each also had its own internal culture. There was no all-purpose, standard-model "Time Incer," and nobody aspired to mold one.

. . . .

In April 1960, the next step in the Time Inc. succession scenario unfolded. It was a classic exercise of Luce management doctrine, in which fairly clear lines of authority could coexist with fairly subtle checks and balances. The amiable Roy Larsen stepped aside from the presidency of Time Inc., at sixty, to become chairman of the executive committee of the board. He was succeeded by James A. Linen, forty-seven, the ebullient supersalesman who had been a highly effective publisher of *Time*. Maurice T. Moore, who had plenty to do as managing partner of the Wall Street law firm Cravath, Swaine and Moore, gave up the title of chairman of the board, and it became a full-time job in the hands of Andrew Heiskell, forty-four, the brilliant publisher of *Life*. Neither Heiskell nor Linen was named chief executive officer, an arrangement that kept both these ambitious and talented executives happy. Luce remained CEO *de facto*, an arrangement that kept him happy. At the same time, he could point out to intimates (and himself) that he was prudently training a successor. It was made plain to me and to them that I was to regard Heiskell and Linen as present and future partners in the senior management of the company. They had outranked me for years in the company hierarchy, but instantly and warmly dealt with me as their peer. It was to be a highly congenial partnership.

Luce, though he thought of himself primarily as an editor, and greatly preferred the title editor-in-chief to president or chairman (he could have had them all if he wanted), was also pleased to think of himself as a businessman. He thought being a businessman was a high calling, and though he was often disappointed with this or that performance of American businessmen, he respected them as a class. He was fascinated by management structure problems in corporations—including, of course, Time Inc.—and we talked often of the subtleties of "organizing creativity." He was sharp with figures and had a powerful interest in earnings and dividends. He could both flatter and shock editors by telling them, "Great issue of your magazine; only goddam trouble, not enough ads." He was an ingenious promotion man—crucial in publishing. And despite a few misplaced enthusiasms, he had a shrewd eye for talent and a belief that talent should be generously rewarded. For years, Time Inc. pay was the best in the business. For a time in the mid-1950s, however, his own salary—to him insignificant alongside his dividends—had become a kind of ceiling on the pay of top editors. Ed Thompson was bold enough to raise the point with him. "What am I paying myself?" Luce inquired. The answer was $60,000. He said he would look into it, and I believe Thompson and Alexander soon received raises; I don't know whether Luce did just then, but by 1959 he had advanced to $80,000.

Harry's absences from New York did indeed add up to about half a year, and I was in effect acting editor-in-chief when he was away. But in Phoenix, by phone and mail, he was prolific with story ideas and big and little questions for all the magazines. These were usually conveyed through me, or at least "cc: Mr. Donovan," but he also felt entirely entitled to communicate directly with his M.E.s, and I had no ambition to interfere. When he was in New York, I did try from time to time to negotiate a division of labor between us—he should concentrate on magazines A and B for a while, and I would specialize in C and D. He would agree in principle, but he didn't really want to be excluded from C and D, and he was constantly inviting me in on A and B. It worked pretty well.

When I reported for work as editorial director, I startled Harry by proposing that I concentrate for a time on *Sports Illustrated*. He found this a somewhat incongruous impulse in an allegedly intellectual sort of editor. He also thought the editorial quality of the magazine was excellent; the trouble was all on the business side— especially in promotion and ad sales. I thought there was plenty of trouble on the editorial side, too. I sent him a rather stiff memo saying: "The estimated financial results for *S.I.* [the magazine lost $2.3 million in 1959] strike me as approximately just. I find considerable encouragement in the fact that *S.I.*, with all its painful shortcomings, can even come as close as it does to making money. But let's not say to the editors of *S.I.* [as Luce had said at a recent lunch], 'How can *S.I.* be made *even better*?' That isn't really the situation. This is not a very good magazine."

Luce indulged me, and for four or five months, I spent much of my time in and around *Sports Illustrated*. For a dozen issues or so, I sent Sidney James, the managing editor, a weekly critique, possibly not his favorite reading matter during that winter. Sid had been an assistant M.E. at *Life*, a genial man with picture sense and good news-desk reflexes—and a cheerfully uncritical view of his magazine. The magazine was publishing some first-class photography and reporting, but this was intermingled with many a journalistic embarrassment. There were mystifying headlines, odd typographical stresses, banal pictures given too much space, outbreaks of cliché, the cutesies, the tasteless. The story mix could get wildly lopsided: In one issue, an article on American antelope, followed immediately by an article on bird banding, followed immediately by an article on French truffle-hunting dogs. There were sad strainings for effect. A perfectly good story on the lift a high school football team had given the depressed town of Braddock, Pennsylvania, got cluttered with a lot of two-hundred-year-old history. "I find it hard to believe," I wrote the managing editor, that "the Poles, Czechs, Hungarians and Negroes now living in Braddock actually felt an 'aura of defeat' because of what happened to Gen. Braddock in 1755." In another issue, I was repelled by an attempt to make the University of Wisconsin football team "to a remarkable degree . . . mirror" the Wisconsin Idea, which had just been defined as "public service and freedom of thought." I pleaded with the M.E.: "Come off it." And I could not resist, in another of the weekly report cards: "Page 78, whoever said 'pretty coeds' should tighten up his standards in coeds, as well as caption writing."

Sid James and the other Time Inc. M.E.s, who over the years received from me a good many hundreds of these critiques, generally replied conversationally: "Sorry you didn't like it; I still think it was a good story." "You're right—it went on too long—just got away from us." "So-and-so would usually be writing that sort of story, but he got sick." The M.E.s figured they had less time for memo writing than I did. In my critiques, I of course employed the "sandwich" technique, enclosing complaint between slabs of praise, whenever praise was plausible. Thus in *S.I.*: " 'A Man Who Knows How to Stuff an Elephant'—Splendid title and a nice story. How much did they charge for stuffing the elephant? Why did the peer want the army officer's mustache mounted? A bet? A deplorable liaison?"

I put in a six-week tour as acting managing editor, while Sid James occupied himself with some "long-range planning," graciously declining my invitation to critique "my" issues. At intervals over the years, I also sat in as acting M.E. at *Life* and *Time*. There was a touch of *machismo* in these exercises. I wanted to show the staffs of these weeklies that I was not enslaved by the stately monthly rhythms of *Fortune*, and especially the people at *S.I.* that I could stay up just as late as they could, coping with the weekend sports results for Saturday and Sunday-night closings. But, more important, these visitations gave me an intimate glimpse into the inner workings of the magazines and the strengths and limitations of their staffs.

I came away from the *S.I.* stint with some big changes in mind—in formula and people. Some of the best of the formula ideas came from André Laguerre. Laguerre was a tough cookie, an unsentimental man with a cool, analytical mind and a powerful interest in the racetrack. He had been an outstanding political correspondent, chief of the Time Inc. news bureau in Paris, then London, when Luce, in one of his most inspired people moves, talked him into becoming an assistant M.E. of *S.I.* André's kind of mind was just what was needed to cut through some of the softness and sloppiness in the magazine, but beyond that, he had a broad journalistic imagination and an especially perceptive view of the way TV (whatever it might do to other publications) was going to help *S.I.* I urged Luce to appoint him managing editor, which Harry already had in mind. He did so at lunch one day in April 1960, and emerged somewhat shaken. After he offered Laguerre the job, and André accepted, all of which took five minutes, neither of them, as Harry told me later, seemed to have anything more to say—an unprecedented vacuum at the Luce lunch table. Laguerre could be as bored with small talk as Harry, but also unresponsive to some lines of big talk; Harry apparently didn't find the right subject that day. Sid James, who had built a remarkable staff and sustained their spirit during tough times, moved on to become publisher of *S.I.*, a job that gave full play to his missionary enthusiasm for the magazine.

I gave Laguerre the story-by-story report cards from time to time, and he went so far as to say they were "quite useful." A piece on a Maryland Hunt meeting: as "the third horse feature in this issue, I could have done without it, and was also antagonized by being told four times in the captions how British it all is."

A few months later:

I think your February 27 issue is one of the best you've ever put out. . . . Permit me a few niggles. . . .

Surely we shouldn't lead off the whole magazine with "Look for an Upset in the Big Ten Swim Meet." Who, including this Big Ten boy, cares? . . .

That's a fine story on Coach Arthur Hayman of Duke. I twitched briefly on the lead. [Duke and North Carolina were only eight miles apart, but "from the bitterness of the battle now raging between their partisans, eight light-years would be a more appropriate distance."] This sticks out only because you've done so well in keeping the sillier sort of sports-page hyperbole out of *S.I.* Incidentally, it might have been more accurate, or at least more interesting [instead of marveling that Duke and North Carolina were such rivals], to say that only two schools so close together, with so much in common, could hate each other so fiercely.

Taylor Spink. I'm prepared to dislike any story-of-how-I-got-the-story, though I must admit [Gerald] Holland has handled it with a very nice touch. Still, the Spink material is so rich, I couldn't help wondering whether more of Spink and less of Holland might not have made an even better story.

P.S. An attentive reader of yours in Phoenix, Arizona [Luce], doesn't share my doubts about the Spink story. Thinks it's one of the best stories *any* Time Inc. magazine ever ran about *anybody*.

A year later: "*S.I.* of September 10 [1962] strikes me as one of the most readable and attractive magazines that ever came out of this building."

Because of my early immersion in the magazine's problems, I became pretty much the acting editor-in-chief of *Sports Illustrated*, even when Luce was in New York. I had more of an affinity for the subject matter than he did. Luce was less deeply interested in sports than in the professional challenge of creating a sports magazine. I labored with Laguerre on his editorial budgets—always a sensitive area when a magazine is losing money—and mediated many disputes between the M.E. and the publisher as to how many "fast-color" pages we could afford. Fast color was crucial to the magazine's ability to exploit the boom in TV sports coverage, and I was usually able to help André get most of what he wanted. *S.I.* finally made a little money in 1964, and it has made a lot ever since. Laguerre was to serve as M.E. for almost fourteen years, and the success of the magazine, journalistic and financial, was in good part his doing.

I felt no need to sit in as acting managing editor of *Fortune*, having been the real thing. I also felt I should stay out of *Fortune*'s hair for a while. I had plenty to learn about the other magazines, and I also thought Duncan Norton-Taylor would have more fun dealing with Luce than with the previous M.E. But Luce felt I knew the *Fortune* problems and cast of characters better than he, which was true enough, and I gradually became acting editor-in-chief of *Fortune*.

I began sending Dunc report cards: "I've read every editorial word in the September [1960] *Fortune*! (F.Y.I., it takes six hours.) . . . A tremendous amount of meat . . . but something is missing—the one or two articles that would give urgency and excitement to the issue as a whole." A picture act on "The Tax-Deductible Cruise" was drab—partly because the merrymakers were Allied Van Lines, "partly because it's familiar Bermuda and the dowdy old *Queen*, partly because the people are so plain (except from the backside). Not really funny, or touching, and certainly not glamorous." A few issues later: "The Colin Clark essay is good, though I wish the familiar refutation of Malthusian worries could have been brisker so as to bring us sooner to the fresher and more provocative part of his argument. Incidentally, why didn't the biographical box note that Clark, no ivory-tower theorist of population trends, has fathered eight sons and one daughter?"

Half a year later (I did not inflict these on Dunc every month):

"What Happened to the U.S. Economy." This immensely important—and convincing—article should be worth the price of a year's subscription to any *Fortune* reader. But I wonder how many *will* read it. We are being tyrannized by charts. Three full pages of them give a needlessly formidable look to the article, and the first two chart pages in fact fail to convey information as briefly and clearly as words could. The third chart page, if it had been the only one, would have been very striking.

After another decent interval:

A dull issue to look at [April 1962], and I think you have quite a problem building up here. Here it is springtime, the G.N.P. running at $550 billion, and capital spending (according to *Fortune*) at a record rate of $50 billion and climbing fast. Very little reflection of this in the editorial pages of *Fortune*. (Much more visual excitement about the U.S. economy in the ad pages.)

The cover is somber (and follows a drab one in March).

Six pages of "Auto Junkyard" do not help matters. Maybe four pages of this would have been O.K. in an issue otherwise alive with interesting faces and the new sights and shapes of American business. I kind of doubt it, though. Too ugly to be funny; not important enough for *Fortune* to get mad about; just plain depressing. Why bother?

That big frontispiece for "Life in Midland, Texas" wasn't very invigorating either. I can't make out whether it's grainy copy, or a dust-storm or what. Caption notwithstanding, you sure as hell can't see "two days in any direction."

Once in a while I would go far out of channels and communicate directly with Mary Grace of the *Fortune* copy desk. I could not stop myself from circling one of the forbidden words that had somehow crept into print—perhaps *hike*, as in wage hike—and sending Mary a brief note: "Mary!"

Whatever the hecklings of its editorial director, the *Fortune* of the early 1960s was doing well in the marketplace, and the editorial staff was as well motivated as editorial staffs can be. Dunc once told me, "I didn't know whether I could carry this off, but I think I did." He did. I knew that *Fortune* in due course would need some younger editors in charge, but there were bigger problems elsewhere.

Harry and I were coeditors-in-chief of *Life*, which was beginning to have difficulties that increasingly preoccupied us both. We tinkered endlessly with format. Luce was deeply concerned with the internal architecture of magazines. The original success of *Time* had come in good part from its orderly departmentalization of the news. Harry kept trying to strengthen and clarify the departmental structure of *Life*'s pages. But *Life* was a different beast.

During *Life*'s triumphant first twenty years, Luce was never absolutely certain why it was so wildly successful. When the magazine began to slip, he was uncertain about remedies. *Life* actually lost a little money in the years 1959–61. Time Inc. management at first attributed this to the short but sharp general recession of that period, but while *Time* and many other magazines were soon rebounding vigorously, *Life* in the 1960s never regained the levels of profitability it had hit in the 1950s. TV was an increasingly serious competitor—for people's attention and for advertising dollars. And the country had somehow changed—it was less cohesive, somewhat more sophisticated.

Luce sometimes brooded that *Life* might simply be like a Broadway hit—no matter how popular, it couldn't go on forever. But he kept fussing with format and kept groping for a new definition of *Life*'s "purpose" that would position it with the audience and with Madison Avenue. It was in fact a Luce reflex when one of the magazines was in trouble to ask whether its "purpose" needed redefinition. He might go away for some days or weeks and worry the question in a long memo, as I had seen him do with *Fortune* a dozen years earlier. It was part of his essential seriousness as a publisher that magazines begin with a purpose, and making money was by no means a sufficient purpose. Much that had been surefire in the great *Life* of the postwar years had begun to seem a little old-fashioned or corny.

At Luce's request, I had gone from my *S.I.* indoctrination course to a more or less full-time exposure to *Life* in the spring of 1960. On emerging, I wrote to Harry:

> I sometimes wonder if "The Good Life," so generously celebrated in *Life*'s last year-end issue is also the enemy of *Life* the publishing property.
>
> As incomes, education and "leisure" increase, more and more people are able to pursue particular interests in quite intense ways. They are actually much busier than they were when they had less money and less time off. . . . This is the top third, roughly, of the U.S. market—the people *Life*'s editors, and advertisers, most want to communicate with. It gets tougher and tougher to compete for their time because there are so many different ways they can afford to spend it.
>
> Below this top third, in the market layers of lower income and lower education, and hence fewer competing interests, you find much more leisure in the sense of "time to kill"—the stray half-hour, the idle evening. Here is the great mass of the adult TV audience.
>
> Among the strikingly successful (in P & L terms) magazines of 1960: *Time, Fortune, The New Yorker, American Heritage, Scientific American*. None is a "mass magazine," each operates exclusively in that top-third of the market, each appeals to a well-defined audience within that third, each is aimed at a quite specific interest or aspiration. Except for *The New Yorker*, none of these five particularly invites the quick leaf-through; the reader can spend one or two or three hours with an issue and have that satisfying feeling that he has *done* something, and had a good time doing it. Maybe, fundamentally, this is not too different from the appeal of golfing, gardening, boating, barbecue cooking, hi-fi, travel, civic bustle.

My report to Luce was a good piece of "magazine doctor" work. Good in the diagnostic area, less useful as to treatment. I proposed: "A substantial appropriation, money and bodies, for an examination of the concept of the mass magazine, i.e., of Time Inc.'s biggest product, in the kind of economy and society the U.S. has arrived at."

Could *Life* compete with small-l life? Possible answers:

> Yes. This just happens to be a sort of sticky period. . . .
>
> Yes, though it won't be easy. There are a lot of factors working against the mass magazine, and it will take a sort of permanent *tour de force* to pull it off, but Time Inc. has the people who can do that. . . .

No. Therefore, *Life* must get ready to appeal more deeply to fewer (relatively) people. . . .

No. *Life* should spin off two, three, four magazines of specialized appeal. Like the Living magazine; the Culture magazine; and what else? . . . The parent publication should become a 10-cent news-and-fun picture magazine for 10 million people?

I was continually urging upon Luce that along with the public promotional "defining" of *Life* we needed a private editorial agreement on what the magazine *wasn't*. But Luce was not ready to surrender any province of what he saw as *Life's* universality. His original prospectus for *Life* in 1936 had been the most eloquent magazine promotion piece ever written (a few touches came from Archibald MacLeish, then a *Fortune* writer):

To see life; to see the world; to eyewitness great events; to watch the faces of the poor and the gestures of the proud; to see strange things—machines, armies, multitudes, shadows in the jungle and on the moon; to see man's work—his paintings, towers and discoveries; to see things thousands of miles away, things hidden behind walls and within rooms, things dangerous to come to; the women that men love and many children; to see and to take pleasure in seeing; to see and be amazed; to see and be instructed.

Thus to see, and be shown, is now the will and new expectancy of half mankind.

Now he tried to match that charter in 1960. The result was somewhat embarrassing—a grandiose document that caused no great stir outside the Time and Life Building and gave no particular guidance to his editors. He proclaimed that *Life* "is and shall be designed to be the magazine of national purpose," same being to "(1) Win the Cold War and (2) Create a better America." This was not quite so pompous as it now sounds. *Life* had just finished running a well-received series on the "National Purpose," contributors including Billy Graham, Walter Lippmann, and presidential candidates Nixon and Kennedy. *Life*, said Luce, must be "A great Magazine of Art. A great Magazine of Science. A great Magazine of Religion. A great Magazine of Politics (grand scale). A great Magazine of Economics (dull word!). A great Magazine of History."

Ed Thompson, whose many strengths included an utter inability to kowtow to the boss, was not bowled over by all the Luce pronouncements. Harry, whose many strengths included a respect for

Thompson's kind of independence, was trying to provoke Ed and others into drafting their own grand charter for a new *Life*. Ed now invited memos from his assistant M.E.s and department heads, and secluded himself for a month or two to try his own "re-think."

Meanwhile, I found some refuge from cosmic thinking about *Life* in occasional nuts-and-bolts memos to the editors:

All in one issue: "Sun sickness; electrical jolts for cats; medical ship *Hope*; Nigerian hospital; *and* osteopathy—a bit of a muchness?"

In another issue: "It makes a long stretch of pummeling and punishing the flesh when you have the *Spartacus* movie 'shockers,' the grisly deaths, followed immediately by the lady astronaut in her 'sensory deprivation pool' and in the doctor's office; followed immediately by 7 pictures on 'delicate surgery' for the ear; followed by short and handsome break for Becket, whose martyrdom mercifully is not shown; followed by poor old Sgt. York in his special bed."

"The only big piece [in an excellent issue] that left me lukewarm was 'Strange Birds That Cannot Fly.' They're strange, all right, and sort of obscene; I didn't care about them eight pages' worth. I would rather have seen these color pages used on something beautiful."

" 'A Swim Just for the Hellespont of It.' This one really antagonized me. The young man seemed insufferable; his parents are fools; lots of people have swum it before; and the chartered DC-3, 35-foot scow, etc., all reeked of publicity-minded adult stage management. Having Sal Mineo on the cover, and that blah about 15-year-old Brenda Lee, 16-year-old Jack Wheeler was especially hard to take.)"

"I hope 're-think' will include some consideration of the stunt-y and gaggy in *Life*, and the role of 'Speaking of Pictures' and 'Miscellany.' This week (and many other weeks) the pictures just don't seem worth the space, and even though they may be meant as strictly take-it-or-leave-it items, it seems too bad to open and close the issue with such outsize trivia."

I sprinkled in plenty of *delightful*s and *superb*s, *lively*s and *splendid*s—not just to keep Thompson and his deputies reading, but because much of the magazine really was those things.

By the end of 1960, all of the top brass of the company were bearing down on "the *Life* problem." Several felt themselves quite expert on the subject of *Life*, and indeed they were. Board Chairman Andrew Heiskell had been the highly successful publisher of *Life* for fourteen years; Roy Larsen, master strategist in magazine circulation, had been *Life*'s first publisher, and Jim Linen had once been the magazine's advertising manager. By memo, lunches, dinners, even office meetings in business hours, we kept wrestling with the formula. Luce, the bombast of his earlier memo behind him ("It wasn't much good," he later decided), was fertile in nongrandiose ideas, publishing as well as editorial, and was as fast as ever to spot somebody else's good idea.

Luce became persuaded, mainly by himself—with some encouragement from me and the business side—that it was time for a change in managing editors. Thompson had been M.E. for twelve years (a tie for longevity with Del Paine's tenure at *Fortune*), and that was a long time in the pressure cooker of a large and complicated photo-weekly. Ed indeed had gloried in the pressure—his closing-night picture-juggling in the layout room just off his office was the only visibly dramatic act of editing in the whole Time and Life Building. Ed would stand there looking a bit like Churchill, fleshy, belligerent face, pale blue eyes, cold cigar, with a dozen or more people in attendance— assistant M.E.s, department editors, writers and researchers, layout people, photographers. I sometimes dropped in on the show, and kept very quiet. As a verbal communicator, Ed was almost as muffled as Del Paine. He would call for more pictures (apparently), shuffle them around, throw some out, and maybe around 10 or 11 P.M. was grumpily content. I had come to like Ed very much. He was defiantly non– Ivy League—he would be wearing a cattleman's gray Stetson as we set out for lunch at some fancy Italian restaurant and I, walking alongside, a bare-headed Minnesotan, thought this is real nerve, him from only as far west as North Dakota. Ed was Phi Beta Kappa and also quintessential Middle America, as his *Life* was—idealistic, compassionate and patriotic, chatty and curious about the world, a basically edifying companion determined to teach you history, religion, and art, also eager to show you desirable women, comic animals, wacky stunts, or a gruesome tragedy.

Life had so many stories, series, special projects in the works for weeks and months in advance that Luce and I decided to split the top editorial responsibility between the Managing Editor and an Editor. The Managing Editor would put out the magazine week by week. Thompson would be Editor, in charge of the various special issues, the editorial page, and long-range projects like the astronaut series.

Ed had masterminded the contract that gave *Life* exclusive rights to the personal stories of the seven original astronauts. I was always uncomfortable with this spectacular case of "checkbook journalism," since the whole venture was underwritten by the U.S. taxpayer. It had all been set in train before I became editorial director, but even if it had come up just after, I'm not sure I would have had the audacity to argue against the deal. It was a competitive coup from out of *Life*'s great dominant and domineering days. *Life*'s "in" with the astronauts and their families led to some gripping stories, and some that were dutiful and boring. The astronauts were brave men, but, except in the original application to be one, they didn't face the choices that confront the classic hero. They were shot up there. It was undeniably exciting to watch launches at Cape Canaveral, as I did, but I thought space was less interesting than the people on the ground who designed the flights and those who waited for the astronauts to come back. I tended to take the technology for granted without being very curious about its inner workings. Years later, *Challenger* served its terrible rebuke to such complacency.

About his new role, Ed Thompson worried he might end up encroaching on the authority of the new M.E., or if he didn't, he wondered whether he would really have enough to do. He took some convincing, but finally accepted in July 1961. The new position was by no means make-work, but it was not quite a natural, either; the undiluted M.E. is a very powerful tradition at Time Inc. What would in many other publications be the role of "The Editor" had been largely filled in Time Inc. by the editor-in-chief and his deputies. Ed took early retirement in 1968, and at age sixty began a second career as editor and publisher of the *Smithsonian*, which he turned into one of the great magazine successes of recent years.

For the new managing editor of *Life*, we turned to George Hunt, forty-two, who had shown great imagination and drive as an assistant M.E. and was himself a writer of distinction and a painter of some talent. I had talked Luce out of a bizarre notion that he might appoint co-managing editors: Hunt plus Philip Wootton, another of the assistant M.E.s. Wootton was a very capable journalist and administrator, but I thought we were going to have enough trouble making the editor–managing editor setup work, without having two M.E.s. Harry thought this might make it easier for Thompson to accept his new role—he would clearly be the senior in a kind of three-man "Office of the Editor." I told him this idea was getting worse all the time.

The new editorial management took a while to settle in, but meanwhile *Life* was edging back into a modest level of profitability. Throughout 1962, I felt increasingly optimistic about the magazine. By December I was congratulating Hunt on three first-rate issues in a row. "This *Life* is an entirely different magazine from some of the merely good *Life*s of last summer. . . . The biggest thing we don't know about 'the *Life* problem' is this: What would be the effect of a year of issues as good as these three?" We never found out, of course. I was proposing an impossible standard, and would have settled happily for two great issues out of three. In my private scorekeeping, over the next decade, I thought we came up just a little short of one out of two.

The coverage of John Kennedy's assassination became the signature of the new George Hunt *Life*. When the first flash hit the Time and Life Building about 1:30 P.M. that Friday, November 22, 1963, I was at lunch with Luce and the managing editors and their deputies in one of our dining rooms on the forty-seventh floor. It was John Steele, chief of our Washington news bureau, who phoned to tell us the president had been shot; minutes later, a factotum of the dining room, a lugubrious-looking man whose face was finally appropriate, came in with the graceless words: "He's on his way out." The *Life* and *Time* editors swiftly excused themselves to get to work downstairs. Even for the monthly *Fortune*, even for *Sports Illustrated*, there were more or less immediate editorial implications. (Would college and pro football games be canceled that weekend?) Within a few minutes, Luce and I were morosely lunching by ourselves, sickened by the event, also uncomfortable—or at least I was, and I suspect Harry too—that there was nothing we could immediately *do* about it, unlike the M.E.s of *Time* and *Life*, who could go down and rip up their magazines. We went down to my office and watched the dreadful pictures played over and over on TV. I phoned Dorothy—the phone companies reported that tens of millions of husbands, wives, parents, children had that same need to be in touch with each other that afternoon—though neither of us had all that much to say.

On *Life*, over that weekend, from his own abundant emotions, his sensitive feel for the drama in pictures, and the talents of a fully fired-up staff (who were not above a little elbow-gouging against the competition), George Hunt created memorable and still-moving journalism about the murder of a Prince. Outside the Time and Life Building, and certainly inside, it was remarked that *Life*'s emotional intensity was much more in tune with the mood of the country than the cooler and more businesslike approach of *Time*, which put the new president of the United States on its cover. (Lyndon Johnson was said to be slightly appreciative, but he never stayed appreciative very long.) I thought both magazines did the right thing: *Time* to ask where do we go now; *Life* to mourn.

There was at least one wrong lesson learned from the tremendous acclamation (and, it must be admitted, commercial boost) that *Life* got from its coverage of Kennedy's killing and his funeral. The people who had put out those issues came to think, as Hunt did, that this was their finest hour. This could lead to a mind-set that saw death, tragedy, devastation as the magazine's worthiest subjects. I remember Luce once barking at Hunt, after looking over some *Life* future-story lists: "Hey, George, why do we call this magazine *Life*? Shouldn't we just call it *Death*?"

Hunt was a big man, enormously protective of his staff but almost physically intimidating to some of them, who had learned that along with his artistic sensitivity there was a strong strain of belligerence. In the Peleliu landing in World War II, he had won the Navy Cross, which he never spoke of, but he did speak often of the Marine Corps. Some of his martial exhortations to the staff, urging them to "hit the beach," "seize the high ground," were a little off-key for the 1960s. Once he raged at me, in a phone call to my home on a Saturday, that I was not being "loyal." (Loyalty down, as noted earlier, is a military virtue, and nowhere more so than in the marines.) My offense was that I was not giving all-out support to a project George had grown very attached to—a New York regional supplement that *Life* began publishing during the 1963 strike of the New York City newspapers. When the strike ended, the *Life* business side wanted to kill the supplement. George wanted to keep it going indefinitely. He saw it as a prototype for regionals for southern California, Chicago, and perhaps other areas, and had come to think the whole future of *Life* was riding on it. I thought we should publish the supplement for up to six months after the newspapers came back, and see how it fared. Results were dim, and I was ready to give up.

After listening to some of his raging, I told George to see me in the office on Monday, and hung up. Over the weekend I wondered whether he should be fired. It was not so much that he had insulted me but I was scared about his judgment—that this accidental New York supplement that hadn't existed a few months ago should now seem absolutely crucial. By Monday, George had calmed down, and I had too. People are entitled to be foolish now and then. (How many times is a tricky question.) And of course I would have felt foolish myself, going to Luce and recommending that he fire this editor whose appointment I had so strongly urged.

Luce thought I was a bit reckless when I went downstairs to sit in as acting M.E. of *Life* in early 1964. He didn't want any damage to his editor-in-chief about-to-be. But I sent Hunt off to Europe and the Middle East for five weeks, and was successfully hand-held by the first-rate team of assistant M.E.s that George had in place. I learned at least a little of the prodigious complexities of *Life* layout and scheduling, including the intractable mysteries of the "face-off"—how clashing ads and editorial material fetch up on the same spread. In pictures, I knew, as they say, what I liked, but I was too smart to try to rough out layouts in front of my betters. My greatest triumph of those weeks was a decision to have a standby cover of Cassius Clay engraved, on the remote chance that he might beat Sonny Liston in a championship fight on the same night our cover had to go to press. Liston was such a heavy favorite (1–7) he wouldn't have been worth a cover when he won. Clay was. His plump, boyish face—"pretty," as he used to say—was beaded with sweat from a sparring workout. The standby cover caption said, "He Did It!" On a newsstand, our photo looked as though it might have been taken right after the fight, though of course we claimed no such thing.

Luce, in those years I was editorial director, remained very much the editor-in-chief of *Time*. That was his baby. He liked to use the original promotional tag, *"Time* The Weekly Newsmagazine," and enjoyed putting down critics who said there was no such thing as a newsmagazine. Why didn't *Time* call itself a journal of opinion? "Because, dammit, *Time* was something new, and I invented the word for it." He was distressed that intellectuals and academics didn't much esteem *Time*; many loathed it. We often talked about this, and I offered my view that some intellectuals would always dislike *Time* because it was so successful; some would always find it too middle-brow; but some were justly alienated because *Time* could be shallow and was often unfair. I had never thought there was any such thing as strictly objective journalism, but I thought (and think) it is possible to be too opinionated. *Time* did not always let "the other side" make its case. *Time* could be ill-mannered, grudging about corrections, sometimes petty in its treatment of other journals and journalists, and none too generous, for that matter, in crediting another Time Inc. publication that might have inspired a *Time* story.

Luce accepted my critique and indeed, in our conversations about my becoming his deputy, I had made it an explicit condition that he should do so. But Luce didn't feel so strongly about it as I did, and was reluctant to do very much about it. I sometimes felt that if some-body (Mephisto?) suggested to Luce that he be editor-in-chief of *Time* for life, and let Donovan be editor-in-chief of Everything Else, he would have asked at least to think about it overnight.

In early 1960, Luce was ready for a new managing editor at *Time*. Roy Alexander had been in the job for eleven years, and was now moved up, or sideways, to Editor. So in less than a year after my arrival as editorial director, the managing editors of *Time* and *Sports Illustrated* were replaced, and in another year, the managing editor of *Life* also. Luce surely knew as well as I did, and doubtless sooner, when one of his magazines needed a new M.E., but he found these decisions very painful, and I think didn't mind if any aggrieved party figured these moves were instigated by Donovan. He also had a gen-erous reluctance to dislodge his M.E.s from their great jobs unless some dignified and reasonably useful new role could be found for them. At *Time*, however, it was much more difficult than at *Life* to break off particular projects and provinces for the Editor to oversee. Alexander was not temperamentally disposed to press for more to do, and his successor, Otto Fuerbringer, was not temperamentally dis-posed to give up any of the highly centralized authority that *Time* managing editors—indeed including Alexander—had enjoyed. Alex-ander became executive assistant to Luce in 1963, after Bill Furth's death, and the Editor title has not since appeared on the *Time* mast-head.

Fuerbringer had been assistant M.E. of *Time* throughout Alex-ander's tenure, and Luce considered him the totally logical successor. I thought at least one other possibility, Thomas Griffith, then foreign news editor of *Time*, should be considered. Harry refused, saying he was committed; whether he meant he had already told Otto he would be the next M.E., or whether he simply meant he was committed in his own mind, I didn't know and didn't feel encouraged to explore. Fuerbringer was an excellent choice, imaginative, energetic, as well organized as *Time* itself, as well informed about everything as *Time* sought to make its mythical cover-to-cover reader. His news antennae were beautifully tuned. He was alert to trends in show business, education, the arts, theology—all the "back-of-the-book" depart-ments that some readers who hated *Time*'s politics found indispen-sable. He had something of Luce's gift for latching onto a scrap of conversation or an obscure item in the paper and seeing a *Time* story in it. Otto was autocratic, a shade more so than other *Time* M.E.s before and since. He could fight rough, in print and in the office politics that had flourished more at *Time*, somehow, than at the other magazines. Fuerbringer, Griffith, and Alexander had all arrived at *Time* in the early 1940s, when there was something of the atmosphere of a "court" around Luce. Even twenty years later, when I came to the *Time* scene, some of the scars of the long strivings for Harry's favor were still visible. It was not entirely flattering that we were spared this at *Fortune*, but there were advantages in being a specialized and somewhat isolated monthly.

Luce promoted Griffith to assistant M.E. and told him and Otto and others that he expected Tom to act as leader of "the Loyal Opposition." It was not a good idea. Tom was a mildly liberal Democrat, Otto a fairly orthodox Republican, but the difficulty was less in political outlook than in temperament and journalistic philosophy. Tom was more open-minded, more judicious in his approach to controversial questions; Otto thought this led to back-and-forthing and hemming and hawing; he was more opinionated and more incisive than Tom, and, interestingly, more "radical"—i.e., more innovative— about *Time* structure and conventions. I used to tell Dorothy the ideal M.E. of *Time* would be the child of a union between Otto and Tom. She thought Caroline Griffith and Winnie Fuerbringer would object.

Tom or Otto would come to me two or three times a year to complain about how difficult the other was to get along with. I would patch this up as best as I could, because I knew Harry set great store by the arrangement, but eventually I had to tell him it just wasn't working—two good men were spending too much emotional energy on a destructive feud. I arranged for Tom to come upstairs as senior staff editor, the extra man I thought Luce and I needed in the overall editorial management of the company. Tom was very effective in this role, Otto was able to appoint a congenial assistant M.E., James Keogh, and everybody was happy—or as happy as people get in a publishing company.

A more intractable conflict was the one between the editors of *Time* and the Time-Life News Service. At its peak, the service had one hundred thirty-five full-time correspondents in the United States and abroad, and all the expensive infrastructure, down to drivers and fixers, that can go with such a corps. The news service had been set up as an autonomous editorial operation within Time Inc., even though *Time* was by far its biggest customer and paid most of its bills (almost equal to *Time*'s editorial budget). The chief of the service was appointed by Luce and reported directly to him. Harry regarded the Time-Life bureau chiefs in Washington and all the major world capitals almost as his personal ambassadors. And with his instinct for checks-and-balances, he saw some virtue in having the correspondents and their bosses not entirely the employees of the editors of *Time*. There was indeed some virtue in the arrangement, but it was also an unbeatable formula for continuous bureaucratic warfare. The *Time* editors naturally wanted full control of their reporting arm, which they were paying for; the news service naturally clung to its Luce-given independence.

Within days of becoming editorial director, I was refereeing some squabble between the *Time* editors and James Shepley, an old friend of mine from prewar Washington, who had been a brash young United Press reporter when I was a brash young *Post* reporter. Jim, a very quick study, was an energetic and combative reporter who was now head of *Time*'s U.S. news service (domestic and foreign were later combined). Shepley and Roy Alexander gave me a whole winter's worth of prickly arbitration cases before Jim went off in 1960 to work in the Nixon campaign. After Nixon's defeat, Shepley came back to Time Inc. and told me he wanted to be a managing editor. I told him he needed some editing experience—maybe he could land on the assistant M.E. level at one of the magazines, maybe he would have to start a rung below that. We explored these possibilities, but because of his pugnacious reputation, he was not an easy sale to any M.E. "Well, since you won't let me edit any of your goddam magazines," he concluded over drinks one evening, "what do you recommend?" I recommended that he try the publishing area. He did, and he became the outstanding example (after Luce himself) of success on both sides of Time Inc. He became assistant publisher of *Life*, then publisher of *Fortune*, then of *Time*, then president of Time Inc.

Shepley was succeeded in the news service by Richard Clurman, another very bright and energetic executive, immensely self-assured, lavish in personal style, and a sharp spotter of journalistic talent. He was a fearless visitor to whatever war was available. I once forbade him, by phone from Germany, to make a trip to Vietnam—he had already been out there at least eight or ten times and I thought he was crowding his luck. Next thing I knew, he was in Vietnam. He told me afterward that "the problem" out there—something about one of his correspondents—had become more urgent since we talked, and he didn't want to bother me again. Couldn't our correspondent have come to New York? No, it was better to talk with him on the scene. Dick's panache—some would have said chutzpah—helped make him an excellent motivator of his troops.

Tension between "the field" and the home office is endemic in journalism (among other places), but it could be acute in Time Inc. Our correspondents, unlike newspaper correspondents filing directly for publication, under their own by-lines—or indeed, unlike *Life, Fortune, Sports Illustrated* people writing for publication, under by-lines—were essentially filing memos to the *Time* editors in New York. For some Common Market story, for instance, from files sent by correspondents in Paris, Brussels, Bonn, Washington, plus some research in New York, a writer in the Time and Life Building on Sixth Avenue would put together his story, to be edited and reedited in that building. Neither the writer nor any correspondent signed the story; it was *Time* speaking. People who applied for jobs in the news service understood this was the system, but it could still be hard to live with when a printed article arrived at a different viewpoint from that of a correspondent—or, worse yet, when reams of material from the field seemed not to register with the editors at all.

The most painful "New York" versus "field" episode of the early 1960s revolved around a *Time* cover story on Madame Nhu of South Vietnam, the Dragon Lady sister-in-law of President Diem, and a subsequent *Time* Press-section story complaining of flagrant bias and defeatism among the American journalists in Saigon—by inference including *Time*'s own bureau chief, Charles Mohr. Charley was a first-rate reporter who had done most of the legwork for the Madame Nhu story. He could also be excitable, not inconsistent with being a good reporter. Mohr, in the *Time* editors' version of events, was at first pleased with the printed article, only changing his mind when other correspondents in Vietnam ridiculed the piece as pro-Saigon apologetics. Mohr then insisted he had been appalled all along by the Nhu article as published. He also felt *Time* in its subsequent story on the Saigon press corps was "shelling its own troops." Clurman went to Saigon—with Luce's blessing—to calm the bureau and develop a second Press-section story that presumably would correct the first.

The resulting article was less of a retraction than Clurman and Luce thought had been agreed to, in a long Saturday session in Harry's office, and more than Fuerbringer was happy with. In the upshot, Mohr quit, Fuerbringer and Clurman—none too sympatico to begin with—became even less so, and *Time* was left looking (1) vindictive, then (2) confused. I missed some of the messiest moments in this sequence because Luce, when he was in New York, liked to come into the office on Saturdays—then *Time*'s closing day—and now and then look at some of the copy. I stayed at home on Long Island on weekends.

But I could have been more vigilant, Monday through Friday, as the Charley Mohr embarrassment was building up.

In some of the literature about Time Inc., notably *The Powers That Be* by David Halberstam (a close friend of Clurman's), the quarreling between Fuerbringer and Clurman looms as the central activity at *Time* for several years. In fact, a good deal else was going on, most of it constructive. Fuerbringer greatly invigorated the appearance of the magazine. *Time* moved away from the slightly fusty look of the 1950s and, without reducing its text content, began using photography with almost as much verve as *Life* and *Sports Illustrated*. More liberal use of color in takeouts on foreign countries and in stories on art, architecture, and the performing arts gave many pages of the magazine something its most ardent admirers had never before claimed for it: beauty.

Fuerbringer was also good at devising new departments. In the early 1960s, he introduced three: World Business, Modern Living, and Law. Given the semisacred character of *Time*'s original structure of sections, almost unchanged since Luce and Hadden invented the magazine forty years earlier, these were bold innovations for a new M.E. I had little to do with them, but cheered Otto on. He overcame Luce's doubts about Modern Living; Law was an easier sell because it had briefly been a department in the early *Time* and was an abiding interest of Harry's. Otto introduced the Essay section in 1965—reflective, even discursive, pieces carrying a by-line, another break with *Time* tradition and to me a real enrichment of the magazine.

Compared to the original magazine, the forty-year-old *Time* had grown a touch wordy. Luce lamented this from time to time. I argued that there was more news in Kennedy's world than in Harding's; *Time* had more resources to cover it, and could afford more paper to print it on. And by comparison with my alma mater *Fortune*, *Time* was still the soul of brevity.

The magazine had long since abandoned the much-parodied *Time*-speak of its early years, though some lazy critics refused to notice. Friends could fail to notice, too, and out on the speech-making rounds, I suffered through more than one introduction in which the toastmaster presented me in what he (or his PR man) fondly thought to be *Time* style. Time prose of the 1960s was at minimum clear and serviceable, often lively, and sometimes distinguished, especially in the critical reviews. I yearned for more of the really good stuff in all our magazines, but of course there are never enough really good writers. *Time*, with its anonymity, its unrelenting rewriting demands, the editings and reeditings, end-of-the-week deadline pressures, was not exactly the perfect writing environment. Some very talented people passed through, moving on to free-lancing, or to *The New Yorker*, to novels, or academia. Some, fortunately, stayed. One of the best of them, Paul O'Neil, wrote of the agony of the *Time* writer, "force-fed by paper" from the correspondents and his researcher, "staring morosely at the wall . . . waiting for his brains to work."

Otto was far readier than Roy Alexander had been to throw away the Tuesday or Wednesday choice for the *Time* cover story if the news at the end of the week suggested something more compelling. Within weeks of becoming M.E., he got the downing of the U-2 spy plane on the cover in just forty hours from announcement to *Time* printing deadline, scrapping some two million copies of a cover already on the presses. The "crash cover" soon became a kind of Fuerbringer trademark, and the magazine was putting on this melodrama every third or fourth week. A decision to switch covers on Friday evening— or even Saturday morning—was the *Time* equivalent of "Stop the presses!" in newspaper lore. These last-minute switches could cost a lot of money, and most of them were well worth it. The *Time* M.E. customarily checked out his cover choice with Luce or me, and if Harry was out of town, it fell to me to approve the crashes. Some of the stories were put together so fast they could add little or nothing to what newspapers and TV were reporting over the weekend. But even these had a certain promotional value, especially vis-à-vis *Newsweek*, which didn't then have the printing schedules (and budget margins) to pull off the crash stunt as often as *Time* did.

The corporation was in an expansive mood in the early 1960s. The management was confident *Life*'s difficulties would be overcome and was actively pursuing new ventures. President Jim Linen was incorrigibly receptive to diversification proposals, and Roy Larsen, still very influential in the company, was usually sympathetic. I was usually sympathetic, too. Optimism overcame my love of argumentation, and I also found it exhilarating to be in on business decisions instead of just writing about them, or editing stories about them, as I had at *Fortune*. Luce tended to be more skeptical, proud that his "little paper" *Time* had already spawned so much else, proud that Time Inc. was able to consider so many new directions, but also wary, occasionally fretful that it was all getting to be too much for him to keep track of, and touchingly, that it was too much to ask me to "edit." Chairman Andrew Heiskell was a good influence in all this: as eager as Linen to enlarge what they had inherited, but more cautious about the numbers.

A richly successful expansion that was mainly Heiskell's inspiration was the creation of Time-Life Books—a conversion of the occasional book by-product thrown off by one of the magazines, mainly *Life*, into an ongoing publishing organization that planned whole series of books, drawing on material we had already printed or had back in our files, but also commissioning more photography and writing as needed. This led to some truly distinguished books, at ridiculously affordable prices, on art, science, countries of the world, and so on. It also led to a lot of work for me. By 1962, the books division had become the third biggest editorial operation in the company, after *Life* and *Time*. So I helped the editor, an imaginative *Life* man named Norman Ross, recruit staff from elsewhere in the company, issued my own book reviews (mainly enthusiastic) to Ross and his colleagues, and of course ate many lunches with them, to talk over ideas for future series. The editors felt they could deliver high-quality books across an enormous span of subject matter—history, culture, nature, science—and were happy to try anything. So it was basically more a marketing decision than an editorial decision as to whether to launch a series on, say, "The Human Body," or instead go for "Great Civilizations."

The publisher of Time-Life Books was Jerome Hardy, a savvy Doubleday executive whom Heiskell had snared for us. Hardy knew the book business and was also very swift in sizing up Time Inc. He saw that senior management would want the traditional Time Inc. appearances preserved, even though he had more of an "editorial" function than any of our magazine publishers. At *Time*, for instance, a story suggestion from the publisher, the lively Bernie Auer, carried about as much weight with Otto Fuerbringer as any other friend's idea on the train in from Greenwich, Connecticut. Hardy had the wit to underplay his large role in deciding what Time-Life Books would write about. Luce/Donovan appointed the Editor of Books, he reported to them (me), plans for new series launchings were dutifully walked past me, and the budget disputes between editor and publisher (not too frequent in that growth stage of Books) came to me much as they did from the magazines.

We had still other publications. *Architectural Forum* had been acquired in the 1930s, and *House and Home* split off from it in the 1950s. Both of these monthlies were consistent money-losers. The Time Inc. of the 1960s had no talent for publishing small, specialized magazines. Salaries, benefits, and general corporate overhead were too high, and there was a hidden cost in the distraction of top management. Though the deficit for the two was nothing staggering (usually around half a million dollars a year), it was a vexatious signal that something was not quite right about these magazines, and this nagged at Luce, Linen, et al. Why can't we seem to fix this? Some of Luce's concerns were promptly shared with me. I agreed with the general view that *Forum* was a distinguished professional journal, and I thought it was losing money in a good cause.* I felt *House and Home* was losing money in a dubious cause. It was a trade magazine, a high-class one to be sure, solicitous of the special interests of the housebuilding industry, often advocating industry subsidies and easy-money policies our other magazines were opposing. I told Luce I would not be involved with *H and H* "any more than ordered to be," and he didn't order. In 1964, I concurred cheerfully in a corporate decision to sell *H and H* to McGraw-Hill. With regret, we divested ourselves of *Forum*, giving it to a foundation.

I also had to pay some attention to *Life International* and *Life en Español*, fortnightlies that shared some of the problems of their mother magazine but had some special difficulties of their own. The world minus the United States and the Spanish-speaking countries is not a coherent audience or market. Nor is Spain plus Mexico, Central America, and South America minus Brazil.

Our urge to project Time Inc. overseas led us into a foolish joint venture with the Italian firm of Mondadori, successful book and magazine publishers. We launched an "upscale" illustrated monthly called *Panorama*, drawing on the editorial resources of both companies and meant to be the prototype for similar magazines in other countries. We were fifty-fifty partners with Mondadori—not a propitious arrangement for editing a magazine. *Panorama* was thought up on "the business side," but I became one of the believers. Luce thought magazines should be thought up by editors; the business side

---

*Even money-losing *Forum*, our smallest magazine, could be snobbish toward the rest of Time Inc. I rebuked the editors for a condescending review of a book on American architecture by Cranston Jones, a *Time* senior editor. "*Forum* is certainly entitled to criticize a book by a *Time* editor but I'm surprised you would publish a review saying in effect this isn't much of a book *because* it's by a *Time* editor."

was then entitled to a judgment on whether a particular idea would sell. Luce had never thought much of the *Panorama* concept, and, reasonably enough, allowed me full jurisdiction over the various editorial headaches that ensued. (In 1965, Time Inc. sold out its half-interest to Mondadori, for about the price of a dinner at Savine and four tickets to La Scala.)

Another interesting distraction arose out of Time Inc.'s ownership of five TV stations. Should Luce (or Donovan) think of himself as editor-in-chief of these stations, and if so, what exactly did that mean? I wrestled with the question in various exchanges with Luce and in speeches to some of the TV station staffs. They welcomed some symbolic link with Time Inc. editorial headquarters, and invited me in on more of their business than I could keep up with. Dick Clurman made some reporting from the Washington news bureau available to our stations, and I offered my "editorial" reactions to documentary films produced for TV under Time Inc. auspices. I concluded that was about as much as Luce or I could do just then (which was fine by him), unless one of our stations in its policy stances was wildly at variance with the views of our magazines, or doing programming so disgraceful as to embarrass us as owner. But the stations' innocuous editorializing tended to deal with local issues, and so far as the general quality of their programming went, it was no worse and no better than TV in general—if we were aesthetically squeamish, then we shouldn't have been owning TV stations at all.

In case we didn't have enough to keep track of, I set up the company's first "research and development" section, to develop ideas in a systematic way for new magazines or new uses of what Time Inc. was already producing. The notion rather amused Luce, who thought inspiration for new magazines was something that arrived while you were shaving. I thought the search for new ideas needed to be somewhat organized (possibly reflecting my *Fortune* exposure to enlightened corporations that went at it that way). My R & D section was a miniature of a Time Inc. magazine—an editorial side and a business side, but only half a dozen people in all. For the first "editor" I commandeered Henry Grunwald, then a senior editor at *Time*. His first assignment was a memo on possible adaptations of Time Inc. material to TV use, his second a hard look at *Life*. I knew I could count on Henry for realism untainted by the promotional brand of "research" intent on proving *Life* superiority over *Look*, *Saturday Evening Post*, TV.

A lively collaborator in R & D was my researcher, Dorothy Ferenbaugh, who worked with me for some twenty years. She not only kept me from telling lies in speeches and articles, but also loved to be turned loose on large questions. If people could read 25 percent faster, would they read 25 percent more magazines? If people are really watching as much TV as the surveys say, are they sleeping less? Also bearing on our business: the nature of memory; the differences between men and women.

I brought in a succession of editorial and publishing people for R & D stints of three to six months. They looked over several new magazine proposals, which we concluded were not for us at that time, though one was the kernel of what became *Money*. They investigated an electronic encyclopedia proposal (no) and the implications for Time Inc. of new technologies in education. This study had some part in Time Inc.'s subsequent decision to form a joint venture with General Electric called the General Learning Corporation, an idea that turned out to be at least twenty years ahead of its time.

I had predicted to Luce that the existence of a corporate R & D department might prod individual divisions of the company to set up their own R & D—and if so, fine. In fact, a very different bureaucratic reaction was soon apparent: It was nice to have this kind of thinking, possibly useful, going forward on somebody else's budget.

Down from the blue-sky stuff, I did a lot of close-in administering. I rather enjoyed administration, and if this reveals a closet bureaucrat, so be it. But I think administration—attentive, sympathetic, imaginative administration, if possible—is more important in organizations of intellectuals than in organizations where more routine is built into everybody's job. People in free-roaming work need to know that somebody is keeping an eye on the outer boundaries, nourishing a tactful support system.

Bill Furth had already relieved Luce of much administering, and when I came aboard, Harry was glad to get rid of the rest, including the senior editorial payroll. With the latter, he knew he was conveying to me a very practical kind of power. Subject to agreement with the publishers on the size of the "pots," magazine by magazine, I became generally responsible for setting the salaries, bonuses, and stock options of all the top editors. I also reviewed with each M.E. his whole payroll—which mattered to him, as a good boss, as much as his own pay. In laboring over the magazine budgets, the M.E.s and I worried about inevitable accumulations of deadwood. I thought Time Inc.'s policy, or lack of one, was very expensive in the long run—the company was not hard-boiled enough to fire people because they could profitably be replaced, but it wasn't very generous in the terms it offered people for leaving. The company gradually developed an attractive early-retirement package; occasionally, of course, the wrong people would opt to go.

I involved myself heavily in recruiting. Time Inc. in general and *Time* in particular had for some years operated on a complacent assumption that all the talent we could possibly use would sooner or later apply for work at the Time and Life Building. The company had not stirred itself to look for talent since the Eric Hodgins sweep of 1945–46. Not just because Eric's exertions had gotten me my job, I tended to think that kind of project was a good thing. I kept prodding the M.E.s about recruiting, and by way of encouragement set up a program by which I would "give" them each an interesting under-thirty writer they would not have hired on their own budget. The M.E. had the writer free for a year, then had to take him on his own budget, or offer him elsewhere in the company. These recruits came to be called (not by me) "Donovan Scholars," and many of them did well. They also caused the magazines to develop more aggressive talent-hunting projects of their own, which had been my general idea.

The editor-in-chief had customarily concerned himself not only with M.E. appointments but also with those just below the M.E. level on each magazine—executive editor and assistant managing editors. These had an obvious bearing on who would be the next M.E., and the incumbent M.E. couldn't just haul off and make these appointments on his own. Here Luce turned over to me most—not quite all—of his scrutiny and veto powers. So I might, for instance, tell Harry that Duncan Norton-Taylor at *Fortune* was prone to spend his big titles too fast, and we shouldn't let him name an executive editor just yet. I also held off, with Harry's understanding, on an executive editor appointment André Laguerre wanted to make too soon.

Lateral movements of upper-level editors from one magazine to another were, of course, a delicate business, and even middle-level movements, which became more numerous as the company expanded, had to be brokered through somebody disinterested—i.e., Bill Furth or me. We said okay if it seemed the transfer would benefit the individual as well as the buyer and the seller. After one tedious negotiation in which the recipient magazine was a shade less enthusiastic than the donor, I reminded Bill of the quip by a British politician when some plodding M.P. was raised to a peerage: "The tone of both Houses has been elevated."

. . . .

But the most compelling aspect of my job was "policy." What should Time Inc. think? We expressed our views overtly in *Life* and *Fortune* editorials, implicitly in many *Time* and *Fortune* articles—not just by what they said but indeed in the selection of subjects and allocation of space. From the beginning of my tenure as editorial director, I sat in on the weekly planning discussions for the *Life* editorial page. I suggested policy stories to all the magazines, reviewed drafts for policy sense and flagged M.E.s when they had printed something heretical. I thought some tone-of-voice differences between the magazines were desirable (as well as inevitable), but I didn't want to see them flatly contradicting each other. Luce's attitude was somewhat more relaxed; he wanted to be able to agree with most of what he read in *Time* and on the *Life* editorial page, and elsewhere would hope for the best. Much as he enjoyed the intellectual back-and-forth of philosophical and political argument, he liked it slightly distanced from any immediate journalistic decision. He had less relish for sitting down with an M.E. and hammering out policy differences on a specific story. He had a generous reluctance to win that kind of argument just because he was the boss, but he was glad if I could win some of them. We were both concerned with cultivating as much consensus as possible among our senior colleagues. A forum of some fifteen to twenty editors, senior political writers, and correspondents was more or less continuously mulling national policy, foreign and domestic. Policy was the usual menu at a weekly managing editors' lunch. Between meals, we wrote each other acres of memos.

While Luce was a registered Republican, and I considered myself an independent, I could sometimes come out more "conservative" than he. I would have liked to see labor unions brought under antitrust law, for instance (John Davenport had convinced me), but Luce thought this was politically unrealistic and would be a ruinous position for any Republican presidential candidate. Harry was, in fact, pretty much of a political independent most of the time, and tended to get very Republican only every fourth year. I had no particular interest in the fortunes of the Republican party as such, or the Democratic party—except that each should win often enough to sustain a vigorous two-party system. I generally preferred Republican domestic policy to Democratic, but on foreign policy, as of the early 1960s, I couldn't discern any distinctively Republican or Democratic positions.

The Time Inc. coverage of the 1960 election was a striking departure from the company's intense partisanship in behalf of Willkie (1940), Dewey (1944 and 1948), Eisenhower (1952 and 1956). *Life*, as a picture magazine, had been carrying on a love affair with Jack and Jackie Kennedy, which the magazine did not call off just because he was running for president. *Life*'s coverage had, in fact, helped make Kennedy a national figure. (Senator Ted Kennedy years later spoke of *Life* as "the scrapbook for our family.") It didn't hurt that Luce was an old friend of Jack's father's and enjoyed seeing all those attractive and ambitious Kennedy children in the pages of his magazines.

When it came time for an endorsement, our council of elders favored Nixon—essentially on the grounds of experience—but were well impressed with Kennedy. *Life*'s editorials supporting Nixon were measured (excessively so, some Nixon people thought) and generous to Kennedy. I was very pleased with the tone.

Time was a tougher case. Much of what I thought most wrong in *Time* was summed up in the magazine's coverage of the Republican convention of 1960. In a memo to Luce and Fuerbringer, I noted that *Time* during the primaries had done four cover stories on the principal contenders for the Democratic nomination

that left all the subjects grateful and, at the same time, left with the readers very shrewd and readable appraisals of these men. (Exception: I thought Symington cover was *too* fair—it didn't make it clear that Stu isn't very bright.) . . . I thought these stories must have won over some of the people who "ought to like" *Time* and don't. . . .

I'm afraid we have lost a good deal of ground with such people this week. Their reaction will be: Yes, *Time* was very fair and interesting about the Democrats as long as they were fighting among themselves, but now the real campaign is on, and here we go again. . . .

For instance:

The Republicans in Chicago "rang out their answers [to Kennedy and the Democrats] last week with a clarity that surprised even themselves." . . .

"Nixon's first move [a fairly forthright press conference, before the voting] had the impact of a grand-slam homer in the last of the ninth." Wait a minute. A grand-slam homer in the last of the ninth breaks up the ball game, unless the home team is four runs or more behind. This game was far from over, as we learn a few paragraphs later in the interesting account of all that Nixon and friends still had to do.

Nixon "deftly assumed the strengthening grasp of leadership." Awkwardness of the phrasing contributes to the general sensation that *Time* is piling it on awful thick. . . .

"The forces of the G.O.P. were now arrayed in new order, ready for command decisions, and the new commander was Richard Nixon." Overheated.

This memo did some good. *Time*'s campaign coverage continued to include plenty of subjective comment, or editorializing, about the performances of the candidates and their stances on issues, but averaging all the stories out, a reader would have been hard-pressed to conclude that *Time*, net, was supporting Nixon. The attitude of the top *Time* editors reflected a lively journalistic appetite for Kennedy as subject matter, an awareness of Luce's relatively tolerant attitude toward this Democrat, an awareness of my arrival upstairs, and the circumstance that Otto Fuerbringer was taken seriously ill in the late summer of 1960. So the leader of the loyal opposition, Assistant Managing Editor Tom Griffith, was acting M.E. during the critical weeks of the campaign. Tom skillfully managed the kind of coverage he had always thought *Time* should give a campaign; I encouraged him, and Luce offered no objection. The glib gossip that it was only because Tom was sitting in that *Time* had a fit of fairness did not make relations easier between the two men when Otto returned to work.

Jack Kennedy was not only an addicted reader of the press (which journalists like in presidents), but also an avid student of the inside dope about office politics—who's up and who's down (not excluding who's sleeping with whom) at the big newspapers, the networks, and the newsmagazines. Kennedy claimed to be able to spot who was editing *Time* week by week, and after Fuerbringer came back full time as M.E., he jovially complained to our White House correspondent, Hugh Sidey, "I thought you assured me that man was at death's door."

Time Inc. was in some respects closer to the Kennedy administration than to the Eisenhower administration it had championed in two elections. President Eisenhower would write cogent letters to Luce (receiving cogent letters back) and invite him to White House dinners now and then, but he had no notion that he needed to enroll Luce to support his presidency. Luce was inclined to do that anyway, and if he weren't, there were plenty of other press lords who were. With Kennedy, I suggested to Luce, Time Inc. might have more influence than we ever had with Ike, because Jack had just squeaked in by a grand total of 118,000 votes, compared to Ike's margin of nine million in 1956. Kennedy would have to pay attention to various powers and principalities, including Time Inc., as he began to build support for his first-term objectives and to think ahead to a second term, as all presidents-elect do, even as the first election-night returns are still coming in.

President Kennedy indeed was attentive to Time Inc. in ways that Ike was not—Jack knew what we were saying and thought it mattered. The White House got a special copy of *Time* a day ahead of the rest of Washington. There is no evidence that Dwight Eisenhower ever devoured the magazine of a Sunday evening. But Kennedy more than once phoned Hugh Sidey at his home on a Sunday to complain about something in the new *Time*—even a picture caption or an unflattering photo angle.

Kennedy's most severe displeasure with *Time* arose out of an article by Charlie Murphy on the Bay of Pigs. A month or so after the fiasco in Cuba, Murphy had come out to my house in Sands Point one evening. Before, during, and after dinner, he talked a thesis he was sure he could document—that Kennedy himself had so compromised the original operating plan, which had been a gamble at best, that it became a certain failure. I had been indignant at all the public acclaim that Kennedy had been getting (his approval ratings in the polls even went up after the Bay of Pigs) for acknowledging that he was "responsible," which of course he was, even as he dumped on the CIA and the military in many conversations Murphy and I were aware of. I encouraged Charlie to go ahead, and his article in *Fortune*, September 1961, was a brilliant journalistic reconstruction of the whole sad venture. It was only when *Time* published a condensed version of the Murphy article that Kennedy exploded. He said at a press conference that the article was the most inaccurate thing he had ever read, and he assigned his military adviser, General Maxwell Taylor, to go to New York and bring us to our senses. Prior to the meeting, the White House sent Luce a seventeen-point bill of particulars; Murphy and *Fortune* M.E. Norton-Taylor drew up a seventeen-point rebuttal. Toward the end of the long meeting in Luce's office, General Taylor and the Time Inc. delegation agreed that a few of the seventeen points could be matters of interpretation. The general was in effect conceding all the others, and he graciously suggested we all had other things to occupy us. I ungraciously objected, reminding him that the president was much celebrated in the press, including the Time Inc. magazines, as a fast and voracious reader, so when he says something is the "most inaccurate" thing he has ever read, that is quite a superlative. Wouldn't the president want now to issue a retraction or at least a modification? "among the less accurate"? "not completely accurate"? I was not letting well enough alone. Max Taylor, gentleman and officer, had been none too happy with his errand to begin with, and he looked relieved when Luce mercifully adjourned the session.

From then on, though not as a result of that confrontation, the Time Inc. magazines were mainly admiring of Kennedy's foreign policy, especially his handling of the Cuban missile crisis in October 1962. *Fortune* and the *Life* editorial pages (partly my doing) zapped him now and then on domestic policy. He remained sensitive, as ever, to anything critical in *Time*, and Luce would usually attend to these complaints personally, by mail or in a visit to the Oval Office. Kennedy's close reading of *Time* tended to confirm Harry's view that he was bright enough to become, maybe, a very good president. Kennedy declined to attend a big fortieth-anniversary bash *Time* gave itself in the Waldorf-Astoria, but he sent a pleasantly teasing telegram: "I hope I am not wrong in detecting these days in *Time* those more mature qualities appropriate to an institution entering its 40s—a certain mellowing of tone, a greater tolerance of human frailty, and most astonishing of all, an occasional hint of fallibility."

With the moderately mellowed Henry Luce, it was still a rigorous sport to talk, argue, ramble, speculate about the news. The only serious policy dispute he and I had in that era lasted only a few days. He had made an ambitious speech about the cold war in which he held up as our "war aims" a world, including the Soviet Union, adhering to such ideals as "open societies," "liberty under law," "government by consent of the governed." Contrary to his usual practice, he had not shown me the speech in advance; I told him I would have argued about it, and he said, "I thought you would." I thought his "terms" were equivalent to unconditional surrender, which we had all come to view as a mistake after World War II. I took a more restrained view than Luce of how provocative the editor-in-chief should be in public; Harry was more inclined to think it was useful to stir up people, including sobersides like Donovan, who now had to think, well, what *would* be acceptable terms for ending the cold war? For me at least, there was high intellectual voltage in the exchanges of those years with Luce. For some years after he died, I would react to something or other in the newspaper: It would be fun to kick this one around with Harry.

Luce was not one to ask, How-are-the-wife-and-kids? and he was generally guarded about his own personal affairs. But there occasionally came an abrupt confidence about some family situation or a financial matter. Sometime in the early sixties—his and the century's—he was having an ill-concealed dalliance with Lady Jean Campbell, who had been a *Life* researcher and was the granddaughter of Harry's friend Lord Beaverbrook. For a time, so I had heard, there was a possibility that a kind of tabloid scandal—not totally inappropriate, all lineage considered—might come into full public glare. Harry, with immense embarrassment, said to me one day that I might be reading or hearing troubling things about him and he hoped I would not be too offended. I was seventeen years younger than he, but it was almost as though he were asking a father's understanding. It was a brief moment of Luce vulnerability. I could only manage some noncommittal noise—it might have come out like a schoolmasterly, "Oh?" or maybe just an Anglican, "Ah . . . ," and we went on to something else. Lady Jean in due course went on to Norman Mailer. She became his fourth wife. Norman in due course went on to number five and number six.

My own domestic life, if less colorful, was rich, made so by Dorothy and three children who were lively company. They went to public schools in Port Washington—we had settled in the suburbs partly to avoid the Manhattan private-school orbit—and then on to Amherst, Mount Holyoke, and Williams. Peter went into banking; the other two took up respectable work: Helen is a deputy managing editor of the *Boston Globe* and Mark a senior editor of *People*.

Dorothy was a dynamo of civic good works and could also see the funny side of organized suburbia. She had developed sophisticated tastes in art, music, decor, food, and she never lost her curiosity to see and learn more. She was not aggrieved at being a Time Inc. executive's wife, and she was a great success at it. Among her many wifely gifts: She didn't always say, You're right, dear.

We put considerable energy into houses. We bought our first in 1949: an utterly conventional 4 b.r., center hall, 2½ b., l.r. wbf, d.r., enclosed sun porch, ⅓ acre, walk to r.r. It cost $17,500. (Three or four owners later, I think it last changed hands at about $400,000.) I put in my "life savings" and took out my first mortgage, and could mow my very own crabgrass until Peter was ten or eleven. Dorothy painted and papered all over the place, her masterwork a treatment of the lavatory in *New Yorker* covers preserved under waterproof varnish, the sort of thing that should eventually have been dismantled in panels and sent to a museum. We couldn't have been more suburban: PTA, Little League, the works. I churned around the landscape considerably, rolling 150-pound cement slabs, end over end, from a sidewalk we didn't want in the front yard to an area in the back where we wanted a terrace. My back has been a little temperamental ever since.

We graduated from that house in 1957 to a place in Sands Point, a lovely white Colonial farmhouse on Hempstead Harbor, one of the bays indenting the North Shore of Long Island. Most of the house dates back to 1719; there were harmonious extensions in 1790, 1820, and 1925. The house rambles—around a corner, up two steps, down one, and be sure to duck here. Dorothy unilaterally declared the place a "Cow Neck Landmark"—Cow Neck was the colonial name for the Port Washington–Sands Point peninsula—and presented me a handsome plaque to that effect. She also found some old survey on which this rather sizable building was identified as "Shore Cottage," and it amused her to put that on stationery under an offset cut of the house—as close as we could come to the airs of the Newport summer people.

Two comments on the property particularly pleased me. The first time Leo Lionni of *Fortune* visited, he said, "You don't have this house because you're managing editor; you're managing editor because you have this house." The day before my appointment as editorial director was to be announced in the papers, I assembled the children on the porch and said I had some news to tell them. "You mean," said Helen, now eleven, "that I can start running the power mower?" (To give the children some sense of my new authority, I would often threaten to make Harmon Killebrew, the slugger for the Minnesota Twins—whom Peter and Mark held in contempt—*S.I.* Sportsman of the Year, or even *Time* Man of the Year.)

Shore Cottage had an insatiable appetite for work and dollars. The property came equipped with a large and very beautiful swimming pool built by previous owners of the *Great Gatsby* era. It was a kidney-shaped pool before there were such things; it had simply been set in the contours of a spring-fed pond that had once been a cattle wallow in colonial Cow Neck. The pool was up a hill at a little distance from the house. We were able to attract the interest of the architect James Polshek before he became famous, and he designed a lovely pool house of Japanese inspiration, its deck cantilevered over the water. It made the architectural magazines. The magnificent trees around the pool consistently contributed vegetation to the water. I once posted a sign for the instruction of guests: This is Not a Dirty Pool. Think of It as an Unusually Clean Pond.

The first time she saw the Sands Point house, my mother said to Dorothy and me, "I admire your courage." My father was more enthusiastic. Never mind the "deferred maintenance," he thought I had made quite a buy. As indeed I had: $57,500 for a dozen rooms, more or less, caretaker's cottage, four acres, 350 feet of beachfront, the pool, and a tennis court fragrant with hollyhocks, dandelions, and daisies growing out of the cracks—the previous owners had once flooded it for a skating party.

In Minneapolis, my father had ostensibly retired, but he continued as a Longyear Company director and consulting engineer; he arrived at work at 8 A.M., instead of 7:30, and took three or four weeks' vacation, instead of two. He and my mother would visit Long Island every year, dividing their time between Sands Point and my brother David's family in Port Washington. Dave had become an account executive and VP with the Benton & Bowles advertising agency. One of his most memorable lines, done for a public-service safe-driving campaign, was "The Life You Save May Be Your Own." His own life ended tragically early. He died of heart failure in his early fifties.

My parents lived on to their early nineties. After they died, I was much moved when Dorothy, devoted daughter-in-law and correspondent, said she missed, terribly, writing to them about our trips. It took some of the point out of the trips. Their approval—all the more cherished because they were so bright, almost but not quite doting—remained important to both of us as long as they lived.

On one of my visits with them in Minneapolis, I was also working on a long-promised speech to the local ministerial association. Some two hundred of the Minneapolis clergy—a stern sight on a wintry Monday morning—bought me breakfast and then had to listen to my complaints about clerical misunderstanding of the economy, in many a sermon I had heard: the implication that selling and advertising, not mentioned in the Bible, are unworthy pursuits; that "money-changing," which is mentioned, pretty much covers the whole sphere of finance; that the chief moral problems facing businessmen are whether to lie and steal. Squaring off, I said the principal ethical dilemmas of the business executive revolve around determinations of what is fair, as between his employees and his stockholders, for instance, or as between the rank and file and the foremen. This can be hard work, I said. My reception was a touch warmer than the December day outdoors.

My father, one of the few laymen in the audience, was somewhat uncomfortable. As a Taft (William Howard) Republican, he certainly did not hold with Socialist sentiments in the pulpit. But as the son of a clergyman, and a deacon of Trinity Church (he had also picked up the somewhat off-key title "Mr. Trinity"), he could be shocked that anyone would argue head-on, out loud, with "the minister"— indeed, two hundred of them. Even at age forty-six, when I gave that speech, I would have been curious, and would have cared, about his report on the event to my mother (both then in their late seventies). I stayed with them overnight but didn't try to eavesdrop. When I later showed my text to Luce—also the son of a clergyman but a less deferential man than my father—he said the speech was good medicine for the ministers.

On another winter visit to Minneapolis, several years later, I had gone out to my sister Elizabeth's for dinner and was sitting up very late plotting with her and her husband, Pete, as to how we might get my parents to give up the old house on Bryant Avenue and move into a manageable apartment. My father in his mid-eighties would still go out and chip ice off the sidewalk. Elizabeth's phone rang about 2 A.M.: It was my father asking if I was still there and didn't she think it was about time I got home. It was unsaid that I might be a middle-aged man, big-shot editor, hardened world traveler and all that, but I was staying under his roof—furthermore, driving his car—and he was responsible. I got right home, and we eventually got my parents into an apartment.

My father finally, definitively, retired from the Longyear Company at age ninety-one. When I related this statistic at a Time Inc. managing editors' lunch, I was rewarded with an uneasy smile or two from younger colleagues.

. . . .

In September 1962, Luce told me he had been "delegated" by the Time Inc. board to invite me to become a director. I offered no resistance. I was the first editor other than Luce to sit on the board. This appointment really sealed the understanding—though we didn't say so out loud—that I was his successor. It was about this time that Harry startled some of our correspondents, in a late-night bull session in Chicago, by telling them—in front of me—that his only complaint about my work as editorial director was that I hadn't already kicked him out of his job. Apparently I was going to force him to retire voluntarily. I said, "In Minneapolis [part of the Chicago news bureau's jurisdiction], we are brought up to be polite." I was not in fact impatient, but I no longer had hesitations. I had by then acted in Luce's stead often enough to think that I could handle the editor-in-chief's job and would enjoy it.

Then, late in 1963, Luce said he would like to turn over the job to me at the time of the stockholders meeting in April 1964. The stockholders annually, obediently reelected the directors, and then the directors annually, obediently appointed (reappointed) the editor-in-chief. The stockholders did not elect the editor-in-chief, who was held, in a point of almost theological gravity, to be not answerable to them, and indeed was further shielded from them by not being an officer of the corporation. But in terms of corporate protocol, the annual meeting was a good moment for the shift. Apart from that, the "few more years," or "ninth term," that Harry had wanted as editor-in-chief were pretty much up. I think, too, he got a kick out of not stepping aside at the conventional sixty-five—he would be sixty-six by April—and maybe he had noticed I would still be in my forties in April, just barely.

There was one little flurry of annoyance when I asked Luce a few weeks before the stockholders meeting whether he had consulted all the directors about his plan. Once more there was the petulant "Can't I just *do* something?" I reminded him that I was going to be responsible to the board in ways he had not been, and I didn't want them to feel they had had no say in my appointment. A few days later, Harry told me with a little stiffness that the directors "are all informed"—it didn't sound exactly like a conference-call New England town meeting.

The only last-minute threat to this orderly timetable came from a well-known scoffer at timetables: the Long Island Railroad. On the morning of the stockholders meeting, my commuter train got stuck in the tunnel under the East River. We were there about forty-five minutes, I suppose, though it seemed longer. I made the 11 A.M. meeting with five minutes to spare. The stockholders, three hundred or so, were not to imagine they were voting on me, but they were permitted to look at me.

IX

Pope Moses II

Shortly after my unveiling at the stockholders meeting, there was a big Time Inc. dinner in May 1964 where Luce, Larsen, Heiskell, Linen, and I all said complimentary things about one another. In his salute to me, Harry said the office of editor-in-chief "is no longer a personal prerogative derived from a legendary and/or murky past." It is now

a very constitutional office by order of the Board of Directors. And from now on, the office of Editor-in-Chief more clearly than ever before expresses Time Inc.'s understanding of that great doctrine of freedom of the press by which we live. Freedom's correlative is responsibility. But to whom is the individual journalist responsible? To whom is the great organization of editors and publishers responsible? Not certainly to any organ of government. Not, we hope, to any vested interests. . . . Freedom of the press is responsible only to conscience, and conscience can only be found in a man. Here in Time Incorporated we strive to achieve a consensus—a consensus of opinion and conviction. . . . But we cannot evade the demand for a general coherence and for a clear sense of direction. Direction through the dilemmas of the present and into the options of the future. And this must come from the Editor-in-Chief. It must come by means of his intelligence and through his conscience. Our great good fortune tonight is that we can trust so fully the intelligence and the conscience of Hedley Donovan.

Luce stopped short of saying out loud Who or What should inform Hedley Donovan's conscience. But I happened to know his answer to that one. His son, Henry Luce III, in a speech given in 1984 at the dedication of Luce Hall at the Center of Theological Inquiry, Princeton, recalls his father explaining that he could not be accountable to "any of the obvious constituencies: not stockholders, who cared only for profit rather than journalistic quality and purpose; not advertisers with their self-evident conflicts of interest; not readers, who could not know what they wanted or needed to read until they read it; not the Board of Directors, a small group of well-meaning but not necessarily wise gentlemen. No," he said, "I decided that my ultimate accountability had to be to my Creator."

Many people who knew Luce had assumed he would never give up the editor-in-chief's office, or if he did ostensibly, he would hang onto the power. They were wrong. He did not retire; he took the title of editorial chairman, which I had suggested (though if I hadn't, I think he might have). He stayed on the board, and he remained the company's largest single stockholder. (Luce and his family and foundation owned about 22 percent of the shares outstanding, Roy Larsen and family and trusts about 12 percent, other directors and officers about 6 percent—constituting effective inside control.) But Luce did turn over the powers and responsibilities of the editor-in-chief to me. He had tactful ways of letting people know, inside and outside the company, that this was indeed what had happened. Among the recipients of the message was Lyndon Johnson.

The president had invited Luce and me to dinner at the White House on a July evening in 1964, just before the Democratic convention in Atlantic City. McGeorge Bundy, still national security adviser, as he had been for Kennedy, was present for cocktails, and energetically serving canapés, but Harry and I were the only dinner guests. Luce and Johnson had come warily to like each other, though Johnson didn't always remember that Harry didn't like to be called "Henry." Each respected power, and LBJ couldn't quite believe that this vigorous man who owned Time Inc. was willing to stop running it. He kept addressing "policy" questions to Harry, and Harry kept passing them along to me. Johnson said he knew "Time-Life is Republican," but just on the chance the Democrats might win in November, who did we think should be their vice president? Harry said, again, that sort of question should be put to me. Johnson did. Telling him "Time-Life" isn't necessarily Republican, I said the Democrats' best VP would be Hubert Humphrey, which of course was Johnson's intention all along.

Luce likewise deferred to me at Time Inc. board meetings when discussions arose about editorial performance, policy positions, news predictions. He was available if I needed backing against any kind of challenge to the authority of a new editor-in-chief who was not Founder and Proprietor. No challenge arose, but it was a very comfortable feeling that he was "there." He continued to be in the New York office about half the year, wrote me and others plentiful letters and memos, did a lot of speaking and traveling, and I think was as close to content as his restless spirit could come.

I believe he was in fact relieved to have somebody else take the considerable heat that went with the job he had loved so much. More or less out of the blue, he told me one day in 1964 that whenever I felt it necessary to change Time Inc.'s China position—i.e., to support recognition of the mainland Communist regime—he would be glad to be informed, but the decision was entirely up to me. I found a special poignance in this, for it was Luce's unswerving support of Chiang Kai-shek and the Chinese Nationalists that more than any other Time Inc. policy stand had made him such a controversial figure—in Washington, in the press generally, in academia. The Luce view was bitterly disputed within Time Inc. as well. He lost two writers he greatly esteemed—John Hersey and Teddy White—because of it.

Luce now sensed that some change in U.S. policy was likely, as China and the Soviet Union developed their momentous split, and as hopes of a Nationalist "return" from Taiwan to the mainland became less and less realistic. And I think he preferred that somebody else be editor-in-chief at such time as Time Inc. might withdraw support from his old friends the Generalissimo and Madame Chiang Kai-shek. As things turned out, we did not change the Time Inc. editorial policy until the late 1960s, shortly before Richard Nixon and Henry Kissinger changed U.S. policy.

On the painful subject of Vietnam, Luce was likewise relieved not to be editor-in-chief. He was generous in praise of a *Life* article and several speeches I wrote in support of the Lyndon Johnson policy in Vietnam. Once, when critics of the war tried to question him after a *Life* dinner, he replied with uncharacteristic testiness (for he generally enjoyed arguing with young staffers), "Read what your editor-in-chief wrote in your own magazine." "Your own" left them gasping; they wanted to feel it *was* their own magazine. But I think Luce would not have been distressed if I had taken quite a different line. If Time Inc. supported Johnson too long and too uncritically on Vietnam, as we did, the fault was more mine than anyone else's. Luce should be entirely exonerated.

As the 1964 election approached, Luce must have felt a few fire-horse impulses, but he suppressed them. We were talking one night that summer about the press treatment of Barry Goldwater, which Luce thought unfair, and I said it wasn't easy to be fair to Goldwater, because he did say some pretty fantastic things. Was the press just supposed to assume he couldn't mean this stuff? I cited chapter and verse. Luce, ever the editor, said, "That's a good *Life* article. Why don't you write it?" So I did: "The Difficulty of Being Fair to Goldwater" (September 18, 1964). Since the article was published under my by-line as editor-in-chief of Time Inc., it was not a big surprise when we went on a few issues later to endorse Johnson in a *Life* editorial. It was the first time that Time Inc. had ever supported a Democrat for president.

Harry was then on an extensive Far Eastern trip—including attendance at the Tokyo Olympics, not normally his kind of thing. I think one purpose of the trip was to be out of my hair at that stage of the presidential campaign. And perhaps also to miss some hassle with Clare, who was an ardent and audible Goldwater backer. She was impeccable, however, when a reporter asked her how come the *Life* editorial: "Haven't you heard that my husband retired? He wouldn't dream of interfering with the policy of the new editor-in-chief, Hedley Donovan." I cabled Luce an advance text of the editorial, not for an okay but to inform him, and heard back that he thought it was good. He never told me how he voted, and I didn't ask.

On winter visits with the Luces in Phoenix, Dorothy and I found them both relaxed and gracious. Total nirvana was not the idea, of course; you could be sloshing around in the swimming pool and Harry or Clare would want to talk about the future of NATO. When I would play golf with Harry on the gentle Biltmore course, he would frequently improve my lie, and his favorite caddy, Pete, did the same for him. He was lenient in counting putts and sand-trap shots, for both of us, and I had some of the best scores of my life.

I was in Canberra, Australia, when Tom Griffith phoned on February 28, 1967, to tell me Luce had died of a heart attack in Phoenix. He was sixty-eight. On the long flight back to New York, I had time to reflect on what a remarkable mind and personality I had been lucky enough to know, and to conclude, once again, that here was a great man.

It was twenty years later that Clare died, at eighty-four. In St. Patrick's Cathedral, in a homily both moving and breezy, John Cardinal O'Connor recalled that after a Good Friday service in which an interminable series of laymen were intoning, "Lord grant Thy servant this or that . . . ," Clare succumbed to the thought: "And Lord, while Thou art up, grant Thy servant a double martini." The cardinal's irreverence moved me to think back to a wonderful moment at a Luce dinner party in their Waldorf Towers apartment.* Ten or twelve people had fallen suddenly, unaccountably silent when Clare brightly spoke up: "Let's talk about sex!" Some of us at her end of the table rallied to the new standard, while Harry got his constituents back to foreign policy.

I remember lively, gossipy lunches with Clare after Harry's death (and she did indeed like two martinis), at the Carlyle or the Plaza in Manhattan, or the Jockey Club in Washington. I was always reminding her of *Life*'s urge to publish excerpts from the autobiography she was always promising she would write. She had had an extraordinary life, and she was brilliantly equipped to relate it—no as-told-to business. She would confess to me, in her mid- and late seventies, long "out of everything," that she got a kick from still "rating a mention" in those polls on the world's Ten Most Admired Women. But she finally wouldn't write the autobiography, and for an honorable reason. Though her love of a good story had made her increasingly inventive in spoken reminiscence (and a source of considerable misinformation in other people's books), she had too much self-respect to publish fairy tales under her own by-line. But she didn't want to publish the full, unvarnished truth, either—about a lot of people, including herself and Harry.

To the end, she expected men to pay attention. I was standing in a black-tie crowd at a *Life* anniversary party in 1986 when I felt a playful finger running up and down my spine. I turned around to see this ethereal beauty in her eighties. "Hi," said Clare.

When Luce announced my appointment as editor-in-chief, I got a note from Alexander Heard, chancellor of Vanderbilt University. "Dear Hedley: It must be like being elected Moses." Alex was right.

---

*The East River triplex came next, as I recall; then, finally, a grand apartment on Fifth Avenue, overlooking the Metropolitan Museum and Central Park.

There was an element of Hebrew lawgiver in the job specs. Also a whiff of Rome. Harry liked to refer to the managing editors as the "College of Cardinals," though Luce as pope was not a perfect analogy, since the M.E.s had not elected him; it was the other way around. Calvin's Geneva and Knox's Edinburgh were also back there in the theological antecedents of the editor-in-chief (both of us), and finally, early republican America, where Madison and Jefferson drew their celebrated line between Church and State.

The Church-and-State metaphor, as I first encountered it at *Fortune*, was Time Inc. shorthand for the company's rigorous separation of editorial operations from business considerations. In practice, of course, the concerns of Church and State were frequently intermingled in the setting and policing of editorial budgets, and every so often in the biggest publishing decisions of all: to start a magazine, or keep one going, or kill one. But these were collegial discussions, not chain-of-command orders by anyone. In other magazine publishing companies, and on newspapers, including the best, even though the editors may be given great latitude, the publisher (or chairman or president) is their ultimate boss. At Time Inc., when I became editor-in-chief, I was accountable solely to the board of directors; I was partner and coequal of the chairman and president; none of us was the other's boss. They also were responsible solely to the board, on which we all sat. The managing editors of the Time Inc. magazines were appointed by the editor-in-chief and responsible solely to him. The publishers, the top business officers of each magazine, were appointed by the president and chairman and officially responsible to them. But until 1960, the publishers had been answerable finally to Luce, because Harry was both Church and State, an editor-in-chief who was also the company's biggest stockholder. Then he began extending the Church-State separation that had prevailed on the individual magazines to the top management layer of the corporation, resulting in a parallel double hierarchy unique, so far as I know, in American corporations.

The Time Inc. board of directors that consented to Luce's "nomination" of the new editor-in-chief was pretty much Harry's creature. There were fourteen members, seven "inside" and four others so long and closely connected with Luce that they really counted as family. That left three truly "outside" directors, each an important CEO: Thomas Watson, Jr., IBM; Frank Pace, General Dynamics; Gaylord Freeman, First National Bank of Chicago. These men were immensely admiring of Luce and Larsen and pleased to be invited onto the Time

Inc. board. They were not exactly hell-raisers, but as Luce and Larsen stepped aside, the outside directors were increasingly willing to ask tough questions of the new management. The directors' questions never challenged the primacy of Church in editorial belief. In my fifteen years as pope, I only once heard a director even remotely suggest he had a vote on the company's editorial positions.

I was responsible to the board for the general conduct of my office for the benefit of the company, but not for my views on public issues, which in the end had to be my views. If the board didn't like the job I was doing, they could hire a new editor-in-chief, but whoever replaced me—unless the whole Luce inheritance were to be renounced—would also be somebody responsible to his own conscience on matters of editorial policy.

Over the years, we expanded the board to about two dozen and kept the mix roughly fifty-fifty between inside and outside. As some of the elderly Luce and Larsen intimates left the board, they were succeeded by more authentically outside outsiders. Among the new directors were Rudolph Peterson, Bank of America; Rawleigh Warner, Mobil; James Beré, Borg-Warner; Alexander Heard, chairman of the Ford Foundation as well as head of Vanderbilt; Washington lawyer Sol Linowitz, former chairman of Xerox; and Matina Horner, president of Radcliffe. Few if any of our busy outside directors would have been interested in being on our board if Time Inc. were simply a large and successful manufacturer of clocks. It was the magazines, the lunchtime conversations about the news, the sense of being somewhat on the inside, that attracted them.

The board seldom challenged a major business proposal by management, but the need for approval by the outside directors was an excellent discipline in the decision-making process. Excellent though not foolproof, as will be related. It was often useful in internal discussions to say, "That's in no shape to take to the board," or sometimes, simply, "The board wouldn't go for that." In a company that was no longer proprietary, an independent board also met important ethical requirements: maintaining a confidential dialogue with the outside auditors, and setting the compensation of the top executives, so they didn't simply pay each other.*

---

*Frank Pace was chairman of the board's Compensation Committee, made up entirely of outside directors. Once, in a company plane, I caught a splendid candid-camera shot of Frank fast asleep, head flopped back, mouth wide open. I autographed an enlargement for him: "Compliments of Hedley Donovan, former member of the Executive Bonus list."

Several of the outside directors looked on our management structure with honest bafflement. They said there just wasn't any other company in the United States that tried to run itself that way, which was true enough, and they felt it was against nature to split the top management responsibility. Not only was management split between Church and State, but State's authority was then divided between Chairman Heiskell and President Linen. These two vigorous executives operated as co-bosses on the business side for about a decade, without backbiting, corridor intrigue, or visible friction.

Jim Linen's hyperenthusiasm for expansion and diversification had led us into the General Learning Corporation venture with General Electric, and also into the acquisition of a 5 percent interest in MGM. We eventually escaped from GLC with a loss of $11 million, and from our MGM investment at about the same price. I had been a believer in the General Learning idea, but argued against the MGM investment. We didn't know anything about filmmaking, and it seemed simply a deal for the sake of a deal. I acquiesced at some point: If the business side didn't interfere with editorial decisions, I shouldn't interfere (too much) with business decisions. I did point out, unnecessarily, that *Time* and *Life* would continue to say what they pleased about MGM movies. Jim was also the prime mover in at least one notably successful acquisition, the Boston book-publishing house of Little, Brown.

Overseas TV was another Linen enthusiasm, and we dropped a bit more money at this, particularly in partnerships with politico-entrepreneurs in Latin America. I rather liked these deals, I suppose from vaguely imperialistic impulses, and Heiskell, normally more cautious about money than Linen, was attracted because he was genuinely interested in Latin America. (He had once owned a house in Spain, spoke respectable Spanish, and, after all, had been publisher of *Life en Español*.)

Heiskell and Linen were also diversifying themselves. They had become heavily involved in *pro bono* activities—Heiskell as founder and first chairman of the Urban Coalition and as a member of special panels and commissions appointed by Governor Nelson Rockefeller and Mayor John Lindsay. Linen was to become president of the Urban League, and also overseer of a wonderful empire of causes and connections in countries where he tended to know the king: Jordan, Iran, Thailand—or equivalent dignitary—Indonesia, the Philippines.

Percy Williams Donovan with his sons.
David (*left*) is six; I'm three. Minneapolis, 1918.

With my sons, Peter (*left*) and Mark. Ravello, Italy, 1979.

The house where I grew up in Minneapolis.

My sister, Elizabeth, age three, with grandmother Mollie Knox Dougan.

Elizabeth, age twenty-one, first woman editor of the University of Minnesota yearbook, *summa cum laude*, all-everything.

In their late eighties, Alice and Percy Donovan listen as
I give a talk at Lake Forest College, Illinois, 1968.

Oxford years, 1934–37: Vacations within vacations

Windy day on the Sussex Downs.

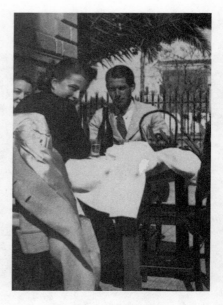

Lunchtime in Sicily.

On the Oxford ice hockey team.

East Geduld gold mine, the Rand,
South Africa.

As a *Washington Post* reporter

Interviewing a Mennonite farmer.

With reporters milling around Japan's special "peace envoy,"
Saburo Kurusu, outside the White House, November 1941.

Questioning Supreme Court Justice Owen Roberts, after his commission
finished its investigation of Pearl Harbor.

1951, appointed associate managing
editor of *Fortune*.

In the Navy, on a courier mission to India, Karachi, 1944.

My first Time Inc. boss, Ralph D. Paine, Jr., and Mary Grace,
head of the *Fortune* proofroom during his regime, mine, and
several more, at her retirement party in 1973.

"Shore Cottage," the 1719 Long Island farmhouse I was emboldened
to buy after a few years as managing editor.
(FROM THE *SKETCH BOOK OF HISTORIC HOMES*, COW NECK HISTORICAL SOCIETY)

With Nikita Khrushchev; Professor Cyril Black of Princeton (*on my left*); and my old Minnesota confederate Richard Scammon (*on my right*). The three of us were an official U.S. delegation to observe the Soviet "election" of 1958. Khrushchev told us he had a Red Army general bigger than Scammon.

Interviewing Premier Aleksei Kosygin in 1969. On my right, George Hunt, *Life* managing editor.

In Red Square, May Day, 1974. I am looking up at the Politburo brass watching the parade from on top of Lenin's Tomb. On my right, John Shaw, *Time* Moscow bureau chief.

USSR Night in Shore Cottage: Dorothy on Russian flute; I manning the Georgian drinking horn (can only be set down empty); the children in Uzbeki caps.

My Grim Look, as it is known in my family, sometimes surfaced
during the Soviet election-watching.

The Grim Look in friendly surroundings—
a Time Inc. board meeting in 1977.

New Delhi.

Troika ride near Moscow, Dorothy at right. My left earlobe
is about to be frostbitten.

Commencement in Pittsburgh (a degree in exchange for a speech).

1980, with Kiki, a cockatiel encouraged by its
master, Secretary of the Navy Edward Hidalgo,
to entertain his dinner guests.

Headgear

Sluggish small talk in Saudi Arabia. King Faisal in his Riyadh Palace.
At left is U.S. Ambassador James Akins.

Golda Meir in Jerusalem.

The Shah of Iran, Niavaran Palace, Tehran,
and Murray Gart (*right*), chief of the *Time* News Service.

Anwar Sadat at the Aswan Dam, and Wilton Wynn (*right*),
Time Cairo bureau chief.

The perpetual Middle East

Henry Luce when he turned over the job of editor-in-chief to me, 1964.
(PHOTOGRAPH BY ALFRED EISENSTAEDT)

Luce's longtime partner (*right*), Roy Larsen, president
and later vice chairman of Time Inc.

My partners in the new management, President James Linen (*right*), and
Chairman Andrew Heiskell, with visiting Korean dignitary.

Vanessa Redgrave at cocktails in London.

In Rome with Richard Duncan, (*left*), News Service chief after Gart, and Leo Lionni, former art director of *Fortune*.

My twenty-fifth anniversary with the company. From left: Louis Banks, managing editor of *Fortune*, later editorial director of Time Inc.; John Dowd, legal counsel; Mary Margaret Banks; my wife, Dorothy; and Robert Lubar, managing editor of *Fortune*.

My secretary, Trudi Lanz, on her retirement, and her original Time Inc. boss, former senior vice president Allen Grover.

Parties Inc.

OPPOSITE, TOP (*from left*): Otto Fuerbringer, former managing editor of *Time*; Bernhard Auer, former publisher of *Time*; Senator Charles Percy of Illinois, at one of America's tonier tennis courts, 1971. OPPOSITE, MIDDLE: With *Time*'s Hugh Sidey and President Gerald Ford, 1975. OPPOSITE, BOTTOM: With Jimmy Carter during his 1976 campaign. At his right, Henry Grunwald, managing editor of *Time*. THIS PAGE, ABOVE: With President Nixon in 1971. Private caption on my own framed print: "Did you ever think of wiring this place?" THIS PAGE, BOTTOM: In the Oval Office as Senior Adviser. Less fun now, 1979: gas shortages, turmoil in Iran, Central America, Salt II hopes fading.

Vietnam, 1965, as guest of the U.S. Air Force on a B-57 strike
against enemy supply lines from the North.

With Marine colonel commanding the Danang air base; Vietcong
mortars on a mountain four miles away.

On the DMZ, Korea, 1965. On my right, Jerrold Schecter,
Time Tokyo bureau chief.

Beijing, 1979, in the Great Hall of the People, with Deng Xiaoping.

Full cycle

Back to work in 1981 as a *Fortune* writer, interviewing President Ronald Reagan at the Century Plaza Hotel, Los Angeles, and George Bush on the vice president's private balcony, old Executive Office Building, overlooking his next stop.

With my two "corporate editors," 1978, Henry Grunwald (*left*)
and Ralph Graves, about to become editor-in-chief
and editorial director.

With my journalistic children, Helen, now deputy managing editor of *The Boston Globe*, and Mark, a senior editor of *People*, at unveiling party for Aaron Shikler portrait commissioned by Time Inc. after my retirement.
Thirty-fourth-floor reception room, Time and Life Building, 1980.

He concerned himself with combating trade protectionism in the U.S., with the plight of Middle East refugees, the encouragement of Western investment in Indonesia. Jim's countries tended to be imperfect democracies, to say the least, and he manfully agreed when *Time*, *Life*, or *Fortune* had occasion to say so. Once in a while he might plead, but not very hard, that we could do a better story on Jordan if we could just wait a week or two.

Jim and Andrew had a strong sense of the corporation as citizen, but their increasingly frequent forays into outside activities also reflected the fact that neither had the satisfaction of complete authority inside. In 1968–69, had Luce still been alive, I think he might have asked, "Who's minding the store?" I could sympathize with my colleagues' urge to be identified with important public issues. I had that satisfaction in every issue of our magazines—not so much because Editor-in-Chief appeared at the top of the mastheads, above Chairman and President, but because I was actively involved in what the magazines said.

In 1969, Linen suffered a stroke, his frenetic travels perhaps a factor, and his doctors ordered him to take things easier. Heiskell and I, with counsel and support from Roy Larsen, now the company's elder statesman, agreed that Linen should step aside as president. Larsen cheerfully offered up his own title—chairman of the executive committee of the board—as a suitable one for Linen, and contented himself with the rank of vice chairman of the board. Jim was not happy; he came to my office one morning after a meeting with Heiskell, and said, with great dignity, "I understand I no longer have your confidence." I had to say that I, too, thought he should give up the president's job, but I had complete confidence in his continuing value as a member of senior management. Whatever hurt Jim felt, he did in fact continue as a wise counselor in publishing matters and an important ambassador and high-level salesman for Time Inc. Jim had his own interpretation of taking things easy; even after a second stroke confined him to a wheelchair, he was still flying all over the map, his indomitable wife, Sally, making it all work.

To succeed Linen as president, I lobbied hard for Jim Shepley. I suspected he would not always be easy to get along with (which proved to be correct), but I thought he was the brightest and toughest among four or five strong candidates. He got the job. Heiskell, Larsen, and I also agreed to end the anomalous division of authority on the

State side of the house. Heiskell became chief executive officer of the company, Shepley chief operating officer.

Church, as evident from these proceedings, sometimes participated heavily in the business of State. The famous "separation" served much more to shield the editors from any possible business-side pressures than to keep the editor-in-chief out of business-side discussions. Indeed, Heiskell and Linen and Shepley regularly invited me into their problems and decisions. I think they valued my views but also—all of them having grown up in the Time Inc. of Henry Luce—felt the agreement of the editor-in-chief lent an extra layer of legitimacy to decisions in their own jurisdictions. Beyond this, there was a relationship of total trust and respect between Andrew Heiskell and me. He knew that I wanted Time Inc. to make a lot of money, that I paid attention to costs, and that I was good at arithmetic. I knew that he believed as strongly as I in the integrity of the editorial process, and furthermore he often came up with good editorial ideas. (Among them, *People*.) Heiskell in fact had started on the editorial side, as *Life*'s first science writer, and Shepley had been a first-rate Washington reporter, so "the news" was a natural part of our ongoing conversation. I kept them informed of policy positions the magazines were about to take—not just as a courtesy but because I wanted their reactions.

In 1967, shortly after Luce died, I told Heiskell, in the presence of a somewhat startled Roy Larsen, that Andrew should be my successor if I didn't come back from a trip I was about to make to Vietnam. This was a touch melodramatic, since my ten-day guided tours of Vietnam were about as dangerous as ten days of driving on the Long Island Expressway (i.e., mildly dangerous). But I had no clear successor in place at the time, and I thought Heiskell could combine my job and his for at least a year or two, during a search for a new editor-in-chief. Two years later, when it became apparent that Linen should step aside as president, Heiskell said he would be glad to see me as chairman and CEO, as well as editor-in-chief, and he could serve as president. Roy Larsen was again a startled witness. "I knew you fellows got along well," he told me later, "but I didn't realize *that* well." I thought Heiskell would make a better CEO than I and that I already had plenty to do. I was inventing the role, as I went along, of an editor-in-chief who was not Henry Luce, and Heiskell was my generous and indispensable collaborator.

When Luce retired as editor-in-chief, he offered me his big office at the northwest corner of the thirty-fourth floor of the Time and Life

Building. Office geography takes on considerable symbolic significance even in a company as informal as Time Inc. (It is also desirable
to have the senior executives collected in a place that can be physically labeled. "The Thirty-fourth Floor," for purposes of general gossip and griping, is much more satisfying than "they.") But I told
Harry he should stay where he was, and he didn't resist. Roy Larsen
tactfully offered me his equally grand suite at the southwest corner
(also including private bath and a little lying-down room, where I
think I lay down twice in fifteen years), and I didn't resist. On the
south, I looked at the slab of the Exxon Building; to the west I had
Broadway and the Hudson, bluffs and towns and ridges beyond, and
sensational autumn and winter sunsets, enhanced by just the right
amount of particulate matter in the Jersey sky. After Harry died,
Andrew asked me if I didn't want to move into Harry's office, and I
said No, why didn't he. I was very comfortable where I was. Andrew
and I received identical salaries and bonuses throughout the fifteen
years of our partnership, increasing over that time from $175,000 a
year to $398,923.* I regularly needled Andrew because his total com-
pensation always came out $400, or some such, more than mine, that
being his director's fee from some Time Inc. subsidiary board that
he was on and I wasn't. We had equal access to the small Time Inc.
air force: two or three planes and a helicopter. We had no chauffeured
company cars—to my mind, the choicest of all New York executive
perks—but we made liberal use of rented limos, sedans preferred
over the long black jobs. Once, to my horror, a stretch limo showed
up for me. I made sure it never happened again.

It helped my relations with the business-side executives and the
outside directors that *Fortune* had taught me a bit about balance
sheets and the like, so I didn't come over as a complete ivory-tower
type. It also helped that I believed strongly in the justice of the box

---

*This strangely precise figure was recently supplied me by the Payroll Department of
Time Inc. For years I had had in mind the amount of $225,000 as my final salary and
$165,000 as my top bonus—for a total of $390,000. Considering the utter clarity of my
memory for such numbers as $25 a week in 1937, it is odd that I should have mislaid
eight or nine thousand 1978 dollars.

In case any IRS agent is reading this book—which in this free country is his right—
I can save him the trouble of looking up my file. For the year 1978, I reported and
paid taxes on a considerably larger amount than $398,923, the excess being various
Time Inc. benefits that were taxable as straight income but not regarded by my employer (or me) as part of my "base pay."

Lest other (non-IRS) readers think all this money talk indecent, I would remind
them of the early discovery (page 138) by *Fortune* and *Time* of the journalistic uses
of all the stuff that publicly held companies must file with the SEC. A Time Inc. editor
is in no position to complain if somebody wants to know: "How much does he make?"

office; if one of our magazines was in trouble, I looked first for editorial reasons. And despite Henry Luce's handsome reference to my conscience, in his send-off speech, I fought off all subsequent efforts to label me "the Conscience of Time Inc.," claiming that everybody in the place, ad salesmen not excluded, had a conscience. I was considered surprisingly cooperative, for an editor, in making speeches at places where our publishers thought it might be useful.

Church/State could come in handy in all sorts of situations. I enjoyed invoking the "separation" when the soft-porn publisher Ralph Ginzburg once wrote me a First Amendment sort of letter complaining because *Time* had rejected advertising copy for his magazine *Avant-Garde*. I replied piously that the Time Inc. advertising departments didn't try to tell the editors what to print and we didn't try to tell them what ads they could accept. (I'm afraid more than once I did in fact stop one of the magazines from accepting ad copy made up to look like editorial material, a persistent problem with special promotional sections offered to *Fortune*.)

One night during the Democratic convention of 1968, I was on Michigan Avenue as Senator Eugene McCarthy's disciples and Mayor Richard Daley's police and the Hippies and Yippies and National Guardsmen were jostling around in the so-called Battle of Chicago. I had been switching back and forth, standing a while with the police, then with the kids, to see what it felt like on both sides, and I was on the students' side when the police started to form up for another of their sweeps. At that moment, a couple of flower children moved right up behind me, and I heard the young man say to the girl, "Just stay behind this businessman and we'll be all right." I thought of explaining to them about Church and State in Time Inc., but decided to let it go.

Time Inc., in my first year as editor-in-chief, ranked number 146 on *Fortune*'s list of the 500 biggest corporations. Our weeklies had a worldwide circulation of more than twelve million. We were the biggest publishing operation in the United States, and indeed had been the biggest in the world until the London *Daily Mirror* group a year or two earlier bought up about 150 magazines. That was fine by me. People may admire an automobile company for getting to be the biggest in the world, but it makes them irritable when anybody is the biggest publishing company, though obviously somebody has to be. Time Inc. took in about 2 percent of all the money spent on all forms of advertising in the United States. Not exactly an octopus. And I doubt that the Time Inc. publications have ever commanded more than 2 percent of the time Americans spend reading or looking at various media of communication. The constitutional right not to read *Time* magazine seems secure. Our revenues in 1964 were about $400 million, profits after taxes about $27 million, a not very flashy operating margin of 7 percent, compared with 8 to 10 percent for successful manufacturing companies. But as an idea business without much money tied up in fixed plant, our return on invested capital was very high. (In 1988, Time Inc. revenues were $4,507,000,000, net after taxes, $289 million. The company was number 102 in the Fortune 500, number 172 in operating margin, number 106 in return on investment. In recent years, the company's flourishing cable-TV business has required heavy capital investment.)

In 1964, Time Inc. had about 7,700 employees worldwide, of whom 1,400 were in my editorial domains (up from 1,200 in 1959, partly because of the growth of Time-Life Books). The company took up about twenty floors of our forty-eight-story building. The publishing areas tended to be furnished in Tasteful Contemporary; the editorial offices were of course more raffish. Though the days were long gone when everybody in Time Inc. knew everybody else, it remained a pleasantly unbuttoned sort of place. Roy Larsen and Jim Linen were wonderfully warm and gregarious men whose good spirits radiated all through the publishing staffs. In the editorial departments, despite the ferocious working schedules as closings approached, the first couple of days in the production cycle could be quite relaxed. These were the favored days for the incessant Time Inc. parties— fitfully restrained during austerity campaigns, always reappearing for ingenious and compelling reasons. A few senior secretaries called senior executives "Mister"; otherwise, first names were Time Inc. etiquette. I'm afraid I just called out "Trudi," through the open door between my office and hers, instead of buzzing Miss (Gertrude) Lanz.

I liked shirtsleeves as well as the open door. I did a good deal of moving about the building and dropping in on people. I suppose "management by wandering around" is the office equivalent of the rural proverb I first heard from a Texas rancher: "The best fertilizer is the owner's footsteps." I knew most of the editorial employees by first name, and at least a hundred or two of the publishing and business people. I was doing what felt comfortable, rather than seeking to be thought "democratic," "accessible," or any of those recommended things. But I also had heard—and was baffled by—the occasional revelation that people found me unapproachable or even frightening. These revelations occasionally came at those office parties (for which I had a mysterious appetite) and might be cast as: "I used to think that you . . . " etc.

The artist Aaron Shikler asked me how I liked an oil portrait he had done of me. I said, "Very much," except maybe I came out a little too stern. (Even my children thought so.) Shikler said, "It's the way you would look to a junior *Time* writer, sitting across the desk from you." Maybe so.

Those 1,400 editorial people—they were my job, and, subject to one or two reservations, my joy. I managed them—to the extent, as previously noted, that such people can be managed at all—by appointing their bosses, and managing *them*. To the extent *they* can be managed.

In moving to *Fortune* editor from *Fortune* writer, I had made the personal passage from work of my own, and the intense ego satisfaction that can bring to the author—at least when he thinks the stuff is good—to the quite different but perhaps equally powerful gratification of putting out a good issue of the magazine. From being a hands-on editor of one magazine, I had now become an editor of editors, and I had another passage in motivations to negotiate. It could be done. And far into my twenty years as editorial director and editor-in-chief, I still got quite a kick out of it when all the Time Inc. magazines on my smoked-glass reading table were looking good, and it did not detract from my pleasure if *Newsweek* and *Forbes* did not look quite so good.

When Osborn Elliott was promoted from editor to editor-in-chief of *Newsweek*, I phoned to congratulate him, and he said, "What do I do now?" I had always thought editor (or managing editor) was as big as you could get on one magazine, so I was tempted to tell Oz the first thing is to get yourself some more magazines. I think I told him to start going home earlier in the evening.

During my tenure as editor-in-chief, I appointed fourteen Time Inc. managing editors (or equivalent), and I claim to have been good at it. Being in office so long, I got to appoint two M.E.s at most of our magazines. I never had to fire an M.E. I did ease two or three out of office a little sooner than they might have liked. It helped that the company's expansion generated some good new jobs at the upper editorial levels, and if one of those didn't materialize, the improvements in the early-retirement package at least made it possible for senior people to leave with little financial pain.

The Time Inc. M.E. was a formidable fellow, and I meant him to be. But I was also looking for men who could share the command of their magazines up (with me) and down (with their staffs)—without feeling their own authority had been compromised. This is fairly complex chemistry. When it jells, a very broad sense of proprietorship sets in.

In their dealings with the editor-in-chief, they had to know, of course, what kinds of things needed to be checked in advance with me: senior appointments; new editorial departments and other formula changes; major projects, series, investigative sallies—matters that might engage valuable people for quite a while, cost noticeable sums of money, and perhaps involve legal and/or political hazards. Considering the inexactness of the tests just stated, it speaks well for the antennae and the loyalty of those fourteen M.E.s that I never felt I had not been given full notice of something I should have heard about.

The M.E.s also knew the kinds of stories I expected to be shown before closings—major "policy" pieces on national issues, stories about our competitors or other areas where Time Inc. was an interested party, and stories on the far edge of the new and volatile standards of "taste." (As far as I knew, no M.E. of my day kept any mental list of particular people or institutions under special protection of the editor-in-chief.) Of course, I could not look at more than a minute fraction—maybe 1 percent—of what our four magazines (then five, then six, to say nothing of Time-Life Books) were about to print. My deputy could look at another percent or two. The essential control was in the quality of the M.E.s. Inevitably, I could be disappointed, even dismayed, by some of the things that could get into print. I spent at least a quarter of my time, I suppose, on cover-to-cover reading of the magazines as they came out, and reviewing with the editors what I did and didn't like. Mostly, I liked.

The intellectuals in the care of a Time Inc. M.E. could be swiftly turned off by inspirational exhortation. They responded to wit, to solid news about their magazines—i.e., numbers, dollars, plans; to a boss who seemed to know what their jobs were like; to a leader who would listen and could also make up his mind and seemed to know where he was going. The place did not purport to be a democracy, and one of the highest arts of the M.E. (and the editor-in-chief) was to know when the point had come for the Yes or No. Nobody had tenure, but the staff for the most part was secretly admiring of Time Inc. and intensely loyal—so long as the boss did not invoke the loyalty as something owed. People were motivated by professional pride in their own work and a personal liking for at least some of their colleagues, including even the boss. They were also interested in plain old-fashioned money.

So a Time Inc. M.E. needed to sense all this, but he wasn't just managing creative people; he needed to be highly imaginative himself. (For the moment, I will not intone "or herself"—we will address this matter soon.) Magazines need continuous creative refreshing and also, issue by issue, acts of inspired curiosity and daring. Good journalism, in short. But magazine journalism cannot offer the daily usefulness and familiarity of the newspaper or the immediacy and marvelous free-of-charge movie quality of TV news and sports. These boundaries that magazines live within were becoming more and more evident, and I particularly prized the managing editors and M.E. candidates who understood where we were positioned and how we might exploit our own possibilities. Here André Laguerre of *S.I.* and Otto Fuerbringer and Henry Grunwald of *Time* were brilliant.

But the Time Inc. M.E. couldn't be just a big-picture man. He had to be a first-rate craftsman—with copy, headlines, pictures, layout. And there was always the matter of running the shop. I considered the administrative role almost as critical as the creative one. Somebody will always pipe up and say, "You can delegate the administration." Yes, but it took a clear sense of administration for an M.E. to do that delegating effectively and to keep track of how the delegated work was going. Some of the M.E.s inevitably had less talent—and less interest—in this role than in the creative. Nobody (starting with the editor-in-chief) is perfect. I myself held onto more administrative responsibility than was strictly necessary, and never turned over to any deputy the authority over top salaries, for instance, that Luce had given me.

In several appointments of managing editors, I thought in terms of a "ticket"—Mr. A for M.E. if he understands he needs Mr. B as his deputy. I had seen the superb Paine-Furth team that Luce set up at *Fortune*, based on complementary skills, as opposed to the futile Fuerbringer-Griffith debate that Luce set up at *Time*. Messrs. A and B both needed stamina, physical and emotional. If they had come up through departmental editing jobs and then survived in the assistant M.E. level, they had the necessary endurance. They needed enough stability

and self-discipline to forgo for themselves indulgences of temperament they would tolerate in people working for them.

It was a plus if an M.E. could speak on his feet—Grunwald and
Richard Stolley of *People* were stars—and would perform cheerfully
at Time Inc. gatherings and in the outer world. It was not a requirement. André Laguerre, asked once to say "a couple of words" at a
Sports Illustrated Christmas party, rose and said, "Merry Christmas,"
and sat down.

The company was rich in editing talent. I often enjoyed the painful luxury of choosing between two highly qualified people for one
choice job. Painful, of course, because I disappointed some very good
people. The challenge then for the winners (and for me) was not to
lose the losers. In my protocol of notifications, the winner heard first,
of course; it was theoretically conceivable that somebody might decline an M.E. appointment, but nobody did. In the same conversation,
we talked about who his deputy(ies) should be; it was entirely conceivable that some M.E.–designate might object if these understand-
ings seemed to be a condition of his appointment—sometimes they
were—but nobody did. Then I told the losers, the same day if possible.
Then the business side (if I hadn't already told them). Then key editorial people who hadn't been in the running themselves, such as
the art director and the chief of research, but who shouldn't have to
learn from the public announcement that they were getting a new
boss. Then give everybody twenty-four hours to tell spouses, children,
secretaries; then the company memorandum: "I am very pleased to
announce . . . ," the press release, and a few paragraphs inside the
Times. Nothing ever got into print before it was meant to; secrets can
be kept if people know they are being trusted—for a couple of days,
anyway.

Following the fourteen M.E.–level appointments that I made,
only two disappointed candidates left the company. One was James
Keogh, after I appointed Henry Grunwald M.E. of *Time*. Jim landed
on his feet, to say the least, in a White House communications job in
the first years of the Nixon administration. The other was Roy Rowan,
a *Life* assistant M.E. who left the year after Ralph Graves was appointed M.E., to work up a magazine of his own, but he later returned
to the company, first to the Time-Life News Service, then *Fortune*.

None of the fourteen was a woman. The pool from which M.E.s
might be chosen consisted of perhaps thirty people—executive editors, assistant M.E.s, major departmental editors, chiefs of major

news bureaus—and in 1964 those were all men, except for the food editor of *Life*, Eleanor Graves. But the number of women in the M.E.–level pool was slowly growing, the proportion of women in the next pool—the writing staffs—more rapidly. The corollary was a sharp increase in the numbers of male researchers and reporters. By the early 1970s, the old Time Inc. caste system—men write, nice young ladies out of the "Seven Sisters" do the "checking"—was pretty well demolished. By the late 1970s, *Fortune* had more male researchers than female. Two women on its board of editors, Carol Loomis and Wyndham Robertson, were among the half-dozen best financial writers in the country. Loomis was invited to become an editor but preferred to keep on writing. Robertson became an assistant M.E. On the subject of sex-blindness at *Fortune*, she said, "We'd hire an orangutan if it could write."

Management on its way to the new enlightenment had taken some stiff prodding. Time Inc. women in 1970 filed a formal complaint of discrimination with the New York State Human Rights Division; the company conceded no past discrimination but in effect promised not to do it again. I was unhappy about the whole business. I thought Time Inc.—even under the old caste system, which included very well-paid women chiefs of research—was offering women a remarkable number of attractive professional-level jobs. The flow of applicants for these jobs certainly suggested that. In the national trends, the steadily rising proportion of women in college enrollments and among applicants for jobs in journalism was going to increase the numbers of women writers and editors. Philosophically, I disliked legal/governmental pressures to compel what was going to happen anyway. But "anyway" was doubtless hastened, in the Time and Life Building, by the discrimination suit.

My first M.E. appointment, after becoming editor-in-chief, was at my old magazine. Dunc Norton-Taylor was now in his early sixties and two of his chief colleagues, John Davenport and Max Ways, were contemporaries. They were editing an ardently conservative *Fortune* of literary and philosophical distinction, but the magazine was beginning to take on a somewhat static quality—visually and in the mix of articles. Dunc made things easy for me by himself suggesting that he return to senior writer status, that Ways and Davenport could then gracefully do the same, and a younger lineup of editors could take over. He thought his logical successor was the versatile Louis

Banks, former News Service reporter, *Time* writer and editor, and briefly a *Life* editor. So did I. Indeed, I had brought Banks on to *Fortune* several years earlier with just such a possibility in mind.

I continued trying to think one or two moves ahead, to position good people in jobs where they would have a shot at better jobs. I encouraged M.E.s to think in those terms, reviewing with each of them at least once a year who their backups were—(a) in case you get hit by a truck tomorrow, or preferably (b) assuming you don't, who might be the long-range candidates. And who might be the back-ups of the backups.

Under our contract with the Newspaper Guild, all employees were entitled to an evaluation of their performances by their superiors at least once a year, and this included even the M.E.s. (In later years, I sometimes entertained myself by thinking of comparable conver-sations, perhaps around Christmas time, between Ronald Reagan and, say, Don Regan or Ed Meese.) I would usually tuck my evalu-ations into some news about salary and bonus. At odd moments dur-ing the year, not by statutory requirement, I might ask M.E.s if they had a good Wailing Wall man, reliable spies, an aggressive enough recruiter. Who are your Young Turks—remember when you were one?—and how much do you get around the floor?

Lou Banks, after a very successful term as *Fortune*'s M.E., ac-cepted my invitation in 1970 to become editorial director, the first time that position had been filled since I held it. He was a superb deputy, and I told him that he was my successor if the truck hit, but unlikely for the long haul, since he was only two years younger than I. Lou, to my regret, decided to strike out on an entirely different career—first becoming a professor at the Harvard Business School, then at MIT.

Banks's departure led me into an experiment in rotation. One at a time, I brought in half a dozen of the M.E.s or their executive editors to serve stints of four months or so as my deputy, with the stipulation that back at the deputy's home magazine, at least one fellow who had never filled in for the M.E. should get a chance at it. (Ten did.) There was a touch of Rube Goldberg about the scheme, but the ro-tatees went at their temporary assignments with tact and energy, and somehow the exercise worked. Top editors learned more about the business side of the company than they had known since the days when Time Inc. was very small. Successor scenarios on the individual magazines and in my own office took on more substance.

I hoped, too, that these "exchange fellowships" for the top editors would dent the clannishness of the separate magazines, without eroding morale. *Sports Illustrated* had become the Marine Corps of our magazines, while *Time* had mellowed under Grunwald. I once sent a memo to Ralph Graves of *Life*: "I count four citations of *Life* in this week's *Time*—and I'm only about half-way through. This must be an all-time record of fraternalism. I hope you plan to buy Henry a good lunch."

The bureaucratic warfare between *Time* and the News Service dragged on, however. I begrudged the drain on many people's time, including my own. I finally declared *Time* the winner, and in 1972 "integrated" the News Service into the magazine. My decree did not exactly transform things overnight. The News Service was a superb professional corps and it was also capable of foot-dragging worthy of an endangered government bureau.

Before launching the rotation of deputies, I felt I should tell my old friend Tom Griffith that I would not be appointing him editorial director. He had been a highly congenial and skillful deputy for several years in the mid-1960s, then editor of *Life*, but he was only one year younger than I, and I felt I owed the company the chance to appraise some of the newer arrivals. I was much touched when Tom wrote of me in *f.y.i.*, the company house organ, after I retired: "When it came to promotions to top editorial positions, friendship had no claims of preference with him; what is remarkable about him is the personal friendships he had retained among those he had to disappoint."

I made at least two mistakes in my appraisals of the top editors— two that I soon realized; perhaps there were more I still don't know about. I subtracted a Mr. B from one magazine before I understood how crucial he was to the effectiveness of Mr. A. On another magazine, I was about to appoint Mr. A, and in our customary collegial fashion, I was telling Heiskell and Shepley about my choice. They urged a different choice. Under the Time Inc. constitution, this was simply conversation, and I could do what I wanted, but the more I thought about what they had said, I decided they were right. I followed their advice, and the appointment was widely regarded as one of my most astute.

In my *Fortune* M.E. days, when Bill Furth came into my office and caught me staring out the window, he would murmur, "Ah, the loneliness of command." The shameful truth, well-known to Bill, was that I enjoyed command. The trick was not to let it be too obvious. I also enjoyed my VIP rank. I felt very important when a *Time* correspondent named Roland Hedley began to appear in *Doonesbury*. Senators, Cabinet officers, governors, corporate CEOs, university presidents liked to be on first-name terms with the editor-in-chief of Time Inc., and he was entirely willing. Vanity certainly came into play, but more important, these friendships were useful in my work. Even presidents of the United States, and certainly candidates for president, found it helpful to have a kind of business friendship with publishers and editors. I was more accessible to Democrats than Luce had been. For Harry, Joe Kennedy's boy Jack was a special case, but Luce had had almost no personal interchange with Truman or Roosevelt. When I became editor-in-chief, I might have been one of ten thousand more or less influential citizens whom a president might think it worthwhile to cultivate, whereas the president (whichever party) was, of course, number 1 on any national editor's list of the people his journalism must try to interpret. Of the four presidents during my editor-in-chief years, two were very complex characters (Johnson and Nixon) and one was medium-complex (Carter). Ford was easier to figure out—which is said in admiration.

Esquire once mentioned me as one of ten nonpoliticians who should be considered for president. (Others on their list included Henry Ford, Justice Potter Stewart, David Rockefeller, and Irwin Miller of Cummins Engine, who was on their cover and who would have been great: a mix of Jimmy Stewart, Mother Teresa, Daddy Warbucks, and add fifty points on the I.Q. I am not sure how Irwin is registered, but I think he is a far-left Republican.) I was prepared to issue a counter-Shermanesque statement: "If nominated, I will run; if elected, I will serve." The statement was never needed.

I knew all the British prime ministers of the 1960s and 1970s, the German chancellors, Japanese prime ministers. I met two popes and General Douglas MacArthur, Kremlin potentates, enough Middle Eastern leaders to start a war, generals of the doomed regime of South Vietnam, and, in a sandbagged headquarters in a slum of Londonderry, an eighteen-year-old bomb thrower who was commander of the Provo wing of the IRA.

That night I was in Londonderry, I had begun the day at Antalya, on the south coast of Turkey. Not an immense journey in miles, but an arduous one, three different jets and a long auto ride at each end.

I wondered whether anybody else in the world had ever made that particular fourteen-hour trip. A few days later, I was poking around a country graveyard, where I understood some of my Ulster forebears might be buried, when I came on the grave of a Lord Leslie, one of our Leslies, who had been a seventeenth-century ambassador from Great Britain to the Ottoman Empire. At least he hadn't had to change planes at Istanbul and Heathrow.

Across several continents, I survived half a dozen *Time* "news tours." These were an inspired promotional device thought up by Jim Linen and Bernie Auer. *Time* would invite a party of twenty-five or thirty corporate CEOs, leavened by some university and foundation heads, on two-week tours of hot foreign-news areas. The guests would pay most of their own expenses, but through the Time-Life News Service, they saw more, and certainly met more foreign leaders, than they could have arranged on their own. That many of the guests were Time Inc. advertisers or potential advertisers was not entirely incidental.

The tours, whatever *Newsweek* may have thought of them, were also something of an endurance contest. I took some pride in my ability, toward the end of these trips, to stay awake while various of the ranking captains of American industry (and alas, even some Time Inc. journalists) were dropping like flies during the countless briefings, speeches, receptions, banquets laid on for us. All my life I have thought of the temptation to fall asleep in public as an invitation to a contest: Am I stronger than this speech, sermon, opera, movie (*Jules et Jim*—oh, boy!) that I am up against? My only clear-cut defeat occurred in Munich in the summer of 1936. Some of us had been drinking the good local beer all afternoon and then went on to *Tristan und Isolde*. In Act II, as the reader will recall, the "action" takes place in a dimly lit garden where the lovesick principals pretty much sit on a bench for half an hour or more. It can be very restful.

The editor-in-chief was entitled to interest himself in everything, and indeed was expected to. So I went to see the Minnesota Vikings lose the Super Bowl in New Orleans and Pasadena. I missed seeing them lose in a couple of other places; they are still 0-for-4. I absorbed a lot of opera at the Met (and outlasted *Tristan* more than once). I went to all the Republican and Democratic conventions of the 1960s and 1970s (none as exciting as my first, the Republicans in Philadelphia in 1940).

I made speeches in London, Frankfurt, Paris, Tokyo, Montreal, Melbourne. Few areas of America were spared. I gave speeches to college graduating classes, business groups, Time Inc. gatherings. I managed to get booed at the University of Rochester for mentioning to the seniors that some of them might soon be in the army, but getting booed on the campus was no great feat in those days. I wrote all the speeches myself, and seldom repeated one. (I would throw up rather than speak anybody else's prose, no matter how elevated, as my own. Take that, Corporate America! You too, Lee Iacocca!) Whatever the effect on the audiences, the speeches were good for me, forcing me to think my way through, if I could, some topic of the day. The speeches helped reassure me that I still knew how to do an honest day's work as a writer. As did the occasional bylined piece for *Time*, *Life*, or *Fortune*.

I rather liked being interviewed, but never got very good at it. I was slow to adapt things I understood perfectly well as a journalist to my occasional role as a personage on the receiving end of an interview. The rather elementary wisdom, for instance, of spending just a few minutes in advance of an interview in thinking of a few—just a few—points you would like to get across, and of quotable language to wrap them in. I was often pleased, especially when I was sitting on some Time Inc. secrets, if I got through an interview without saying anything the reporter could use in his story. The higher skill would have been to make some extraneous positive points, about Time Inc. or even myself, while giving away nothing about the topic at hand. I was also slow to recognize for myself (though I had written about it as a political reporter) the perils of sarcasm or joke-cracking, especially dry-type jokes. An interviewer once asked me if I did any daydreaming. "He replied that he preferred to call it thinking." In cold print, murderous.

Journalists (including this one) tend to be extremely thin-skinned when they get written about. They bleed—more than politicians, about the same as professors and businessmen—at the quote taken slightly out of context, the quote divorced from tone of voice, the wounding adjective, the ignoring of things that are going well (at Time Inc., Harvard Law School, wherever), the heavy stress on the things not going well. At a time when *Fortune* was having some difficulties, the managing editor, Robert Lubar, was interviewed by the *Wall Street Journal*. "Now I understand," he told me afterward, "why businessmen hate the press."

. . . .

I suppose I became a fully paid-up member of the Eastern Establishment when its generally acknowledged chairman, John McCloy, asked me to become a director of the Council on Foreign Relations, of which he was also chairman. McCloy was one of that remarkable breed of lawyers and bankers (including Dean Acheson, Robert Lovett, Arthur Dean, Douglas Dillon, the Dulles brothers) who for a generation moved so fluently between Wall Street and Washington, sought for defense and foreign-policy posts by presidents of both parties (until Nixon, who felt uncomfortable with these types). I told Jack McCloy I would need a few days to think about my calendar. He came fairly close to spluttering; I gathered one did not *think* about accepting an invitation to the council board. After my few days, I accepted, of course.

As a director, it once fell to me to introduce Senator Ted Kennedy at a council luncheon. It was at the time when Kennedy was warming up for his challenge to President Jimmy Carter for the Democratic nomination, and he drew a capacity crowd. I proposed that "future historians will mark this date, April 2, 1979, as the final fall of the Eastern Establishment—the day that the Council on Foreign Relations served a box lunch."

I was richly rewarded, soon after becoming a council director, by the most interesting board meeting I have ever attended, nonprofit or corporate. People spoke up heatedly, and there was actually a vote, a close vote. The question was admission of women to the council. The general temper of the board at that time may be deduced from the fact that David Rockefeller and I, favoring the admission of women, were considered Young Turks. There was a lovable Old Guard arrayed against us. Hamilton Fish Armstrong, diplomatic historian, longtime editor of *Foreign Affairs*, offered the marvelously Edwardian argument that when you were off some evening at a council meeting, your wife at least knew you were not sitting around with other ladies, but if there were women members, who knows? (This seemed especially touching when I learned some years later, from reading a book, that Ham Armstrong had had his first wife stolen away by Walter Lippmann, no less. But not at a council meeting.) We voted to admit women—9-to-7, as I recall.

For all its genteel style and resolutely nonpartisan character, the council had managed to make itself controversial. It was Exhibit A in the "hidden government" theories of the John Birch Society and other Far Right crazies. When Rockefeller and other members formed the sinister-sounding Trilateral Commission (to encourage informal dialogue among influential Japanese, Europeans, Americans), it became Exhibit B. I became a director there, too. So did some high government officials, former and/or future. (When I congratulated George Bush on his election as vice president in 1980, I said I hoped he didn't mind receiving correspondence from a member of the Trilateral Commission, to which he had belonged. He scrawled a card of thanks, and said, "Sh-sh-sh" about the Trilateral stuff. I have kept this exchange secret until now.)

I took on other board memberships that kept me in close touch with some important regions of Time Inc.'s subject matter and kept me close, too, to some men and women who were very good company. At one time or another, I served as a trustee of the Ford Foundation, New York University, the Carnegie Endowment for International Peace, Mount Holyoke College, the nonprofit Aerospace Corporation, the Asia Society, the University of Minnesota Foundation, the National Center for the Humanities. I evaded proposals that I become chairman of the trustees at various of these places. I didn't want to commit that much time, and I also disliked the fund-raising role. Ever since my *Fortune* M.E. days, I had held to a judgelike posture that I shouldn't be shaking the tin cup, for this or that worthy cause, at people who might then turn up in my office asking for this or that favor in print. Just being a trustee, of course, left me open to an occasionally awkward "story idea" from a fellow trustee—or, once in a long while, from the trustee's PR man hinting that his guy might be willing to sit still for a *Time* cover story. But this sort of thing isn't really that hard to deal with—or if it is, you shouldn't be editor-in-chief of Time Inc. Or managing editor of *Fortune*. Or a reporter on a respectable newspaper.

Apart from my trusteeships (or the occasional corporate donation lobbied through the board of directors), I worked at enlarging Time Inc.'s journalistic relationship with the university world. There were a lot of stories for us in that world—and I also wanted it to think well of Time Inc. I assembled Time-Life-Fortune-Books delegations to spend two or three days in lively academic settings: Cambridge, of course; the University of Chicago neighborhood; the Research Triangle of North Carolina (I even made my troops go to a miserable Duke vs. Wake Forest football game); and the Bel Air Hotel in suburban Los Angeles—yes, heavy thinkers from Cal Tech, UCLA, Scripps Institution of Oceanography, the Rand Corporation were quite happy to converse there with us. It was always fun to introduce two local intellectual eminences who had never met before, but it was still more satisfying, of course, to see in print something that had started from the dialogue in these floating think tanks.

I imposed medium-monastic restrictions on myself, and the editorial staff, concerning political and governmental involvements. I didn't want Time Inc. people moonlighting as speech-makers for presidential candidates, and in 1960, as editorial director, I had put out an edict to that effect. I required staff members to take a leave of absence, for a minimum of three months, if they wanted to work for candidates for national office—i.e., politicians our magazines would be writing about. Our people were free to work for candidates we wouldn't be writing about, or indeed to run for the local school board if they felt like it, and a few did. We had staff members on leave with the Nixon and Kennedy campaigns in 1960 and the Nixon, Rockefeller, Humphrey, and Robert Kennedy campaigns in 1968. I didn't try to stop anybody from contributing money to campaigns, but never did myself. I would write the candidate or his handlers promising that the money thus saved would go to "churches and colleges of the liberal arts."

I served on a presidential task force on education, one of the nonpartisan "Great Society" panels that Lyndon Johnson assembled in 1964. This was interesting work—quite a lot of work—and I declined a couple of invitations to serve on equally interesting and arduous-sounding study groups in the first Nixon term.

There could be dangers in getting too close to presidents, as I thought Luce had done with Eisenhower. I never felt we were in that difficulty in the 1960s and 1970s. Lyndon Johnson tried to lean on us a few times, but we didn't give. During Watergate, Nixon's operative Charles Colson (in the bad old days before he was Born Again) tried to pressure me once or twice but wasn't very good at it.

In fifteen years as editor-in-chief, I was asked once by the director of the CIA to withhold publication of a story. William Colby appealed to *Time* and several other publications not to print their discovery that the *Glomar Explorer* had succeeded in lifting one section of a Soviet submarine, accidentally sunk in the Pacific, from the ocean floor. The section might be rich in intelligence booty, and the Soviets might not be aware we had it up. I thought the request made sense and complied. A day or two later, the *Los Angeles Times* published the information, and then the rest of the press followed, *Time* included. As the *Times* reasoned, too many people knew about the story for it to stay secret very long. I was content that we weren't the first to break it.

The heaviest pressure on the editor-in-chief came not from Washington or "business" or the board of directors, but from those 1,400 editorial people—and their expectations of the company—and from the competitive position of our magazines. Which brings me now to the long fight to save our biggest magazine.

X

The Big Red Goes Down

Long before I had any responsibility for *Life*, I had a personal relationship with the magazine. I first met *Life* in England—an American student two years away from home, devouring everything in Vol. I, No. 1, November 23, 1936. It showed me the latest doings of Franklin Roosevelt (the editors thanked him for having such an expressive face), construction of the Fort Peck Dam in Montana and Saturday night at the nearby saloons, Helen Hayes and her new play, the NBC studios in Rockefeller Center, and a good-looking Kappa cheerleader at Northwestern (same sorority as my mother and sister, though they were not cheerleaders). There was "local" picture news for me, too— Edward VIII opening Parliament; a dance aboard HMS *Valiant*; Winston Churchill, caught by candid camera at some white-tie banquet, fingering a sore tooth. There was a Russian peasant taking a shower, Rio de Janeiro's beautiful harbor by night, Mussolini strutting, a Spanish militiawoman ready to fight. What a world to be seen for ten cents (from an American newsstand), $7.00 a year by sea mail to the United Kingdom.

A little later, having now become a newspaper reporter, I might even claim some distant professional kinship with *Life*. While I was covering fires, shootings, and civic meetings in Washington, D.C., and even pulling some assignments that rated a photographer as well, *Life* was creating American photojournalism. The magazine unleashed the power of the printed picture, and it hit me both as reader and as aspiring reporter. If as an editor in later years I was somewhat more attentive to the visual than many word men are, it was in part the effect, a kind of shock effect, of the first few years of *Life* arriving in my first few years as a journalist. The traditional word-minded approach to the telling of a story, the explaining of a situation, could grant pictures a certain supporting role: "Here, by the way, and in case you wondered, is what Senator 'Cotton Ed' Smith of South Carolina, this fellow I am telling you about in print, looks like." The idea that the picture could tell you as much, or even more, than the journalist was hammering out on his typewriter was something to think about. I never thought, then or now, that a picture was axiomatically worth ten thousand words—depends on the picture, depends on the words. But the picture is indeed a mighty force in itself, and I was lucky to learn that at a time when it was not a commonplace in journalism.

In my next experience with *Life*, during World War II, I marveled at the enterprise and courage that so often put *Life* photographers in the midst of the battles that I was studying in dispassionate intelligence documents. The documents and the *Life* pictures were each a part of the reality.

After the classic Alfred Eisenstaedt photo of the sailor kissing the nurse in Times Square on V-J Day, *Life*—like everybody else—had some postwar adjusting to do. And in fact, though not quite ten years old, *Life* was already being "re-thought." But a freshman writer on *Fortune* had no need to know about that and could enjoy a little of the glamour that *Life* conferred on everybody who worked for Time Inc. And by the 1950s, it seemed as if *Life* and the era were made for each other. *Life* was now the biggest magazine in the world, and, through most of the 1950s, the richest. This was the magazine that could publish a complete Hemingway novella, *The Old Man and the Sea*, in a single issue; cause the U.S. Air Force to fly twenty-one different types of operational planes in a single formation for a "group portrait"; order all the governors in the United States to stand on an outsize map of the country, holding up state signs. (Well, almost all: Tom Dewey stood on New York, over near Buffalo, but wouldn't hold up his sign.) For all its free-spending ways, *Life* was sweetening the Time Inc. profit-sharing accounts of everybody who worked for *Time* and *Fortune*, and it was helping subsidize the costly start-up of *Sports Illustrated*. Even when Luce and the brass in the early 1960s officially declared the existence of a *Life* "problem," the mood of the staff, publishing as well as editorial, was gung ho. "The Big Red," the ad salesmen called their magazine, like a football team or an army division.

So now, April 1964, I was editor-in-chief of this great American institution. And one of my problems was to keep it from seeming institutional. For all the pride my new place on the *Life* masthead gave me, and for all the fun that came with it, *Life* was now my toughest job. In spite of the good picture sense I thought I had, I knew I had less general feel for *Life* than for our other magazines. And I grasped—though incompletely—some of the commercial hazards waiting out there for *Life*.

After the long round of *Life* "re-think" described in chapter VIII, and the succession of George Hunt as M.E., the recovery from the small but shocking losses of 1959–61 had continued, but this was still not a robust publishing property. In 1964, *Life* made just $4,465,000 on revenues of $192,000,000, a precarious 2.3 percent.

Hunt had a talented and expensive staff of about 320 people, not a few of whom, on any given night, were struggling to create the magazine's squared-off captions. The fate of nations might not depend on it, but it was imperative to get five characters out of a particular sentence (in a story that just might touch upon the fate of nations). Not several words, which would be easy enough, but five characters. No more, no less. This kind of thing could keep people up until 2 A.M. But still, and mainly, they loved it—the rigors a part of the esprit, of course, and the magazine's appeal as a place to work almost undiminished. The proximity to the famous photographers, the glimpses of an actress or statesman in the corridor (doubtless on the way to lunch with the M.E.), the constant parties—quite a place. Some unknowable number of bright young people who would have sought out *Life* in the 1950s may have gone to TV in the 1960s, but the magazine was still attracting plenty of first-rate talent.

The *Life* this staff was putting out in the mid-1960s was to me a better magazine than the *Life* of ten years earlier. George Hunt was accelerating some of the changes in *Life* that Ed Thompson had started toward the end of his long tenure, and George was introducing more changes of his own. This *Life* was usually powerful, often beautiful. There were majestic treatments of classical Greece, Rome, Alexander, the Bible, ancient Egypt, including the very modern technology of moving the treasures of Abu Simbel to high ground before Nasser dammed up their stretch of the Nile. (All of these special acts and series were of course put to profitable by-product use by Time-Life Books.)

Life's superb corps of staff photographers, some two dozen—spending raw film and expense-account advances with equal vigor—brought in their take from all over the world. Editors and story "designers," hunched over layout tables and light boxes, culled this prodigious harvest. On the Hunt *Life*, they liked to play pictures big, often "bleeding" to the edge of the page. (The distinctive red band was even stricken from the cover, so the photo could bleed to the bottom.)

This *Life* was a little more sophisticated than the *Life* of the 1950s, a little less folksy. It also was more a magazine of mood, even emotional vulnerability. The journalism was more personal. Signed columns and reviews were introduced. Writers of big text pieces, staff as well as outside contributors, were encouraged to *feel*, in print.

The feeling could sometimes slop over. The editors wanted to do a big story, soon after the Kennedy assassination, on the national "climate of hate" that, they felt, went far to explain Lee Harvey Oswald's deed in Dallas. I suggested to Hunt that there was in fact less racial, religious, ethnic hate in America in the 1960s than throughout most of our history. I reminded him: "Of the fifty-odd Congressmen who opposed U.S. entry into World War I in 1917, at least half (including the sainted Bob La Follette) were openly anti-Semitic, and thought 'Jewish bankers' plus J. P. Morgan were dragging us into the war. Hatred and fear of Catholics? Compare 1960 Presidential election with 1928." What *Life* finally published was not the original indictment—the printed article called Oswald "a lone fanatic"—but a sufficiently caustic profile of particular "fear mongers" and a reasonably sober appraisal of their following.

I was griped by a *Life* excerpt from a new book by the Trappist monk Thomas Merton, deploring pretty much everything about America, especially the pretensions to culture. "Some striking language here and there but in general a banal sort of indictment, and just plain foolish in a good many spots. I must admit also that I'm irritated, perhaps uncharitably, at hearing all this from somebody who's shut himself away from the world for 25 years."

The magazine was uneven, as anything put together by so many people, in so many different journalistic modes, dealing with so many different subjects, is bound to be. I say that calmly enough today, but twenty and twenty-five years ago, I found it harder to accept. I would complain of "jangly-jerky-jumpy visual quality . . . too many different typographical styles . . . too many top-of-the-lungs headlines." A fair number of pictures were played *too* big, and stories could certainly go on too long—sometimes one spread too many, sometimes worse. "Too much Existentialism," I noted one day in 1964, "straddling 26 pages of the magazine. Too many more or less identical pictures of Sartre, who isn't all that much fun to look at." I could never reconcile myself to some of the atrocious advertising face-offs. "I know we need the ads but we can at least control the nature of the editorial matter that's going to have to contend with them. It ought to be text whenever possible. Certainly it shouldn't be *The Last Supper* overwhelmed by Sucaryl tablets and Rambler station wagons." And the quality of reproduction was a chronic affliction, accentuated by retrenchments in paper weight. I pleaded: "Shouldn't there be somebody around here who can say, 'This is lovely film as we look at it on the light box, but it's the kind of thing that just doesn't come out well in print in the magazine'?" I had known some previous frustrations in asking this question as M.E. of *Fortune*, and I didn't get a good answer at *Life*, either.

Despite the changes in attitudes and atmospherics, none of *Life*'s basic editorial interests had been abandoned. The magazine kept its keen hard-news instincts, and the increasing availability of fast color gave a new dimension to its coverage of great events. Hunt liked to rip up the magazine at the last minute (as Thompson had). These crash closings had to be cleared with me; I don't recall ever refusing one.

For Winston Churchill's funeral, Hunt went all out. He postponed the normal closing deadline by three days, chartered a DC-8 to fly to London, set up a photo lab on the plane, then flew forty people to Chicago, where they arrived with all film developed and the story spreads laid out, ready to be rushed to the R. R. Donnelley plant. (George invited me to ride along, but I thought I shouldn't take up space the working press might need.) The result, in the issue of February 5, 1965, was a magnificent twenty-page color story: the lying-in-state in Westminster Hall, the procession to St. Paul's, the services there, the march to Waterloo Station. (Sir Winston had planned the proceedings himself.) *Life*'s story was on the presses in Chicago a few hours after the burial at Blenheim, ancestral seat of the Churchills.

I didn't ask how much the DC-8 had cost. It was worth it. In fact, I knew it was not all that much; the bill for the chartered plane (minus individual airfares, to be exact, for all the *Life* people who needed to be in England and/or Chicago) would have been small change next to all the other costs of a large-scale, late-closing, fast-color lead. And George's flying photo lab became another chapter in the *Life* legend, along with *Life*'s preemptive purchase of the Zapruder film in Dallas (he was the amateur who happened to catch the JFK assassination) and the sequestering for some hours of Lee Oswald's wife and mother.

Death and violence abounded. *Life* covered the Six Day War in the Middle East and two thousand and more days of Vietnam, including the immolation of Buddhist priests, napalm bombing, the horrors of My Lai, the savage battles for Hue and Khe Sanh. Paul Schutzer, a *Life* photographer, lost his life advancing with Israeli troops near Gaza, and another, the great Larry Burrows, was killed covering the "incursion" from Vietnam into Cambodia.

Life and the astronauts were practically family, especially to Loudon Wainwright, who knew them better than any other journalist. When Grissom, White, and Chaffee died in the fire on the launching pad, in 1967, there were no pictures of the hideous event itself, but Loudon's captions for *Life*'s photo-album story of the three men and their wives and children might have hit the reader just as hard as "live" camera coverage.

The next year, Martin Luther King and Robert Kennedy were murdered, and *Life* preserved what everybody had already seen on TV and some depths and details everybody had not seen. In its treatment of the battlefields at home—Birmingham and Ole Miss, Watts, Newark, Detroit—*Life*'s long-standing civil rights sympathies were plain in pictures and text.

Hunt brought investigative reporting into the magazine; exposés of political corruption, the Mafia, and in 1965 a searingly intimate photo essay on a young Manhattan couple destroying themselves with cocaine. "We are animals in a world no one knows." It was a more remarkable story then, of course, than it would be today.

The lighthearted *Life* was still publishing, as attentive as ever to Hollywood, Broadway, anything new in entertainment, fashion, fads and parties, scandal, glamour. This was a magazine wise in the ways of press agents, with its own touch of tabloid instincts and cynicism, a pride in being with it, an awareness that *Life* was in show business itself. Looking over Hunt's schedule of upcoming covers one day in 1964, I had to ask him: "What's this . . . August 28 . . . BEATLES?" George patiently explained that these were four young men from Liverpool who would be starting their first American tour that week, and they were going to be big stuff.

Life, the tour guide, the professor of pain-free courses in science, medicine, geography, nature, was still very much on the job. I thought the best animal story *Life* ever did was the "Great Cats of Africa," a series that brought the reader extremely close to the action—especially in an unforgettable encounter between a leopard and a doomed baboon in the Kalahari Desert. The photographer was John Dominis, deploying Land Rovers, beaters, couriers, and (so he liked to claim) glass beads for trading, but above all courage and patience.

But of everything the instructive *Life* did during my tenure, I was proudest of a special issue on Picasso, December 1968, because so many *Life* talents and resources came together to create an extraordinarily perceptive and inviting introduction to this artist, for 8,500,000 subscribers—and, as we then claimed, another thirty to thirty-five million pass-along readers, many of whom surely regarded this as pretty weird stuff. Along with magnificent reproductions of the man's work (magnificent for such a massive press run), brilliant appraisals of his meaning and influence (brilliant for any size magazine), there was of course a splendid photo essay, "His Women: The wonder is that he found so much time to paint."

Hunt, along with the original inspiration, contributed a charming account of his exploratory call upon the great man, "as hard to see as de Gaulle himself." The day Hunt was to see him, a message came that "the Master was at work and in no mood to see anyone.... Picasso is, after all, Picasso." George waited around for several days at Mougins on the Côte d'Azur—not too rugged duty—before the imperial nod finally came. (I was reminded of the tendency of dictators, tin-pot as well as big-league, to make the journalist come to the capital and wait, when on a very different mission, George and I were soon to share the waiting-room experience in Moscow.)

George eventually was received, and after his audience, Picasso's wife Jacqueline "nudged me and whispered, 'Kiss him, kiss him.' Picasso is 5 feet 3 inches; I am 6 feet 3 inches. I bent double and did so on both cheeks." The issue was two years in the making, and once when I expressed some impatience to see something in print, Hunt launched into a fervent argument that the final product was going to be the greatest issue in *Life*'s history, or if not, he would resign. "Oh, come on, George," I said. From there on, my supreme contribution to the Picasso issue was not to interfere with any aspect of it.

"Picasso" crowned a great editorial year for *Life*. It was a year of nonstop news, highly pictorial news: the Eugene McCarthy campaign—the derided "children's crusade" that helped drive Lyndon

Johnson from office; the rioting that followed the Martin Luther King assassination; the King and Bob Kennedy funerals; turmoil on the American campus and among the young of Western Europe; the tragically brief "Prague Spring"; black American athletes giving the clenched-fist salute as they received their medals at the Mexico City Olympics; the Democratic convention that triggered violence in the streets of Chicago; Hubert Humphrey and Richard Nixon; Jackie Kennedy and Aristotle Onassis.

But even in this glorious year for photojournalism, I was uneasy about *Life*. We had finally abandoned the idea that *Life* could be for everybody. We told ourselves we were aiming at the top third of the audience, by income and education, and Hunt refined that further: In case of doubt, aim at the upper half of the top third. But if *Life* was not for everybody, it was still about everything. This made it all the more urgent, I felt, that the many separate strengths of *Life* should be melded into a magazine of clear editorial personality. In 1968, to the barely muffled groans of the editors, I summoned them once more to the "definition" drill. (There had been one of those only two years earlier, with Harry Luce a vigorous participant just months before he died.) *Life* editors, managing and otherwise, were powerfully tempted to pick up the latest issue of the magazine and say, "Dammit, *that's* what *Life* is!" A better answer, I told them, was to pick up a month's worth of *Life*s—"That's what we are!" But in July 1968, I had picked up three months, thirteen issues, and "I came away from my re-reading still uncertain just what our formula is."

I opened the conversation, in a memo of course, with a sketch of magazine personalities:

> I suppose the shortest history of the fall of the *Saturday Evening Post* [it had just folded] is that its comfortable small-town personality of the 1920s and 1930s became obsolete, and it never found a new character. *Collier's*, more sophisticated than the *Post*, more daring, more urban, more liberal, did very well competing against the *Post*, then was outflanked by *Life* and never found a coherent new personality for itself. *Reader's Digest, New Yorker, Playboy*—all huge successes and easy for readers (or detractors) to characterize in a word or two. I don't think of *Look* as having a clear-cut personality; I would be nervous if they developed one.

Hunt's top 16⅔ percent of the U.S. audience was better educated and generally more sophisticated than it had been in 1960; it was busier, more deeply and broadly curious, but at the same time much more easily bored. "These people," I suggested, "may have changed even more than *Life* has in the 1960s." I urged:

> urbanity, sharper wit, bite and more of a sense of irony than in the present magazine, more intellectual reach and critical depth—all good things in themselves but more important, they might also be the qualities that could connect all the other *Life* strengths into a rounded, complete personality.
>
> Ponder, please, the implications for *Life* itself of a story *Life* has been covering very extensively: the Eugene McCarthy phenomenon. Most of his votes in the primaries, all the analysts agree, came from upper and upper-middle income, upper-education neighborhoods, heavily suburban. Precisely *Life* territory, in other words. And what is the McCarthy "style" these people find so appealing? Cool, calm, understated, sardonic, etc.
>
> Just the point of view I would have liked to see applied, for instance, to the article on the "Human Potential Movement" instead of the essentially earnest and sympathetic approach we took. Why can't *Life* get just as mad at the intellectually pompous, pretentious or half-baked, as it does at more obvious malefactors, like the Mafia? Or why couldn't we have looked with some wit and detachment at "The New Rock," instead of trying to establish a spurious identity with it, through frenetic typography and utterly uncritical point of view?
>
> If we kidded the HPM weirdos at Esalen, or had some fun with New Rock, we would of course shock some of our readers (and staff). That would be a very good thing.

And I couldn't refrain from a plaintive note about *Life* fashion stories: "I am generally entertained and left feeling well-I'll-be-damned, but I'm not sure that's the idea." I kept urging fashion stories about what actual people actually wear. No sale.

I spared the busy editors from writing memos back, and we chewed over my July memo in a long round of meetings and meals. The senior editors agreed that more "bite and urbanity" would be fine, but the general sense of their response was that there was nothing wrong with *Life* that a lot of strong stories, even more than they were already running, wouldn't fix. All of us, as it turned out, were wrong or just irrelevant. If you could ordain the news, it would have been hard to arrange for a bigger pictorial year than 1968, and it didn't do much for *Life*. And the kind of magazine personality, tone, embracing point of view that I was asking for required some reflective, almost detached, qualities that didn't necessarily go with getting this big brute to press every week, full of the requisite hard news in great pictures, soft news in great pictures, stretches of beauty, self-improvement, features, fun. I was probably asking for the moon.

Early in 1969, Hunt punctiliously reminded me that I had told him, when he was appointed managing editor in 1961, that I thought seven or eight years was a long enough term for the M.E. of *Life* or *Time*. I don't know whether George was hoping I would ask him to stay on longer, but I didn't. The years of volcanic enthusiasms and explosions had a cost, and I thought George deserved to take things easier. I also thought the magazine was coming into a period when a cooler style of editorial administration, as well as fresh editorial perspectives, would be helpful. (I am happy to report that I last saw George turning seventy, in 1988, busy with family, painting, sailing, in cheerful transit between his homes in Florida and Maine.)

I appointed Ralph Graves, age forty-four, an unflappable fellow with a fine *Life* résumé—correspondent, writer, Chicago news bureau chief, articles editor, assistant M.E. Ralph had sharp news instincts, taste and wit, and a strong sense of order. When I appointed Tom Griffith as editor of *Life*, replacing Ed Thompson, I had borrowed Graves from *Life*, to serve a while as my deputy. I had a very good look at him in this role, and confirmed my impression that he was the right man to succeed Hunt. Griffith was effective in the editor role, presiding over the editorial page, reviewing all text pieces and columns with "policy" coloration, and serving as a tactful counselor to the M.E. The two got along very well.

The glorious job I gave Graves became the toughest any Time Inc. M.E. has ever held. The M.E. of a new magazine that is struggling to make it—*Sports Illustrated* in the 1950s, *Money* in the 1970s—is under heavy strain. So, too, if only briefly, the M.E. of a flameout like Time Inc.'s launch of *TV-Cable Week* in 1984. But these stresses scarcely compare with those pressing in on the editor of a long-renowned magazine that is—slowly—failing.

None of us knew for sure that *Life* was failing, but the top management was privy to grim figures unknown to the outer world or to *Life*'s own staff. I kept Ralph almost totally informed. Competitors, advertisers, ad agencies could count *Life* ad pages for themselves, but they didn't know the magazine's costs or bottom line, and behind that, the crucial circulation renewal rates. These were the most sensitive figures of all, and they were discouraging.

The ruinous "numbers war" among the big picture magazines grew out of their increasingly desperate attempts to match the audience figures the most popular TV shows could claim. By the late 1960s, TV had long since achieved "saturation"—one or more sets in 99 percent of the households in America—and whatever might be said about the quality of the programming, the technical quality of the picture had improved steadily, and almost everybody was seeing it in color. For coverage of fast-breaking news—especially Vietnam and the Middle East—TV's new skills with the hand-held camera and satellite transmission were a potent resource. As a medium for advertising toothpaste, cereals, detergents, and other products differentiated mainly by their brand names, TV had become more cost-effective (horrid coinage) than the big magazines.

Fighting back against TV and each other, the magazines virtually gave away circulation to whomp up the numbers. More and more audacious claims were developed as to "audience"—paid circulation times four or five, equaling numbers of people supposedly looking at a magazine, thus arriving at thirty to forty million—as big as the audience for a hot sitcom. At one point in this destructive cycle, *Life* was charging less than ten cents a copy in some new-subscription solicitations for a magazine that was costing twenty-six or twenty-seven cents a copy to produce, let alone mail. New circulation brought in at these distress-sale prices naturally did not perform well when asked to renew at prices closer to *Life*'s true costs. The need to replace, once or twice a year, these large layers of unnatural subscribers with millions more equally fickle readers imposed punishing promotion and mailing costs on *Life*, *Look*, and the *Saturday Evening Post*.

The *Post* was the first to fold, in 1968. (Its president later reflected that the three magazines were running "a race to the poorhouse.") *Life* bought some of the *Post*'s circulation, and in various ways acceptable to the SEC and Anti-Trust helped this much-beloved publication off the stage. I was among the Time Inc. executives pleased with the deal. *Look* had been outsmarted. One down, one to go. (Not to be said out loud, of course. What do we have lawyers for?) In that hour of brief euphoria, *Life* raised its circulation guarantee from 7.5 million to 8 million in October 1968—and, effective January 1969, to 8.5 million—and now claimed an audience of forty-eight million, "larger than any other single communications medium." (I had been wiser when I was younger. In a 1960 memo to Luce, I had urged stabilizing *Life* circulation at seven million, and from there on, "just grow with the country" and "let *Life* be passed by whoever thinks they can stand the gaff.")

The costs of maintaining these new numbers now added new strains to the shaky P & L. *Life* had had very respectable profits as recently as 1966, its best year in a decade—a net of $10 million on revenues of $165 million. But in 1967, the net fell by half, and in the fabulous picture-news year of 1968, the magazine barely broke even. In 1969, *Life* went into the red, never to get out.

It fell to Ralph Graves to carry out painful staff retrenchments, to adjust to economies in paper weight, to fortify staff morale, put down panicky rumors, and all the while get out the magazine and keep hunting for the editorial miracle that would turn everything around. As ad pages declined, editorial space had to shrink, by two to four pages an issue. Editors had always fought for more pages for their favorite stories, and now these in-house struggles grew more heated; Graves had to arbitrate. He asked me more than once if he couldn't just do away with the editorials, releasing a page for pictures. I thought since *Life* was hospitable to so much opinion and emotion— in pictures as well as in text, from staff as well as from outside—that it was especially important for the magazine to have a visible spine of principle and viewpoint. Though it could sometimes be one huge headache, as I readily admitted to Graves, deciding exactly what *Life* did stand for. This despite the vigilant oversight of the page by Tom Griffith (and Ed Thompson before him) and distinguished writing over the years by the versatile John Knox Jessup. (When I once told Jessup I was a descendant of John Knox, he politely told me Knox had never married and I must be a collateral descendant, as was he.)

State-of-the-world ponderings, for editorial-page purposes, often blended into state-of-*Life*. I treasure a communiqué Graves sent me after a long session where four or five of us had been earnestly pondering a *Life* editorial on various threats to freedom of the press: "Hedley—It is my impression that neither 'editorial integrity' nor 'freedom of the press' nor 'prior restraint' nor 'Third World censorship' can hold a candle to 'belt tightening' as a heartfelt issue."

Graves once sent me a striking list of "used up" stories and proposed an editorial on how fast the press and public can lose interest in topics that seemed red-hot only a few months or weeks earlier. I thought it would be an unfortunate subject for an editorial. "It hits pretty close to home. Some of what ails *Life* is this speeding up of the whole news consumption cycle and with it the public's increasingly 'high' standard as to what is sensational. Partly the doing of TV, partly the dramatic skills of the best newspapers and magazines, notably including *Life*, and in good part the high rate of history in the 1960s."

Only a week or two after Graves took over, however, he was putting together one of the most talked about and influential articles *Life* ever ran. He invited me to his layout room one morning to look at the lead story he proposed for the issue of June 27, 1969: "One Week's Dead in Vietnam." It would consist of the individual pictures, high-school-album size, of the Americans killed during the week of May 28 to June 3. There had been 242 of them—about the normal weekly toll in that season of the war—and *Life* had been able to track down pictures of 217.

The story was the idea of Loudon Wainwright, who had written a spare and deeply moving text block of just two paragraphs; the only other type in thirteen pages would be beneath each picture— name, age, service, rank, hometown. Wainwright, Graves, and a few others stood by silently while I read the text block and looked for a long time at the young faces on two sample spreads. The editors were not at all sure I would let them run the story—which added up to a devastating statement against the war, even one more day of it—at a time when the *Life* editorial page and *Time* articles were arguing for a phased American disengagement to protect whatever possibilities of survival remained to South Vietnam. (Time Inc. views on Vietnam, and mine, are related in more detail in chapter XIII.)

I told Graves to go ahead. Wainwright, in his book on *Life*, recalls that until I was safely out of earshot and off the editorial floor, "We kept our elation to big grins and noiseless hand-clapping. Middle-aged schoolboys who'd turned the principal around. We were high with it, very high." I had not, in fact, been turned around. I still thought gradual withdrawal was the right American policy, but I also thought it was right for *Life* to show the heart-wrenching cost. Only the day before, by coincidence, I had seen on a Harlem street corner an immensely dignified black woman, dressed in black, eyes glistening behind her glasses, standing alone and holding, as though on a tray, a fresh American flag, folded in the proper triangle. She disposed me toward Loudon's story.

I also decided, in the minute or two it took me to make up my mind, that we owed the story to those two hundred and more families who in pride and numbness had loaned those treasured pictures to

Life. (Imagine telling them the article wasn't going to run after all.) I remembered, too, as a young Washington reporter hating myself for intruding on some grieving family to ask for a picture of a son or daughter just dead—an auto accident, a suicide—and marveling at the courtesy, even gratitude, with which I was received. Many families felt the picture in the paper lent some importance to their loss.

The Graves *Life* was not the consistently magnificent magazine of my pipe dreams, but it was sometimes superb and seldom less than very good. The Vietnam roll call got Ralph's *Life* off to a strong start, and within weeks came two big news events that furnished the magazine great raw material: the first walk on the moon, and Woodstock. The two events also defined an editorial difficulty for *Life*. The moon walk, for all the advanced technology that went into it, was a venture born out of the "old" America: patriotic, persevering, optimistic—some dollars and guts and know-how can get anything done. A part of *Life*'s heart was still with that America, and much of the country still felt at home there. Woodstock was a different America, 400,000 of the young drawn to a muddy pasture to listen to rock and celebrate the counterculture. This was the America of long hair, pot, coed dorms, gentle in its peace ballads, fierce in its shouted obscenities, frightening or outrageous to many *Life* subscribers, as some of them wrote us, especially when *Life* seemed to identify with the revolt—as indeed many of our younger staff did. Kent State followed in 1970, and even at the Miss America contest in Atlantic City, Miss Montana raised a clenched fist to protest Vietnam. The split within America accentuated *Life*'s long-standing "personality" problem.

A *Life* coup, most welcome in that painful period, was the capture of the reminiscences of Nikita Khrushchev. This remarkable material may have come our way as an indirect result of an interview George Hunt and I had in January 1969 with Soviet Premier Aleksei Kosygin, co-boss with Leonid Brezhnev (though Brezhnev was gradually becoming more equal). It was the first interview Kosygin had given Western journalists in two years (the sudden summons came after we were kept waiting three days), and *Life* made a big splash of it, with a cover and fourteen color pages. In the Middle East, said Kosygin, the United States was "playing with fire." In Vietnam, we were waging "a dirty war," our bombing was "barbaric," and our allies in Saigon were "a bunch of dregs." Kosygin's mournful face remained completely calm through two hours of this, but his interpreter, Victor Sukhodrev, put so much animation into his work that Hunt, as he said later, found himself incensed at the messenger. The tirade had reached a kind of climax where Kosygin was denouncing "your shameless aggression, your Fascist generals," your this and your that, when he had to get up to answer his phone. As he left the table where we had been talking, he spoke a few more words. Victor translated: "Not you personally, of course." When Kosygin came back from his phone call, I said, "Thank you very much," and he almost smiled.

The Kremlin's top press people thought the interview had gone very well, and they were cordial when I brought up a long-standing request for the reopening of *Time*'s Moscow news bureau. The Soviets had closed it down four years earlier because a *Time* cover story on Lenin included the fact that he had had a mistress. (Once in Washington, when I was pursuing the Moscow bureau question with the Soviet ambassador, the genial Anatoly Dobrynin, he said, "How would you like it if some Soviet publication said Abraham Lincoln had had a mistress?" If you can document it, I said, we would think it was a hell of a story.)

Time's Moscow bureau did get reopened, and we sent as our correspondent Jerrold Schecter, a resourceful fellow who soon showed a flair for working in and around the seemingly monolithic façade that confronted an American journalist in Moscow. Soon after he got there, Schecter was notifying his boss, Murray Gart (who had succeeded Richard Clurman as chief of our News Service), that he could have access to a mass of material that purported to be Khrushchev's own words about his rise to power and his days in power— recorded in the obscurity of his retirement. Schecter came to New York to brief me. Gart went to Moscow to deal with the Soviet intermediaries and to listen to a sample of the tape.

Eventually, *Life* and Little, Brown paid $750,000 for 180 hours of tape and 820 pages of transcripts, all rights worldwide—book, magazine, newspaper—to Time Inc. We retained Voiceprint Laboratories of Somerville, New Jersey, and they confirmed that the voice on the tapes was indeed that of the man who spoke (and waved his shoe) at the United Nations in 1960. Strobe Talbott, a Rhodes scholar who had been a summer intern in our Moscow bureau, broadened his Oxford studies of Russian literature to include the translating and organizing of the Khrushchev material. Edward Crankshaw, the English Kremlinologist and biographer of Khrushchev, wrote an introduction. Another key figure was the fellow who put up *Life*'s share of the money, Garry Valk, who had just been elevated to the toughest publishing job in Time Inc. "How would you like to be the brand-new publisher of *Life* . . . ," I asked at a staff dinner. "You have begun to sense that your office is not exactly rolling in unexpended monies, and a couple of fellows come by and close the door and outline this somewhat, shall we say, unconventional transaction. . . ."

Life published four articles, and Little, Brown produced two volumes, *Khrushchev Remembers* and *Khrushchev: The Last Testament*. In the first volume, we were not allowed to label the work "memoirs." "Reminiscences" were permitted, and he could "Recollect" or even "Remember," but it had to be clear that Khrushchev had not actually *written* this. This "deniability" was important to Khrushchev and his family. In the second volume, published in 1974 after his death and excerpted in *Time*, we were allowed to call the work a memoir.

Among Soviet scholars in the United States and Western Europe, after some initial skepticism (well aired by other publications that would have loved to have the stuff themselves), it gradually came to be accepted that this was the real thing. After Khrushchev's death in 1971 ("I'm tired, almost too tired to go on," he says in one of the final taping sessions), Time Inc. presented the original tapes to the Oral History Collection at Columbia University.

"I now live like a hermit on the outskirts of Moscow," the book begins. "I communicate only with those who guard me from others— and who guard others from me." About Stalin: "Something admirable . . . something savage . . . unquestionably something sick." He heard Stalin say toward the end of his life, "I trust no one, not even myself." Khrushchev told more than the West had previously known of his own maneuverings in the years after Stalin's death in 1953, and how he destroyed or neutralized political rivals to become the undisputed leader by 1958. He insisted, however, that he believed in collective leadership, not dictatorship by one man. He wanted somewhat more openness in Soviet life, and stressed that he was a good Communist "who wants a more enlightened Communist society." He told nothing of how and why he was himself deposed in 1964, though he revealed of one of his successors that for a time under Stalin, the career and life of Kosygin "was hanging by a thread. I simply cannot explain how he was saved from being exterminated." (It would have been an interesting question for George Hunt or me to have asked that skillful survivor.) Khrushchev obliquely criticized Brezhnev for the 1968 invasion of Czechoslovakia, but was by no means soft about NATO or Wall Street. He thought Presidents Eisenhower and Kennedy, despite the capitalist stain, shared his central idea about foreign policy: "I certainly was afraid of war. Who but a fool isn't?"

Only three or four Time Inc. people, not including me, knew for certain who the Soviet intermediaries were and how the Khrushchev material was moved out of the USSR. (That information is still locked in a Time Inc. safe.) If you asked the classic Leninist question, Who gains?, it seems to me likely that the project had the blessing of Yuri Andropov, then head of the KGB. "Liberals" are sometimes to be found among the secret police—an anomaly that runs back to czarist times. The police know more than most Soviets about the country's true condition, and may feel a little more security in thinking about it.

Andropov had been a protégé of Khrushchev's, and believed in his de-Stalinization policies—though this did not stop him from joining (as a member of the party secretariat) in the overthrow of Khrushchev in 1964. By 1969–70, Brezhnev was halfway rehabilitating Stalinism, or, as Khrushchev wrote, "They're starting to cover up for the man guilty of all those murders." The Khrushchev material would not be published in the Soviet Union, of course, but Andropov may have seen it as some kind of message to the West that there were still anti-Stalinist influences within the leadership. A dozen years later, when Andropov succeeded Brezhnev, he was the chief patron of Mikhail Gorbachev. Across two decades of Kremlin politics, the Khrushchev reminiscence sends a prophetic signal.

And now, in the age of Gorbachev, there is apparently a possibility that the authorities will allow Khrushchev's words to be published within the Soviet Union. In 1988, Time Inc. and Columbia University turned over the original tapes and transcripts to the Khrushchev family.

Ralph Graves, throughout his tenure as M.E., had to cope with intermittent critiques from his editor-in-chief, though I was generally admiring of his *Life*, as I often assured him. He usually took my natterings in good humor. Not invariably. "I hope you feel . . . as pissed off as I do," he wrote another editor about an issue I liked less than they did, by "Hedley's niggardly praise." Another *Life* editor thought my critiques "sometimes read like a finicky teacher's notes in the margins of high school essays."

I was not deterred. "I don't think an editor can simply declare a picture extra-interesting by playing it big. . . . I don't like question-mark heds [headlines] for questions that aren't going to get answered. . . . Hugh Sidey writes better and better. Sometimes he seduces us. He is allowed [in a report on Nixon's trip to China] to overplay the mysteriousness-of-it-all: We won't know for 50 years what really happened, etc. I suspect Hugh himself will very shortly be telling us almost everything that happened." In an otherwise good story on drug smuggling, why should a magazine claiming forty million readers try for "such hard-breathing identification with a few thousand smugglers—The Big Crackdown Is On and Its Target Is You!" A Germaine Greer cover story "had an unfortunate tone of marveling that a feminist should like men."

I was vexed when the leftish journalist Robert Sherrill was signed up to review a book by the newly leftish Ramsay Clark, former attorney general, and still more vexed when the book-review editor replied to my complaint that after this he would try to avoid "known radical names," and it was probably a mistake to review the book at all. "Please," I pleaded, "that is not the point! A 'radical' reviewing a 'conservative' or vice versa is fun. Buckley reviewing de Toledano would not be fun. I think Clark's book *should* have been reviewed (his transformation into New Left hero is a good story), preferably by somebody at least a little Right of him."

A returning Vietnam veteran, billed as being "in limbo": "Some fine pictures and perceptive reporting, but too many maudlin patches. 'Limbo' isn't really quite borne out by the story: he has his '71 'Cuda, apartment, babes, even feels more at home in Midland than he did before he went to Nam. (Incidentally, do girls old enough to go to a man's apartment really chew bubble gum in Midland, Texas?) The fact that he hasn't yet been able to find a part-time job (a fairly recent search, one gathers) doesn't seem too desperate a situation (he can still afford 'action in bars and clubs'), and it's not convincing that 'Vietnam somehow left him without the potential for making new plans and having new dreams.' "

Marlon Brando, by Shana Alexander, pegged to the appearance of *The Godfather*: "Splendid layout and cover. Much of the text is very good indeed, though I do begrudge some of the indulgences and insider-asides of such personal journalism. Between the Editor's Note and Shana's own text, quite a bit is made of her being assigned to the story seven years ago, but then, so what? 'I weave, fate unweaves, or lawyers do. . . .' Tell us more, or less." Well, she did tell us more. She and Brando have been seeing and debating each other, off and on, and "we have become yoked together, two oarsmen rowing in opposite directions in the same boat. Actor and writer, extrovert and introvert, Aries and Libra, yang and yin and you-name-it—could any two creatures be more unlike than Marlon and me? We do not understand each other at all." Odd provenance for a profile, but maybe a little bit of a grabber, after all. However, I couldn't refrain from a few Old Journalism questions: "Somewhere along the way I would like to be reminded where Brando came from, what movies he's been in other than *Streetcar*, how old he is these days, current wife, if any. It used to be joke subject-matter that he was so wooden but Shana says she and 'most people' now consider him the greatest natural-born actor alive. This was news to me and very interesting—do the critics generally agree? And is he good in *Godfather*? (Is it a good movie?)"

The most serious editorial disagreement I ever had with Graves arose from a series on "The Brain," published over two months late in 1971. This was built around remarkable pictures by the Swedish photographer Lennart Nilsson, showing things that nobody but a brain surgeon had ever seen before. And more than the surgeons had seen. It was wonderful stuff but I thought it went on much too long, sixty-nine pages spread over four issues, some of the pictures repetitious or indecipherable, some of the diagrams and captions almost impenetrable. I thought it had the makings of three superb pieces for a total of thirty-five to forty pages. It seemed especially wrongheaded, I told Ralph, that at a crucial moment in *Life*'s circulation promotion efforts, three *covers* should have been given over to textbookish treatment of the same (however useful) piece of anatomy.

In several tight-lipped conversations, Ralph was unshakable in defense of the series as printed. At one point, I wondered out loud if he and I were really discussing the same magazine. As he told me many years later, he did not take this as the rather ominous remark I meant it to be. In fact, I thought for a while of replacing him with André Laguerre of *S.I.*, a move that at least one or two of my business-side colleagues had advocated. I decided that Ralph this once was entitled to be wrong in a big way. (I didn't consider it remotely possible that it was I who was wrong on this one.) I also thought that relieving Graves would be making him the scapegoat for all the *Life* troubles beyond his control.

Within weeks, Graves and I were sharing, in total harmony, a colossal journalistic embarrassment. This was the great Howard Hughes hoax, sold to McGraw-Hill and *Life* by the gifted con artist Clifford Irving. Hughes loomed as an El Dorado to book and magazine editors: the eccentric billionaire—back when that was a lot of money—collector of Hollywood stars and starlets, aircraft designer, expert pilot, owner of the mysterious (except to *Fortune* readers) Hughes Tool Company. If he would ever tell it, what a story! It was Clifford Irving's essential inspiration that Hughes's highly publicized eccentricities—his secretiveness, reclusiveness, phobias, quirks, paranoia—could be used to explain away every sort of doubt about a purported "authorized biography." Irving approached McGraw-Hill, which had published his biography of the art forger Elmyr de Hory, and claimed that he had sent that book to Hughes, who was then holed up in the Bahamas, and that Hughes wrote him back a kind of fan note, which then led to a correspondence in which the recluse agreed to have Irving become his biographer. "It would not suit me to die," Hughes/Irving grandly pronounced, "without having certain misconceptions cleared up and without having stated the truth about my life."

McGraw-Hill asked Graves if *Life* would be interested in the magazine rights. *Life* would be. Graves informed me and his publisher, who told his bosses, Andrew Heiskell and Jim Shepley. Knowledge of the deal was very tightly held within Time Inc. Hughes/Irving insisted work on the book proceed in total secrecy, which of course suited McGraw-Hill and *Life*, who did not want news of their sensational publishing property to leak until the book was written and ready for the presses. It was a break for Irving, whether or not he was aware of it, that the editor-in-chief of Time Inc. had had those long and weird phone conversations with Hughes ten years earlier (chapter VI), and was thus disposed not to be surprised at any strange Hughes stipulations—and there were many before we were through—that Irving invented. Graves, McGraw-Hill, and Irving were now seeing a good deal of each other. Irving was diligently forging "Hughes" letters and titillating the editors with tidbits from his voluminous "interviews" with the mystery man, from which the book would be wrought and the *Life* articles excerpted.

Somewhere in those weeks, I told Graves that the next time he was seeing Irving, I would like to sit in. This was out of sheer curiosity, not a hunch that anything was fishy. Ralph said Irving and his McGraw-Hill handlers wanted as few Time Inc. faces at the table as possible. I was all too understanding.

On December 7, 1971, McGraw-Hill announced publication for March 1972 of a biography based on hundreds of hours of interviews with Hughes. *Life* would run excerpts for three weeks in a row, just before the book came out.

The Hughes Tool Company, acting for their master in the Bahamas, immediately denounced the book as "a fake and a fraud." The scam began to come apart—slowly, because Irving had constructed it very ingeniously and because he got some lucky breaks. He took a lie-detector test with inconclusive results. A handwriting expert said of the most crucial of his "Hughes" letters that there was not one chance in a million that it was a forgery.

By late January, however, the whole hoax had unraveled. Instead of three articles *by* Hughes, *Life* got two cover stories *on* Hughes, Irving, and his swindle. The cover for the first was a drawing of "Hughes" by an artist friend of Irving's (probably not a bad likeness, based on old photos and allowing for subsequent wear and tear). The second cover was a glamorous photo of a Danish baroness, Nina van Pallandt, who said Irving had been busy with her in Mexico part of the time he claimed to have been interviewing Hughes. *Time*, keeping any trace of a brotherly smile completely wiped off its face, ran one cover story on the affair. Irving was even more opportunistic than our magazines. After he got out of jail (seventeen months for conspiracy to defraud, forgery, perjury), he brought out a book called *Hoax*.

In a postmortem at Time Inc.'s February 1972 board meeting, I told the directors I was sorry I hadn't read Irving's previous book, *Fake*, much sooner than I did. "Perhaps I would have been moved to ask Graves some astute questions to ask McGraw-Hill to ask Irving. Perhaps not." When I did read it, I found it "a tiresome, repetitious book, and unless you happen to be very much interested in modern art and especially the world of art dealers, which there's no evidence Hughes ever has been, it's a terrible bore." But when Graves first relayed the McGraw-Hill proposition to me, no money asked up front, I thought we were getting a shot at "a fabulous journalistic property. . . . Or putting it another way, I would have hated to wake up some day last summer and read that *Look* was about to publish the autobiography or authorized biography of Howard Hughes." The directors retroactively shared my competitive reflex. I concluded my recital: "I think we have to assume there is going to be some harm done, at least temporarily, to our reputation . . . a certain credibility gap to overcome. Some nice people come up to me and say you have had millions of dollars worth of free publicity, or what wonderful innocent fun you've given all of us, etc. No doubt these are offsets to the embarrassment of being fooled, but not quite total, I think."

One of the outside directors, the Chicago banker Gaylord Freeman, asked if I had considered firing Graves. I said, No, Graves had kept me fully informed all the way. I had approved all his major commitments and decisions, and if anyone was to be fired, it would have to be me. Nobody offered a motion to that effect.

The directors, considering the gruesome numbers they had been looking at for so long, remained remarkably good-tempered about *Life*. There were no recriminations from the board over past follies in circulation policy, and there was never any board pressure to set a deadline for *Life*'s survival. Losses were now running at an annual rate of seven to eight million dollars. And in 1970, Congress approved a Postal Reorganization Bill, which would lead to increases of 170 percent in *Life*'s postal costs projected over the years 1972–76. *Look* had retired from the circulation war, cutting its base from 7,750,000 to 6,000,000. In 1971, we had considered (not for the first time) taking *Life* biweekly, which would have produced big cost savings and, of course, big revenue losses. Studied in detail, the fortnightly did not seem promising. We considered possible narrowings of subject matter and audience (Youth? Women?), but were daunted by the difficulties of converting an established magazine into something its readers and advertisers were not expecting. We considered more special issues and supplements, but the risk was a blurring of character. The impending postal-rate increases made a reduction of trim size superficially attractive, but the big page was as much a part of the trademark as the famous logo. So we decided to fight it out as the recognizable *Life*, the only big-page, fast-closing pictorial weekly. We cut the swollen circulation to seven million. We had belatedly conceded the mega numbers to TV. Then, in September 1971, *Look* decided to fold, and *Life* took over a part of its subscription list. But within two months, we were again cutting back our circulation (now to 5.5 million), lowering ad rates, and raising subscription prices.

We were running out of places to retreat to. By the beginning of 1972, Jim Shepley had concluded the situation was hopeless, and so had Arthur Keylor. A former general manager of *Life*, now group vice president for all our magazines, Keylor was a very sharp analyst of magazine economics. Andrew Heiskell, publisher of *Life* in its golden years, was torn between sentiment and growing dismay at the numbers. I was insistent that *Life* deserved at least one full year to see what would happen with *Look* out of the way. *Life* got the year. As things turned out, the disappearance of *Look* did *Life* no good at all, and indeed may have contributed to the feeling among many advertisers that the big picture magazine was simply obsolete. I was in San Francisco in September 1972, on an election-year political tour, when Heiskell phoned me with news of a disastrously weak response to the latest circulation mailings. Advertising bookings, none too healthy to begin with, were also slipping badly.

As late as November 1, however, I still had an outside hope that some new inspiration in defining *Life*, and sorting out its ingredients, might somehow save the magazine. I showed Heiskell and Shepley the rough draft of a long memo I had written over several late nights, thinking it might be included with the *Life* materials that would go to the board for its November meeting. They complimented me on my memo, but Heiskell in turn showed me some 1973 P & L projections even more dismal than figures I had seen only a fortnight earlier. I had to give up.

In November, on management's recommendation, the board authorized "suspension" of *Life* with the issue of December 29. Suppliers and advertisers—all of them important to the other Time Inc. publications—deserved notice, and it looked as if December 8 would be the last decent date. For legal reasons, the final formal decision to suspend had to be delayed until a meeting of the Executive Committee of the board in the late afternoon of December 7. The scenario required that this decision should be taken after the closing of the New York Stock Exchange, that the exchange should be asked before it opened the next morning to suspend trading in Time Inc. stock, and that the Time Inc. unit of the Newspaper Guild be notified of the decision before it was announced publicly.

Earlier that week, keeping a long-standing commitment, I had gone to a "Dartmouth Conference" on Soviet-American relations in Hanover, New Hampshire, and I had been planning to fly back to New York on the morning of December 7. The day before, it began snowing hard, and my flight was canceled. During an all-night bus ride through the blizzard, down from White River Junction to the city, I thought about *Life*, and about the grievous things I would have to do in the coming hours. From the short, sad Executive Committee meeting in Heiskell's office I went to a short, sad meeting in my office with the top *Life* editors. I had told Graves two or three weeks earlier—I couldn't leave such a close comrade in the dark—and he then had the excruciating job of assigning stories for the January 1973 issues as though they would be published.

On the morning of Friday the eighth, the management faced several hundred *Life* editorial and publishing people, assembled by over-night notice, in the company auditorium. I told Dorothy at breakfast I would rather be shot than do what I was about to do. This was only a slight exaggeration. I had told Heiskell and Shepley I would lead off so it would not seem as though the business side was dragging me along. So I stood up and announced the news, learned overnight or by then guessed by many of the staff, but still there were gasps, murmurs of "Oh, no," and tears. And, inevitably, wisecracks—Associate Editor Frank Kappler, *sotto voce*: "That's the strongest rumor yet." I said *Life* had been losing money four years in a row and we were looking at still worse numbers for 1973 and 1974. (At a press conference afterward, I gave out a figure of $30 million for the four-year loss. The 1973 projection, which I did not specify, was for a loss of $17 million.) "We have persevered," I said, "as long as we could see any realistic prospect, within a reasonable time span, of a turn-around in *Life*'s economy. We can no longer see such a prospect. We believe the publication of *Life* beyond 1972 could begin to be a burden on the other magazines and activities of Time Inc. and on the long-term growth of the company."

It was the most painful day of my professional life, though my pain was hardly to be compared with that of people losing their jobs. About half the editorial staff were soon placed within Time Inc. Many found good jobs elsewhere. Some availed themselves of the generous severance settlements and early-retirement pensions to take things easy, and some, despite the severance pay and the company's place-ment efforts, had a very tough time. I doubt if any of the editorial staff were particularly thrilled to read that Time Inc. stock shot up six points after trading was resumed that Friday.

And in that way, a familiar presence in American life disap-peared. When a long-established newspaper is forced to fold, the sense of loss in one city can be intense. When a great national magazine goes under, the sorrow is more diffuse but no less real. The closing of the *Saturday Evening Post* in 1968 brought on a national wave of nostalgia—for the freckle-faced newsboy, the gatherings around the stove in the country store, the Sunday-afternoon spin in the new family car, and all the rest of the vanished America of Norman Rock-well. But *Life* was very much about midcentury America—about it and a part of it. It was about New York and Los Angeles and Chicago, as well as Minneapolis and Brainerd, and it was about the whole great world beyond. People wrote us that they would always remember just where they were and what they were doing when they heard the news about *Life*.

For me, as a believer in the justice of the box office, there was an unavoidable sense of failure as well as loss. The marketplace had no civic obligation to keep *Life* going. That was up to us who worked there. For years afterward, I brooded as to what we could have done differently. To this day, I haven't come up with it. And to this day, I am glad we kept trying for one last year after rational analysis said we should give up.

XI

Inventing New Magazines, Improving Old Ones

As *Life* was going under, all of us in management found some relief in the fixable problems of the other Time Inc. magazines, and in ideas for new magazines. I relished the nonstop effort to make our successful magazines still more successful, and just as each managing editor wanted to think he was putting out a better magazine than the one he had been handed, so too, the editor-in-chief, multiplied by the number of Time Inc. magazines.

I found the invention of new magazines, under the roof of a big and complicated corporation, a challenge not only to creativity but also to a range of management skills, including the political. We were not working in a garret. The company had great resources—in talent, dollars and reputation—to put behind a promising new idea. The corollary was that a new magazine was born with "the Time Inc. standard of living," all the fringes and comforts of a benevolent company—premium office space in mid-Manhattan, lush expense accounts, free flu shots. When and if a new magazine was meeting all of its out-of-pocket costs and carrying its share of Time Inc. overhead, it was considered to be in the black. Then, when its return on investment reached a rate comparable to the ROI for other Time Inc. publications, it could be considered successful. Those who had brought the magazine to that happy point were denied the biggest thrill—and hazard—of the entrepreneurial calling. The new magazine was not going to make them rich, but if it had flopped, they weren't going to go broke. They would be well paid either way. Ego satisfaction was also subject to some limitations. Credit for a successful new publishing idea needed to be shared generously—this came easy because it corresponded to the facts. Blame for a fiasco— fortunately, we didn't have one—would have been well distributed. And finally there was the job of shepherding the promising idea past one or two layers of publishing and editorial executives, then the directors. Andrew Heiskell and I had the final word, subject to the board's approval, as to go or no go, but we also cared—within reason—about the views of the top dozen or so editors and publishers.

From a romantic view of how seminal thoughts get thought, it may seem that I have just described a perfect formula for sterile groupthink. But I would argue, to the contrary, that in just half a dozen years in the 1970s, Time Inc. developed three important new magazines, within—not despite, and maybe even because of—the corporate environment. The three creations were *Money*, *People*, and a monthly *Life*; the conversion of *Fortune* from a monthly to a fortnightly was not unlike the launching of a new magazine.

I had always been fascinated by the extraordinary burst of American magazine-making that brought into being, within two years in the early 1920s, *Time*, *Reader's Digest*, and *The New Yorker*. What was it, and could it be bottled? We have never seen anything comparable since, and I doubt if Harold Ross ever sat down with DeWitt Wallace and Harry Luce to talk it out. (I'm not sure Luce and Ross ever spoke to each other after the 1936 Wolcott Gibbs profile in the *New Yorker*.) But I took satisfaction, in the very different climate of the 1970s, not only that Time Inc. could come up with new magazines, but also that our size and success were in no way inhibiting the launching of new magazines by others. Some of the others indeed were Time Inc. alumni. I was not ready to fret about monopolistic tendencies in the media, or see Time Inc. as any sort of juggernaut. *Time* had spawned scores of imitations all over the world, some very successful. More than a hundred *Life*-like magazines came out after *Life* invented the form. *Scientific American* was rebuilt, and made highly profitable for some years, by former *Life* science writers. *Newsweek*, started ten years after *Time*, was and still is full of former *Time* editors and writers. And so on.

In 1970, we began to go at the invention of new magazines in a quite systematic way. My old R & D section evolved into the Magazine Development Group, headed by Bernie Auer, the former publisher of

Time, and Otto Fuerbringer, who had stepped down two years earlier as managing editor of *Time*.

After the original burst of magazine-making by Luce and his colleagues—*Time*, *Fortune*, and *Life* all created within thirteen years—it was eighteen years before Time Inc. tried again. After *Sports Illustrated* was launched in 1954, Luce's stubborn persistence during the long years of red ink came in part from a determination that nobody should say this middle-aged company had lost its creative flair.

I had had a small and indirect part in the decision to start and stick with *S.I.* As managing editor of *Fortune*, I was publishing a series of analytical pieces on "The Changing American Market," industry by industry, and these articles became an influence in the strategy of many corporations. The whole series stressed the growth of the "moneyed middle class," and one of the articles offered spectacular projections of the growth in demand for leisure-time products and services; these projections figured in the Time Inc. calculations of the circulation and advertising potential of a sports magazine. From *Fortune* days on, I felt reasonably comfortable with income statistics, demographic trend lines, and the like, and this was helpful in digesting some of the research of the Magazine Development Group.

The real engines of growth for Time Inc. (and other successful publishing companies) in the 1960s and 1970s were three: national prosperity; the explosion of news—in Washington, the world, the economy, science, technology, medicine, culture, entertainment; and expansion of the "serious audience," mainly a function of population growth and the spread of education, but also in part the work of journalism itself, including Time Inc.

Even as the serious audience was expanding, the rise of TV represented a vast broadening in access to mass audiences. People intent on characterizing "American taste," *the* American audience, *the* American public, could become confused by all the different things that were going on. Today, except for television, in almost every form of address to the American mind, the appeal is toward higher levels of education and sophistication, and there are now tens of millions of people on these upper levels. So magazines of a high order of intellectual appeal can have audiences of a size we wouldn't have dreamed of a generation ago. The great impact and force of television should not be allowed to obscure all the other changes in the quality of the American audiences.

It is a pity, in a way, that TV could not have been invented around, say, 1850. Then, if some philanthropist had put a set in every home, we would now think of it as part of that wonderful historic process of giving some education to everybody—extension of the free public-school system, Americanization of the immigrants, the opening of Andrew Carnegie's free libraries in several hundred towns. We could think of TV as one more step in the growth of a reasonably literate democracy, which in time would embrace many audiences, some of them highly discriminating.

So Time Inc. management was trying to understand, and if possible anticipate, the underlying forces that shaped the markets and audiences for Time Inc. services. To find a new magazine somewhere in there, the editors had to see a worthwhile editorial purpose, had to see that the magazine could be something Time Inc. would be proud to publish. And if it looked all that good editorially, did it have, by the best hunch of our publishing executives, a better-than-even chance of making good financially? Could it compete against all the other things out there for people to read, look at, do?

From a long list of piled-up magazine ideas, Auer and Fuerbringer proposed that four were worth dummying (printing up sample layouts and text) and testing: *Money*, *Well* (health), *View* (movies, TV), *Camera Month*. Auer developed the concept of a magazine "cluster." None of the four possible magazines felt like a weekly, and the economics of a monthly could be very difficult, but four monthlies could share publishing staff people, particularly in circulation, and offer a respectable total circulation, perhaps up to two million, salable to some advertisers as a package. In market tests, *Money* and *Well* did best, and the other two were put on the back burner. (I was glad a little later to let *Well* go there, too. Health and medicine have always bored me journalistically—a considerable blind spot.)

Fuerbringer developed a very convincing prospectus for *Money*, which would help the reader make money through smart career and investment choices, save money as a consumer, and still have some fun at spending money. I was enthusiastic about everything except the flat-footed name. I had always liked the allusive quality of *Time* and *Fortune* as magazine names. But you can't beat something with nothing, and *Money* it was. (The runner-up name, which I found positively unpleasant, was *Advantage*.) When and if a magazine becomes successful, its name, of course, sounds absolutely right.

So after another pause of precisely eighteen years in magazine-inventing—the interval between *Life* and *S.I.* was 1936 to 1954—Time Inc. launched *Money* in October 1972. It was a proud moment for me: the first new magazine start-up during my tenure as editor-in-chief. If *Money*'s paternity was a collective, as with most Time Inc. ventures even in Luce's day, I was still one of the three or four Founding Fathers. Fuerbringer was the most Founding. My final okay, along with Heiskell's, was the one that committed us.

The first issue had a nice heft to it: one hundred pages, almost half ads. The ad bulk didn't mean much, however; selling a lot of space in the first issue of a new Time Inc. magazine is no great trick. Circulation was 225,000, a bit under budget. Much of the editorial content was useful "service" journalism, some even useful and lively—a much-to-be-desired combination—and some was amateurish. In menu balance and tone of voice, the issue betrayed considerable confusion as to whom we thought the magazine was aimed at. Vol. I, No. 1, accurately foretold some persistent editorial problems.

Still, it gave me comfort that this new Time Inc. magazine, frail and ill-defined as it might be, was out there in the marketplace on the day that I had to announce the folding of *Life*. The Magazine Development Group that created the original *Money* dummies had not been set up as a hedge against the death of *Life*. But when *Life* did go under, the young *Money*, Vol. I, No. 3, just out, suggested that Time Inc. believed it still knew how to think up new magazines.

A further symbolism was that the managing editor of *Money* was thirty-two, the youngest Time Inc. M.E. since Luce and Brit Hadden were trading the editorship of *Time* back and forth. He was William Rukeyser, lured from the *Wall Street Journal* to *Fortune* a few years earlier, then spotted by Fuerbringer for the *Money* job. I liked the message, inside the company and outside, that Time Inc. was still a place where a very young man could get a shot at running a magazine. Bill was in for a more strenuous opportunity than either he or I anticipated.

Within a year, it was plain that *Money* was going to fall far short of the company's original projections. Instead of breaking even in 1974, after total losses of only $2 million, we were now looking at break-even as far off as 1978 or 1979, after losses of at least $7 million. Circulation had not advanced much, despite a onetime bonanza when a surprisingly large number of former *Life* readers opted to receive *Money* for their unexpired subscriptions. (The black-humor line around the office was that these people thought they were going to get regular small-m money.) Advertising volume was fairly healthy, but rates had been held low and subscriptions priced relatively high, on the theory that our readers should pay something like the true cost of producing this magazine that was going to help them save and make money.

The editorial content of the early issues was tilted heavily, however, toward the young modest-income consumer, and some of the articles had a kind of nagging Naderite quality, while the promotional mailings had attracted older and more affluent readers who thought they were going to be getting sage investment advice. Renewal rates suffered accordingly. Illustration that was erratic and sometimes downright ugly did not help matters. I labored with Bill on the art, which was not his strongest suit. He was thoroughly savvy about our subject matter, however, prolific in story ideas, and a brisk and sensible text editor. Not the least of his virtues was the ability to operate on a lean editorial budget. I spared him a few of the nastier financial projections, but he knew the general precariousness of his work, and went about it with admirable confidence. He had to put up with an army of editorial kibitzers. While Lou Banks was still editorial director of Time Inc., I asked him to take *Money* under his wing, and then he continued regular critiques as an MIT professor (and Time Inc. consultant). The series of deputies who rotated through my office in the mid-1970s offered Rukeyser their advice, and of course I made mine plentifully available.

Slowly a *Money* personality began to take shape. We began awarding a bit more income to our mythical typical reader, a somewhat higher level of spending choices, and we adopted an assumption that if he didn't already have interesting investment decisions to make, he expected to be there soon. At the same time, subscription and newsstand prices were cut and we conceded to ourselves that circulation would have to climb to at least 800,000, more likely a million, for the magazine to be viable. The other publications in the original four-magazine "cluster" were not going to come out at any time soon, if ever, so *Money* would have to make it on its own, not as part of a nice little family of monthlies. *Money* circulation did build, to 300,000, then 400,000, and 500,000 was in sight, but at heavy promotion costs. So there was no immediate improvement in the bottom-line figures, and the projected cumulative losses kept worsening.

By early 1975, Jim Shepley was ready to kill the magazine, and Heiskell was leaning that way. There were published rumors that

Time Inc. was about to give up on *Money*. These had to be denied, of course. Folding a magazine is like devaluing a currency; you have to deny right up to the last minute that you are considering any such thing. Nobody, as the Madison Avenue cliché runs, wants to advertise in the last issue.

Compared with the decision to kill *Life*, this one would have been almost painless. *Money* was very small and new, the staff could be absorbed elsewhere in Time Inc., and the company had no great sentiment invested. I had a hunch, however, that with just a little more time, the magazine could show it would eventually make it. I came up with an argument I still admire: Time Inc. had been saying publicly that *Money* was making good progress and we had also been saying publicly that *People* (started in 1974) looked like it was going to be a great success. Wouldn't our truthful claim about *People* come under suspicion if we were now to confess we had only been kidding about *Money*? I proposed: Let's give *Money* until the end of this year to look healthier; if it doesn't, we can kill it, and by then we should have solid enough figures on *People*'s success that we could safely make them public.

We did give *Money* until the end of the year, and it did get healthier. (At a May board meeting, we formally committed ourselves to folding the magazine in December if the outlook was not greatly improved.) Circulation finally began to expand at more acceptable costs, and in December had passed 600,000. Rukeyser had carried out several editorial improvements, including more attention to ways of having fun with money, as well as a redesign of the graphics. Indeed, we kept reinventing the magazine, issue by issue, all through its first three or four years.

In early 1976, in the elevator lobby on the thirty-fourth floor of the Time and Life Building, we put on a little ceremony in which the copper cover plates of the first issues of *Money* and *People* were bolted to a ceiling composed of plates for notable issues of all the other Time Inc. magazines. (One of my own works is up there—the twenty-fifth-anniversary cover I designed for *Fortune*. Nervous employees have sometimes wondered just how safe it is to stand under all that metal. For myself, if there had been some engineering miscalculation, I wanted at least to be standing under my own cover.) The ceiling party (there was a party, of course) was by way of saying that these two new magazines had arrived, for good. In the case of *Money*, this was a rather audacious ritual, and nobody from the SEC was invited. We were scooping the P & L statements by a good many quarters. But toward the end of 1977, *Money* was breaking even on an out-of-pocket basis, and in 1981 it made money after assuming its full share of Time Inc. overhead. It has been making plenty of it ever since. Whew.

I once told a *Money* staff meeting that Time Inc. management did not aspire to have *Money* compete with *Sports Illustrated* for the house record for most painful magazine start-up. "Since statistics, records and superlatives are so important in the sports world, we're going to let *S.I.* hold the all-time record—most money invested in a Time Inc. magazine before it broke even. That trophy has been retired." In the event, *S.I.* barely edged out *Money* for years in red ink (ten versus nine, before meeting overhead), but was far ahead in total cumulative losses—a monthly can't leak money as fast as a weekly.

People had zoomed off on a totally different trajectory. When *Life* folded, two of its assistant M.E.s came to work in magazine development. Phil Kunhardt, a superb originator and editor of mood and "feel" stories (a shy, sweet man who seemed to be permanently blushing), was working with a small crew of ex-*Life* people on the *Camera Month* possibility. The other was Richard Stolley, who was working on a dummy for *View*, focusing on the world of entertainment, which of course had been one part of the old *Life* franchise. Stolley was one of the few top Time Inc. editors who would have been good at putting out a tabloid newspaper. (Ed Thompson was another, and, oddly enough, so was Luce. Harry had interesting insights about things that might matter to "the subway straphanger," and when I once asked him how long since he'd been on the subway, he said that wasn't the point.) Stolley was aggressive with fast-breaking hard news, knowing about the softer stuff, an ingenious and inexhaustible fellow who thrived on pressure. Which, as things turned out, was just as well.

Fuerbringer, one morning in March 1973, was on his way to update me on the various mad-editor experiments going on in his lab. Outside my office, he ran into Andrew Heiskell. Andrew, on his way somewhere else, tossed off a billion-dollar idea (maybe two billion at today's prices). "Hey, why don't we start a magazine called *People*? Sometime when you're not too busy, might be fun to think about it for a couple of weeks." Otto thought so and was still beaming when he tried it out on me. I said, Sure, why not, though I had no more idea than Otto of exactly what we were talking about.

Otto began finding out. He recruited a small team headed by Phil Kunhardt to work with him on an editorial outline. With characteristic energy and enthusiasm, he delivered within weeks a detailed and persuasive description of a *People* magazine. A publishing prospectus was worked up—circulation, cover price, ad rates, budget projections. The editorial team produced a pasteup dummy good enough to encourage us to proceed to a printed dummy, dated August 20, 1973. An even-bustier-than-usual Elizabeth Taylor was in the foreground of the cover photo, Richard Burton in dark glasses in the background, "Split Up" as caption. (Cover billing also for "Ethel and Kids," Joe Namath, Ari Onassis, Liza Minnelli, Bardot, Loren, and a dozen other celebrities, as well as "Topless Beaches.")

The managing editors of our other magazines were not captivated. I had invited their reactions to the Liz-and-Dick dummy, and they obliged, in person and by memo. "Sleazy . . . cheap . . . popcorn . . . frivolous . . . fan magazine." Henry Grunwald of *Time* wrote me a judicious memo, but I heard secondhand he "hated the thing." From Cambridge, Lou Banks wrote me in anguish. "Crushingly depressing. A palpable piece of market research journalism without so much as a glow—as it stands—of a constructive idea. And obviously doctored in editing to exploit the baseness of the market . . . an exploitive publication that must by its very nature undermine and erode the substance of *Time, Life, Fortune, Money,* and those wonderful books."

The friendliest word came from Bill Rukeyser of *Money*. With some special sympathy, perhaps, for colleagues struggling to bring off a new magazine idea, Bill summed up: "A lively short read."

Bill was right. The dummy was very brisk and entertaining reading (I have never been able to speak of "a read"), and I thought the many things wrong with it—e.g., cheap-looking typewriter type, lots of smirking and leering—would not be too difficult to fix. Unless one felt that the whole idea of an easy-reading magazine about people (and no issues, problems, questions except as they made particular people interesting) was entirely unworthy of Time Inc. I felt, to the contrary, that our Time Inc. journalism should be versatile enough— indeed, democratic enough—to create a *People* the company could be proud of. I suppose there was also a personal, professional challenge to me somewhat similar to the one *Sports Illustrated* posed to Harry Luce: Could I help create an important new national magazine of which I myself was not necessarily the first and most natural reader?

The dummy issue had been printed in a run of 110,000 copies and "test-marketed" in eleven cities chosen to equate with a national draw of one million. (Luce would have been disgusted. Editors and publishers should simply *know* whether a magazine will work.) The elements in the dummy that bothered me, and my M.E.s so much more so, didn't seem to trouble people in Seattle, Minneapolis, and Houston all that much. The issue tested sensationally well.

Shepley was ready to go from Liz-and-Dick to launch, but I wanted to see a better dummy, produced in something approximating a real-time news week. Fuerbringer and I gave Dick Stolley a shot at putting out this one. (He had once confessed to me the laudable ambition of "running something.") Phil Kunhardt was put in charge of the single-subject special issues of *Life*—he had already brought out a handsome one for the twenty-fifth anniversary of Israel—by which we hoped to keep that valuable logo alive.

The next *People* dummy, Billie Jean King and husband Larry on the cover, was more professional than the first, greatly improved in typography and more assured in tone of voice. Public opinion in the Time and Life Building, in the latrines and elevators, at the M.E.s' luncheon table, was less hostile but scarcely admiring. I didn't invite M.E. reactions this time; I didn't want to put them on record a second time against something I was now convinced of. I did remind them that when *Sports Illustrated* was launched, many *Time* and *Fortune* editors were snooty: Why on earth is Time Inc. publishing a sports magazine? And though none of us had been around at the time, I suspected that when the original *Life* was being discussed, there were *Time* and *Fortune* people who thought it was a disgraceful lurch into sensationalism.

I was ready to go bail in a memo to the board of directors, October 15, 1973:

"Why *People*? Well, why history, literature, movies, news?

"*People*'s purpose is to tell things that are worth knowing—and fun to know—about people in the news, people in action, people on the way down or up, people acting like people. Some of *People*'s people will be famous. Some, not yet famous, may deserve to be.

"*People*, without being preachy about it, will have a point of view, a set of standards, an attitude about celebrity as well as the celebrities.

"*People* is not a gossip magazine—but people will certainly talk about it."

The first issue, dated March 4, 1974, was strikingly similar, in pace and mix, to the *People* that came out last week. It was Fuerbringer and Stolley who really thought up the magazine, taking off from Heiskell's one-paragraph idea. Andrew had in fact thought more seriously about the magazine than his casual style of idea-dropping suggested. Mindful of Church/State sensitivities, he had the tact and wit to let the editors do the detailed inventing. For myself, I claim one managerial virtue that helped *People* get started: the ability to become enthusiastic about somebody else's good idea. And perhaps also: the ability not to get flustered if my enthusiasm is not shared by people I respect.

One of the Founding Fathers was a woman, Clare Luce. She had been very sympathetic, in correspondence and conversation with Heiskell and me, during the final painful months of our struggle to keep *Life* going. She was quick to see the potential in *People*, and when Andrew sent her a courtesy copy of the first printed dummy, she was much more pleased than my M.E.s. She also fired back six pages, single-spaced, of perceptive critique and catchy story ideas. She foresaw, quite accurately, that our problem, if any, would be advertising, not circulation. (The reverse of *Money*'s problem.) When I told her in a subsequent letter that I thought of her as "one of the principal parents" of *People*, she did not demur. She may have suggested something very like it at one time or another, as indeed had many people in and out of Time Inc. I might have dug out my 1960 memo speculating on a "10-cent news-and-fun picture magazine" (see chapter VIII). Harry Luce, had he been alive, might have claimed *Time*'s continuously popular "People" page, introduced in 1923, as the real progenitor. But the catalyst was the disappearance of the big picture magazines in 1971–72 and the availability in 1973 of *Life*'s expert photojournalists for other work, and it was Heiskell who saw how they might come together.

Mia Farrow, pensively touching a pearl necklace to her lips, as she was about to do in *Gatsby*, was the inaugural cover. Fifty cents and fifty editorial pages. The stories inside included Marina Oswald: "Finally at peace with herself"; Alexander Solzhenitsyn: "From his own writing a chilling account of a good man's arrest"; Gloria Vanderbilt: "A fourth marriage that really works." The magazine sold 978,000 copies and carried twenty ad pages, both slightly below forecast.

For *People*, it was the beginning of a very rugged year. Getting out this magazine every week was very different from assembling two dummies, over two months, and then one issue for real. Stolley had to create a whole network of stringers and freelance photographers all over the country; the old *Life* network helped, and *People* lined up a field force with remarkable speed. There were times during that first year—hard to believe later—when I really worried whether there was enough material to keep this up. How soon could we go back to Liz or Frankie or Jackie after just doing them, and if there was some limit to that (I surely hoped so), where were the "fresh faces" deserving to be famous? Some of the faces fresh to me were not to me all that deserving. Stolley recalls having to explain to me three or four times during the first year that the unfamiliar name I saw scheduled for next week's cover was an immensely popular rock star, and that I finally asked him, "Dick, how many more of those fellows *are* there?" The other Time Inc. editors continued, for the most part, to condescend, which *People* people resented, though it may have helped build a healthy underdog morale.

The publishing side had to contend with sluggish ad orders. Madison Avenue had helped decree that "big picture magazines" were obsolete, but it was uncomfortable with a magazine that did not fit an established category. What *is* this *People*? Clearly not the doomed old *Life* or *Look*—they were a category, at least—or the vigorous *Time* and *Newsweek*—choose one or the other, but many advertisers had to be in a "newsweekly." Not one of the women's "books" (dreadful ad lingo) or the shelter "books," or *Fortune-Business Week-Forbes*. Understandably, *People* was not keen to be "positioned" alongside the *National Enquirer* or *Playboy* or *Photoplay*. Gradually, the vitality of the magazine itself overcame the concerns about category. But first the business side had to master a critical distribution problem. An essential element in the publishing strategy had been to avoid the punitive postal rates that had been so damaging to *Life*'s prospects. *People* would be sold at newsstands, drugstores, supermarkets; subscriptions would be filled on request but not solicited. But Time Inc. had had no experience with a magazine wholly oriented toward newsstand sales, and it took months before *People* was receiving effective display—especially in the crucial supermarket racks.

Then in 1975, *People* took off. Within eighteen months of launch, it was making money out of pocket, and very soon after, paying its share of company costs. Like *Sports Illustrated*, *People* benefited from TV. Some of its subject matter was created by TV, and *People* could deal more candidly than TV with the personalities of the entertainment world. The magazine also benefited from the change in national mores that made many celebrities willing to discuss their personal lives with a frankness that would have been unthinkable only a few years earlier.

Even after *People* had made it, I wanted the M.E. to know I was still reading attentively: "Once more *People* seems intent on affronting mature readers like Mr. Heiskell and myself. Zsa Zsa—the Managing Editor should look so good—is called an 'aging beauty.' Omar Sharif, a mere 43, is described as an 'aging boulevardier.' Actually, beginners-slope training for a boulevardier does not even start until 50."

"Personality journalism," Stolley called it—not new of course, but *People*'s success influenced other magazines, newspapers, and television. The magazine also became a handy label of derision, as in "too trashy even for *People*." If *People* could be vulgar, I felt it was vulgarity in the good sense, *of the people*. I also thought the magazine was making good on my promise to the directors that it would tell us about some people worth knowing. In one issue of early 1975, there was a moving portrait of Dr. Eugene Balthazar, a surgeon retiring from private practice who opened a free clinic in the decaying downtown of Aurora, Illinois, funded from his own savings. There was a lively portrait of Maurice Cullinane, third-generation Irish cop, who had just become chief of police in Washington, D.C., and ordered his motor-scootermen to dismount and walk for at least half of their shifts. "People in the community don't feel the police understand their problems if they're driving around all the time." Also a nice piece on James Herriot, the Yorkshire veterinarian who was writing those gentle books *All Creatures Great and Small, All Things Bright and Beautiful*. Also Nelson Rockefeller, then vice president, and his wife, Happy, and Secretary of State Henry Kissinger and Nancy, vacationing at Dorado Beach, Puerto Rico. Celebrities at a Rockresort, but at least not rock celebrities. The cover of that issue, to be sure, said, "Elvis is 40!"

I found it utterly unembarrassing to head the *People* masthead as editor-in-chief, and as the magazine prospered, I noticed the attitude of other Time Inc. editors mellowing. This was not just appreciation for a new contributor to profit-sharing, but a recognition that the magazine—not for everybody, any more than *S.I.* or *Fortune*—was becoming increasingly professional at what it set out to do. As *People*'s reporting grew more thorough, I even had to plead with Stolley, as I so often had with M.E.s of *Time* and *Fortune*, not to let stories get too long—*keep it moving*.

In 1977, *The New York Times* tacitly conferred a "category" on *People*: They brought out an imitation called *Us*. "Somebody once said," I reminded a *People* staff convention, "that the final test of fame is to have a crazy person imagine he's you. . . . Perhaps you just achieved the final test of fame."

In the same speech I went on to some general musings about fame and celebrity and journalism:

> I predict our cast of characters will grow over the next few years, not merely because we don't want to repeat ourselves too often, but I think the people of interest to *People* are in fact increasing in number. There are fewer toweringly great people in the landscape today than at other times in the twentieth century, but there are more quite famous people than ever before. It may be that as the public becomes more sophisticated, it simply is harder for anybody to be perceived as being great, while all the various engines of exposure make it possible for many people to be quite well known. Many deserve their renown. And that really should be one of the tests of a democratic society, if it's completely healthy, that it is constantly producing more people who merit some attention, and certainly one of the tests of the social value of the press in a healthy democratic society is whether the press is telling us about those people.

When another Time Inc. magazine was in its youth, I once or twice heard Harry Luce talk about *Sports Illustrated* in a way that sounded to me dangerously high-minded. He was tempted to erect a whole moral philosophy of sport. I didn't want the editors—small danger—to think they must intellectualize all the fun out of sports. Nor would I have wanted the editors of *People* to heavy up their magazine with visible moral seriousness. Again, small danger. *People* sometimes made me wince, but I generally found it lively entertainment. It was informative about people worth knowing about, as well as some trashy people I couldn't help reading about, and some others that I could skip. But then I don't read everything in *Foreign Affairs*, either.

On the bleak morning in 1972 when I had to announce the folding of the weekly *Life*, I was careful to speak of it as a "suspension." We were still doing business in the Time and Life Building (and in Time-Life buildings in Chicago, Paris, London), publishing Time-Life Books, putting out Time-Life Films and record albums. We had no interest in selling the *Life* name to anybody, or seeing it picked up off the street. Within weeks, Ralph Graves and others were coming up with ideas for a new *Life*, monthly or bimonthly, quarterly, fortnightly, something. We decided to show the flag with an occasional *Life* "special report," and the first came out in June 1973—Kunhardt's salute to "The Spirit of Israel." This was the big-page, heavy-paper *Life* of the great old days, and despite a cover price of $1.50 and almost no promotion, it sold nearly 600,000 copies. We dutifully noted to ourselves (like politicians) that the subject had a fervent special constituency, but we were still encouraged enough to bring out, in December 1973, "The Year in Pictures." This sold 850,000 copies and from then on, for the next four years, we brought out "The Year in Pictures" each December and a single-subject special issue sometime during the year. These were "One Day in the Life of America" (beautiful vintage Kunhardt, title and idea cheerfully appropriated by the Collins publishing operation for a later book); "100 Events That Shaped America" (965,000 copies—a Bicentennial sellout); "The New Youth" (ho-hum); and my own favorite, "Remarkable American Women." This was a fascinating gallery of 114—including Calamity Jane, Mother Seton, Emily Post, Gloria Steinem, Marian Anderson, many others less obvious, and in the final place of honor, of course, "a tireless partisan of the best in all of us": Eleanor Roosevelt. (I was less worshipful but would not have dreamed of tinkering with the long and rapturous *Life* caption.)

Leading off the year-end special report on 1976, in the last of a dozen or so articles and editorials I wrote for *Life* over the years, I indulged myself in some Bicentennial reflections. First I used my unlimited expense account to take the shuttle to Boston to meet a new governor who sounded interesting:

"Michael Dukakis, son of Greek-born immigrants, sits in his lofty-ceilinged office in the splendid Bulfinch Statehouse, behind him the portrait of a predecessor, Samuel Adams (1794–97). Outdoors there is a December drizzle, and the Governor is remembering a golden weekend in July, 'When the Tall Ships were in Boston Harbor—that was something!'

"Indeed it was. And also in New York, in Chesapeake Bay, Philadelphia and Newport. A Tall Ship even reached Chicago."

America's third century, I thought, was "just too big for the mind to take in; in a collective act of good judgment, journalists, politicians, professors and clergy generally refrained from speculations about how things will be in A.D. 2076." Though if the Bicentennial celebration "was light on bombast," the year was touched with national pride, of a neighborly, good-humored sort. Still, there was "our deepest domestic wound and abiding national shame, racial bigotry. Boston, of the glorious history and brisk young Governor, also supplied us the disgraceful scene on pages 34–35, 'A sad day for Old Glory'."

The photo showed a South Boston demonstrator against busing using an American flagstaff as a lance in a charge against a black man.

The strong sales of the *Life* specials, and the immense success of three anthologies—*The Best of Life, Life Goes to the Movies,* and *Life Goes to War*—all fortified our urge to bring back the magazine itself on a regular basis. In December 1977, Kunhardt summed up the case in a very appealing memo, and I asked him to do a dummy of a monthly. This was also persuasive. A publishing prospectus was almost equally so. By now, sentiment was taking over, and even flint-hearted business-side types were not immune. For all of us in that generation of management, the fall of *Life* was the only serious Time Inc. failure we had known. Even the runaway success of *People* didn't cancel it out. The *Life* chapter cried out for a happy ending. In April 1978, with the blessing of the board, we announced publication of a monthly *Life*, starting in October.

The new magazine carried the "Big Red" logo, even bigger than before, and a colorful cover on hobbyist ballooning, the great red, yellow, blue, gold bags straining the borders of the glorious fourteen-by-eleven page. The issue ran to 138 pages, fifty-six in ads. There were delightful four-year-old pictures, never published before, of President Ford, Secretary of State Kissinger, and Defense Secretary Donald Rumsfeld at a famous Kyoto geisha house where grown men play that game of trying to detach a straw that a girl is holding between her upper lip and nose, while she is trying to steal yours. (I had played the same game at the same house, also a game that was a variant on scissors/paper/stone, also "The Nothing Game," which I thought I had invented to torture my children, but which turned out to be a geisha staple. I vanquished several of the girls—you just stare at your opponent and see who has to turn away first—but the senior geisha broke me.) Another exclusive in the new *Life* was a six-page color story on the Shah of Iran's beachside compound at the Caspian Sea, "a perfect refuge from the tumult of Teheran." The tumult within months was to drive him from his throne. There was a chapter from the new Mario Puzo novel, *Fools Die*. Also nature stories, fashion, animals, archaeology, movies, football, family life, bullfighting, and a touch of discreet cheesecake. The closest approach to hard news was a spread of a teenaged Sandinista ready to fire on Somoza national guardsmen, and five pages of stately color on the investiture of Pope John Paul I.

The issue was a nice $1.50 worth of interesting and inviting stories, the old *Life* mix of beauty, education, action, entertainment skillfully revived but lacking in the topical urgency of the weekly *Life*. The magazine sold very well, however, far exceeding the initial guarantee of 700,000.

Within two years, average circulation approached 1,400,000. But advertising, after the initial bulge, trailed off: the what-is-it problem again. Minus a strong news component, this was clearly not the old *Life*, but it was not easy to say just what the new *Life* was. The editors had to keep on creating the form through most of the new magazine's first decade.

Decisions against the launching of a new venture can also be interesting work. They are not without elements of risk—lost opportunity, lost reward—or abyss avoided?

The most elaborately examined new magazine we did not publish was *Woman*. Over the years, it had tantalized many Time Inc. editors and publishing executives that there were all those women out there, 52 percent of the adult population, doing all that reading and all that spending, and we had no magazine specifically addressed to them. Harry Luce had found this a profoundly uninteresting question. He knew a number of women who read *Time* and *Life* (*Fortune* and *S.I.* did not purport to be for them), and as for sewing patterns, menu suggestions, home decorating tips, and even a bit of gossipy chitchat, well, in the magazine business there was enough work to go around. I was more challenged: What if we could create a magazine centered on the vastly changed place of women in American life? Not a competitor of the *Ladies Home Journal*, nor of *Ms*. We envisioned an audience that would include many readers of the newsweeklies and of the upper-quality newspapers, but we would offer something different from the service any reader, female or male, could get from *Time* or *The New York Times*.

Off and on, over four years in the mid-1970s, we tried to find that "something different." Two of our best woman journalists, Patricia Ryan, a senior editor at *Sports Illustrated* (she had started there as a secretary), and Eleanor Graves, food editor of the weekly *Life*, each had a shot at it. They assembled small staffs and worked up story lists and dummies. We experimented with a *Time*-size mock-up, a *TV Digest* size, a monthly frequency, and a weekly.

I never thought we had it quite right. Nor did the potential readers; a dummy that was test-marketed in several cities in 1977 sold poorly. We set aside the idea, after having spent something over $1 million—not too stiff a price for finding out that a magazine won't work. Eleanor Graves and Pat Ryan went on to top jobs at magazines for men as well as women—Graves as assistant M.E., then executive editor of the revived monthly *Life*, Ryan as assistant M.E., then M.E. of *People*, then to *Life* as M.E.

Thinking up new magazines was only a little more difficult than thinking up ways to improve long-running magazines that were already very good. As successor to Henry Luce, I aspired of course to be more than a curator of the famous magazines he turned over to me. (The New York Public Library calls its more generous contributors "Conservators"; fine for a library.) Most executives, to be sure, consciously or not, are in competition with their predecessors. In magazine journalism, this personal motivation merges with a marketplace imperative: Even the most successful publications must keep improving or eventually go out of business. In my M.E. days at *Fortune*, I had already observed this law as it applied to one magazine, and now I saw it at work more broadly. Newspapers in one-paper cities are under less pressure to improve, but there are no "natural monopolies" in the magazine business.

As editor-in-chief, I believed *Time* and *Sports Illustrated*, as well as *Fortune*, were simply required to get better, and their editors, out of the same mix of personal and institutional motives, felt the same way. The terminal case of not "getting better," which I could never forget, was the weekly *Life*, which was in so many ways a higher-quality magazine in its failing days than in its golden days, but was clearly not "better" in relation to its audience and market.

But if the editor competes indirectly with his predecessors, he competes head-on, right now, with the opposition. This means not just *Time* versus *Newsweek* and *U.S. News and World Report*, but *Time* versus the best newspapers and the television evening news. The alert editor will not be too proud to pick up good ideas from his competitors, and he will certainly look for weaknesses in the competition that can be exploited. But some of the same weaknesses were also noticeable—more often than I liked—in our own magazines.

On the long list of things wrong with the American press, which I brought with me to the editor-in-chief's office, the first item was: inaccuracies. I had learned within my first week on the *Washington*

Post that it is harder than anyone might think to give a totally accurate description of even a quite uncomplicated event. Thirty and
forty years later, as head of a very large and expensive journalistic
operation, I still had occasion now and then to reflect on the maddening difficulty of simply getting the facts straight: "You fellows do
a wonderful job telling me about NATO but when you're writing
about the chemical industry (or Kansas City or Princeton or diabetes)
there's always something that isn't quite right." Very irritating, and
sometimes true, despite all of our elaborate precautions.

We were endlessly concerned with readability—none of the effort
matters, of course, if people aren't moved to read/look at it. Our
magazines could have been better written—a permanent description,
to be sure, of all the magazines in the world—but some of the writing
was so good that the unevenness rankled all the more. And always
in magazine journalism, there is the need to think three to thirty days
ahead—will people still be interested in such-and-such when they
get their magazines next month or next Wednesday?

Around the Time and Life Building, points of journalistic crafts-
manship could generate arguments more heated than grand questions
of "policy." Not everybody cared deeply about Vietnam; everyone
cared about journalism, especially his own story. But does the story
have to be that long? Aren't there any better pictures? Could anybody
but a Ph.D. in econometrics understand that chart? Do we want three
California stories in one issue? Feelings could run very high.

We needed acute antennae. We were trying to practice a journalism of intelligent anticipation, catch change "in the air," and at
the same time spot the big, simple, in-a-way-obvious thing that has
suddenly become journalistically ripe. We wanted to be ahead of the
procession without being so far in front that nobody else was ready
to be interested. Being right at the wrong time counts, in journalism
at least, as being wrong. And journalism being as competitive as it
is, an inflation on language can set in, and with it comes the danger
of spotting some change that isn't really happening yet, and perhaps
never will.

When I wanted a change of pace from magazine journalism, I
could indulge in one of my favorite jobs: editor-in-chief of Time-Life
Books. So I enjoyed the long lunches every two or three weeks when
we talked ideas for future book series—and I cheered on the editors
as they left the table to cope with the deadlines of that afternoon. I

was never tempted to sit in as acting editor of Books. I had put in some hard work as editorial director of Books when the venture was getting started in the early 1960s, and felt now I had earned a more leisurely role. The books rolled off the presses—one every ten days— and the editorial achievement was as pleasing as the financial. The general strategies and techniques developed at the start worked beautifully for a dozen years. By 1970, Books had become the company's second most profitable publishing operation, after *Time*.

When Norman Ross left Books in 1965 for the new General Learning Corporation, our joint venture with G.E., I appointed as his successor Maitland Edey, another *Life* alumnus. Edey was an adventurous outdoorsman, a gifted writer, and an editor of great taste. During his tenure as editor, Books brought out 161 titles, with total sales of more than thirty million copies. These series included the Time-Life Library of Art, Foods of the World, Time-Life Library of America, This Fabulous Century (by decades, starting from the 1870s).

To my regret, Edey insisted on retiring in 1970. He had turned sixty, he wanted to do some writing, spend more time out in the weather, and I think also he had been under some personal compulsion to prove he could run something, and now he had. On Edey's recommendation, I appointed Jerry Korn to succeed him. Korn, ex-AP, *Collier's*, *Life*, was a meticulous editor who approved every word and picture, an incorrigible workaholic who would never take more than a week's vacation at a time. This way, he insisted to me, he got "refreshed" four or five times a year; I suspected he just didn't want a whole month's copy flowing to press while he was up at his place in Maine. It later fell to Korn, and to me as his boss, to face up to some creakings and groanings in the marvelous money machine.

But it was still warming to me to encounter all over the country customers whose only complaint was that they were running out of bookshelves. They were especially enthusiastic about the effects of our books on their children. (I would hope that a survey today would show large numbers of thirty- to forty-year-old Americans gratefully recalling Time-Life books.)

Once when I was giving a speech in Indianapolis, in the Nixon-Agnew heyday, I found my Books credentials especially helpful. The toastmaster was familiar with my views on Nixon and Agnew, and he warned me this was a very conservative audience who might send up a little flak in the Q-and-A period. He particularly pointed out a florid man who he said was state treasurer of the Republican party, and was considered to be very possibly the most reactionary man in the whole state of Indiana, a considerable claim. He said, "You can probably count on a question from him." So when the Q-and-A period began, I kept this man in view, but he never got up at all. At the end of the proceedings, however, he was standing off to one side of the dining room, obviously waiting to meet me. I thought, Well, here it comes. When he finally was introduced, he said, "Mr. Donovan, I really just wanted to meet you to be able to compliment you on the *World of Turner* book in the Time-Life Library of Art." We had a very congenial discussion about Turner and our Time-Life book. I was later told that he was the biggest private collector of Turner prints in the United States. He was very critical of a Turner book the Museum of Modern Art had recently put out. I'm not sure I had seen it, but I promptly agreed that it was disgraceful.

My latter years as editor-in-chief of Time-Life Books were not so much fun as the first years. Korn put out some attractive series— Time-Life Encyclopedia of Gardening, American Wilderness, Time-Life Library of Photography—but the equivalent of the old blockbusters of the 1960s was elusive. Profit margins shrank, and "magazine-type" editorial costs and procedures came under tougher scrutiny. Spectacular success in overseas sales only partially masked the weakness in the domestic market, accentuated by the recession of 1975–76. There was speculation as to how often you could ask the same people to buy your magazines, books, phonograph records— the chilling clinical phrase was "list fatigue." Korn had to lay off about a tenth of his staff. A succession of first-rate publishing executives had grappled with Books economics in good times and less good, and now it fell to one of the best, Joan Manley, to consider whether we had done all the obvious series, and some not so obvious, and now perhaps should count our money and retire from the business. But of course publishers and editors (and Time Inc.) are not inclined to give up.

Joan was the first woman publisher in Time Inc., and our first woman director, and she put through a cost-cutting measure that would have reduced many male Time Inc. executives to jelly: the transplanting of a whole corporate division from Mother Manhattan to Alexandria, Virginia. Only a third of the staff chose to make the move, despite many blandishments, but most of those who chose not to go were replaced without too much difficulty (some didn't need replacing), and the shift did save a lot of money, freeing Books to rise and fight another day.

....

Sports Illustrated was an almost entirely carefree aspect of my portfolio. After the heavy exertions of the early 1960s that helped create the finally successful *S.I.*, the magazine needed very little editor-in-chiefing. M.E. André Laguerre and I, neither exactly garrulous (André could out-taciturn me), had many a congenial conversation about this enormously enjoyable magazine that he had done so much to shape. I no longer zapped him with many of my story-by-story report cards, but I did it just often enough to let him know I was paying attention. The quality of the writing in *S.I.* was good enough to allow the staff to think it was the best-written magazine in Time Inc., and Laguerre kept improving it. I have never cared much for the cliché that the best writing in American newspapers is on the sports pages (and I don't think the best places to eat are where the truck drivers stop), but the fact was that *S.I.* offered writers—staff as well as outside contributors—the time and space to unfold some very polished narrative reporting. *Time*, with its compulsion to compress, couldn't allow such leisurely storytelling, nor could the increasingly businesslike *Fortune*.

A notable Laguerre innovation was the bathing-suit issue. Casting about for something to enliven the issues between the New Year's football bowl games and the start of the baseball season (this was before the huge popularity of pro basketball), André ran a nineteen-page piece on swimming and snorkeling in the Caribbean. The historic date was January 20, 1964. The emphasis was on travel and sport, and the pictures of girls in bathing suits were more or less incidental. The issue was a vast success and became an annual fixture: exotic settings all over the world, more and more pages, more and more expanses of girls, less and less bathing suit. By 1988, at Phangnga Bay, Thailand, the girls were occupying thirty-four pages. I hoped it was not a sign of advancing age that I wondered if it was almost too much of a good thing. The *S.I.* staff runs an annual office pool on the mail responses to the issue (dependably the heaviest of the year) and the number of cancellations ("I thought I was giving my 11-year-old son a *sports* magazine for Christmas"). The all-time record was three hundred and three cancellations in 1975; the toll was a mere seventy-three in 1988.

S.I., despite its growing reputation as a money factory, never attracted a head-to-head weekly competitor. (*Newsweek* briefly published a monthly *Inside Sports*, then sold it.) The daily sports sections of the newspapers, as well as TV, fed readers and topics to *S.I.* Perhaps the Sunday sports sections of the best newspapers came closest to being competitors, but *S.I.*, with the full weekend results in hand, its superb color photography, and its distinguished text pieces, was simply a different medium. And for many years, *S.I.* far excelled both TV and the newspapers in the courage and candor of its investigations of the seamy side of sports: the corrupting influence of gambling, the pious hypocrisies of so many franchise owners and college authorities, the calculated brutality in pro football and hockey, the frightening drug plague, the prevalence of racism—some subtle, some not so subtle—even as blacks were supplying more and more of the stars. It is only in recent years that the best newspapers have sufficiently liberated themselves from home-team coziness to tackle these stories in a serious way. For Laguerre and his staff, I thought it was a remarkable journalistic achievement to dig into this dirty stuff, look at it unblinkingly, and still maintain a fresh curiosity and enthusiasm about sports—illustrated—that I (child of Minnesota) totally shared.

I did a lot of worrying, in discussions with the *S.I.* editors and publishing people, about the effect on the fans (and on the *S.I.* audience) of the opportunism of owners in moving franchises all over the map, of the astronomical player salaries and bonuses that TV revenue was making possible, and of the ascendancy of minority athletes. Might the mainly white middle-income spectators get tired of watching overpaid mercenaries, many of them black or Hispanic, purporting to represent Boston or Cincinnati or Wherever? It just never happened. As sports fans, the white middle-income Americans seem to be all for equal opportunity (however they may feel about their schools or neighborhoods), and they seem to be utterly unenvious of the multimillion-dollar contracts those twenty-four-year-old left fielders sign. Perhaps it is no more complicated than a democratic admiration for excellence in fields where everybody would love to excel. The fans do get sore when the rich club owners decamp to another city that promises bigger and better parking lots at municipal expense.

Laguerre was such an effective M.E. it was perhaps unimaginative of me to dislodge him just because he had been there so long. But as his tenure stretched on past ten years, he agreed it would soon be time for someone else to have a crack at the job. These were perfectly pleasant conversations with André, and we were each enthusiastic about his executive editor, Roy Terrell, as his successor. When Terrell did take over in 1974, André had been M.E. almost fourteen years, a Time Inc. record (surpassing Ed Thompson of *Life* and Del Paine of *Fortune*, tied at twelve).

It had been a glorious run, but Laguerre was embittered when I failed to come up with another solid job for him in Time Inc. At fifty-seven, he was only two years younger than I, too near my age to be a possible successor in my job. (The editor-in-chief also needs to be able to speak in public at least a little more than André was willing to do.) We didn't have any more new magazines coming up in the immediate future, with the possible exception of *Woman*, for which Laguerre would have been spectacularly miscast. I asked him to explore the feasibility of a European edition of *S.I.*, and I had to persuade him this wasn't make-work. He did an interesting report recommending a British *S.I.* as an attractive gamble, but when I reluctantly turned down the proposal, his original suspicions about the assignment were doubtless confirmed. He left Time Inc. and founded *Classic*, a handsome monthly on thoroughbred racing, but it lasted only a few years.

I was very uncomfortable about Laguerre's departure—not only because of my respect for the man and his talents but also because I myself was not inclined to retire short of age sixty-five, and younger men who might be interested in my job would just have to be patient. Time Inc. has never figured out—or at least I never did—how you can appoint relatively young people as managing editors, a highly desirable policy in an idea business, and then find good jobs for all the "old" M.E.s as other young people get their turn. The expansion of the company created some new jobs at the top editorial levels, but not enough to take care of everybody.

Some M.E.s, like Mait Edey at Books, chose to leave the job and the company of their own accord, acted indecently happy about it, and I couldn't seem to reason with them. Another such turned out to be Laguerre's successor, Terrell. Roy was a first-rate writer who at one time or another had covered almost any sport you could name, and had himself played a lot of them. Roy was an excellent M.E.—not a major innovator, but major innovation was not called for, an exacting text editor and shrewd manager who helped some new talents rise. He made the magazine even more professional than it already was.

I thought I knew Terrell quite well personally. We played some golf and tennis once in a while, and shared the more strenuous sport of Long Island Railroad commuting from the same suburb. But I found I didn't really know him after all. I was astonished to learn that he wanted to give up the M.E.'s job after just five years and avail himself of our earliest early-retirement option, at age fifty-six. He wrote me a most moving letter about his decision. I told the people at his farewell dinner that Roy's letter was so subversive I wasn't going to quote from it, for fear nobody in the crowd would turn up for work the next morning. I will risk it now:

> For almost 40 years I have been earning a living, raising and educating a family, pursuing a career, and now I am tired of getting up and going to work every morning. I want to go fishing instead.
>
> 1978 was an exceptional year for *Sports Illustrated*, yet I find myself only quietly pleased with our triumphs and success and only mildly stimulated by the thought of future challenge. . . .
>
> I am less and less enamored of those constant and pervasive New York irritants—crowds, noise, filth, bad manners, miserable winters, exorbitant taxes, etc.—and I would prefer to live the rest of my life somewhere else.
>
> My mother is 83, my father 84, and both are declining rapidly in health. I want to spend more time with them before they go. My children are growing older much too fast, and I would like to spend more time with them, too. Actually, I haven't seen all that much of my wife in the last five years, either. . . .
>
> And finally there are the many things I want to do . . . many are at least mildly adventurous, and some are physically demanding, involving boats and oceans and mountain trails and streams. I must get started on them while still relatively young.
>
> . . . It would be presumptuous of me to assume that you will attempt to try to talk me out of this decision, and therefore it would be doubly presumptuous of me to counter your (imagined) arguments here. . . .

I did try, and got nowhere. Roy moved to the Florida Keys and did go fishing.

So I appointed Gilbert Rogin to succeed him. This happened just a few weeks before I retired as editor-in-chief, and in introducing Rogin at Roy's party, I said he better be good because he was going to be my last M.E. appointment, unless things very suddenly went very sour at one of our other magazines. He was good.

....

I was never afflicted with a yes-man as a managing editor, but for my stoutest no-men, I would have to call it a tie between Ralph Graves of *Life* and Robert Lubar of *Fortune*. Lubar had been a navy destroyer officer during the war, then a *Time* correspondent in New Delhi, London, Mexico City, and Bonn. Mary Johnston, *Fortune*'s chief of research and a brilliant recruiter of talent, had been impressed by Lubar's files from overseas and urged me to offer him a writer's job on *Fortune*. I followed her advice (as good a day's work as Mary and I ever did). It was Lubar who wrote the tax-reform articles of 1959 that caused Charlie Stillman to suspect Communist infiltration at *Fortune*. Lubar rose rapidly to the Board of Editors, then to assistant managing editor, and was my choice to succeed Lou Banks as M.E. in 1970.

The Banks *Fortune* had been a generally lively, well-paced magazine with persistent weaknesses in illustration. I gave Banks story-by-story critiques of his first two or three issues, also advising him: "You will be pleased to hear that this is not a regular monthly service from my office." But meanwhile:

> When the scheduling of *Fortune* stories is fully computerized, and you and I have both been thrown out of work, I think the machine would not have allowed *Color TV* and *Natural Gas* in the same issue. Too much similarity in *texture*—i.e., industry-wide "battles," large and complex cast of corporate characters, and a kind of clothesline story structure, in which we have to be taken along from Company A, to B, C, D, etc.
>
> *Aluminum*. Excellent story (much improved since the draft I saw). The illustration doesn't seem just right. The cover strikes me a little too much like some fancy promotional brochure; the frontispiece is good, but the two of them together set up a strictly impersonal sequence, carried on through the charts and the not very interesting blue-light photos on pp 110–111. This was a story about *people*—interesting executives, important politicians, none shown.
>
> *Is Technology Taking Over?* This is a remarkable essay, brilliant in stretches. (And again my compliments to the editor, pls.; I felt for him when I read the first draft.) But I don't think we ever notify the reader with any exactness what the piece is going to be about and where it is going. The title (apart from my prejudice against question-mark titles) poses a terribly hackneyed theme with no suggestion that we have anything fresh to say, which in fact we do. The photo

is a real stopper, but neither it nor the valiant caption does much to define the story.

A couple of years later:

> *How to Think About the Russians.* Herman [Kahn] spreads himself very thin, and there are things in here he shouldn't be allowed to get away with. Still, this is very interesting conversation. But it's an essay, surely, rather than a *Fortune* lead. And that would have spared us the frontispiece. This relates to my point at lunch the other day: maybe *Fortune* needs better month-to-month operating options more than it needs better long-range imagination (at which it's already so good; maybe even too good? Is such a thing possible?).
>
> *Why It's Harder to Keep Good Executives.* You were right; this is an excellent story.
>
> *The Fastest Richest Texan Ever.* You have been so successful in hammering down the length of *Fortune* stories that I even occasionally am disappointed they end so soon. Probably that's as it should be. I found myself, for instance, wanting to know more about Ross Perot's personal aspirations and plans for his money. Also, his price-earnings ratio is fantastic enough, but his price-revenues ratio (is there such a thing?) seems absolutely astounding to me. Has there ever been such a high one in the history of the world? This surely would have been worth some discussion.

A memo addressed jointly to Banks and Henry Luce III (Harry's son, then publisher of *Fortune*, hence responsible for the magazine's business affairs, including physical production): "Dreadful reproduction quality in the August [1969] *Fortune*—or is it just my make-ready?" These were the first-run copies distributed inside the building. Alas, the full-run quality was not much better.

Banks was an idealistic man almost evangelical in his enthusiasms. He had an exalted view of the social responsibilities and possibilities of the American corporation. He was seldom preachy about it in print, however, so we had no serious clashes between his concept and my less-lofty approach. I was becoming more inclined to the view that the first duty of the corporation is to make a lot of money (lawfully) and then let well-paid employees, well-served customers, well-rewarded stockholders fulfill whatever social responsibilities appeal to them as individuals. I did not apply this doctrine, of course, to Time Inc., which I considered, perhaps self-righteously, to be engaged in a higher calling than your average corporation. In any case, Banks and I were both sympathetic to Lyndon Johnson's Great Society vision, and *Fortune* was, too.

Bob Lubar was not necessarily more conservative than Banks politically (I think of him as a right-wing Democrat, and of Lou as a far-left Republican). But he had a wonderfully prickly independence, and a down-to-earth skepticism about anything high-flown. Bob's outlook was reflected in some tough analytical pieces he published: "The Social Engineers Retreat Under Fire," "The Bad News About the Federal Budget," "How Equal Opportunity Turned Into Employment Quotas," "The Revolution of Rising Entitlements." Lubar had strong opinions, verging on the choleric. I prize the memory of an evening on the Long Island Railroad—a very long evening—when the train was mysteriously delayed at the Great Neck station, while Port Washington (end-of-the-line) passengers, Lubar included, fumed, played bridge, read, slept. Having been an LIRR commuter for more years than Bob, I had long since settled into the stoic mode—some might call it apathy—in which I had no curiosity whatsoever as to what might be the trouble up the line. The train would start moving again when it wanted to, and that was life. But Bob, who was sitting next to me, was getting redder and redder in the face as conductors would walk through the car explaining nothing. Finally, he caught the eye of one of these zombies and loudly demanded: "What is the meaning of this comedy?" I wonder if commuter *angst* has ever been expressed more economically.

I offered Bob occasional report cards: "I think it could be a rule that there just isn't the makings of a *Fortune* editorial when the conclusion has to be let's have a study, or let's have a national debate." "I thought this was a very meaty issue and generally attractive in looks. Also a fair number of bugs here and there. The cover was drab (and out of focus?). With that whole rich World Economy as our theme, there should have been something more compelling. Roundup, lead editorial and lead article were all excellent. *Fortune* economic analysis at its best—and with brevity, too. Worth the price of the issue. (Good charts.)" "Minor curiosity: How does Arthur Louis [a *Fortune* writer] get to say 'I' so often?" "I have read about two-thirds of the current issue with great satisfaction. Nothing wrong with the other one-third; just that I haven't read it yet." "I continue to be concerned at the lack of visual excitement."

Fortune, even as Lubar was taking over, was running into heavy weather. Circulation had edged up to half a million in 1969, and the magazine's profit was the highest ever. But in 1970, ad pages fell off by more than 25 percent, and suddenly the magazine was barely breaking even. All magazine ad volume was off that year, but *Fortune* was hit harder than most. Competition from the rest of the business press for readers' time and advertisers' dollars was getting rugged. Even within the family, *Fortune* sometimes lost business to *"Time B,"* a demographic edition that offered advertisers the same editorial content as the regular *Time* plus split-run ad pages aimed at more than a million business executives (*Fortune* didn't think there were that many in the country) among *Time's* four million subscribers.

We began some strenuous grappling, not for the first time, with *Fortune* costs. Paper weight had been cut down several times since the good old days (this accounted in part for my endless unhappiness with reproduction quality), but the magazine was still printed on a big page, and still running a spacious middle-of-the-book "well"— usually forty-eight pages of unbroken editorial space, an art director's dream—and never mind if some subscribers disliked the story continuations to the back of the book. With the issue of September 1972, we cut the page size from 13 x 10¼ to 11 x 9 (still bigger than the newsweeklies), for a considerable saving in paper and postage costs. The old "well" was broken up by ad pages, stories stopped jumping to the back, and typography was generally freshened up.

More wrenching change was impending. The possibility of converting *Fortune* to a fortnightly had last been studied in 1967–69, but the publishing projections were not encouraging. By the mid-1970s, however, the business side was convinced the fortnightly made publishing sense. *Fortune* was doing well again (profits at a record $4 million in 1976), and this was the ideal climate for expanding—not from weakness but to enlarge success. A fortnightly would offer advertisers twenty-six issues a year, make a briefer, less bristling issue for the subscriber to pick up, but still offer 30 percent more editorial space over a year.

The top editors thought it was a terrible idea. Their essential concern (apart from disliking a disturbance of familiar routines) was that shorter articles would necessarily be superficial, that *Fortune* would give up the thoroughness that had been at the core of its reputation. This worried me, too, and I was a little scared at the size of the risk we were taking—a greater risk than the launching of a completely new magazine. In *Fortune* we had a going operation; if we converted it into something quite different and that didn't work, we couldn't just say, Oops, and go back to the monthly; we would have to go on to the still bigger gamble of a weekly. We could end up with no *Fortune* at all.

But the ongoing *Fortune*, momentarily profitable as it was, had ongoing readability problems its editors hated to acknowledge. I became convinced that the fortnightly, for all the risk, was in fact the prudent direction.

The editors were pretty well dug in. Executive Editor Dan Seligman: "The editorial concept of the biweekly just seems like a mishmash to me. As we move . . . into the short-article world, what's our selling point?" Assistant M.E. Allan Demaree, who had headed an editorial task force studying the fortnightly idea, concluded: "We shouldn't make the move. . . . We give up part of our monopoly franchise to get into a very competitive swim." Bob Lubar wrote me a stern memo, saying he had "moved from a skeptical position to one of firm opposition." More memos, meetings, lunches, including a not entirely casual comment by Bob Lubar that he wasn't sure he would be a good editor of a fortnightly.

We had reached one of those situations where the boss must finally make like a boss. I told the editors in May 1977 that we were going ahead with the change, effective January 1978. By the time we had our ceiling-bolting party for the first fortnightly cover plate, the editors' morale had perked up noticeably. It helped that they had been extremely busy. They had done a remarkable job in getting out strong issues of the old monthly through the summer and fall, while turning out inviting pilot issues of the new magazine. Nobody quit.

The changes at *Time*, during the years I was editor-in-chief, were more radical than those at *Fortune*. Many were important innovations in form, but more significant was a change in journalistic approach. The change sounds simple enough, but it was not easy to execute and it carried some risks: I wanted to see the magazine become more thoughtful and more fair-minded. Since *Time* was the company's best-known publication, perhaps the best-known magazine in the world, I gave a very high priority to this effort, and I believe it led to a major enhancement of the reputation of Time Inc.

In my inaugural at the "Luce-Donovan dinner" of May 1964, just as a presidential campaign was warming up, I said: "The vote of Time Inc. should never be considered to be in the pocket of any particular political leader or party. The vote of Time Inc. is an independent vote. Not an independent vote in the sense of some snooty or finicky disdain for political parties. And certainly not independent in the sense of any wishy-washy confusion as to what we believe. But independent in the sense that we are in no way beholden to any party, have no vested interest in any party as such."

Tom Griffith had volunteered to read the drafts of my speech and Harry's in advance of that dinner (we weren't showing them to each other) supposedly to make sure there were no "long overlaps"—but really, to catch serious contradictions, if any. Tom showed the paragraph cited above to Luce. "He read it and thanked me in the manner of a man who knew there would be a passage like that from Hedley Donovan."

But you don't just press a button at 10 A.M. some Monday and command *Time* from now on to be fair. The people who wrote and edited the kind of political commentary I objected to were (except for the occasional opportunist) expressing their honest convictions in a *Time*-honored tone of voice. The portentous all-knowing tone could be slowly changed, and was. The honest opinions that I differed with were argued out head-on. If I won more often than I lost, I liked to think this was logic more than rank.

I wanted to achieve fair-mindedness without losing sharpness and snap, arrive at balance without drifting off into dithering. It could take more lines of type to be fair, and still convey a *Time* point of view, than simply to be dogmatic. There was a real hazard there, for *Time*'s traditional briskness had been one of its great strengths. "I have sometimes heard it said," I recalled at the Luce-Donovan dinner, "that it will be a sorry day for Time Inc. if we ever run out of enemies. I consider this such a remote danger I refuse to worry about it. We do indeed have some enemies to be proud of, and we want to keep them. We also have some unnecessary enemies whom we acquired rather carelessly."

Though the "we" ostensibly referred to all our magazines, I was speaking mainly to Luce and the *Time* editors, as they were well aware. And for the first two years or so of my tenure, there was something of a contest of wills between the new editor-in-chief and the strong-minded and effective editors, particularly Otto Fuerbringer and his trusted deputy, Jim Keogh, who were putting out *Time*. But I found enormous professional satisfaction in my *Time* responsibilities. The top editors were fine journalists, and the magazine's whole mechanism was beautifully tuned to perform on short notice. I got a kick out of selling a story idea to Otto on a Friday and seeing it in print on Monday, on its way to five and a half million subscribers worldwide. Sometimes I might see a few lines of my own prose, or even a few paragraphs, that I stuck into some story that had been run past me.

Otto had to put up with the occasional critiques, several provoked by Vietnam stories. But if the editors wanted a little time off from Vietnam, I suggested in a note to Otto, we might have a lunch-time seminar on sex, specifically whether "The Sex Quota per issue has got too generous." In an issue that included a two-page essay on homosexuality, sex-centered stories had also turned up in People, Law, Theatre, Religion, Modern Living, and Cinema. "In this rather steamy atmosphere, Books' references to Truman Capote as 'wispy,' etc., struck me as gratuitous; they had no relevance to the work under review [*In Cold Blood*]." I assume the lunch was held; alas, my archives do not disclose what was said, or whether any women were invited—probably not.

Fuerbringer got a chance to issue me a report card after I sent him on vacation for four or five weeks in the summer of 1967 so I could sit in as acting M.E. He was a kindly critic. When he read the first couple of Donovan issues, Otto could tell "you were still sort of finding your way around the floor" (which was true indeed). "But then after that I could see you really had the machinery running" (which was generous).

It was a heavy hard-news month that I had stepped into—lucked into, the insensitive might say. Vietnam was growing more costly and more divisive, almost week by week, and, perhaps not surprisingly, the tone of *Time*'s stories began to get very close to what I wanted. It was also the "long hot summer" when the Newark and Detroit race riots burst, and we did cover stories on both. Newark began to get serious toward the end of a week, which is good—in a *Time*-centered view of the human condition—in that the magazine brings its coverage to the subscriber very soon after the event, but is also bad because *Time* correspondents, writers, researchers, editors, even the acting managing editor, sometime editor-in-chief, must work very arduous hours.

Time's official closing day had retreated over the years, a day at a time, from Monday of this week to Friday of last week, but whatever closing day was set, a huge volume of work would stubbornly pile up just behind the deadline. I used to figure that about three-quarters of the *Time* staff's serious work got done in the last two days and nights of the week. I didn't feel the company was shortchanged by this because those last two days were long and rugged, and you never knew what useful ideas might have been marinating during the "easy" part of the week. *Time* people occasionally conducted light-hearted arguments as to what was the ideal *hour*, not merely day of the week, for a newsworthy catastrophe to occur. Early afternoon of closing day—say, 2 P.M., EST, was often nominated.

Shortly after my stint as acting M.E., Fuerbringer invited me to a weekend retreat for his senior staff at a pleasant oceanside inn in East Hampton, Long Island. I handed out a good many compliments, complained some about *Time* layout—"I'm not sure it's good for *Time* to go on looking quite so much like *Time*"—and wished out loud that more of the magazine were as well written as the best of it. "What magazine do you find well written?" asked one senior editor. "If it were later in the evening and we'd had more drinks," the transcript records me as answering, "I might make an argument that *Sports Illustrated* is better written." It did get later, and somewhat abrasive, when I argued that *Time*'s editors needed to take *Newsweek* more seriously. Several said they were tired of hearing how much *Newsweek* had improved; there was room for a number 2 out there. I agreed, but don't get too tired, I said, because we have a tougher competitor than the one we used to dismiss.

In early 1968, I asked Otto to step aside as M.E. He was surprised, said he still felt a great zest for the job and had hoped to hold it at least ten years, which would have brought us to 1970. He was also disappointed, though less surprised, at my choice of Henry Grunwald as his successor. He shared my high regard for Henry as a journalist, but his favored deputy had been Jim Keogh, and in my contingency conversations with Otto, he had always supported Jim as the stand-by M.E.

I told Otto that just as *Time* had been greatly invigorated by his own accession, I felt we were approaching that point in the cycle again, and that I didn't want to make the change during or just after the 1968 presidential campaign, lest it seem to imply some sort of reproach about *Time*'s coverage. I was able to offer Otto an excellent assignment—to head up a small group exploring possible newspaper acquisitions, a subject that had interested Time Inc. off and on for decades (Luce had been slightly tempted by the old *New York Herald Tribune*). Otto had worked ten years on the *St. Louis Post-Dispatch*, before coming to *Time*, and with no visible sulking, he plunged back into the newspaper world. None of the big-city papers that Fuerbringer looked at seemed just right for us, but he conceived an imaginative "lateral entry" scheme in which we bought two Chicago suburban newspaper groups—attractive properties in themselves and a possible base for creating a new metropolitan-area daily. As things turned out, we didn't pursue that possibility, and many years later sold the suburban papers, but meanwhile Fuerbringer went on to the great round of magazine-inventing described earlier in this chapter.

In changing managing editors, I was indeed hoping for the stimulus to innovation that a new boss brings. But I was also concerned, as the national agony over Vietnam deepened, that *Time* should be instinctively sensitive to what was involved—and, so far as my own responsibilities ran, that I should not too often be in the position, after the event, of telling Fuerbringer why I was distressed by something he had printed.

If some of the staff thought the departure of Fuerbringer meant that a hundred flowers were about to bloom, they were badly mistaken. Grunwald was almost equally autocratic, though his personal style was a little less formidable, and his political and cultural center of gravity was a bit to the liberal side of Fuerbringer's. Henry's distinguished Viennese family had left Austria soon after the Nazis took over in 1938, moved to Paris, left just ahead of the German army, and came to New York. Henry started as a weekend copy boy for *Time* while studying at New York University. He rose many rungs on the *Time* ladder at precocious speed—he was a senior editor at age twenty-eight—and in remarkably few years was transformed from a "possibly obnoxious" (his own measured phrase) youngster to an urbane and elegant intellectual of faintly bohemian aura. Henry has a brilliant mind that would have been fruitful in several fields, I thought, but it was beautifully employed in journalism. A Jewish friend paid me a tactless compliment on Henry's appointment: "I admire your courage in choosing a Jew." I counted to ten and told her it took no courage at all.

Grunwald was even more innovative than Fuerbringer. He introduced half a dozen new *Time* departments—Behavior, Environment, Energy, The Sexes, Economy, Dance. These didn't necessarily run every week, and some did not survive for long. Here he was extending the Fuerbringer recognition that *Time*'s table of contents need not be graven in stone.

He took up an idea of his energetic business editor, Marshall Loeb (later M.E. of *Money*, then *Fortune*), that *Time* should possess its own board of economists, convene them quarterly, and report their views on the business outlook. The board was a very successful device, and it was a nice testimonial to *Time* and to Loeb's persuasiveness that a number of eminences—including seven past or future chairmen of the President's Council of Economic Advisers—were happy to serve. One of them was Alan Greenspan, chairman of the Federal Reserve since 1987. Alan, during a spell of back trouble, contributed a certain éclat to the board's meetings by lying down on the floor as soon as he arrived and issuing his carefully balanced judgments from that position. I knew most of the *Time* economists, generally understood what they were talking about, and enjoyed the editor-in-chief's privilege of asking a question now and then. I had first encountered Greenspan in the early 1950s when Sandy Parker, *Fortune's* eccentric economist-genius, asked me if I would let him spend $5,000 to farm out some heavy statistical research to this bright young guy who was just trying to start up his own consulting firm. I said fine, and then for two or three years I okayed the billings (very reasonable) from the Greenspan office. Finally I said to Parker, who was badly overextended and needed to enlarge his staff, "Look, you like Alan's work, he seems to be putting in about half-time with us anyway, why don't we just hire him full time?" Sandy, I think, whiffed danger on his own turf, and I didn't press. Alan's career did not seem to suffer.

Under Grunwald, *Time* stories took on more depth. They got longer, too, sometimes too long. I wrote Henry: "As you know, I applaud the idea of more variety in story lengths, with some in a 'natural' way running longer than we once would have allowed. . . . But the corollary was supposed to be some 'naturally' short items as well, just a couple of paragraphs, or even a single sentence. These seem to be very scarce. More disturbing is the large number of three- and four-column stories that could have been cut by a quarter or a third with great benefit to the general briskness and pace of the magazine. If the space thus saved went to quick treatments of other subjects, we would have had a richer and snappier issue." But a subsequent Beverly Sills cover story was "excellent—including that we came and went in five pages."

Some essays, striving for due respect for complexity, suffered from a kind of excess of fairness. It was a complaint I had never thought I would have to make about *Time*. But I sometimes counted within a single article up to eight or ten on-the-other-hand shifts back and forth between the con and pro of some controversial issue. I urged putting all the best con arguments in one place, faithfully rendered, and then letting the good guys (us) have their say.

Not too many sparrows fell unnoticed. "The incomplete statistic, an old *Time* problem, is still with us. 'This year alone, at least 463 Catholic clerics in the U.S. have left the priesthood.' Is that a lot?" On a story on state and local election results in November 1968: "The G.O.P. commands 31 statehouses . . . made a net gain of only 36 state legislators . . . added more than 500 county offices." As national totals, I complained to Grunwald, "all the figures are meaningless except the one on statehouses (luckily I know there are 50 of those)."

A book review needed "a sentence or two of straightforward scene-setting and explaining. This latter service was over-done in *Time* for quite a while, and often came out dull and didactic. Now we may be erring in the other direction. We are more complex and allusive, and give the better half of our readers credit for more literary sophistication, all of which trend I like, but we may be neglecting some simple little touches which would let the other half of our readers more fully in on things."

Another book review in the same issue: "Well executed review of an unsuccessful and unimportant and unlikely-to-be-talked-about book [*Terra Amata* by J.M.G. LeClezio]. I've never understood our rationale about these. Sometimes I used to think they made the section because of some lurid sex, or 16th century Ottoman torture, or some such, but that doesn't seem to be the case with this item."

After Chappaquiddick (1969): "The Teddy Kennedy story is excellent. I do regret the lack of any reference to Rose—it must have been quite a week for her. . . . We do not mention one of the most glaring new questions raised by Teddy on the TV: why did his side-kicks Markham and Gargan allow this man with a bad back, suffering concussion, etc., to make his second swim, without plunging in after him, or grabbing a dinghy, or phoning police, or a doctor, or something?"

And always the pictures: "I marked up a couple dozen or so cuts in here [a 1971 issue] that particularly distressed me. Some cases are bad reproduction, some perhaps bad copy to begin with . . . some of the ones that bothered me are doubtless wirephoto, but maybe we shouldn't use wirephoto except for very interesting action or historic moments we couldn't have any other way? I doubt if one more statesman at one more airport, e.g., Secretary of State Rogers in Ankara, qualifies."

The magazine became less impersonal. Grunwald introduced by-lines all through the departments (previously only the reviews were signed), a courageous step that did not come easy, because we seemed to be tagging along after *Newsweek*. *Time* also began running signed columns, notably The Presidency, intimate and richly readable reporting by Hugh Sidey, which had first appeared as a feature in the weekly *Life*. Tom Griffith did Newswatch, perceptive commentary on the press. Outside contributors were courted to write for the Essay section. Even the editor-in-chief was allowed to unburden himself there, usually in the form of excerpts (very generous excerpts) from speeches.

An innocent pleasure that came with my office was the pondering, starting every September, of the choice for *Time*'s Man of the Year. Nominations were invited from the news bureaus all over the world, from writers, researchers, department editors in New York, and their sales pitches could be impassioned. Melodramatic precautions were taken to preserve security. The top editors did their secret winnowing of the names, several writers might be assigned to camouflage stories, and one team went to work on the real article.

Subscribers—and subjects—could get quite stirred up. The subject had to be let in on the secret, of course, so he would give our people the necessary interviewing time, and let them rummage through old photo albums if need be. Thus informed, Henry Kissinger, national security adviser, uncrowned secretary of state, phoned me at home one night in December 1972 to "plead"—just for the record, I suspect—that he not be made co–Man of the Year with President Richard Nixon. He said his boss wouldn't like the joint billing. We thought it was warranted by their collaboration in détente with the Soviets and the efforts to wind down the Vietnam war. When I told Kissinger, no, it was going to be the two of them, he tried to work on Grunwald, who came up with an answer I wished I had thought of: that if the professor didn't stop bothering us, we might leave him on the cover all by himself. A faint doubt lingers in my mind as to how deeply this outcome would have distressed Dr. Kissinger.

Nixon had just been The Man, all by himself, the previous year, for his China opening and other foreign-policy initiatives, and because we felt we owed him one—most new presidents made it for the year of their election, or if not, for the first year in office. Nixon hadn't. Four of us went to the Oval Office to interview him for the M.O.Y. story one Sunday just before Christmas; he came in from a staff party, relaxed and genial in a maroon blazer and slacks. We had asked to tape the interview but were told, never mind, Army Signal Corps people would do it. Afterward, it turned out their equipment wasn't functioning. We immediately reconstructed the entire two-hour interview from memory—journalists jogging each other can do that—and the White House accepted our transcript as complete and authentic. Taping snafus a few months later would have been a nice break for Nixon. (Many years after Watergate, interviewing Nixon for a *Fortune* article on the Reagan presidency, I asked an aide if I might bring a recorder. He said the interview would go better without— "He's not too comfortable with those things.")

Another presidential Man of the Year, Lyndon Johnson (for 1964), first said he would not be interviewed—the story "can only make my job more difficult"—then gave our reporters as much time as they wanted, then let it be known he liked the printed article but disliked the very flattering cover painting by Peter Hurd. The right shoulder was much too big. But not big enough to keep the original off the wall of his office, as I later noticed at the LBJ ranch.

When *Time* made the Ayatollah Khomeini Man of the Year (for 1979), I took considerable heat around the White House, where I was then employed. Frank Carlucci, then deputy director of the CIA (later Defense Secretary), confronted me in the Situation Room and asked how he could explain the cover to his children. I said if the Carluccis had a dart board around the house, I bet the kids could think of something entertaining. There was a precedent for this, in a good many American basement rumpus rooms, on the occasions when Hitler and Stalin had made Man of the Year.

Long out of Time Inc. office, I still got a kick out of reading that President Reagan at the Moscow Summit had asked for autographs on a dozen copies of the Mikhail Gorbachev cover of January 4, 1988. The Man obliged.

Grunwald was vigilant, as Fuerbringer had been, in ensuring that *Time* should not seem prim about sex. A 1973 cover story on Marlon Brando's then-shocking film, *Last Tango in Paris*, triggered more than twelve thousand letters, almost all angry and more than half canceling subscriptions. Among those addressed to me personally were some from Minnesota people who had known my parents and felt mortified for them. (The previous record was seven thousand letters brought on by a 1966 cover story slugged "Is God Dead?" A number of outraged readers thought the question was blasphemous; some heavyweight theologians liked the story.)

Henry once took some *Time* writers and researchers during the lunch hour to one of the nearby hard-core movie houses. The public porn phenomenon was *Time* subject matter, and the M.E., like an alert teacher in a progressive school, was leading the kids on an educational field trip. Several of them walked out before the movie (there is some scholarly dispute as to which one) was over—"boring" was the general verdict. But that always struck me, as an editor, as begging the question. There was a real tension, I thought, between the entitlement—unquestioned as far as I am concerned—of various minorities to tastes and preferences repugnant to the majority, and the right of the majority to move about, exist, live (not only raise children) in a society in some approximate harmony with their values. Or was the latter no right at all? The simplistic "boring" does not really address the question. Nor did *Time* (or *Life*) do so convincingly during my tenure. Admittedly a very tough question—as our courts, all the way up to the Supreme, have so often demonstrated.

Grunwald and I were very comfortable ideologically. In domestic political outlook, he was a shade more "liberal" than I—which is easy to be—but open-minded, curious, and very astute in his judgments of public figures. In the Reagan years of the 1980s, I think Henry somehow got over onto the conservative side of me, but by then presidents and *Time* editors were no longer in my care.

Henry had an extraordinary range of knowledge and interests. His early life in Middle Europe may well have enhanced his feel for American idiom and the American temper. Along with his sophistication in world politics, in philosophy, in all the back-of-the-book regions, there were one or two gaps. He knew nothing of sports, and didn't pretend otherwise. Economics was not his strongest department, and a certain amount of foolishness in this field could slip past his pencil. I complained about a *Time* story reproaching Nixon for a Labor Day speech that I generally admired. "I applaud his audacity in speaking up in favor of hard work"—his two references to welfare loafing were "at most one too many"—but "I would fault him (and *Time*) for not pointing out that one of the chief fruits of rising productivity is increased leisure, which is not to be confused with loafing on the job. . . . When people are supposedly at work, work should indeed be performed."

A *Time* story on deregulation of natural-gas prices assumed that "consumers" had "lost" because instead of artificially low prices, they were going to have to start paying something closer to the real value of the product. Surely, I pleaded, "Everybody, including 'consumers' (who are also producers of other products, often stockholders directly or via pension funds, and Americans with a general interest in an efficient economy) gains when scarce products are realistically priced, encouraging production and discouraging wasteful consumption. Sure, I know a lot of consumers *think* they lose in such a situation, but *Time* shouldn't encourage the delusion. (I am assuming that the industry in question is running its business lawfully and obeying the anti-trust laws.)"

In the fall of 1975, I encouraged Henry to go off on a trip, and I sat in again for a month as managing editor. I was pleased to find that I could still stay up most of Thursday and Friday nights, which was when the M.E. earned most of his pay. I also felt that an M.E. who could figure out some way not to earn most of his pay on those two nights would deserve a big raise. I let myself be talked into an unfortunate cover story on the much-ballyhooed movie *Barry Lyndon*, which turned out to be a colossal flop. I had fun writing a new lead for an early December football story on the Minnesota Vikings: "Decembers can be pretty cold in Minnesota, but deep winter does not set in until the Vikings have lost the Super Bowl in January."

I had a chance to do more writing, as editor-in-chief, when the Time Inc. unit of the Newspaper Guild went on strike. Management had tried to lower the "cutoff point" below which the Guild contract determined salaries—strictly by length of service—and overtime rates. We were not seeking to bring down total compensation to the staff—indeed, we pledged the total would not be lowered—but to gain, or regain, control over more of the payroll, opening the way for more merit raises at the discretion of management and fewer automatic raises ordained by contract. The Guild, naturally enough, saw this as a diminishing of its role, and, combined with long-building grievances about those late nights at *Time*, and edginess in Books about layoffs, there was swelling sentiment for a strike. The Guild usually had quite a low proportion of eligible employees—20 to 30 percent over the years—as dues-paying members (especially if it had just raised dues), and some of the bosses (myself included) were occasionally tempted by the notion of calling for an NLRB election to determine whether the Guild in fact represented a majority of the employees. But such a vote in itself would probably have pulled a wave of new members into the Guild. In any case, membership tended to increase whenever contract negotiations grew tense, and by the spring of 1976, it had reached 60 percent of the eligible staff.

A strike vote carried—by the huge margin of 454 to 11—and on June 2, about six hundred employees walked off their jobs. A good many others who were not Guild members (including my son Mark, then an *S.I.* reporter) respected the picket lines. But enough people did come to work to get out the magazines; editors reexperienced the writer's life; secretaries became researchers; pickup writers were recruited in the corridors—including Jim Shepley (to Law) and myself (to Nation). Morale was high among the strikebreakers and out on the picket lines as well. But as it became apparent that none of the magazines would be forced to close down—*Time* had been the prime target—the strike ran out of steam. The Guild voted by another huge margin—411 to 31—to accept the contract that had been on the table when the strike began three weeks earlier. So management "won," but we took care not to gloat. It was the first strike by Time Inc. editorial people, quite civil as strikes go, and there has not been another one since.

Time's influence on American journalism had been profound, and by the 1960s and 1970s, much of the competitive pressure on *Time* came from the successful adaptation by other publishers of the original Luce-Hadden concept. Indeed, the magazine held no patents to prevent others from doing *Time*'s own stuff better, if they could, than *Time* did it.

In their original prospectus, the two youngsters just out of Yale wrote that *Time* (not yet in existence) "is interested not in how much it includes between its covers but in how much it gets off its pages into the minds of its readers." The stress on readability made many newspaper and magazine editors sit up and take notice when *Time*, for all the brash amateurishness of the early years, became an early success. The *Time* insight that important and difficult subjects could be approached through a personality—a cover story on a physicist or banker—eventually permeated American journalism. So much so that *Time*, in recent years, almost bored with *that* invention, devotes most of its covers to treatment in graphics of topics, ideas, questions in the news. I am not harrumphing on the porch of the Old Soldiers' Home; good journalism knows when a device has had its day.

The greatest Luce-Hadden insight was that "news" was not just politics, crime, sports, and some canned business-page stuff to dress up the stock-market quotations. It was everything that people did and cared about—medicine, science, religion, education, manners and morals, even chatter about other people, sometimes inconsequential, sometimes important; hence the "People" page of *Time*, hence ultimately *People* magazine. Today all the good newspapers, and some less good, treat these "back-of-the-book" subjects as a major opportunity. *The New York Times* is the prize specimen: a newspaper and a daily magazine, publishing pop sociology and psychology; interesting stuff about food, furniture, decor, trendy people; endlessly concerned about your health (the paper as neurotic as much of its audience); raking in the ad revenues—all this helping support the "old" paper and its purists (as I have argued with some of them) in their pristine state. It was still true that the best newspapers could help condition some of their readers to want *Time* as well, but other readers could feel these increasingly lively daily magazines left them in no need of the weekly newsmagazine.

For *Time*, the head-on competition remained *Newsweek*. (The third newsweekly, *U.S. News and World Report*, was considered a somewhat marginal competitor by both *Time* and *Newsweek* because of its concentration on political and business news; its own promotion stressed no-fluff.) *Newsweek* had begun as an unabashed imitation of *Time*, and slogged along in that role for some years, until Philip Graham bought it for the *Washington Post* in 1961. My old friend Phil—he by then publisher of the *Post*, I editorial director of Time Inc.—used to tweak me for deserting the *Post* after the war, and I would complain to him about the miserable *Post* pay.

Phil began giving *Newsweek* more character, but after his death, his wife, Kay, became a still better publisher (of the *Post* as well as *Newsweek*). *Newsweek* began to pay well, almost as well as *Time*. During the 1960s, *Newsweek* improved in more obvious ways than *Time* did; there was indeed more room for improvement. *Time* continued to improve in the 1970s and throughout remained the better magazine, in my subjective view—fortunately supported by the objective measurements of circulation and advertising income. But *Time*'s profitability was somewhat erratic during the 1970s, in part because of heavy editorial costs.

I had once advised the board of directors that the company didn't choose managing editors on the basis of "budgetary ruthlessness," so it comes "as a bonus when somebody is an extremely good editor and also reasonably good at financial control." That bonus, as the Time Inc. company history discreetly puts it, "was slow in coming under Grunwald's editorship." A succession of cost-conscious *Time* publishers leaned on Henry, and on me to lean on him some more. Well-organized deputies in due course brought the editorial process partway under control. I did not try to stop Henry from ordering up new story drafts late in the production cycle, editing, reediting, rewriting, fiddling with words. I had some of the same urges myself. "Again and again after closing an issue of *Time*," Henry recalled later, "I would wake up in the middle of the night with a start, suddenly remembering something that should have been included in a story." And it would be included—if he could raise somebody at the office. He was an expensive editor, and he put out a superb magazine.

XII

Who Edits the Editors?

For the Grunwald-Donovan *Time*, I collected warming compliments as I moved about in New York and the world, but I never encountered an admirer who would say, "Oh, and one other thing, I just love your bias." As I had learned in long years of argumentation with professors, students, industrialists, politicians, other journalists, "bias" is what somebody has when you disagree with his or her opinion. If you agree with the opinion, you are allowed to admire the courage, integrity, decency, compassion, insight, vision, whatever, that attends it, but certainly not any *bias*. As a believer in bias (mine especially, but everybody was entitled), I enjoyed encounters with people who imagined they were innocent of it.

Among many Q-and-A knockabouts on campuses, I engaged several times in long evenings with Harvard's Nieman Fellows, outstanding youngish journalists awarded a year of academic stimulus. They were overwhelmingly liberal, and after one three-hour session when they had been beating me about the head and ears for *Time* "bias," circa 1966, I said I was surprised they hadn't even mentioned the most flagrant, consistent bias of *Time* ever since the magazine started up in 1923. They looked suitably blank. I said it was *Time*'s consistent championship of civil rights from the magazine's first year, including regular publication of a box score of lynchings. This bias indeed led to some circulation and advertising difficulties for *Time* in the South. But this was not bias to the Nieman Fellows—never mind what folks think in Birmingham, Alabama—because on this issue the Niemans so completely agreed with *Time*.

I not only defended the journalistic right to be biased, but the inevitability of being biased. How could any journalist with any sense or sensitivity deal with a controversial subject and not have opinions about it? And how do you write or edit a totally antiseptic story uncontaminated by these opinions? Fair-mindedness, as opposed to an impossible "objectivity," was my aspiration. There were many degrees of "subjectivity," ranging from minimum unavoidable to moderate, assertive, outrageous. In my *Washington Post* days, I had tried for minimum unavoidable, especially on the biggest and most controversial issues. In my old scrapbooks I can also find some stories with pretty high opinion content. But the beginning of fair-mindedness is to recognize the presence of your opinions in your work, and the respect owed other opinions.

For an editor dealing with outside contributors, the "fair" ideal could sometimes require strenuous exertions on behalf of views I didn't agree with. In *Fortune*'s twenty-fifth-anniversary series in 1955, I had signed up Adlai Stevenson as one of the contributors, and Stevenson had signed up my colleague Eric Hodgins, who had been one of his 1952 speechwriters, to draft the article. Hodgins was a Democrat of somewhat old-fashioned (even for that time) populist tendencies, and he was putting some words in Stevenson's mouth that I (setting aside my vote for Eisenhower) thought quite out of harmony with the governor's elegantly measured and sophisticated form of liberalism. In one exchange of marginalia, Eric angrily demanded: "Who's writing this piece, Adlai Stevenson or Hedley Donovan?" I refrained from the obvious cheap shot. Eventually, in various mediations by mail and phone from Libertyville, Illinois, Stevenson judiciously gave each of his surrogates a few victories, and came through with some fresh and graceful passages of his own.

I had a somewhat similar encounter in 1969 with Clark Clifford, the Democratic elder statesman and lawyer's lawyer who took over the Defense Department in 1967 after Robert McNamara moved, or was moved by Lyndon Johnson, to the World Bank. Soon after arriving at the Pentagon, Clifford concluded that the Vietnam War was hopeless. After he (and Johnson) left office, he was ready to write his views for *Life*. I regarded this as an important article, though there was much in it I didn't agree with. I pressed Clifford and his editor, Tom Griffith, for changes that I thought would protect the piece against unnecessary attack. Clark, after a flare-up or two, recognized, I think, that I was acting as a lawyer of sorts, trying to help my client make his best case.

Some of Time Inc.'s biases had simply accreted. What we had said over the weeks and months and years about tax reform or Poland or pornography became the policy. But researchers and editors and writers could and did ask, "Why must we always say *that*?" And events could demand new policy positions. In arriving at these, I tried to make sure that all the people whose judgment was most relevant felt they had been brought into the decision process. They couldn't all win, but I was proud that nobody in Time Inc., so far as I know, ever resigned on a point of policy or principle during my fifteen years as editor-in-chief. (Though I can almost hear Henry Luce asking, Should you be proud? Yup, I am.)

It was during that tenure that the U.S. press first came under serious attack from the Right. The classic attack had been from the Left, and it had seen the press as an indispensable tool and partner of "the interests," the capitalist system. This was the perspective of some of my University of Minnesota professors in the 1930s and certainly of the state's dominant Farmer-Labor party. Even Franklin Roosevelt, scarcely a flaming radical, found the newspaper publishers a useful political foil; he goaded them mercilessly and gloried in their near-unanimous opposition to his reelection in 1936. Adlai Stevenson in the 1950s, more in sorrow than in triumph, complained of the strongly Republican cast of the country's editorial pages. By the middle 1960s, from Berkeley on, the rebels of the counterculture had freshened up the old liberal and radical vocabulary. Now the attack from the Left was on "the Establishment press."

The momentous new assault also came in the mid-1960s, and I felt it as it hit. In some of the speeches of Barry Goldwater's backers at the San Francisco convention of 1964, it was the *Republicans* attacking the press—"the Eastern press," to be sure, but to Goldwater's Sunbelt delegates, this was grand raw meat. Some of them gestured at the press section, where various of us effete Eastern editors were on display. (In the same proceedings, Dwight Eisenhower, who had enjoyed overwhelming support on the editorial pages, contributed an ungrateful attack on the press.) Most of the country's newspapers, in the event, supported Lyndon Johnson, which Goldwater's followers could interpret as confirmation of their champion's view.

Then a demagogue (which Goldwater was not) of devilish gifts, George Wallace of Alabama, took up the issue. In the South, he could play his segregationist views against the "Northeastern media." He delighted in publicly recognizing a *Time* or *Life* reporter or photographer—a *New York Times* correspondent or CBS man would do as well—at the press table at his rallies, and using these foreigners as straight men. The journalists provided more satisfaction than "pointy-headed Northern professors," whom he could not call out by name in his audiences.

But for the populist-Right offensive against the press, the Democratic convention of 1968 was the catalyst. The ugly confrontations between Chicago police and the youthful hippie demonstrators—for peace/McCarthy/McGovern, against Humphrey/Johnson/Mayor Daley —went all over America by TV. Daley's police generally got the worst of it on TV, and the protest came over as brave idealism. In many American living rooms, a great truth dawned: TV can choose what news to show you. "They" may not fabricate the news back there in New York, but they might as well, because they decide how much of which news to put on the air.

The Chicago police were singling out journalists for deliberate beatings, according to a telegram to Mayor Daley signed by the publishers of *The New York Times, Washington Post, Los Angeles Times,* and *Chicago Daily News*, the heads of the three TV networks, and the editor-in-chief of Time Inc. "The obvious purpose," we said, "was to discourage or prevent reporting of an important confrontation between police and demonstrators which the American public has a right to know about." Later I was not so sure about "the obvious purpose." The cops overreacted; maybe we did, too. In *America in Our Time*, the British journalist Geoffrey Hodgins calls the telegram "one of the most remarkable joint demarches ever made by the acknowledged peerage of the American news media," perhaps "the historical high water mark of the radicalization" of the press Establishment. It would have startled some of my Time Inc. colleagues to hear that I had been radicalized.

The TV reporting of Chicago, despite the Right's response, did the Democrats considerable damage, and the immediate beneficiary was the Nixon-Agnew ticket. The new Republican administration displayed no gratitude to the networks. Spiro Agnew latched onto the George Wallace themes, and in picturesque ghostwritten language attacked the "nattering nabobs of negativism"—the media elite who ran TV, the Eastern newspapers, the newsmagazines.

As portrayed by Agnew, the press, far from being part of the system, was an ultraliberal enemy of the system and of the values of Middle America, constantly stressing and magnifying bad news, giving excessive publicity to malcontents and oddballs, manufacturing unnecessary "problems" and "crises." Private citizens who felt many of these same resentments of the press now found it entirely respectable to voice such opinions; after all, they were agreeing with the vice president.

Following a critical *Time* cover story on Agnew, the mail ran heavily pro-Agnew and anti-*Time*, including many cancellations. Some of the letters may have been triggered by an unfortunate difficulty with mailing labels; about 300,000 copies of *Time* went out from our Atlanta printers with the mailing sticker pasted over Agnew's mouth. Of Time's half-dozen printing locations, conservative Atlanta would be the last to be suspected of a deliberate plot against Agnew. The cause was exceptionally large cover type in the lower-lefthand corner—"Agnew: Nixon's Other Voice"—taking up a lot of space. *Time* had a preference that the mailing sticker should not cover any type, so in Atlanta some excessively bureaucratic adjuster of the machinery went to the nearest space next to the type. I'm not sure we ever persuaded Agnew this is how it happened.

We don't hear much of Agnew these days, but the hostilities that he articulated have persisted and indeed sharpened. They are fed by the fact that the United States, as Agnew had noticed, finally developed a "national press." A commonplace for more than a century in the centralized nations of Western Europe, in Japan, and in some of Latin America, a national press evolved here only with the arrival of TV network news as a powerful national medium. By the mid-1960s, the three networks, along with the three newsweeklies, *Time*, *Newsweek*, and *U.S. News and World Report*, and three newspapers more and more national in their reach, *The New York Times*, *Washington Post*, and *Wall Street Journal*, were increasingly perceived as an elitist monolith.

In arguments with the fevered critics who saw Time Inc. as part of a leftist conspiracy, I declined to take responsibility for something somebody didn't like on the TV news last night. I did point out that most TV news was in fact quite neutral, not to say timid, in political coloration; that the *Wall Street Journal* was well to the right of the mainstream, *U.S. News* a bit to the right, *Time* and *Newsweek* well to the right of *The New York Times*; and that in any case we did not meet every week in some secret headquarters to decide on "the Eastern media" line. I thought sometimes I had made a bit of a dent.

But a senator from, say, Nebraska, who once would have concerned himself with what the *Omaha Herald* and other home-state papers were saying about him, now had to keep in mind the circulation of the national press in Nebraska. Perhaps some speech or legislative proposal lands him one week in both *Time* and *Newsweek*, maybe for a few seconds on the CBS evening news, and in *New York Times* and *Washington Post* news stories and columns syndicated in Nebraska. Perhaps all these treatments happened to be unflattering. It could be hard to convince the senator there was no Eastern media conspiracy.

The rise of a national press along with the growing influence of the press, especially the pervasiveness and technological brilliance of TV, had sharpened the question of accountability. It was the question of accountability that was at the heart of the American public's unease with the press, and it was not just a question of who are you to tell me what to think, but who are you to tell me what to think *about*?

Some editors and publishers and TV executives reacted to the offensive from the Right with bashful, "Who, me?" protestations, pleading that they really didn't have much of any influence. Some of the same people could also react with almost hysterical alarm if a federal judge said a cross word about the press—words, they argued, that could cause the dread "chilling effect" on press freedom. In this jittery view, the First Amendment was in constant peril. TV stations, subject to federal licensing, had more sober cause for nervousness than the gloriously unlicensed printed press. Perhaps to compensate for these anxieties, TV stations in the 1960s and 1970s could wallow in profit margins of 30 and 35 and 40 percent. Except in the remote case the FCC did not renew it, the license was to print money. (Competition from cable and VCR later cut into those margins.)

My own view was that the press should admit to having substantial influence, should be grateful for a remarkably broad degree of freedom, and should go about its business unafraid. We were famously good at dishing it out; we ought to be able to take it now and then. Agnew was nothing to get panicked about. Indeed, I thought certain of his criticisms of the press—ones that various journalists, myself included, had been making for some years—had merit. I shocked one or two media audiences by asserting that a statement does not become automatically untrue by being spoken by the vice president.

I was not an absolutist about the First Amendment. The freedom of the press was not there so Hedley Donovan should enjoy his work, but so the citizens of a democracy could be informed. But their right to be informed could come into collision with other rights of citizens, including the right of privacy (however difficult to define) and the right to a fair trial, which can be jeopardized sometimes by an enterprising press. Here we think first of a defendant, but I also thought the prosecution—the state, theoretically representing all citizens—had a right to a fair trial of *its* case.

My conviction that freedom of the press was not necessarily the supreme freedom in our system carried over into the sensitive areas of "security." Perhaps my four years as a Naval Intelligence officer inclined me toward more sympathy with the government side of secrecy arguments than most editors felt. But I did believe there were legitimate government secrets, despite plenty of examples of preposterous "overclassification" (sometimes to avoid political embarrassment, more often from sheer bureaucratic force of habit). I would have agonized if Time Inc. had been offered the "Pentagon Papers," the Defense Department's 2,900-page report on American involvement in Vietnam that Daniel Ellsberg turned over to *The New York Times* in 1968. I would have questioned how much major news there was in it (there was much fascinating detail that needed a lot of space), but for me the real rub would have been: Will I go against the claim of the White House, State Department, Defense Department, Justice Department, that publication of this material would endanger the security of the United States? The *Times*—where, I was glad to learn later, there was anguished debate on this very point—went ahead. The Supreme Court narrowly approved, studious readers were modestly enlightened, the national security was not undermined.

In 1973, following a sharp increase in the number of court subpoenas to journalists, Time Inc. reluctantly supported proposals for a federal "shield law" to affirm the confidentiality of news sources and to define closely the very limited exceptions to this principle. The reluctance rose from a concern that one legislative definition of the First Amendment could lead to another and another, and the eventual effect could be to limit press freedom. But I was also bothered increasingly by the image of the press as crybaby. I wondered whether it wasn't better to fight each subpoena case by case in the courts, and maybe now and then a reporter would have to go to jail. Colleagues (including Time Inc. counsel) persuaded me that a federal shield law would discourage the subpoena impulse and bolster the case of the press when we did have to go to court. The federal legislation was not enacted, but some thirty states now have shield laws.

As a rather retrograde press statesman, one of my last acts, a few weeks before retiring as editor-in-chief, was to decline to associate Time Inc. with an *amicus curiae* brief that a dozen or more publications were filing on behalf of *The Progressive*, a small Wisconsin weekly. *The Progressive* had been enjoined by a federal district court judge from publishing an illustrated article telling how to assemble an H-bomb. The magazine said all the information could be dug out of unclassified materials, but the Justice Department, acting under the Atomic Energy Act of 1954, argued that, even so, such material, "drawn together, synthesized and collated," endangered national security. That struck me as fairly silly, but still, when you got right down to it, why should an American magazine publish this how-to article if there was even a remote possibility it could be a timesaver for Colonel Muammar Qadhafi, the PLO, the IRA, or who knows? I couldn't believe the injunction represented any serious threat to press freedom, but while the issue was still being argued before an appellate court, the government dropped its case, conceding that all the information was readily available to anyone visiting the library at Los Alamos.

I never liked the Nixon concept of the press and government locked in an "adversarial" relationship. The watchdog role of the press is in fact indispensable to effective government in a democracy. It can cause embarrassment, even politically fatal damage, to particular individuals in public office, but to see this as a result of permanent press-government war betrays a poor grasp of our constitutional system. I saw the press as one of our beautiful American checks-and-balances (baffling and excessive to many foreign observers), comparable in a way to the judiciary, which can seriously inconvenience both the legislative and the executive branches, but is in no sense their "adversary."

The view of the press as an implacable enemy of people in politics was by no means confined to the Nixon-Agnew administration. By 1972, Ed Muskie was blaming his loss of the Democratic nomination on the press, and the winner of the nomination, George McGovern, was soon blaming *his* problems on the press. Defeated or self-destructed presidential candidates of both parties have been doing it ever since (Gary Hart, for instance, in 1987), and successful candidates—Jimmy Carter for one term, Ronald Reagan for two—have been prompt to blame the press for magnifying and distorting anything that goes wrong after they take office (Carter seething over press pursuit of Bert Lance and brother Billy, Reagan wondering why TV must focus on some unemployed fellow "in East Succotash"). Meanwhile, the steady growth during the 1960s and 1970s in the number of independent voters naturally distressed organization politicians of both parties, and when they wondered where the independents were getting some of their screwy ideas, suspicion centered, with some justice, on the press.

At least a few journalists, alas, took up the "adversarial" posture with self-dramatizing relish, and their conceits tended to reinforce the paranoia of the politicians. The relentless skepticism, arrogance, and plain rudeness of a few of the journalistic prima donnas hurt the repute of the press as a whole.

Some of the worst offenders were TV celebrities—presidents learned to run against them in press conferences—but there were also amply swollen egos in print. In the fall of 1979, while I was "senior adviser" to Jimmy Carter, Teddy White asked to talk to me about the White House reaction to Ted Kennedy's attempt to snatch the Democratic nomination from the incumbent president. I was in general not talking to the press, but White was working on another "president" book that would not come out for at least a year. He was an old friend, and on a not-for-attribution basis, I told him an hour's worth of pretty good stuff, bought him a couple of drinks, and treated him to several phone calls at the Metropolitan Club. As we were getting ready to leave, I politely asked, "Well, how does it [the 1980 election] look to you?" Teddy froze (did *I* imagine I could interview *him*?) and volunteered, in toto, "One thing I've learned, they're all different."

By contrast with the TV boors, I always thought a part of the appeal of Hugh Sidey's *Time* column on the presidency was an old-fashioned respect for public office and a certain kindliness toward the people standing in that light. (Good writing and acute powers of observation helped, too.)

Where the attacks from the Nixon-Agnew forces and from the counterculture came together was in questioning the legitimacy of an unelected influence on the political process. The press was seen as one of the pillars of the Establishment, along with the university (also attacked from Left and Right), the corporation (attacked from Left), the union movement (fitfully attacked from the Right but no longer relevant enough to draw much fire), the churches (which were doing their own attacking from both Left and Right, depending on which church). The media were the ideal target; everybody could read their stuff and look at it and be at least a little expert about the product.

In the incongruous Right-Left agreement, the media and their self-appointed, self-perpetuating leaders were accurately seen as enjoying extraordinary protection and privilege. Their privileges were even written into the Constitution—though the press consists of nakedly capitalistic, profit-seeking enterprises, unlike the universities (however corrupt in other ways), or the churches, or the unions with the possible exception of the Teamsters. There is a kind of moral and aesthetic vulnerability attaching to the press, I must admit, just because it does perform its indispensable role in our political process "for money." We don't mind Supreme Court justices drawing salaries, but we wouldn't like to see the Court showing a big profit—bonuses and stock options to the judges—at the end of a good year.

Still, I found the Right-Left attack deeply subversive and felt it should be fought hard, not whined about. I had always believed it was one of the glories of the American system that there were so many centers and sources of private influence standing between the individual and the state, exercising influence without invoking the coercive power of government. And for the press, private ownership and profitability were the keys to its independence of government and its ability to tell special interests to go to hell. But by the late 1960s, to the critics Right and Left, the press had simply come to have too much power.

What was once metaphor—"a fourth estate" (Thomas Macaulay, 1828), or *The Fourth Branch of Government* (a 1959 book by Douglass Cater)—was now regarded as reality. To many, the press was no longer seen as a counterweight against other authorities but as an overbearing authority in itself—an unanswerable branch of government.

I remember back-to-back evenings the week after the 1969 Woodstock festival when I endured Republican friends condemning *Life* for (1) "glorifying" the event out of political sympathy and also (2) using it to "sell papers," and then at dinner the next night listened to some far-Democrats (excessively influenced by their still farther children) who thought *Life* was "condescending" toward the rock culture. And *Life* was intolerant about Woodstock, I was advised, because it would spoil the magazine's "image" with its advertisers if the tone were otherwise.

I hasten to add that I am not one of those journalists who think that by citing criticism from both sides of some controversial issue you establish the unassailable wisdom and justice of your own position. Not necessarily so. But "attacks from both sides" could in fact teach an editor something, illuminating some issues and the surrounding popular emotions in ways not always evident on the thirty-fourth floor of the Time and Life Building. The two-flank attack could also sharpen your debating reflexes; standing up to it was, in my case, part of what the editor-in-chief was paid for.

I was proud to realize it did matter what the Time Inc. publications said. I liked to think—but never said out loud—that Time Inc. was perhaps worth two senators, good ones. On the most inflamed issues of my tenure, Vietnam and Watergate, it could be said, as I will be relating in following chapters, that *Time* and *Life* simply marched up the hill and then back down again. But I think our final position in each case gained force from our earlier views. I always resisted proposals that *Time* should run a regular editorial page lest it seem a concession that the magazine shouldn't or wouldn't entertain opinions elsewhere in its pages. With the weekly *Life*, to the contrary, I insisted to the end that it keep its editorial page—not just for the sake of being on the record, in case somebody should ask where we stood on some issue, but actually in the hope of influencing people.

I never imagined, however, that the political influence of Time Inc. was as great as our influence on the forms of American journalism or indeed on the culture generally. The great *Life* series on art, history, science, nature—and their spin-offs in Time-Life Books—surely opened more eyes than the editorial page ever did.

So what can or should serve as restraints upon the considerable power of the American press? I would not have wanted, for myself or anyone else, the power to enforce a uniform "code" upon the media. But I hoped I had enough character to enforce my own code on myself, and the ability to make it stick in Time Inc. I never tried to write it all down in any one place (nor had Luce before me), but in various speeches and memos and case-by-case decisions, I kept working the question. It does not lend itself to a crisp list of rules. For every press abuse and excess, there are at least a few remedies worse than the complaint.

It is easy enough for an editor to say he doesn't want any reporter of his to impersonate a gas-meter reader or plainclothesman. But I don't think a responsible editor can say that no investigative reporter (or foreign correspondent) can *ever* withhold his identity. Nor can he say, "I just don't want to know about it." It's his business to know when it's being done and why.

It went without saying that Time Inc. publications would not fabricate quotes, but I did not believe we should deny ourselves all use of information and comment given anonymously. Granted that "off the record" and "not for attribution" can be grossly abused, by source and journalist. They can still be a legitimate stimulus to the flow of news. Much of the early coverage of the Watergate story, especially that of the *Washington Post*, but also *Time*'s, depended on unnamed informants, their veracity amply confirmed in later court and congressional testimony.

By contrast, *Time*'s difficulty in defending itself against General Ariel Sharon's libel action of 1982 turned largely on a correspondent's reliance on sources he could not identify, as authority for a conversation that "reportedly" took place. The allegation occupied only two sentences in an otherwise-well-documented cover story of four thousand words on the massacre of Palestinians in two Lebanese refugee camps. But so far as the jury was concerned, the two sentences were false and libelous—though *Time* had not known they were false, hence had not published them maliciously, hence in law "won" the case and paid no damages. Less technically, it could be argued that Sharon and *Time* both won, or that both lost, but in my view, *Time* was the bigger loser—in heavy legal costs, distractions of a long trial, and damage to professional repute.

At the height, or depth, of the Agnew offensive against the press, I wrote a statement for the Time Inc. annual report for 1969: "Who Edits the Editors?" It was run as a full-page ad in *The New York Times* and elsewhere by my defiant company. The argument: Your constitutional right not to read our publications is well established. "Freedom of the Press does not guarantee that anyone will pay to read us. We believe the right to be read must be re-earned with each fresh issue of our publications." So it is the readers, of course, who edit the editors. "Our franchise is up for renewal every week, and we would not have it any other way."

This was good free-press philosophy and polemic, but over the years I came to believe it did not fully meet legitimate concerns about press power. The audience could indeed act as "the market" and impose corrections—or even a death sentence. But the time lag could be long, many specific offenses could go unpublished, and death sentences when they came, as to *Life*, usually had nothing to do with abuse of press power. (*Life*'s capital offense was failure to compete effectively against TV for mass-market advertising.)

I was opposed, however, to any kind of monitoring of ethics by some press-wide body. In 1973, when some well-meaning editors and professors, including several friends of mine, set up the "National News Council," to hear complaints and issue findings on press misbehavior, I declined to let Time Inc. join the sponsors:

> We believe that any council that might sound like a single institutional voice for the press, or an authoritative judge of press performance, would accentuate what are already widespread misconceptions about the workings of the American press. . . . Too many politicians and others are already disposed to discuss "the press" or "the media" as though all the thousands of magazines, newspapers and news organizations of TV and radio could be considered a single institution. . . . We will continue our policy of responding directly, without prompting by a press council, to all criticism of the Time Inc. publications, making corrections when called for, or explaining why not. We believe that our primary contract is with our readers and that we are not in any degree responsible to any "industry" body.

The council folded ten years later. Press support was spotty (*The New York Times* also refused to join), and many papers had refused to cooperate with the council's investigations or to report its findings.

I was also unsympathetic to occasional suggestions that Time Inc. install an ombudsman. Thirty or more newspapers maintain full-time ombudsmen to investigate complaints of unfairness, inaccuracy, questionable ethics, and they have occasionally produced some very blunt criticism of their bosses and colleagues (notably at the *Washington Post*, where the job is set up as a final assignment before retirement). But I felt the ombudsman was something of a cop-out for editors. On newspapers where he appears on the op-ed page amid all the contending views of the syndicated columnists, he easily becomes just one more opinionated voice. He isn't "the paper" itself speaking. For Time Inc., I didn't want any in-house Designated Critic relieving the top editors, myself included, of their responsibility for investigating and acknowledging breaches of our standards.

I believed we should admit cheerfully to fallibility as well as bias. Though the American press is the best in the world, it is not as good as it claims to be and does not quite deliver all that our system assumes from it. Nobody is going to pay $2 for tomorrow's *New York Times*, or $10 for next week's *Time*, which might buy the kind of omniscience our blurb-writers sometimes claim for the press. Speed and the scarcity and cost of first-class people are the biggest quality limitations. Early in my editing days at *Fortune*, I convinced our economic forecasters that it was good for the soul to call attention to past predictions that had not panned out. It also enhanced the credibility of everything we didn't have to correct. In the 1960s, I had a long tussle with the editors of *Time* to get them to admit error in print a little more often and more gracefully than had been their habit. By the 1970s, I think all the Time Inc. publications were reasonably hospitable to the notion that they could be mistaken. But the time and money limitations on quality—the costs of accuracy and depth—were not easing, and the audience was getting tougher. Ironically, the better the job done by parts of the press, part of the time, the better equipped people were to pick apart poor performance by the press. Time Inc. had helped train its own critics.

I thought the Time Inc. publications, like much of the press, succumbed too easily to the bad-news syndrome. Here I was in partial agreement with Agnew. But this failing of the press, the VP to the contrary, did not spring so much from some negative view of American society as from the old journalistic canon that the exception is news. This is the man-bites-dog doctrine: airliner-falls-down, news; airliner-stays-up, not news. Of course the exception does make news, and the exception is often violent, often shocking. Very little of the world's great literature, it must be admitted, deals with good people leading ordinary lives. But I didn't consider that we were in competition with Aeschylus. The chief constituent of news, especially for magazines, is simply change, and change is in no way abnormal in America. Indeed, it is the rule: change in social conditions and customs, change in the nature of the economy and the living standard, changes in education, taste, political life. Something is different from what it was last week or last year. Some of the changes will be for the better, and journalism can celebrate such discoveries without fear of going soft.

But a responsible journalism will never lose the capacity to get mad. It is not necessarily "better to light one candle than to curse the darkness." Sometimes the press must establish that it is dark, then perhaps the press can help locate the candles.

I agreed with Agnew that "the Northeastern press" was too provincial (not that he was all that cosmopolitan). At one gathering of several hundred Time Inc. editorial staffers, I speculated that there were more people in the room who had been to Saigon in the previous year than to Buffalo. "You may say there's no story in Buffalo," I added, "but I wonder." I am not sure anybody actually was inspired to go to Buffalo, but at least one droll memo was soon circulating, listing some terminally boring Buffalo "story ideas." I did, however, nudge some Manhattan-based editors and writers into travels to various Southern and Middle Western cities not on their normal coastal orbit, sometimes by hauling them along on my own "soundings" trips in election years. I took one group some eight miles northeast of the Time and Life Building to the desolation of the South Bronx, where most of them had never set foot. This was before the South Bronx had become famous—and for a couple of elections an obligatory presidential campaign stop—which happened perhaps in small part because of attention in *Time*, *Life*, and *Fortune*.

I concluded—in the South Bronx, in the Time and Life Building, Buffalo (I did go there once), Saigon (several times)—that my own first and continuous act of accountability must be to understand as well as I could the stories and scenes and situations the Time Inc. publications were reporting. I took pride in never sloughing off some criticism with a yeah-sure-well-that's-*Time*-for-you. (I enjoyed needling my friend John Oakes, always sensitive about real or fancied slurs in *Time* against *The New York Times*, on things I found objectionable in his paper; he had no responsibility, and took none, for anything that happened outside his editorial-page sanctum.) If any Time Inc. publication had done an injustice, I thought it was entirely reasonable for the aggrieved party to tell me about it and expect me to do something about it. I couldn't always, but that's where accountability starts: with the name, address, phone number of an individual empowered by his organization, and temperamentally disposed, to stand up and answer.

The next requirement of accountability was that I should make my own standards very well known within Time Inc.—on fairness, depth and balance, taste, the mix between the light stuff and the serious, our dedication to the public interest. If I could get all this well understood within the building, the further phase of accountability was to make clear in the outer world that these were indeed our standards. I tried to accomplish this in various speeches and, at least as important, in the handling of complaints.

A rather rigorous experience in accountability grew out of a 1977 *Time* article charging that Synanon, a once-respected California program for alcohol and drug addicts, had degenerated into a "kooky cult" given to mandatory divorces and remarriages, enforced vasectomies, and high living for the leaders. (The first major national publicity ever given Synanon, ironically, was a large and admiring story, some years earlier, in *Life*.) Synanon brought a $77 million libel suit against Time Inc. and also began a campaign of harassment against the company's management, particularly the editor-in-chief, whom they correctly held finally accountable for what *Time* said.

Their language was menacing, and it was not all bluff. Two Synanon members were convicted of attempted murder for putting a rattlesnake in the mailbox of a Los Angeles lawyer who had crossed them. In one deposition, Synanon's chief guru, Charles Dederich, said that if he should die of the emotional distress *Time*'s "hatchet job" had caused him, and was no longer here to control the actions of his followers, "I would almost be tempted to say: God help your children, Hedley Donovan, if you have any." In a speech, Dederich said, "Don't mess with us. You can get killed dead. Physically dead." Synanon people picketed the Time and Life Building from time to time, as well as my New York apartment building, carrying signs saying, among other things, "Hedley Donovan is a murderer" (because *Time*'s story might prevent people from seeking lifesaving treatment at Synanon). The New York Police Department took them very seriously and advised Time Inc. to do the same. Jim Shepley and Andrew Heiskell wore bulletproof vests to a stockholders meeting during this period. I declined a police offer to drive me to and from work, but did arrange contacts in the department for my children, and we all studied a list of recommended precautions. One of these warned against badly wrapped or strangely shaped packages, and when one such arrived at Sands Point, it was opened at a safe distance from the house. It proved to be a present from a notoriously inept wrapper, my sister Elizabeth.

Synanon had some clever operatives. They somehow gained access to my schedule for a rather complicated trip, booked through the company's travel department, that I was making to Paris-India-Rome-London. As I was leaving my apartment for Kennedy Airport (via the garage, as recommended by the Police Department, instead of the front door), two pickets were awaiting me. One with a microphone said, "We are going to ruin your life, Mr. Donovan." At JFK Airport, I found Air France had no reservation for me—"your office" had called yesterday to cancel it. Fortunately, the plane wasn't full. It turned out that my reservations had been canceled halfway around the world. My schedule was put back together again, and all carriers were firmly instructed to ignore telephoned cancellations. It was never proved that Synanon was responsible for tampering with my travel arrangements, but the circumstantial evidence was, to say the least, suggestive.

When I returned to JFK after three weeks away, on the Concorde from London, as originally scheduled, a customs inspector emptied my luggage, checked all the linings, took everything out of the toilet kit, squeezed toothpaste and shaving-cream tubes, shook pills out of the jars. All the other passengers had long since been waved through, and I was boiling. I had taken the Concorde (against my principles, even on company money) only so I could do a business dinner in London and then make the Time Inc. board of directors meeting at 11 A.M. the next day.

The inspector insisted it was just "a random check," but when he finished, two plainclothes customs agents appeared, showed me their badges, and escorted me to a little room where they said they would conduct a strip search. I said, "Help yourself," but suggested it was not a very smart career move they were making. I'm afraid I may even have said that Mike Blumenthal (then secretary of the treasury) would be interested to hear of my experience. The agents were getting uneasy; one of them later said I didn't "look quite right"—meaning, in this context, like somebody who should be searched. I asked them if they had ever heard of Synanon—they did remember the rattlesnake story, and I told them more. They said they had received several anonymous tips that a passenger named Donovan, who would have traveled to all the places I had in fact just been, would be on that Concorde flight, smuggling jewels and drugs. After a little phoning around, the agents wanted to carry my luggage out to my limo, and I let them. I told them they might see a couple of Synanon types out by the car, and sure enough, there they were, with picket signs and a mike: "Did you have a pleasant trip, Mr. Donovan?" I missed the board meeting, but got to the Time and Life

Building in time for the directors' lunch, where the recitation of my adventures may have been more gripping than anything I would have said during the business session.

In 1979, the Synanon suit against Time Inc. was dismissed in the Superior Court of California. In the early 1980s, Synanon was entangled in a number of legal actions, and began losing members and resources. I haven't heard from them for some years, which suits me just as well.

I have always thought it would enhance accountability if the press would attack the press. Why shouldn't a publication unleash its skepticism, investigative skills, and polemical talents against competitors? *Time* from 1923 on had run a Press section, operating on the then-novel notion that the press itself was news. But the stories generally lacked critical bite. *Time* made an exception for *The New York Times*—the "good gray *New York Times*"—and I thought some of its digs, especially during the Fuerbringer administration, were snide. The paper being as influential as it was, I thought it deserved serious critical appraisal. When *Time* ran a Press-section story on *Times* columnist Cyrus Sulzberger, portraying him as a lone voice of reason on Vietnam, amid the general dovishness of the *Times*, I caught a heavy barrage from John Oakes. John was especially incensed that *Time* quoted a Joseph Alsop column that said a *Times* editorial "all but crowed" over an apparent U.S. defeat in Binh Dinh province. John thought the Alsop attack "a vicious distortion" and *Time*'s use of it equally contemptible. I wrote John:

> I think it is Press news when one of the three or four best known columnists in the country [as Alsop then was] attacks the best known newspaper in the country on matters involving the treatment of the biggest news story before the country.
>
> I have never tried to add them up, but I suppose on any given day the *Times* brings me anywhere from 5 to 50 cases of polemical onslaught by somebody on somebody else. I find almost all of them interesting, some of them important, and in general feel that the *Times* is serving me well by telling me about all this. I doubt if any of the onslaughtees ever agree with what was said about them. I am sure they often consider it "a vicious distortion," and there must be at least a few of them who think it was irresponsible of the *Times* to print the thing at all. Surely the *Times*, a much more conspicuous and important force than so many of the embattled people it reports

upon, and itself so strongly committed to controversy, cannot avoid drawing some heated and harsh language upon itself from time to time.

The traditional press "industry" reflex was that one editorial page, or columnist, or magazine, or network, attacking another was damaging to the whole business. I applauded when Jody Powell, on leaving the White House after service as Jimmy Carter's press secretary, urged the media to get rougher with the media. And, more recently, my old colleague Richard Clurman, in his book *Beyond Malice*, has forcefully developed the same argument. I feel that if *Time* is the equivalent of two senators, as I ventured earlier, *Newsweek* surely counts at least as one, and why shouldn't they have at each other, just like real-life senators? Likewise the networks, the national newspapers—the press should cover itself as rigorously as it covers other national institutions. Who edits the editors? Along with the readers, competing editors should.

XIII

Vietnam

I don't think there was a day in my first decade as editor-in-chief that Vietnam didn't figure in my work. It was always there. Indeed, there were many days and weeks of my working life totally dominated by the war. It can still haunt. With fellow pilgrims on a warm spring day in 1988, I walked very slowly beside that eloquent black granite wall in Washington, incised with 58,156 American names. Even there, within sight of the beloved monuments to Lincoln and Washington, I thought the Vietnam Wall might well be the most moving memorial in America.

I have already told of Harry Luce's relief in handing the Vietnam question over to me, of the fight between the *Time* editors in New York and our Saigon bureau chief over a cover story on Madame Nhu, of *Life*'s heartbreaking picture album of one week's war dead. But now I want to give a fuller account of Time Inc.'s involvement, and mine, in that tragic national experience.

I first approached Vietnam via "Munich," the lesson so many Americans of my age had learned or overlearned. "Munich" was of course the all-purpose metaphor for appeasement: Let Hitler have a slice of Czechoslovakia, next he'll want the rest of the country, then Poland, then all Europe, "tomorrow the world." I never thought the Communists would be landing in Santa Barbara (interesting meeting though that might be) if we didn't stop them in Vietnam, but I did think several dominoes might fall: Laos and Cambodia certainly, very possibly Thailand, Burma, Malaysia, Singapore. This would put pressure, at the least, on the none-too-robust regimes of Indonesia and the Philippines.

I shared the view of the Kennedy administration, carried over for at least the first two years of the Johnson regime, that the fissures apparently developing between the Soviet Union and China were less important than the common interests that still bound them, and that the Communist regime of North Vietnam and the Viet Cong guerrillas in the South were essentially the proxies of the big Communist powers. Here the Munich metaphor was reinforced by the relatively recent real-life experience of Korea, where the North's 1950 invasion of the South was authorized by Stalin; armed with Soviet tanks, planes, artillery; and soon supported, with Stalin's approval, by 300,000 Communist Chinese troops, as well as Soviet advisers. So several American presidents were not entirely benighted to believe we had something at stake in another anti-Communist republic, flawed as it was, on the rim of China—a nation that, in late 1964, had become a nuclear power. But the perceived strategic threat to American interests was very long range (there was certainly no immediate economic or territorial interest involved), and in that sense I saw Vietnam as the most idealistic war America had ever undertaken. We had promised to help defend the independence of South Vietnam—this eventually came to be dressed up in the worldly language of "credibility"—and we tried to keep our word.

These views were reflected in *Life* and *Fortune* editorials, and in the tone of *Time* stories, as the American commitment deepened in the first year of the Johnson administration. As the first American combat units were committed to Vietnam—the marines went ashore at Danang in March 1965—and as the bombing of the North began, the Johnson policy had overwhelming support in public-opinion polls, in Congress and the press. The correspondents in Saigon were largely in agreement with the policy, though they had a more realistic view than their bosses (or the politicians) of what it might take to carry out the policy.

I made four trips to Vietnam, the first in November 1965. I thought I should see firsthand some of the places and people our correspondents and photographers were covering and get some feel of what this assignment was like. The correspondents in turn had a chance to press their favorite story ideas on the boss and register a gripe or two. They got in on some interviews with people ordinarily difficult for the reporter to see. But they also had all the headaches of "advancing" a VIP tour. "Come back any time," I was told in a

touching farewell at Tan Son Nhut, the Saigon airport, "but preferably not next week."

Eventually more than fifty *Time* and *Life* photographers and correspondents served, in stints from several months to several years,
in Vietnam. Three lost their lives. Two or three dozen New York
writers and editors came through briefly. I have never felt apologetic
about making short visits to the sites of big and complicated stories—
the Middle East, Poland, the USSR, Vietnam; you will learn at least
a few things you couldn't have picked up just sitting in New York.
The wisdom, of course, is not to imagine you learned more than you
did. But I thought I brought some pertinent professional experience
as a journalist, sometime intelligence officer, even lapsed history professor, to what I was looking at. And as an antidote to excessive
humility, it was good to remember that people could spend years in
Vietnam and still misread the place. In varying degrees, both the
visiting firemen and their hosts were in the dark.

The touring editor had a further difficulty in a place like Vietnam.
On the one hand, I did not want to be flabbergasted by what I saw
because that would imply that the American press, including the
Time Inc. magazines, had not done a very good job of informing me.
But on the other hand, I liked still to think of myself as a reporter
and rather prided myself on retaining some powers of observation. I
wanted to run across at least a few things that I had not quite been
told, no matter how faithfully I had read my own magazines, *The
New York Times*, and everything else.

So I thought the American press had almost but not quite prepared me for Saigon itself. No longer "Pearl of the Orient" or "Paris
of the East," of course, but it still struck me as a place of charm and
unforgettable character: the dignified nineteenth-century French colonial city of leafy boulevards, squares, parks, a proper cathedral,
and comfortable villas; the Chinese world of Chulon; the teeming
Vietnamese quarters swollen by refugees from the war; the capital
of Vietnamese Buddhism, attended by its temples and saffron-robed
priests; the wartime capital of an endangered government but not to
be confused with London in the days of Churchill and Hitler. There
were the graceful rivers of girls cycling in their *ao dai* gowns, and
there was the noise and stink of traffic jams, especially on the road
to Tan Son Nhut. There was corruption in some ministries and certainly in the streets, wherever American soldiers and the handsomely
paid civilian construction crews were dispensing their wages. But for
every child who wanted to sell you his sister, there was another who

just wanted to hold your hand and look at an American. And of course there were Saigonese of all ages who wanted nothing to do with Americans one way or another.

The first evening I was in Saigon, colleagues took me up to the roof of the Caravelle Hotel, where there was a bar, a faint breeze, a fine view of the city, and flares and artillery fire in the distance. "H and I," my friends said, meaning "Harass and Interdict"—the periodic shelling of trails and roads the Viet Cong might or might not be using that night. "No incoming," it was agreed; that would have been VC mortar fire at Saigon targets. There was a whole Vietnam vocabulary—a rich mixture of military and bureaucratic terminology and euphemism in Saigon and the earthier language out closer to the action. "In-country" in Saigon, "Nam" in the field. Our allies were the ARVN (Army of the Republic of Vietnam). The enemy in Saigon briefings were the NVA (North Vietnamese Army), a.k.a. PAVN (People's Army of North Vietnam), and the VC, the Southern guerrillas. Via the radio call letters, "Victor Charlie" became "Charlie" in the field, or the sardonic "Charles," and sometimes "the Cong," but more commonly, zips, slopes, gooks (applied, alas, about as often to our South Vietnamese allies as to the other Vietnamese we were fighting). Gooks were often "greased," and they took too many of our "grunts" with them. "The world" was anywhere but Nam, R & R havens like Hong Kong and Bangkok, but above all the United States of America (Uncle Sugar of World War II days had been retired, likewise the G.I.).

I made a point of not using the Nam-speak out there, or back in New York; I didn't think I was entitled. For the same reason, I refrained from wearing jungle fatigues or the foreign-correspondent safari suits the Saigon tailors would run up for thirty-five dollars. For looking around out in the countryside, I wore ancient two-dollar khaki shirts, finally being fully amortized from my navy days, and my worst old Long Island yard-work pants. I think some South Vietnamese province chiefs and well-starched U.S. brigadiers, ordered to make time for this VIP, had expected a more imposing presence.

Thrashing along at ninety-five knots, the helicopters could give you a considerable intimacy with Vietnam. They flew low enough and slow enough to let you see details: a goal barely missed in a schoolyard soccer game, a glint of sun on the concertina wire strung around a militia outpost. They went fast enough, in a week or so of dawn-to-dusk days, to show you a lot of a big country and to put you down in most of Vietnam's many varieties of terrain—physical, political, and military. As one cheerful colonel said, "How did we ever used to have wars without helicopters?"

Another colonel, less cheerful, snapped at a chopper pilot over the intercom: "Get your ass the hell up to 2,000 before we get shot." The pilot quickly steepened his climb. Over Viet Cong–controlled country, 2,000 feet—some preferred 3,000—was considered prudent altitude. Approaching an isolated landing zone or fire support base, the pilots would fly crazy patterns meant to baffle the unseen anti-aircraft gunners below. A Japanese photographer who had done superb work on the war told me he never had a moment's peace in helicopters because of the unspeakable damage that might come from A.A. fire up through the seats. I was able to put this out of my mind; the panorama from the chopper was just too interesting.

From Saigon I flew across the Mekong Delta—the whole intricate network of waterways; the big reddish-chocolate river with all its fingers and mouths; the ditches, canals, lagoons; the miserable mangrove swamps; the wet rice paddies glimmering in the sun. I was taken to prosperous and somewhat secure towns and villages, and told about the "pacification" and "nation-building" programs that—despite the VC and the considerable corruption (including complicity with the VC) and incompetence among "our" Vietnamese—did make some laborious progress. I was flown to the marshy southern tip of the Delta, relatively peaceful country held by a not-very-belligerent ARVN division, the 21st, the "Paddy Rats."

An American lieutenant taking me by Jeep to one of the several villages in his care told me things were much improved: "You know, a few months ago we had mortar and rifle fire every night. We don't get it more than once or twice a week now. And you know, Mr. Donovan, this road we are on—I don't think we have had a daylight incident here for at least two weeks."

The war in the Delta was essentially ARVN and its U.S. advisers versus the VC. Neither the North nor the United States made heavy troop commitments in the Delta. The Delta rice bowl was important to the well-being of the South, but the culture and the saturated geography discouraged both sides from trying for complete control. The war would be won or lost on harder ground farther up north.

This nine-hundred-mile-long country was spectacular from the helicopter and sometimes on the ground. North from Saigon there were endless miles of dazzling white sand beaches, near the coast an intricate mosaic of neat green-and-yellow fields, red clay hills, strange little pointed mountains, and running up the spine of the country the big blue mountains of the Annamite chain, here and there miniature Yosemites sparkling in the folds. One staggering sight was CamRanh Bay, one of the great natural harbors of the world, utterly undisturbed six months earlier, now pulsating with U.S. pile drivers and earth movers shown me by proud colonels and majors, and about to surpass Saigon as the principal port of South Vietnam. The bay was as beautiful as Hong Kong or San Francisco but with magnificent beaches; I thought what a superb resort, complete with long jet runways, it would be after the war. Today, of course, it is a Soviet naval base.

Another world was the Central Highlands, where there were "big sky" effects that reminded me of Montana and Wyoming, which some American soldiers and correspondents told me was not the way they thought of it at all. The trouble with the Highlands was that the open, rolling terrain (good for cattle grazing and mobile warfare) was overlooked by sinister, mist-shrouded, jungle-clad mountains where God-knows-how-many enemy platoons, companies, battalions could be waiting.

The natives of the Highlands were the Montagnard tribesmen, many in U.S. employ, tough troops when they wanted to be. They were ready to receive guests with ceremonious servings of miscellaneous goat and sheep organs, fortunately not on the menu at the camp I visited. When I mentioned this good luck to one American who worked with the Montagnards, he said, "Are you sure?" I was given a brass bracelet of brotherhood, later useful for one-upmanship on Long Island, in the days when people were wearing copper bracelets to stave off tennis elbow. In nearby Pleiku, sleeping in a U.S. Air Cavalry barracks, I was roused by a midnight alert and reported to the bunker in pajamas. Sniper activity, no mortar fire, as it turned out, but people were jumpy. It was here, in a sense, that the American war had started. The mortaring of these barracks in February 1965, in which eight Americans were killed, was the immediate provocation for Lyndon Johnson's decision to send in the marines.

I rode north in an Air Force transport, its troop-carrying capacity stenciled on the fuselage: 90 US 135 VN. This was not racial discrimination; a Vietnamese soldier did in fact tend to weigh only about two-thirds as much as an American. We had the full 135, mainly fragrant Montagnards.

The marines showed me some of their problems around Danang,

pointing out a VC-held mountain only four miles from the air base and guiding me around Hill 22, where there had been hard fighting a few days earlier, some of it sacrilegiously invading an ancient cemetery. My hosts were very careful as to where they and I stepped; only an hour or two after I left, several marines were killed when their truck hit a mine just outside the camp's gate. The marines tried to be helpful to the local authorities in various health and education programs, but weren't solemn about their civic good works. "Grab them by the balls," said a mess-hall sign, "and the hearts and minds will follow."

From Danang, with Frank McCulloch, a doughty ex-marine who was our Saigon bureau chief, I was taken on "Yellow Bird 02," an air strike against a North Vietnamese artillery position concealed under triple-canopy jungle in the mountains bordering Cambodia. The enemy guns had been giving trouble to South Vietnamese Rangers operating out of Duc Co, a jungle camp I had visited two or three days earlier. Seen from the camp, the jungle was a green wall. The view from the B-57 Canberra twin-jet bomber was of a carpet. The pilot came appallingly close to the vertical in diving down to the treetops for half a dozen bombing and strafing runs, and then in roaring back up. McCulloch, who was riding in the plane behind us, told me afterward we had drawn heavy antiaircraft fire. "Lots of those red winks," he said, "fifty millimeter," but I hadn't noticed because I was so busy experiencing the G-forces.

I felt very safe and clean that evening, having had a shower and a big steak and ice cream dinner aboard the USS *Oriskany*. I stayed up most of two nights on the carrier, listening in on the briefings of the crews that were about to take off on bombing missions against North Vietnam. The *Oriskany* had been on station in the South China Sea for almost six months and had only four more days before being rotated out of the combat area. The tension on the flight bridge was palpable as men waited for the bomber crews to come back. They all did.

I read a navy press release about Rear Admiral Ralph Cousins, commanding Task Force 77, *Oriskany* his flagship. I couldn't help noticing that the admiral was born in 1915, making me the oldest of the four thousand men aboard, most of them not long out of high school. I felt it in the legs, going up and down all those ladders, down I-don't-know-how-many decks to the engine and boiler rooms, up from the "black hole" to the flight deck and up again to the bridge.

Back in Saigon, I met with many of the American civilian and military brass, impressive people not yet worn down by the war. I was able to bring greetings to General William Westmoreland from Dwight Eisenhower, whom I had recently seen in New York. "Westy's as good as we've got," said Ike. "It's going to be tough out there." Ambassador Henry Cabot Lodge hospitably turned over the embassy residence to me; he was off to Bangkok for a visit with his wife. He showed me how to summon the servants, assured me the ground security was impeccable, but said the American ambassador's house was, after all, something of an attraction, and he couldn't guarantee against mortar attention. Just stay away from the windows.

I had heard so much mortar talk that when I got back to New York I suggested to *Time* an article examining the effect of the new lightweight metals on the technology of guerrilla war in populated areas. I had been told that three Vietnamese could carry, in three pieces, a mortar or rocket launcher tolerably accurate up to seven miles. This meant that the defense of cities, military bases, and other fixed positions required continuous and intensive forward patrolling, out beyond the static defenses, dangerous work voracious for manpower. I debriefed myself of this and various other Vietnam story ideas in a couple of long lunchtime recitations to the editors. George Hunt asked me to write some of it as an introduction to a special section on Vietnam he was planning for the *Life* of February 25, 1966. This ran as a four-page editorial: "Vietnam: The War Is Worth Winning."

My article was quite realistic about the problems but overconfident about our ability to master them. One reason, perhaps perverse, was that I had learned more than I previously knew of the desperate military situation only six months earlier. The country had been very close to defeat in the spring of 1965; the ARVN at one time was down to a dozen mobile battalions—fewer than 10,000 men. But a turnaround did begin in early summer; by then, the United States had 75,000 troops in South Vietnam, and on July 28, Johnson announced that another 50,000 were on the way. In October, in the Ia Drang Valley, the 1st Air Cavalry won the first major American victory of the war, inflicting heavy losses on three regiments of North Vietnamese. It all contributed to a sense of momentum, and I speculated in print that the "big-unit" war, battalion-size engagements and up, might be over by 1967, but that this would take a U.S. commitment of at least 400,000 men. After most of them came home, it would be up to the ARVN to deal with the VC, I wrote, and the guerrilla war might go on for years.

Through 1966, the Time Inc. publications continued to support the Johnson policy, but I urged upon our magazines respect for opponents of the policy and respect for the dimensions of the whole undertaking. I felt the war was bringing on some of the old excesses in *Time* advocacy. Describing Senator William Fulbright, one of the first congressional opponents of the war, *Time* said: "The trait that has made him a Senate storm center for two decades is not hard to define. Put simply, it is an emotional and intellectual reluctance to believe that Communism is a monolithic doctrine of belligerence based on a fanatical dream of world domination."

I told the *Time* editors:

> That sure *is* put simply. He has been fairly generally disliked in the Senate, not I think for his views about Communism, but for his maddeningly weary style of suggesting how stupid everybody else is. As to his views about Communism, he is generally too relaxed about it, but I think *Time* in turn got itself stuck with an unrealistically rigid view of the Communist world. . . . My quarrel with the Fulbrights is not that they state the obvious truth that Communism is no longer a monolith, but that they don't seem to recognize how and why Communism became non-monolithic and how it might be fractionated further. It is snide to point out that Fulbright's "Old Myths and New Realities" speech was delivered to a "nearly empty Senate chamber." We all know, and many of our readers must, too, that long set-piece speeches don't draw much of a crowd in the Senate. . . . I think *Time* has important things to say about Vietnam, and I don't like to see our argument weakened by imprecision in defining what we're against, or petty treatment of personalities.

A few months later, when U.S. planes first attacked Hanoi and Haiphong, *Time* ran a cover story on Defense Secretary Robert McNamara. I told Otto Fuerbringer that the story had a lot of excellent detail on the raids, their planning, and the results—the best report on this I'd ever seen in one place—but I was distressed by much of the surrounding commentary, both substance and tone:

> I disagree strongly with the assertion that the U.S. must be determined to win in Vietnam "at any price." We are all long since agreed that it is very important for the U.S. to win in Vietnam, and worth a very substantial effort, as indeed we are making. But I have never believed that Vietnam is a life-and-death issue for the United States. It is not worth "any price."

Occasionally a kind of cheerleader tone turns up in our treatment of the war and Washington decisions about the war. The effect is to make us sound like uncritical champions of an official line rather than thoughtful, independent supporters of a policy which, God knows, has its agonizing aspects. The cover slash, *Raising the Price of Aggression*, bothers me on this score. It offers the rather boring prospect of a defense of the Administration's decision and in no way suggests that we have a lot of fascinating stuff about the strikes and their planning. In the captions I didn't like *Relentless reply to relentless aggression*, or *Said the Aussie: "All the Way!" Said the Filipino: "About Time!"* I wince at returning pilots "rhapsodic" over bombing results (even if they were). And we demean our own forces when we ridicule the enemy. "Trafalgar as directed by Charlie Chaplin" is an entertaining phrase [*Time*'s description of a recent sally by North Vietnamese torpedo boats] but if those had been U.S. PT boats attacking Japanese destroyers in World War II, we would have considered them "heroic" and if they had been Japanese PT crews we would at least have credited them with being "fanatical."

Fuerbringer conceded minor infelicities, but stood up for the story: "*Time* has not been and does not intend to become a Johnson cheerleader. . . . The U.S. had taken a major and necessary decision; the Hanoi-Haiphong bombings were a military masterpiece. Thus the story had a strong and justifiedly admiring tone."

On a *Time* story defending the constitutionality of Johnson's policies, I wrote Otto: "The business about how Presidents have sent troops abroad 150 times or so without asking Congress is pretty familiar, and has surely been in *Time* before, and isn't really the point. Vietnam has become our third biggest foreign war, which ain't Tripoli pirates."

It was in late 1966 that the war began to be deeply divisive for America. In the polls, support for the war was declining, restiveness was rising in Congress, and the ugly "class" character of the war had emerged. The draft, which for years had meant nothing more than an obligation to register, was now beginning to draft—to take young men from their homes and send them overseas to be shot at. The draftees were mainly from lower-income families, as were the men who volunteered a step or two ahead of the draft. Paradoxically—or maybe not so paradoxically—the youthful protest against the war came most heatedly from the campuses, where educational deferments protected the young men as long as they stayed in college. Presumably there were elements of idealism and disinterested analysis involved in campus attitudes toward the war, as well as the instinct for self-preservation. Female college students, it should be noted, and faculty members beyond military age tended to be at least as much opposed to the war, especially at the elite institutions, as the male students. Within Time Inc., the younger editorial people were turning increasingly skeptical about the war, and some of the middle-aged, even like some congressmen, were torn between faith in the familiar verities of American foreign policy, 1941–65, and concern for their draft-age sons and for the arguments their children brought home from the campuses. Could a college sophomore perhaps be right?

I went to Vietnam again in April 1967. Saigon was dirtier, noisier, smellier than a year and a half earlier, and somewhat more stable politically. The flamboyant premier, Air Marshal Nguyen Cao Ky, came to dinner at our *Life* villa, and the more sedate president, General Nguyen Van Thieu, invited me to dinner at his house in a heavily guarded military compound. The president was all too hospitable; he kept plying me with canapés spiced up with *nuc mam*, the noted rotten-fish sauce, and the next day up North, during a long round of Jeep and helicopter rides, the U.S. Marines had to allow me a good many comfort stops. Thieu and Ky were wily political rivals (the corridor between their offices in Independence Palace was said to be the longest one hundred meters in Vietnam), but Ky later in 1967 acquiesced in the results of a somewhat democratic election that gave him the vice presidency and left Thieu president. After several years of revolving-door regimes, Saigon was always ripe for rumors of another coup, but none came. Indeed, Thieu was still in office eight years later, and when he left, it was only because the North Vietnamese Army was closing in on Saigon.

The countryside in 1967 was also more stable, in a spotty way, than in 1965. Parallel to a sizable stretch of National Highway No. 4, the most important road in the Delta, I was given a helicopter ride at six or eight feet above ground level, so I could admire the peaceful Sunday-afternoon traffic—pedestrians, cyclists, bullocks, trucks loaded with farm produce, buses jammed with people, surprising numbers of private cars. The deck-level flight would not have been prudent a year or even a few months earlier. The stiffest definition of a fully pacified hamlet—few could meet the test—was a place where the hamlet chief slept in his own bed instead of going at nightfall to the nearest ARVN or militia post. But in valleys near Danang, a helicopter inspection trip that required an escort of two gunships in late 1965 could now be made in a single chopper, and no riflemen needed to be posted around the villages where we stopped.

Away from the more or less pacified regions (none of the forty-three provinces was rated 100 percent secure, and no more than a dozen of the 241 administrative districts), there were more conventional battlefields. At Khe Sanh, in the northwest corner of the country, some of the marines called their encampment "Little Bighorn." The terrain in fact more closely resembled Dien Bien Phu, where the French in 1954 suffered their final defeat in Indochina—a modest plateau sitting in a bowl of mountains. There had been some shelling of Khe Sanh shortly before I visited, a heavier barrage was to come a week or two later, and then for eleven weeks in 1968, the marines withstood violent night-and-day bombardments. A sergeant at Khe Sanh: "Could I ask you something? I have to be here, but why are you here?" I said Khe Sanh kept turning up in the news, I was never going to know what it was like to be stationed there, which was fine by me, but at least I knew now what the place looked like. I ended up with the names of some people to phone in Philadelphia to say he was okay, and I hope he stayed that way.

I visited some of the Special Forces camps—perimeter perhaps six hundred meters across—hacked out of hostile and mysterious country close to the Cambodian border, manned by six or eight gung-ho Green Berets and several hundred Vietnamese, some not so gung ho, a few very possibly working for the VC. The camps were like something out of *Beau Geste* or the American Indian wars—old-fashioned "forts" plus a helicopter pad. At a camp where I caught the smell of decaying bodies, the lieutenant in charge was in no way apologetic: some VC got partway up the embankment the other night and there hadn't been time to dispose of them yet. His outpost had been under mortar and sniper fire almost every night for weeks. He was on his third tour of duty in Special Forces camps, said he probably shouldn't say this, but he enjoyed it. He was one of the literally hundreds of young officers I met on my trips to Vietnam who, at least to a visiting editor, conveyed a strong sense of conviction about the importance of the war, along with a very sober view of what we— they—were up against.

I toured a 25th Division training base where newly arrived soldiers were shown some of the VC techniques in laying land mines,

setting booby traps, preparing that ancient Asian snare, the camou-
flaged punji pit. (In the nuclear age, several hundred American soldiers died of wounds inflicted by sharpened bamboo sticks, the tips
sometimes smeared with poison.) I was a guest of the 25th in crawling
through a demonstration maze of VC tunneling of which the division
was very proud. The tunnels were bigger than VC diameter but still
a tight fit for a 200-pound editor (age fifty-three). I was drenched with
sweat when I finally squirmed out. A soldier slyly asked me, "How
were the rats?" I wasn't going to be the new kid on the block. "Not
too bad today," I told him, but I was just as glad I hadn't run into
him before I went down.

In the Mekong Delta, I talked with the legendary Colonel Sam
Wilson, a kind of one-man State Department/Information Agency/
CIA/Development AID/Community Chest/Pentagon. Wilson, after six
months in Long An province southwest of Saigon—VC-infested for
years and a major corridor for enemy movements to the South—
would claim only that population under government control had been
increased from about 25 to 30 percent and territorial control from 5
to 10 percent.

Back in New York, I wrote a *Life* article, "Vietnam: Slow, Tough,
But Coming Along" (June 2, 1967). I acknowledged that it was a very
different war from the one predicted in my previous article, but I still
thought we could "win" in some conventional sense and start bringing our troops back by 1969. "The war will be over, goes one definition, when the V.C. are no more than 'a very bad police problem.' "
By that test, I ventured that V-VN Day could still be five or six years
away.

I also talked about Vietnam in a commencement speech, "On the
Possibility of Being Wrong." James Hester, the president of New York
University, had invited Lyndon Johnson to be the speaker, but the
White House was not committing the president very far in advance
in those days, especially to campus appearances, which had increasingly disagreeable possibilities: "Hey, hey, LBJ, how many kids did
you kill today?" So Hester needed a standby. I was one of his trustees,
and would not have my feelings hurt if I were invited to perform, or
disinvited, at the last minute.

I told the graduates (unaware that they were listening to the
understudy) that it would be clear within a year or two that the
Johnson policy was succeeding or it was failing. When that time came,
I hoped those who had been wrong—politicians, professors, clergy-

men, even journalists—would have the grace to say so; if not, we could live in a very sour political and intellectual atmosphere for years to come. I continued:

> After a war we Americans do a beautiful job of binding up the wounds of the enemy. Look at Japan and Germany today. After Vietnam, I think many of the most serious wounds will be internal, right here at home. . . . We might begin even now to let a certain measure of modesty and generosity into the dialogue. As to what will or won't work in Vietnam, we might begin by admitting that we are all to some extent guessing. Nothing is guaranteed. So far as the morality of the policy is concerned, we might do well to credit all parties to the debate with decent motives and a normal sense of human compassion. We might also try, even as we go on arguing, to reawaken some sense among us of community. As Americans we have come a long way together; our history, when you get right down to it, really reads pretty well.

My own concerns about the domestic damage grew over that summer of 1967. I was impressed by the evidence of rising opposition in the Middle West, by no means confined to the young or the liberal, and in my own very Republican suburb on Long Island, the war was steadily losing support, especially among women.

I was influenced, too, by some observations by my son Peter, Amherst '66. He may have been one of the few liberal-arts graduates of his year who actually went out of his way to go to Vietnam. Turned down by all the military for bad eyesight, he got into the International Volunteer Service, the Vietnam equivalent of the Peace Corps (which was not allowed to operate in combat areas), and was sent to a village in the Mekong Delta. He spent a little time with me during my 1967 visit to Vietnam, and in our conversations there and correspondence afterward, I found him somewhat discouraged about the war. The government officials and ARVN detachments he saw in his province did not inspire confidence. Peter was later transferred to an IVS unit in Saigon, and was there during the Tet offensive of early 1968, when the VC assault on the cities of South Vietnam got such spectacular TV display in the United States. Tet was felt at the Donovan dinner table. Dorothy, who had originally believed in the war, was now ready for us to get out of Vietnam, then and there: "But my son is out there!" "I know, so is mine." Inconclusive.

In the fall of 1967, I held a series of Vietnam discussions with the top editors of the magazines and the writers and Washington correspondents most involved with our coverage of the war. The Saigon bureau was asked to file voluminously. About twenty-five people took part, and, as I recall it, all but Daniel Seligman, executive editor of *Fortune*, John Steele, chief of the Washington news bureau, and perhaps one or two others, thought we should end our all-out support of the Johnson policies. I had come to that conclusion myself, but I wanted all my colleagues to be heard, especially those who disagreed with me.

Several of the editors were clearly relieved, though they didn't quite put it that way, that I had finally arrived at views they had already held for some months. These included two senior *Life* people, Editor Tom Griffith and Assistant M.E. Ralph Graves, and the chief of the Time-Life News Service, Dick Clurman, who had been going to Vietnam two or three times a year for several years, and was becoming increasingly pessimistic. *Life* M.E. George Hunt, originally an ardent believer in the war (and proud of the valor of the marines out there), was moving at about the same pace as I, increasingly troubled by the military odds, also tugged along, as he told me, by his own "campus," the younger *Life* staffers.

The shift began. A *Time* cover story in early October called the siege of the marines at Con Thieu "a symbol of cumulative frustrations in a complex war," and acknowledged "pressing reasons for disquiet" in American opinion. We began to prepare a *Life* editorial advocating a pause in the bombing of North Vietnam and serious probing of the possibility of peace talks with Hanoi. It was originally intended to run in the October 13 issue; at the last minute, I had it pulled. This led to rumors that we had succumbed to "administration pressure." There was a bit of pressure, as a matter of fact (requests from Lyndon Johnson and Secretary of State Dean Rusk that we reconsider), but we had not succumbed. I pulled the editorial for a prosaic reason: so the writer could have more time to tighten the argument. The author of the editorial was Curtis Prendergast. Writing of the episode many years later, in the company history, he graciously explained that the earlier draft "showed too much of the writer's late-night sweat." Curt's revised draft ran in the issue of October 20, 1967.

Though we continued to support the prosecution of the war in the South, ground and air, we also urged in an editorial in January 1968 that the possibilities of a "negotiated peace" in the South should be explored. The notion that there could be meaningful peace negotiations with Vietnamese Communists, North or South, was of course a naive misreading of Vietnamese Communists, as later events demonstrated. But *Life* had considerable company in that view—in Congress, elsewhere in the press, in academia. The view also rested on misconceptions about the anti- and non-Communist Vietnamese—that they had almost as much political and military vitality as we wished they did. But the Time Inc. policy shift of those fall and winter months of 1967–68, modest though it may sound today, was at the time momentous to me and my colleagues, worth debating, worth agonizing over.

I received a *cri de coeur* from my researcher, Dorothy Ferenbaugh, a thoughtful observer and a sharp listener to what people were saying. Dottie, self-confessed "square" and patriot (daughter of a retired major general), wrote me that the credibility of the Johnson administration was "all but totally destroyed," so far as she was concerned; that George Romney, the Michigan governor who said he had been brainwashed in his briefings on Vietnam "may have had a point"; that our military intelligence seemed to be "drastically poor"; and that it was crazy to stick the marines into such "a rathole" as Khe Sanh.

Lyndon Johnson was bitter about the Time Inc. shift. He told people I had "betrayed" him. Much of the press had already turned against the war, but he liked to think, so he said, he could depend on Time Inc.—and CBS. Then, in a special report broadcast in February 1968, Walter Cronkite went into opposition. I heard the president was saying Cronkite and Hedley Donovan had cost him the war.

When I saw Johnson one evening in March 1968, he used on me a variant of the lament he had addressed at least once to Robert Kennedy as Kennedy turned against the war: "I was just trying to carry on what your brother believed in out there." I don't know how Kennedy answered, but when Johnson told me he was just doing "what you fellows always said I should do out there," I said I thought we had been wrong. By "we" I meant primarily myself and *Time* and *Life*, but if Johnson wanted to include himself, he could. In longer exchanges with him on other occasions, I had observed his gift, remarkable in a powerful man who loved to talk, of listening very patiently and attentively to someone else, then picking up his own stream of thought with no acknowledgment whatever of what the other person had said (though he might bring it up some other time). In our brief exchange on Vietnam, the debate-type response to my confession of error would have been to ask what made me now think that I/Time Inc./he had been wrong. Instead, he simply said, "This wouldn't have happened if Henry [again he forgot the "Harry"] was still alive." I let that go.

When Lyndon Johnson abdicated, and his loyal vice president, Hubert Humphrey, became the Democratic candidate, I preferred Richard Nixon in good part because I thought he was home free on Vietnam. Not to "cut and run" (the LBJ phrase), but to maneuver vis-à-vis U.S. opinion and Vietnam, both South and North, and to wind down our commitment in ways that gave the South a chance to make it on its own. Nixon as president never attacked the Democrats for putting us in Vietnam, and was intent as a politician, but I think also as a point of principle, not to be the president who "lost Vietnam" or ditched an ally.

In February 1969, I made another visit to Vietnam. I broadened my naval experience by spending a day with the U.S. "brown water" fleet, fast patrol boats scanning the banks of Mekong branches and bayous where enemy troops might be surprised. (Sometimes, of course, it was the patrol boats that were surprised.) Otherwise, I was looking at places and military maps I had seen before, and measuring progress, if any, since previous trips. Our commitment was now up to 540,000 troops, the toll of American dead in an "ordinary" week was running at two hundred to three hundred. At one military briefing, the arithmetic was stark: In 1968, in Tet and other defeats, the VC and NVA had probably suffered at least 100,000 casualties, and they had been able to bring down from the North at least 200,000, maybe 250,000, reinforcements.

To the leadership in the North, the war was truly life-or-death. They would send down the Ho Chi Minh Trail and its tributaries more than enough men to replace their losses; they would use cease-fires and bombing pauses and even signed peace agreements, when those came, to further their unwavering purpose of overthrowing the "puppet" regime in Saigon and driving out their American masters, as they had driven out the French imperialists. They would outlast us, whatever it cost.

American policy, following our propaganda defeat (and military victory) in the Tet battles of 1968, and the return to Texas of Lyndon Johnson, was now infected with a fatal reasonableness. It was desirable, very desirable, for us to "win," but it was tacitly admitted that it was not imperative. Nixon in 1969 began a slow withdrawal of American troops, stressed "Vietnamization" of the war, and quietly developed feelers to Hanoi. In Washington more and more often, one began to hear the words "decent interval"—meaning the time that must elapse, after we started leaving Vietnam, for people elsewhere in Asia, in Western Europe, the Soviet Union, the Middle East, in our own country, to feel America had given its ally South Vietnam a shot at surviving.

In my own thinking, at the time we shifted the Time Inc. stance, it was the injustice of the war within America that weighed most heavily. Perhaps this was parochial, perhaps I should have cared more deeply about the suffering of the Vietnamese, but I must honestly record that I didn't come at it that way. The Vietnamese were capable of abundant aggression toward one another and their neighbors in Laos and Cambodia. One of the gentle, lotus-type politicians of Laos called the North Vietnamese the "Prussians of Asia." They could have conducted a brutal war among themselves, without our presence, and indeed they did before we arrived in force and after we left.

No, I was troubled by the increasingly dubious morality of the war as it bore upon Americans. In the nineteenth century, in a small professional army, Rudyard Kipling's Tommy could fight for the queen's shilling or just for adventure, out on the fringes of empire. But was it right for a democracy to send draftees to die far from home for less than vital national interests?

I was outraged by the instinct in Nixon (as in Johnson before him) and his vice president to treat dissent as though it bordered on treason. I wrote in a *Life* editorial in October 1969:

> Our Constitution specifies no fewer than nine matters, none as serious as war, which require a two-thirds vote for congressional approval. When we are in a war which has never had explicit congressional sanction, and never even been legally "declared," being fought in good part by draftees (chosen by a fantastically capricious system), a war which many (*Life* included) have thought important to win but almost nobody has ever claimed was imperative, and when this war has dragged on inconclusively for years, the wonder is not that there is protest but that there is so much willingness to serve and sacrifice. Mr. Nixon and Mr. Agnew too would do better to marvel at the stability and patience of the nation they are privileged to lead, rather than purse lips and wonder how Hanoi is reading our students today.
>
> What an irony that we should be on fairly good terms with Communist Russia, talking cautiously about a possible thaw in relations with Communist China, and still so bitterly embroiled with one of the smallest Communist states.

It was also in October 1969 that several hundred Time Inc. employees signed a petition requesting use of the company auditorium for a "Moratorium Day" peace rally. The moratorium was conceived as a dramatic interruption of normal business in corporate offices, stores, campuses, government buildings all over the country, as a protest against the war. Time Inc. management, with some misgivings about the precedent, made the auditorium available. The proceedings were calm and not very heavily attended, but over the course of the day, 645 signatures were collected for a telegram to Nixon demanding the withdrawal of U.S. troops. (Lest I fall into the previously mentioned sin of the unmoored statistic: There were then about 2,500 employees in the Time and Life Building.)

Moratorium Day was just the kind of incident that brought out the worst in Nixon. Even as he pursued his Vietnamization of the war, pulling out U.S. troops stage by stage, talking up the growing role of the Saigon government and ARVN, sending Henry Kissinger to trade subtleties in Paris with Hanoi's agents, he kept up his divisive and inflammatory rhetoric within the United States. I thought he was encouraging the stab-in-the-back reaction he and Dr. Kissinger professed to fear: the postwar legend in Weimar Germany that the home front had betrayed the army. I think Nixon, from one set of special personal circumstances, and Kissinger for very different personal reasons, could not grasp the full extent of the dismay of a so-to-speak "normal" American at seeing his country torn apart in this way. Most Americans were not driven by Nixon's suspicions, nor his view of life as a continuous crisis, nor were they seized with Kissinger's melancholy view of the burdens of power. I still liked to think we were The City Upon the Hill, and it was excruciating to see The City fighting itself in the streets.

Throughout those bitter days, many Time Inc. employees felt our editorial position was insufficiently critical of the administration. After Nixon's "incursion" into Cambodia, and the Kent State shootings, I had received a staff petition with 332 signatures asking that *Time, Life,* and *Fortune* condemn Nixon's action, and, if the editors would not do so, the staff dissent should at least be reported in the magazines.

I said in a memo to the staff that I respected the concerns expressed in the petition, that I was aware that other publications might report on it (they didn't), but our magazines would not: "I must reaffirm a general principle of editorial responsibility in Time Inc. Our readers are entitled to assume that our editorial position on any topic is based on the views of the Time Inc. people professionally assigned to that topic, working under the direction of the editors identified on our mastheads. This system does not guarantee infallibility, but it does clearly locate responsibility. I think it makes for stronger journalism than if our editorial positions were based on samplings of general sentiment within the staff." The petitioners were scarcely mollified. One wrote accusing me of "gross insensitivity."

Looking back on it today, I am uncomfortable with my unbending reply. If the press is to report on the press as fully and energetically as it reports on other institutions (as I advocated in chapter 12), then the dissent of the 332 Time Inc. employees was surely (in the useful *Time* coinage) "newsworthy." So *Newsweek* and *The New York Times* should have reported it, and it would have been odd for Time Inc. itself to take no notice of the story.

All kinds of difficulties instantly suggest themselves. Were the magazines in some introductory comment entitled to point out that of the 332 men and women who signed the statement, only fifteen, or seven, or whatever the number, had assignments involving Vietnam? Were the magazines entitled to say the 332 were only a fraction of those who might have signed? If so, how to determine the fraction? Of all editorial employees in New York? That would have been about 25 percent. But a few business-side employees had signed—would it have been fair to say only about 12 percent of the company's New York employees had signed? Would that precipitate a demand for a fully organized vote—organized, of course, by good old Time Inc. itself? Electioneering during business hours? And if the precedent is fully established for the future, how many dissenters must there be, on how big an issue, for the Time Inc. magazines to be obligated to report that not all the staff members agree with the editors? These problems were not insoluble. The resolution, ironic perhaps, was that the editor-in-chief, from the authority unquestioned even by the dissidents of 1971, could have said this or that staff protest doesn't merit notice in our magazines, this one does. That one did.

In a forceful *Life* editorial in April 1971, Tom Griffith wrote:

The U.S. has done a great deal in, for and to Vietnam—probably too much. According to President Nixon, one of his major difficulties in Vietnam is that "Americans are very impatient people; they feel that if a good thing is going to happen, it should happen instantly." This is an almost unbelievable complaint for a U.S. President to make in 1971. Americans have been extraordinarily patient in waiting for a resolution of the Vietnam war—the longest and most inconclusive in U.S. history and the most marginal to our vital interests.

Though we do not ask the President to say this, his statements should permit Americans to conclude that if worse came to worst, Communist victory in the South could be borne more easily than an indefinite U.S. role in an endless war: this indeed would be to become the "pitiful, helpless giant" of Nixon's midnight fears.

I caught heat from the hawkish side. In that same spring of 1971, I gave a speech to an audience of Middle Western business executives on "Coming to Terms with Vietnam." The audience, I suppose by definition, was heavily pro-Nixon, and several ostentatiously walked out as the drift of my talk became apparent. I tried to spell out where I thought I had gone wrong (and helped Time Inc. go wrong) about Vietnam, and the speech was reprinted as a *Time* essay: "We must all begin by recapturing some sense of astonishment that the U.S. is still engaged in this war." Our major intervention began in 1965; three years later, campaigning for the presidency, Nixon said, "It was essential that we end this war," and "end it quickly," and now, still another three years later, we were still in it.

Nixon should set a firm date, I said, by which all U.S. forces— land, sea, air—would be out. I continued:

> We have now done what we could. President Nixon should stress more often that America has made an enormous effort, far beyond anything that could have been considered a diplomatic or moral contract with South Vietnam. . . . Despite tremendous effort, we were not able to project American power into a very complicated little country 8,000 miles from San Diego in such a way that a non-Communist government was certain to prevail. We are having to settle for a possibility that it will prevail.
>
> I happen still to think the U.S. was right to try in 1965 to prevent the forcible takeover of South Vietnam by Communism, and that such a takeover would have happened if we had not moved in as we did. I would say now, though I did not see it then, that we went on in 1966 and 1967 to expand the U.S. effort far out of proportion to our original purposes, and that this enlarged commitment then began to take on a life of its own and even to work against our original purposes. It took me the better part of those two years to begin to see that. I wish I had been wiser sooner. . . .
>
> If the country is to come to terms with the Vietnam experience, the process must begin with a good many individuals acknowledging their own errors. Such a process could help arrest any wave of na-

tional bitterness and recrimination. . . . We first became involved in Vietnam to contain China, and our contain-China policy first developed in the days when China and Russia seemed to be a monolithic Communist bloc. If it is now safe for us to trade with China and safe to negotiate an ABM agreement [banning defenses against missiles] with Russia, it should be safe, at last, to bring our soldiers home from Vietnam.

The Time Inc. retreat from Vietnam was still too gradual for some of our staff. It hurt, in May 1972, when I received a bitter letter from Maitland Edey, the former editor of Books, who was still writing for us, a friend and colleague I greatly respected. He wrote of endless official lying, as he saw it, in U.S. policy in Vietnam, and urged that Time Inc. advocate an immediate cessation of the U.S. military effort. He listed some eighteen examples of government lies.

I didn't have the time or heart for a case-by-case critique of his letter. Had I attempted it, I would have conceded that the naval incident in the Tonkin Gulf on the night of August 4, 1964, simply didn't happen, so the Tonkin Gulf Resolution, in which Congress gave Lyndon Johnson sweeping warlike powers to pursue his policies in Southeast Asia, was indeed based on a "lie." I would have argued that the resolution was not all that decisive, however, since Congress could have repealed it any time it wanted to (it finally did in 1970), and that Congress could have withheld support of the Vietnam War any time it chose to, by cutting off the money to fight it. I would have agreed that the whole business of the "body count" was riddled with lies, small and large. I would have pointed out, however, that in a war without territorial objectives (for our side), enemy corpses—if honestly identified and counted—were a legitimate, if ugly, measure of "progress." I would have noted that even in "the good war," World War II, U.S. and Allied communiqués rather consistently exaggerated enemy losses. Our own losses in Vietnam were reported more fully and more promptly than our losses in World War II. I would also have reminded Mait that most of the raw material for his bill of lies came from dispatches filed from Vietnam without censorship (unlike World War II) by correspondents who moved around the countryside in U.S. government vehicles.

Instead, I wrote Mait very briefly, enclosing as my answer an advance copy of an editorial by Tom Griffith, and adding that when the time came to try to put the country back together again, "it surely won't help if all misguided hopes, inaccurate predictions, mistaken promises of the past [i.e., most of Mait's exhibits] are now declared to have been lies." Edey wrote back that the *Life* editorial was good so far as it went, but "this war has got to stop." Now. And he was talking about "the lies that were lies." He went on: "You sadden me because I sense in you a lack of moral passion on this issue. . . . Please, make your commitment, and do more." I found this a somewhat self-righteous way of saying he and I disagreed, and let it go unanswered.

I made a last visit to Vietnam in April 1973. In Paris in January, Kissinger and Le Duc Tho of the Hanoi Politburo had initialed the agreements that ostensibly ended the war. Saigon that spring was animated and mortar-free. I was told of scattered skirmishes in the nearby provinces that I visited, but life looked deceptively placid in these places once so heavily bombarded. U.S. and South Vietnamese officials offered encouraging reports of political and economic progress, and ARVN capabilities were said to be improving. The progress was not illusory, but it was not enough.

Nixon and Kissinger had agreed to the continued presence in the South of the Northern troops in place—at least 100,000—at the time of the Paris accords. The North in return dropped its long-standing insistence that no peace could be negotiated while the Thieu regime remained in power. But the concession was meaningless, since the North had no intention of treating the Paris agreement as the basis of a lasting settlement. Hanoi began at once to marshal all its formidable military resources for a decisive blow against the South.

Thieu thought he had assurances from Nixon and Kissinger that he could call for American military supplies, and above all air support, if the North violated the agreement. But once Congress and the public thought America was at last "out," it was doubtful that any Northern violations, no matter how flagrant, could have brought us partway back "in." The violations did become flagrant, but by then Nixon was being consumed by Watergate. When the North sent fourteen divisions of regulars against the South in the winter of 1974–75, Thieu begged for help. But by then, even with Nixon gone and their old buddy Jerry Ford in the White House, congressmen would not come up with a mere $300 million in emergency shipments of ammunition and fuel—on top of the $111 billion we had already spent. The country had had enough of Vietnam.

As General Van Tien Dung closed in on Saigon, the U.S. Embassy was devising evacuation plans for American civilians, including correspondents. But Time Inc. and other news organizations could get no assurances as to what, if anything, could be done for the Vietnamese who had worked for the American press. Murray Gart, the head of our News Service, and Roy Rowan, Hong Kong bureau chief, plunged into this problem, chartering planes, outwitting bureaucracies, regrouping when the bureaucrats won one—e.g., Saigon airport police, in a bizarre display of integrity, scorning a 100,000-piastre bribe to let a Time Inc. busload through the gates.

Gart and Rowan eventually got thirty-seven Vietnamese out: all those who wanted to leave, among the people who had worked for us—people who would have been in danger as soon as the Communists came in—and their wives, husbands, children, uncles, aunts, truly "extended families." Several got Time Inc. jobs in New York or Los Angeles. Some of their children went to law school and medical school, there were some nice entrepreneurial success stories, and maybe a sad story somewhere, but all in all a wonderful microcosm of the latest wave of Asians in America. It wasn't just that Gart and Rowan got our people out, which we owed them, but they then enriched this country.

One of our reporters who chose to stay behind was Pham Xuan An, a stringer promoted to correspondent, thought by envious competitors of Time Inc. to be the best Vietnamese journalist in Saigon. An was highly energetic and dazzlingly knowledgeable about South Vietnam political and military figures. It turned out that An had belonged all along to the VC; he was in fact a lieutenant colonel.

In Douglas Grade School in Minneapolis, when I was growing up, it was very generally known that America had never lost a war. When I was in high school, a fine history teacher named W. W. Williams ("Willie," but not to his face) thought we were old enough to hear that in the War of 1812 our young country had to settle for a tie with the British. Half a dozen years later, at Oxford, I tried to enlighten English friends about the War of 1812. They had never heard of such a "war." They thought they were quite busy at that time with Napoleon. Many years later, I thought Dwight Eisenhower was right to settle for a tie in Korea: We had defended a non-Communist South Korea but could not, at acceptable cost, destroy the Communist regime in North Korea.

But in Vietnam, unmistakably, we lost. Or did we? The makings of a revisionist school appear now and then in arguments that our effort in Vietnam gave the other nations of Southeast Asia valuable time, and that we even accelerated and deepened the split between China and the USSR, by putting the Soviets in alliance with Hanoi, and causing the two big Communist forces to back opposite sides in Cambodia. I find this fairly farfetched. It is easier to argue—all this with hindsight, of course—that these things were going to happen anyhow, and certainly one of the postwar developments, the Soviet presence at Cam Ranh Bay, is scarcely to our advantage.

As to ruinous consequences of our failure in Vietnam, none has materialized. No dominoes fell, except for Laos and Cambodia, which had been associated with Vietnam in French Indochina for more than a century. American "credibility" did perhaps suffer for a time, but the damage was not lasting; there is no evidence that our allies, or the Soviets or the Chinese, fail to take us seriously. Vietnam can be overinvoked in foreign-policy debates (as "Munich" once was, to opposite effect), but the experience has not plunged us into isolationism.

Looking back now, it is clear enough that we should not have gone into Vietnam at all unless we were prepared to win. This does not imply the use of nuclear weapons. But it would have meant putting America on a war footing in 1965, moving at once against the enemy supply lines and sanctuaries in Cambodia and Laos, and from the outset bombing the North as heavily as we eventually did. Victory in such a war would not have been cheap—or certain—but it would have been preferable to our defeat in the very costly war we did fight. Such a war would have been bigger but very possibly shorter and less punishing—to Vietnam and ourselves—than the actual war of 1965–75. We can be fairly confident today that China and/or the Soviet Union would not have "come in," though that was not all that obvious at the time. We can sympathize, too, with Lyndon Johnson's concern that war legislation should not supersede his "Great Society" programs. Given the unwillingness of Johnson and his advisers to make it into a big war, they and we should have been ruthless enough to let South Vietnam fall in 1965, instead of ten years later.

But ruthlessness, of course, is not one of our dominant national traits. The American attributes that did operate in Vietnam included—along with idealism and generosity—a certain insensitivity to other cultures, unrealistic assumptions about the exportability of American models, excessive faith in technology. It was not only the limitations of American power that were illuminated in our defeat, but also the limitations of American wisdom.

I did not believe we had been morally soiled, however, or lastingly weakened, by Vietnam. I thought we might even have learned something—and that we might even be smart enough not to read Vietnam into situations where it didn't apply. Those personal reactions in the immediate aftermath of our defeat seem to me to have been reasonably well vindicated in later years.

XIV

A Severe Case of Optimism

In my attitudes about Vietnam and other national issues of my editing years—in my public philosophy, if that is not too grand a phrase—I suppose the unifying principle was optimism. An odd inclination, one might say, in a journalist, one of those specialists in delivering all the bad news as fast as possible. Odder still in a journalist who has experienced, presumably with open eyes, three-quarters of the years of the twentieth century.

This century has not had a good reputation. Leon Trotsky advised people who aspired to "a quiet life" not to be born in the twentieth. "The terrible century," Churchill once called it. But there I was, born in 1914, and here I am, writing away in 1988, and for some reason or reasons, still optimistic about my country. Was it something in the water in Minnesota? No, a good many of my Minnesota contemporaries hold to more somber views.

Ever since I was a child, I have had an uncontrollable weakness for seeing the good side in unpromising situations. After a Donovan baseball broke a neighborhood window—assessments to my brother David and me—I can remember telling my mother it was a good thing, because I had been wanting to change the backyard batting rules anyway. To grounders only. At age sixteen, after my first (and so far only) automobile accident, in which I brought the family car to rest against a tree, I announced that it had been a good thing because for only thirty-five dollars I had learned what not to do after you start skidding on ice. "Only thirty-five dollars" (the fender repair bill, paid by me) was fairly daring language in the Donovan household in the winter of 1930–31.

So this young Dr. Pangloss grew up. Once, in my editing days at *Fortune*, when I had just finished an especially exhausting forty-eight-hour stint rewriting the "Business Roundup," the monthly economic forecast, I was in an airliner that seemed to be lost for hours in fog over La Guardia Airport. It would drop down for a landing approach, then abruptly change its mind, and surge back up, and I kept thinking to myself, "Well, at least I wouldn't have to edit the Roundup any more."

I have never, however, attained the serene certainties of Andrew Carnegie, whose Endowment for International Peace I served as a trustee for many years. A famous passage from Mr. Carnegie's instructions to his original board in 1910 was often read—somewhat tongue-in-cheek, I fear—at trustee dinners later in the century. When wars have been ended, the Founder charged his future trustees, they should in their "widest discretion" determine "what is the next most degrading evil" the endowment should tackle, and go to it.

Out of my interpretation of America's history, and from my own cheerful chemistry, I did develop an almost unshakable confidence in this country. It certainly influenced my work as an editor—sometimes, perhaps, at some cost in realism.

I am reminded of a *Time* essay "The Good Uses of the Watergate Affair," which I wrote about halfway through the scandal. If Richard Nixon, I wrote, were "as jovial and gregarious as, say, William Howard Taft, he might have needed a Robert Haldeman ('I'm Nixon's s.o.b.') to protect him from his own openness. That is not his problem." Now he had been forced to fire Haldeman and John Ehrlichman, and it would be difficult for him, if not impossible, to construct another palace guard "as arrogant, zealous and narrow." I noted that Nixon, "belatedly but generously," had actually praised the press for its coverage of Watergate and that his press secretary, Ron Ziegler, had apologized for his contemptible attacks on the *Washington Post*. "Watergate could be a turning point, after several years of Government hostility and harassment, toward a renewed national perception of why a fully independent press (with its abundant faults and excesses) is essential to the American system." And: "Most salutary of all, Watergate could be a historic check upon the long and dangerous aggrandizement of the Presidency. The Federal Government is not really the same thing as the United States: it is one institution in America; and the President is not really synonymous with the Federal Government; he is the head of only one of its three branches." In the work of Congress, the judiciary, the press, as they dealt with Watergate, we were seeing, "in short, that the American democratic 'system,' an even grander and more important thing than the Presidency, is still running."

My optimism was inseparable from a romantic belief in the American as a special being in a special country. But it is not easy arriving at definitions equal to the subtleties, exceptions, and varieties within any national culture, and especially the American culture. "We are not a nation," Herman Melville wrote, "so much as a world." Over the years, I labored—in articles, speeches, memos to colleagues—with the nature of the American. If I could have wangled a five-year grant from the Ford Foundation, I might have written a book on the national character (possible conflict of interest, since I was a trustee), but come to think about it, Time Inc. gave me an even longer grant. And I have continued, even off company time, to try to understand the American identity.

America was uniquely dependent on an idea. Our idea, of course, was freedom, not merely from the British Crown, but for the individual to pursue his "unalienable rights"—unalienable because granted by God, a power above any state—to life, liberty, and the pursuit of happiness. We were not a piece of well-defined geography to begin with, and we were by no means one people or folk in any racial or ethnic sense.

When the "known world," for Americans, consisted chiefly of ourselves and the European monarchies, it was easy enough to define the unique character of this country: We were a republic. When sea captains and missionaries brought Asia and Africa into our view, America's sense of identity was in no way challenged. And when much of Western Europe became fairly democratic (Victoria's constitutional monarchy, the Third Republic in France) we were still special: The New World.

But we now live in a greatly expanded world of immense diversity. Because the American journalist and businessman and tourist can jet anywhere in hours, it is a commonplace to say the world has grown very small. I argue, to the contrary, that the world has grown very large—so much of it out there waiting to be seen, so accessible to so many. It has not made us citizens of "one world." Instead, we have been confronted, far more directly than our parents and grandparents ever were, with the vastness and variousness of the world.

Who we think we are is necessarily something we perceive in comparison with other nations, and it gets harder to define America against all of today's rich variety of national societies. I doubt if it clarifies our thinking to keep talking of ourselves as the leader of "the Free World," embracing as it does so many kinds of governments and degrees of freedom, down to zero; nor does it help to speak of it as "the Anti-Communist World," for not all of it is all that rigorously anti; we simply mean the non-Communist world, 140 or so countries, most of whom decline to think of America as their leader. And to the extent that we have been defining ourselves by our adversary, we were in further difficulty, for the "Communism" of the late 1980s, as best we understood what was happening in Moscow, seemed as much an envious student as a sworn enemy of the West.

It may not have been lovable of us, but for generations we believed we were God's elect. John Adams wrote that it was the design of Providence to use America for the "illumination" and "emancipation" of all mankind. Thomas Jefferson proposed that the Seal of the United States should show the children of Israel led by a pillar of light. The notion of America as the land of the Chosen People was one of his favorite themes; this very urbane man could say, "God led our forefathers as Israel of old." He called us "the world's best hope," and we hear echoes of that when Abraham Lincoln, amid the anguish of the Civil War, said we were "the last best hope of earth." More cautiously, he called us "this almost chosen people." And the great historian George Bancroft, trained at Harvard, Heidelberg, and Göttingen, believed (as another historian has written of him) our history was really "the story of the wonder-working of the hand of God in the American forest." It is hard to imagine any Harvard Ph.D., or Wisconsin or Stanford either, looking at it just that way today.

Yet well into the twentieth century, the belief persisted. The debate over our entry into World War I, 1914 to 1917, could be read, on one level, as a clash between men who believed it was enough for America simply to stand here in its goodness, as example and beacon, and more militant men who believed America must carry its truths across the oceans.

Somewhere after World War I, many Americans lost that confidence that God's hand was especially upon us. The war itself came to seem a mistake and a failure, something America had never felt about its other wars. It was generally a time of rising sophistication and cynicism; the traditional religious beliefs were weakening; the memories of the frontier were fast receding; increasingly large blocs of the American population lacked any ancestral share in the classic early chapters of American history. For Americans who did still have faith in the God of their fathers, it was hard to believe that the spreading of the urban industrial landscape could enjoy quite the same divine favor as the crossing of the Continental Divide. And if anything of the old idea of the Chosen People had survived the 1920s, the Great Depression of the 1930s surely did not burnish it.

For a large, literate democratic society once to have held so strongly such a righteous and spacious view of itself, and then in a few years to see it so threatened, could have been a profoundly unsettling experience. But we never really had the experience. For at just that moment, Americans were confronted with Adolf Hitler. The Nazis and the Japanese did not require us to think about deep meanings of America. They required us to defend ourselves, and that was meaning enough.

If the defeat of the Axis powers had led to a stable peace, a search for a modern sense of American mission might have started soon after the war. But Stalin, almost overnight, took the place of Tojo and Hitler. The cold war was on. Once more we believed ourselves to be holding a worldwide line against tyranny. Once more we were relieved of asking ourselves what else America is all about.

The cold war eased some in 1953, after Stalin's death and after the Korean truce, and then it eased some more around 1963. The previous autumn, the Soviets had started installing missiles in Cuba, the most blatant thrust they ever made outside their own acknowledged sphere of influence, and John Kennedy coolly stared them down and eased them out. By the summer of 1963, he was making his highly conciliatory American University speech and laying the groundwork for the nuclear test-ban treaty.

But once again, just as one set of foreign dangers seemed to be receding, still another crisis, perceived as a major danger to ourselves and our allies, came to dominate our thinking about foreign policy. That, of course, was Vietnam.

When the U.S. effort there finally wound down in 1973, we had been through a forty-year crisis: the Depression, World War II, the cold war, Korea, Cuba, Vietnam. All Americans in their forties, fifties, and sixties—most of the leadership generation—had spent most or all of their adult lives with a view of an embattled, endangered America. But in the early 1970s, the cold war was ameliorated by, of all people, Richard Nixon, with his SALT I agreement with the USSR and his opening to China. And the cold war may finally have been called off by, of all people, Ronald Reagan, in his meetings with Mikhail Gorbachev in 1987–88.

With détente, however, there came no inspiring new definitions of America and the American. Indeed, President Nixon came up with a stridently vulgar definition: "We're number 1." "We must remain number 1," he said. "We don't want to be number 2. You don't want your children to be number 3." Applied to our own civic life, the great American urge to be better than the other fellow has been highly productive. People write big checks and work their heads off so the local symphony or art museum or university can be one of the country's "top ten," or "generally considered the best in the South." But slathered across the world, the boastfulness can be ugly. If the United States is number 1, who will we allow to be 2 or 3, and can we expect all the rest to line up in an orderly way in the back of the queue?

President Gerald Ford, as an old football player, was perhaps more naturally entitled than Nixon to locker-room metaphor. This otherwise sensible man pushed the "number 1" theme to appalling lengths. In a speech at La Crosse, Wisconsin: "America's industry is unsurpassed. Our military capability is second to none. But there is one thing that is even more important than all of that. America is morally and spiritually number one, and that will be the driving force to keep us moving so that America and all its people, its government, will be number one forever."

In a speech of my own, at Lehigh University, I said, "If this extraordinary language embarrasses us, how must it sound to the rest of the world?"

Jimmy Carter, alas, ratcheted the claim one notch further. A man of disciplined precision in private speech, he could be carried away in public to wild hyperbole. Returning from an economic summit meeting in Venice, he said it was good to be back in "the greatest nation *by far* [my italics] on earth." So much for the allied nations he had just been conferring with.

I preferred, I must confess, Ronald Reagan's "Morning in America" music. I wasn't sure exactly what was meant by this motif of his 1984 reelection campaign, but it seemed to convey hope and confidence—without condemning any other country to the twilight. (I voted against him, however, because he went beyond this vaguely benign message to imply a Republican monopoly on patriotism and because I felt he brought religion too far into politics. And I was fond of Fritz Mondale of Minnesota, who was clearly about to be clobbered.)

In the best tradition of American patriotic oratory, going all the way back to the Revolution, the stress was never so much on biggest or greatest or most, as on uniqueness, the idea that America was a special venture, different from any country that had gone before. Lincoln's last best hope of earth was not exactly a bashful claim, but it did convey a certain nobility of purpose and vision.

By the decade of 1965–75, many Americans would have found the Lincoln claim laughable. These were the years when the country seemed to be tearing itself apart: Watts, Newark, Detroit, Vietnam, the Martin Luther King and Robert Kennedy assassinations, the campuses in upheaval, militant feminism, the counterculture and "the Movement," obscenities, trashings, bombings.

In one of those angry years, 1969, I received a touching letter from a marine private first class, Daniel Walsh, writing from Camp Pendleton, California, presumably on his way to Vietnam or on his way back:

> I am confused, bewildered, disillusioned and increasingly suspicious. Confused by what is happening all around me, to my country, my countrymen, the world in general. . . .
>
> Bewildered by war, death, dissent, protests, placard carrying and flag waving, name calling and division of the country and her leaders. My upbringing [earlier he told me he was Irish Catholic] dictates that I use a "My Country, Right or Wrong" bumper sticker on my car. An unquestionably patriotic slogan, but somehow it curtails one's ability to change, to add or subtract from his stated beliefs.
>
> As of now I am opinionated on few subjects. (I like girls. I want to go to college.) How does everyone else know exactly how they feel about, say, Vietnam? Inflation? Must the Marine Corps be as dehumanizing as it is?
>
> Mr. Donovan, I realize that you are extremely busy, but please

take time to answer my questions. I have written to a Bishop, long ago, with no answer, and recently to a Senator of my state, with, as yet, no reply.

My first reaction was smart bishop, smart senator, but I thought better of it, and wrote Private Walsh that he should of course go to college, that something coeducational was probably indicated, and perhaps he should call on Time Inc. after he graduated. Then I inflicted on him several Donovan speeches addressed, approximately, to some of his questions.

If I was not as torn as Private Walsh, it was because I had lived (and doubtless read) more chapters of American history. I thought some things of value were being said by "the Movement," especially on the subject of racial injustice and on the inequity of sacrifice in Vietnam. But some of the protesters, healthy college men, were themselves prime examples of the Vietnam inequity. The protesters were also beneficiaries of the postwar prosperity they tended to look down upon. They didn't have to worry about finding a job when they got out of college. But for the first time in our mobile, striving society, we also had some millions of young people who couldn't reasonably aspire to "do better" than their fathers did (because father had done so well). I thought this contributed to the unmooring of the most affluent of the young. Their attacks on the U.S. government—or, for that matter, the press—dismayed me less than their assault on the university itself, for this was the institution that had created so much of the national leadership of which they were potential members. The campus, of course, was a convenient target—most of the angry young were already right there.

But "confrontation"—much-used word at the time—was precisely what did not take place. The angry young and the Establishment were talking past each other. And adult sympathizers with the protest could say some fatuous things. The *New York Post* (very liberal in those long-ago days) was constantly fretting that leftist violence would strengthen "the forces of repression." Trashing of a Bank of America branch in Santa Barbara would "play into the hands" of the governor of California, Ronald Reagan. Bombing of an army mathematics lab at the University of Wisconsin was "cruel, senseless terrorism," but more ominous, it could "touch off right-wing political hysteria; Mr. Agnew has already begun to press the frenzy-button." And Mayor John Lindsay, calling the New York office-building bombings "reprehensible," couldn't let it go at that. They were reprehensible "and self-defeating."

The climax of America's internal crisis came in 1970, in the "days of rage" following Cambodia, Kent State, and Jackson State. It was the time of sit-ins, lie-ins, petitions, vigils, draft-card burnings. When construction workers, wearing their hard hats and carrying flags, marched to protest the protesters, some Americans familiar with the German and Italian experience of the 1920s and 1930s even thought they saw the lineaments of a native fascism. My colleague Andrew Heiskell, who had grown up in Europe in those years, was of that view. And I remember the very low-key, level-headed Tom Griffith remarking, "Some mornings when I finish the papers, I'm not sure this country is going to make it."

To me that was unthinkable. As a country, we had come through worse. I couldn't refrain from asking for a little research on the New York City draft riots during the Civil War. Following a drawing of draft numbers on July 11, 1863 (at an office at 46th Street and Third Avenue), Manhattan erupted in three days of arson and looting, sabotage of telegraph and rail lines, assaults on blacks and police. The dead and wounded were estimated at a thousand.

If America looked over the edge of an abyss in the spring of 1970, we didn't like what we saw. By the midterm elections of 1970, the beginnings of the conservative reaction were discernible. In the presidential election of 1972, I saw the candidates as a kind of caricature of the nation's choice between the protest and the tradition—the pleasant, mild, "impractical" George McGovern versus the devious, belligerent Richard Nixon. And the scarcely charismatic conservative won in a landslide. The underlying trend was soon obscured by Watergate, and Ford's pardon of the disgraced Nixon contributed to Jimmy Carter's narrow win in 1976. In the same year, *Harper's* could publish an article entitled "Silence on Campus: A Professor Laments Student Apathy." The conservative tide was still running in the three presidential elections of the 1980s.

We are politically conservative in a deeper sense that has little to do with who is in the White House. After Switzerland, America has the world's oldest essentially unchanged governmental system. (And the Democrats are the world's oldest political party.) The Constitution ratified in 1788 set up a system still entirely recognizable two hundred years later. And after the first dozen amendments were adopted, the Constitution was amended only fourteen times between 1804 and 1971.

Our remarkable political stability helps make possible an economic and social environment in which radical change is the norm. I think of the allegedly conservative American businessman as one of our leading radicals, constantly introducing new products, new ways of making them, new ways of distributing them, with new implications for the way people will work, where they will live, how they will live. I would maintain that most of the changes, since I started to notice such things, are to the good. Two of my favorites are the automatic transmission and air-conditioning. The computer and I are not too congenial, but I am prepared to believe it is useful to others.

The dynamism of the economy created for most Americans an extraordinarily wide spectrum of choice as consumers and workers. As a reporter and editor I had seen, after the Depression decade, the great revival of American "upward mobility." I suppose I was myself a case in point. But whether the evidence was anecdotal (as in many a *Fortune* story) or analytical (as in many a *Fortune* article), it was clear that from the 1940s on, Americans in extraordinary numbers were again satisfying their historic compulsion to "get ahead."

There weren't too many sociologists around, for better or worse, when the Republic was getting founded and the West was being won. But upward mobility was much of what America was about. The upwardly mobile could be more poetically defined as people pursuing the American Dream. I never thought that phrase was an embarrassment. It might be that the dream consisted essentially of the dreaming—both for those who reached the dreamed-of places and for those who didn't. But the freedom to dream—indeed, society's expectation that we should dream—and the perception that no dream was totally preposterous, was very much a part of the American idea.

The fluidity of class and the conservative-radical mix in the national temperament contributed to my bias toward optimism about America. That optimism has always disqualified me as a classic conservative. I am a low-church conservative. I do have some general respect for things as they are—they are that way for a reason—but changes can often be essential and are not impossible. I had no notion of the perfectability of man, but I thought I saw in American history, along with all the improvements in man's material lot, a considerable amelioration of man's behavior.

As to "number 1," we had been tied—*pace* Presidents Nixon, Ford, and Carter—for strongest military power. We were the strongest single economy (though outweighed by the total of the other industrial democracies). We were no longer the richest nation per capita, nor the most democratic of the democracies, and certainly not the most law-abiding. As the American system generally flourished, the exceptions to its bounty became the more poignant, and the excesses of opulence could approach the obscene. But I still thought that, all in all, the promise and the dream were alive and working.

The greatest flaw in an optimistic view of America was, of course, the situation of Black America. Ever since the end of the Depression, I had considered racial injustice our greatest domestic weakness—and disgrace. Once while I was M.E. of *Fortune*, I was interviewed by a British journalist who was asking a hundred American "opinion makers" to list the country's most serious problems. I was amazed to have him tell me afterward that I was the only one who had put race relations first. I haven't changed my ranking, and now the closely connected drug and crime pathologies would reinforce it. But of course I have long since had to concede that my generation of idealistic white northerners was innocently overconfident about solutions: abolition of the poll tax, subsidized public housing, desegregation of schools. And from the early 1970s on, the well-meant welfare programs became disastrously counterproductive. Still more painful to me professionally, I came to feel that our Time Inc. reporting was sometimes so uncritically "pro-black" as to cost us credibility, and undermine realistic approaches to appalling but perhaps not hopeless problems.

Life in 1968 ran an ambitious series on black history that left me uneasy. I wrote the editors: "We seem to imply there was a profusion of important contributions by individual blacks to the early history of the Republic, slighted in the bias of white history, but really there were precious few—for entirely understandable reasons. This indeed is the poignancy of the search for the black past in America. And it is deepened by the difficulty of finding a fully satisfying black past in Africa."

In 1970, *Time* carried off an eye-catching special issue on Black America, with all the usual departments—Art, Theater, Religion, National Affairs, and so on—devoted to black achievements, and the barriers. Managing Editor Henry Grunwald made a farsighted cover choice: a twenty-eight-year-old Chicago clergyman named Jesse Jackson. But I wrote Grunwald that *Time* took "the minimum view of black progress to date, put the harshest interpretation on white behavior, and seemed extremely reluctant to criticize any blacks for anything." This approach seemed to me basically condescending. All through the issue, there was the "general implication that 'discrimination' somehow keeps down the numbers of blacks in book-publishing houses, theater, business, medicine, etc. Well, of course, it does 'in an historical sense'—two centuries of slavery, and many decades more of discrimination. But it surely isn't as though a lot of present-day talent was being ignored or frozen out.

"The Press Section says some blacks 'have already demonstrated that they're among the best newsmen in the U.S.' I guess depending on the definition of 'some' and 'among,' this could be cleared past a researcher, but it gives a misleading impression." As Time Inc. well knew. After belated but finally vigorous recruiting efforts, we still had very few blacks at professional levels on the editorial staffs. (After another two decades of "reverse discrimination," which I had advocated, that is still the case.)

"In Behavior we say whites have 'prejudices' about blacks, and blacks have 'fixed notions' about whites." Interesting distinction.

"In Law we say, 'blacks are clearly underrepresented in law enforcement and overrepresented in crime and punishment.' The whole argument cries out for some information about *applications*—does the Detroit Police Department take 50 percent of all white applicants and only 15 percent of all blacks, or what?" In Books, "We are terribly indulgent toward nonsense when spoken by blacks. . . . Strange argument in Sports. Why is the high proportion of blacks in the all-star games presented as a grievance? It would seem to show how unbiased the coaches, sports writers, fans are in picking the all-star teams."

Perhaps because of the cover, Jesse Jackson, the next time I was in Chicago, guided me around a part of his turf, the embattled Mother Cabrini housing project, kids yelling at him all the way: "Hey, Jess!" He was telling me of his conviction that blacks along with righteous anger must feel responsibility, that for the young especially it was crucial to believe that they themselves, not just the white world, had something to say about what they became. I liked that message in 1970, and on that point at least I thought Jackson gave the best presidential campaign speeches of 1988.

But when I gave a lunch in Chicago for Jackson and several other black politicians, professors, clergymen, I was naively surprised at how much time they felt they had to spend in competitive denunciation of the white Establishment and the media, including Time Inc. (all this quite contrary to Jackson's conversation at Cabrini), before we could talk seriously. Everybody was proving they weren't Uncle Tom. Mayor Richard Hatcher of Gary, Indiana, an economic and racial disaster area, said, "Blacks are allowed to be mayor when it's no longer worthwhile." Somebody else, to general mirth, said when a few blacks get to be mayors "it shows the system isn't perfect." And: "When the air that whites breathe is polluted, then we have an environment problem." An instructive meal.

A few months later, I wrote the M.E.s: "After forests of journalism, there seems a kind of lull in discussion of the 'race question.' I would be interested in a thoughtful estimate of where we are. . . . On Fifth Avenue yesterday I ran into half a dozen of those heartbreaking Harlem classroom outings, the seven-year-olds holding hands, name tags in Christmas-tree cutouts safety-pinned to the coats, the sweetly frazzled teachers leading them past Steuben and Tiffany. Do we dare be slightly hopeful for them?"

In a Time Inc. farewell speech on May 30, 1979, the evening before I retired as editor-in-chief, I couldn't resist one last round of story suggestions. I urged that our magazines "renew their concern that America should achieve civilized race relations. Our failure to do this is surely America's most serious social weakness, but just because it is so familiar, journalism tends to get bored with the problem when it is not in full crisis. Our own magazines have done some magnificent reporting in this field, and some good preaching, too. I believe we should try again."

Once at a meeting at Vanderbilt University, in Nashville, I was a speaker on the same program with Martin Luther King, Jr. He closed his moving remarks—a sermon, really—with the words, "We've come a long, long way, we have a long, long way to go." He put equal stress on both statements, and the words are still true, two decades and more later.

I persisted in seeking a contemporary, humane concept of patriotism, what the great English historian G. M. Trevelyan called "an elevated and critical patriotism." I believed that patriotism, in spite of all the follies committed in its name, has been a powerful organizing principle in human affairs, certainly so in America; it has gotten a lot of work done, and added an extra dimension, even a nobility, to many lives. I doubt that "mankind" or "humanity" is yet capable of evoking comparable efforts or loyalties or personal satisfactions.

Ever since *Life* was working up its "National Purpose" series in 1960, to volleys of editorial memos back and forth, I had been convinced that large collective purposes are suspect—except as they serve the opportunity for individuals to pursue their purposes. I never moved very far off Donovan's "General Theory," as once proposed in a memo to Harry Luce: "Private action must be supreme in our society, and the burden of proof is always on those who propose exceptions. They will often have such proof—for reasons of national defense, or for good anti-cyclical reasons, or for reasons of humanitarianism, or for the furtherance of 'consent' in our society." But for many Americans, including me, it is one of their individual purposes that their country should be just and generous, should "do good." I need the state to defend me from the Soviets and to collect my garbage, but I need it also for moral and emotional reasons, including the satisfaction of belonging.

The yearning for America to do and be good heavily influenced my ideas about foreign policy. The bedrock purpose of our foreign policy was, of course, to preserve the independence of the United States and, behind that shield, the individual liberties and opportunities of our citizens. Everything else was ways and means.

Still I looked for that moral dimension, too. I always thought we should appropriate more for foreign aid than Congress did, not just as a matter of self-interest but because it was right. I used to needle my friend Paul Hoffman on this point. Paul was a legendary salesman (once president of Studebaker) and a deeply idealistic man who had been administrator of the Marshall Plan, and then the general foreign-aid program, and then the U.N. development programs. He had spent hundreds of man-hours testifying to Congress that all the aid was essential to U.S. defense (and useful to the economy). I would argue that some of his favorite projects had nothing to do with American self-interest, but we should help out just because it was right. "If you ever have to go up to the Hill," Paul said, "stick to self-interest—none of this because-it's-right." I never had to go up there. So I was free to write in a *Time* essay: "In the close choices, of which there are a good many in foreign policy, I would come down on the side of generosity and a willingness to take some chances on behalf of liberty."

I liked to think that our alliances with countries that shared our values were as much in their interest as ours. My concept of "goodness" in foreign policy included an aspiration not to be sappy. I could get fairly worked up in conversation with one school of Europeans who seemed to believe that NATO was essentially a favor to America. More than once, I resorted to what my wife had come to call "the Okinawa gambit." Dorothy had been with me at a dinner where six or eight delightful Okinawan politicians and professors were complaining interminably about various aspects of the U.S. military presence on their island, and finally I said it might be simplest if we just pulled out. They were appalled (not for fear of invasion but for the effect on the local economy). I used a legalistic variant in Bonn one evening when some distinguished and disputatious scholars were fretting at some length about the American troops and bases in West Germany. I ventured, with a meaningful throat-clearing, that nothing in the U.S. Constitution actually *requires* us to maintain a large army in the middle of Europe. A considerable shifting of gears ensued.

I was a medium hard-liner about the Soviet Union. I thought the nuclear "balance of terror" had done much to preserve the peace; by 1988, the period since V-J Day had lasted twice as long as the interval between World Wars I and II. I was in favor of bigger defense spending for most of three decades, from Truman through Carter (and permanently skeptical as to how well the Pentagon was spending the money it already had).

I had very limited faith in the United Nations, and no readiness whatever to accept Third World pretensions to some moral superiority over the West. I never warmed to "human rights" as a phrase—something unctuous and squishy there. (It has led inevitably to "animal rights.") I preferred the older battle cries: Freedom! Liberty! I agreed with Jeane Kirkpatrick's eloquent *Commentary* article of 1979 urging that we distinguish between totalitarian systems, which had never yet evolved into democracies, and old-fashioned autocracies and military dictatorships, which sometimes did—witness Spain and Portugal in the 1970s. But two communist states, Poland and Hungary, were apparently evolving, a decade later, into quasi-democratic, pluralistic societies. And even the Soviet Union was attempting a fateful experiment: a little freedom.

I never entertained illusions that every country in the world was cut out to be just as squeaky-clean democratic as Denmark or New Zealand or Oregon. Democracy is not necessarily the talent (or desire) of all mankind. But for countries where history and literacy make it possible, I believed America must work for free and open societies, enhancing the lives of those peoples as well as our own security. It must be noted that the basic political freedoms, especially freedom of speech, matter more to those who use them most—i.e., journalists, professors, and politicians—than to many in their audience. The most elementary freedom of all—the freedom to walk the streets in safety— is better assured in a good many dictatorships, Left and Right, than in America.

Repression in Cuba, China, the newly, forcibly unified Vietnam, the black African states, was as odious to me as in South Africa, Chile, South Korea. To some of the most fervent "human rights" guardians, regimes more or less on "our side" somehow seemed more reprehensible than the Marxist states. I would have found that mind-set more acceptable if it came from the simple practical argument that America has more leverage over countries on our side than on the other.

Pinochet, Cambodia, Saudi Arabia, Greek colonels—everything in our greatly enlarged world mattered to America. I used to cite Paraguay and Afghanistan as rare and refreshing countries of no moment to the United States. I believe Paraguay is still a safe example.

Almost any of these distant places and peoples could generate controversy within America. It was Vietnam, of course, that had torn apart the twenty-five-year consensus in American foreign policy dating from Pearl Harbor. But the acrimony spread far beyond Vietnam. From the press gallery in Miami Beach, I heard something sweetly nostalgic in the plea of my fellow Middle Westerner George McGovern, of South Dakota, in his acceptance speech at the Democratic convention in 1972: "Come home, America." But we couldn't come home from the world.

One legislative reaction to Vietnam was the War Powers Resolution of 1973, prohibiting the president from stationing U.S. forces in a combat area for longer than sixty days without explicit congressional authorization. Nixon vetoed it and was overridden; three presidents of both parties have grumbled about it since: How can we operate a foreign policy with 535 secretaries of state? I was in favor of the resolution. I thought the considerable inconvenience to presidents was outweighed by the desirability of reclaiming for Congress a voice in decisions that can lead to war or that amount to undeclared war.

The congressional aggressiveness, post-Vietnam, has extended across the whole spectrum of foreign policy. It has often taken the form of undebated riders tacked on appropriations bills on the House or Senate floor—indeed a weird way to "legislate foreign policy," as presidents and their lawful secretaries of state have noted. They complain of the slack state of party discipline on Capitol Hill ("Who can you go to?"); the proliferation of staff (up to twenty thousand), many of them powerfully attracted to foreign policy; the proliferation of congressional committees and subcommittees—up to three hundred, at least a third with some claim on some corner of foreign policy. But I believe there still must be some way for Congress to have a say, a responsible say, and through Congress as well as the president, for this democracy to register foreign-policy views even between elections. I have never figured out the formula, but I know I dislike the idea of foreign policy as the preserve of a priesthood answerable only to a president who "has the information" and knows best.

Despite the breakup of the old consensus, and the executive-congressional tensions, I saw certain continuities persisting in our foreign policy. In both parties, and at both ends of Pennsylvania Avenue, there was solid support for NATO (and permanent vexation with the allies for not "doing more"), solid support for our defense commitments to Japan and South Korea (and indignation about their trade practices). When Republican administrations succeeded Democratic, and vice versa, the shifts in foreign policy tended to be less sweeping than the preceding campaign oratory might have suggested. Outs attacked Ins, of course, for anything in the world that was disappointing to Americans—there was never any shortage of material—and on getting In, learned more respect for the incorrigible character of some of the situations out there.

The continuities in our foreign policy, the underlying strength of the political and economic systems, the reserves of good sense and goodwill—these have continued to reassure me. And they mightily impress many foreign observers (and investors). I have even written these lines in 1988, in the midst of one of the dreariest presidential campaigns of the twentieth century.

XV

Leadership in Several Sizes

Out of the sound-bite campaign, incongruously, comes the man who will take charge of America's dealings with the other five billion people on earth. And it is perhaps equally incongruous that our presidents, created in an electoral process increasingly separate from the realities of governing, usually represent us well. The president will deal with prime ministers and presidents chosen in democratic elections, some more edifying than ours, and with every conceivable stripe of despot. Over some thirty years of journalistic travel, I met a good many of the foreign leaders our presidents did business with, and was strengthened in my general prejudice that the president earns his pay.

The world out there is a highly nationalistic place, and few of its leaders got to be leaders by preaching internationalism. The nation-state is a remarkably durable organism, despite all the logic of larger groupings and despite the realities of economic interdependence and nuclear menace. As an editor, I saw the whole postwar explosion of nationalisms transform the world that journalism works in. I toured much of the new terrain and went back many times to some of the biggest stories.

When the European colonial empires were dissolved, some seventy new nations came into being in Africa, the Middle East, Asia, Polynesia. Some were better governed, I believed, under the old regimes, but independence had profound appeal to the colonial peoples—and indeed some appeal to fatigued imperialists, especially in

London. As successors of the British Raj, India and Pakistan became proud and important states, uncowed by their large Soviet and Chinese neighbors or by distant America. (Later, a third successor nation on the subcontinent would be sad, disaster-prone Bangladesh.) In the Middle East, the success of the Israelis in creating their own nation, and the nationalist aspirations of the Palestinians, have kept a sensitive area in turmoil for forty years. In the Soviet Union—which may or may not be "evil" but is certainly an empire—some of the burdens of empire have lately become more noticeable: nationalist stirrings on the southern and western marches—in Armenia, Azerbaijan, Estonia, Latvia, Lithuania. And within the Soviet orbit in Eastern Europe, Hungarians continued, even before the Gorbachev era of *glasnost*, to be Hungarians, and Poles continued, spectacularly, to be Poles. West Germany and East Germany, utterly artificial and seemingly temporary entities defined by the farthest Soviet and American military advances across Hitler's stricken Reich, have now been separate nations for well over forty years. They have taken on many of the attributes of individual nations, and they have lasted more than half as long as the unified Germany (1866–1945) they succeeded.

So no country has been here forever. Countries do have to be born—in war, revolution, or even in a peaceable evolution in political ideas. People, led people, bring nations into being, and then over years—and centuries if they are granted centuries—clothe them with the singularities of nationhood. What a gloriously complicated construct modern "England" is, and France and Spain, to say nothing of Italy or our big seniors China and India. The richness of the known history leads back eventually to the still-disputed origins of the tribes and stocks who first settled those lands. Yet even the most sophisticated Frenchmen and Italians think of themselves not as European but as French or Italian—and they are right.

I had been challenged, ever since my Oxford days, by the whole subject of national characteristics—not just ours. There were always pedants and fusspots who would say you mustn't "generalize" about whole nations, and dreamy types who want to think all peoples, deep down, are "just human beings." But it seemed to me a matter of simple commonsense observation that there are national characteristics. Americans *are* different from the British, Germans from Italians, Russians from Indians, Japanese from everybody. And these differences make the world vastly more interesting—and more dangerous—than if we were truly one species.

. . . .

Out in that interesting and dangerous world, there was quite a picturesque variety of autocrats, bosses, strongmen, dictators, and I had a chance to meet a good many of them. I met General Suharto, ruler of Indonesia; the gloriously British Field Marshal Ayub Khan, president of Pakistan; President Julius Nyerere of Tanzania; Prime Minister Robert Mugabe of Zimbabwe, and the man he dislodged, Ian Smith of Rhodesia; Prime Minister Balthazar Vorster, of the stubborn Boer directorate in South Africa; the dour General Park Chung Hee, president of South Korea; and Marshal Josip Broz Tito of Yugoslavia. I was in Belgrade in 1966, at a time when critics of the U.S. presence in Vietnam were saying that if the Americans would just get out, the Vietnamese would not become Soviet and/or Chinese puppets but would evolve in an independent "Titoist" direction. I cooked up what I thought was a clever question: "Since you are something of an authority, Sir, on Titoism, do you feel it is adaptable to Southeast Asia?" The marshal was not beguiled: The United States should get out. Period.

In Manila in their heyday, I saw Ferdinand and Imelda Marcos. Once when I had to cancel a lunch with Imelda in New York, to be with my wife, who was very ill, she sent to the hospital a floral "arrangement" so huge and hideous that Dorothy (whom she had never met) broke into tears. "There must be people in the Philippines," she said, "who could have used that money." How true.

In the Hispanic world, I met one Marxist *caudillo*, Fidel Castro; one Fascist *caudillo*, General Francisco Franco of Spain; and two leaders best described as entrepreneurs—presidents of Mexico's peculiar one-party "democracy" (recently evolving toward real democracy). One was the colorful Miguel Alemán, said to have left office worth as much as a billion dollars, and the other was the solemn Luis Echeverría. Despite the anticapitalist tone of many of his speeches, it can safely be said that he did not disdain the profit motive. When I interviewed another *caudillo*, General Augusto Pinochet of Chile, he was wearing a heavy tweed jacket, brown slacks, and loafers. I wrote for *Time*: "A ruddy thickset man with the look of a prosperous Swiss dairy farmer in town for the day. One half-expected a General's braided visor, the dark glasses and cruel lips seen on all the anti-junta posters from Sweden to Berkeley. 'You can see I am not so horrible,' said Pinochet, 'that I don't eat babies.' "

Possibly the most arrogant man I ever interviewed was the Shah of Iran, when he was at the peak of his power, the oil revenue pouring in and the United States falling all over itself to supply him arms. He was given to lecturing the West on political and economic policy: "If the oil of this part of the world is denied to the so-called Western world, you are dead." He spoke of a program for selling 49 percent ownership in Iran's factories to the workers: "So the workers and small landowners are in the forefront of our revolutionary movement and are with the regime. De Gaulle tried to do the same in France. He could not. I can, because of the very special relationship that exists between the King and the people in this country."

Another royal pain was the boss of Sinagpore. I reported to Otto Fuerbringer the gist of a lunch with Lee Kuan Yew, mainly taken up with Vietnam: "(1) You shouldn't be there; (2) You're doing everything wrong; (3) Also, you are pretty stupid generally; (4) But don't go, of course."

I traveled many times to the Middle East, saw many of the same leaders on more than one visit, and over these intervals had a good chance to measure progress toward peace. The progress was usually meager to nonexistent. I interviewed Gamal Abdel Nasser in his rather modest Cairo villa and found him surprisingly likable for a fellow who could do such foolish things, including the precipitation of the Six Day War and a wholesale dalliance with Soviet military advisers. Nasser's death and the succession of Anwar Sadat led to one of the rare easings in the intractable difficulties of the Middle East. Henry Kissinger and Richard Nixon had the good sense to cultivate Sadat, and he had the courage to reopen diplomatic relations with the United States. He had the further courage to accept the Camp David agreements brokered by Jimmy Carter, and then to sign a peace treaty with Israel, for which, as he knew he might, he paid ultimately with his life. He had a brilliant smile, teeth as dazzling as a Kennedy's—and vision. In conversations with him at his villa by the Aswan Dam, at the nearby Cataract Hotel, at his home in the Nile Delta (near his native village), and in New York and Washington, I came away convinced that this was a statesman.

I would not have said that of any of the other Arab leaders I met nor of the Israelis. I admired Jordan's King Hussein for the skill with which he played a not-very-strong hand, doing nothing bold on behalf of a broad settlement but protecting the independence of his country. His hilltop compound outside Amman was the most heavily guarded residence, royal or presidential, that I visited in the Middle East; Hussein had survived at least six assassination attempts. Another spectacular survivor was Syria's Hafez Assad, a Shiite Muslim in a heavily Sunni Muslim country that is prone to violence and fanaticism, himself ruthless in suppressing opposition. My first interview with him was the first he had ever given an American reporter, one of those journalistic coups that can sometimes be more interesting to the journalist than to his readers. As I wrote in *Time* (1974), Assad "is a rugged man with a grave and gentle conversational style. There is an utterly calm and somewhat pedantic quality in his harshest comments on Zionism, Israeli aggressiveness and U.S. foreign policy. . . . Assad showed some 'give' here and there. Just a little."

I could feel a faint sympathy for Syria when I looked out from the farthest Syrian outposts to the Golan Heights. This was Syrian territory, bordering northern Israel, taken by Israel in the 1967 Six Day War, held in the 1973 Yom Kippur War after the biggest tank battles since World War II. On a fine spring day in peacetime, it had taken me only an hour to drive out from Damascus. If the wars had not ended when they did, Israeli armor, rolling through open country sloping down toward Damascus, could have reached Assad's capital in a day or two. Through Syrian eyes, I was looking uphill at a bristling mini-superpower, a high-tech Western state implanted in the Arab world, armed with the latest and best American weaponry. Syria had ample Soviet equipment, but they didn't use it, especially the planes, as proficiently as the Israelis used their American arms. And of course when you toured the Golan Heights on the Israeli side of the lines, the military guides said it was intolerable to have Syrian mortars sited to "fire down" on the peaceful Jewish settlements north of Galilee.

"Anyone who wants to hurt Israel," said the indomitable Golda Meir, "cannot resist the temptation when they are up there and we are down below. No other country in the world has this problem—neighbors who are dedicated to the idea that you must be destroyed." She was still chain-smoking, at seventy-five, the last time I interviewed her. "Forgive me," went one of her favorite formulations, "but we do not care to disappear." (Variants: be driven into the sea/commit suicide.) She could still speak of Israel "creating new facts" with its settlements in occupied territory and still dismiss the Palestinians: "Who *are* these people?" They were no nation, so far as Golda was concerned, but simply Arabs, welcome to stay in the Jewish homeland if they wished, but why didn't the various Arab states who professed such concern about the "Palestinians" take them in? She was at least as tough as any of the men who succeeded her—Rabin, Begin, Shamir—and I didn't find any of them exactly wimpish. I have often suspected that some of the Israelis' intransigence about the Palestinians comes from the striking similarities between the two. There are three to four million of each people in the Middle East. The Palestinians are dispersed among many countries—Jews know something about that. Palestinian families are close-knit, ambitious for their children, intent on education. In Lebanon, Jordan, the Gulf States, the West Bank, I met Palestinian doctors, lawyers, professors, engineers, politicians—impressive people, some defenders of terrorism included. I had to ask myself: Is it only victory that transforms a terrorist into a patriot? Do Begin and Shamir, once the commanders of the Irgun and Stern "gangs"—as the British authorities in the Palestine Mandate thought of them—ever wonder about that?

In Beirut one evening, I made the mistake of explaining to some militant Palestinians that a part of America's sympathy for Israel went back to the Bible, old Sunday school lessons about the Holy Land, the Christian sense that we too were children of Judea and Samaria. Some of the Palestinians turned out to be Christians who knew the Bible better than I did. I could console myself that they were the beneficiaries, one or two generations removed, of American and European missionaries and educators who carried the Word back to where it started, to the Near East—or Asia Minor, as it was known at Trinity Church, Minneapolis.

In the nonstop debate that a visiting American editor could get caught up in (or foment), the greatest difficulty for me was to hear something I partway agreed with carried to such silly lengths that I found myself arguing, in effect, against myself. When Arab government officials and "kept" editors told me the American press and Congress were dominated by "Zionists," I could handle the press part of that without too much trouble. It was important not to pretend that there were not many Jews in high positions in the American media. But I knew who was who much better than the Arabs did, and the details and shadings of editorial stances. The Congress was a more difficult case. There was no denying that Congress was extraordinarily sensitive to Israeli interests. For maximum political influence per capita, I said it might be a tie between "the Jewish vote" and "the farm vote"—each comprising about 3 percent of our population— and each listened-to for many good reasons, historical, geographic, emotional. The farmers may have confused the Arabs a little.

I could agree halfway, two-thirds of the way, with the wonderful modern Hebrew warriors, female and male, and still find myself so impatient with their extremism that I might come out sounding unsympathetic to their whole cause. This is a hard valve to regulate. People more diplomatic than I—indeed, diplomats by trade—have told me they have known the same difficulty. A surefire invitation to polemical excess was for some foreigner to lead off, "Well, of course, you Americans always seem to think. . . ." I fought down the "Listen, Buster" reflex, and usually adopted a false-polite, "Please allow me to know something about my own country."

Of course each "side" has an answer to every argument from the other side. We had to do Q—how else could we respond?—because P had been done—and on and on back through the whole chain of grievances, back to the Balfour Declaration of 1917, to the colonial policies of the Ottoman Empire, back even to the Crusades, even to Masada. The visitor gets to know the whole sad sequence by heart, and may even indulge a fantasy—What if he could pound on the table and declare a moratorium on history? What do you propose for the present and the future, as of 10 A.M. tomorrow, and no further reference to the past is permitted! A fantasy indeed, for of course the heart of the quarrel *is* the past.

Another tragic argument about history runs hopelessly through the grim towns and lovely green countryside of Northern Ireland. I was drawn twice to visit the miserable little war in Ulster, in part perhaps because of my ancestry on both sides of the blood feud.

The Ulster war, unlike the Middle East wars, had absolutely no geopolitical significance. World War III was never going to start in Belfast. But Northern Ireland was an exhibit of sectarian fanaticism from out of the late Middle Ages, somehow preserved in amber, in the highly civilized northwestern corner of Europe. A terrible anachronism, and humbling—or it should have been—to prideful Irish, South and North. In the Middle East, the antagonists, though all "Semites," were at least from very different worlds—the belief and culture of Jews (including the secular) versus the encompassing faith of Islam. However misguidedly, the Israelis and their neighbors saw themselves fighting for their very existence—which is worth fighting about. In Northern Ireland the war, scandalously, was between professed Christians of marked piety. I interviewed high churchmen, Protestant and Catholic, Unionist and Sinn Fein politicians, British army officers, Ulster paramilitary, businessmen, editors, the murderous romantics of the IRA. I couldn't see any ending; I hoped I was wrong. For the six counties of the North, the war is a running torment (think of a childhood there!). For the twenty-six counties of the South, the amiable Republic of Ireland, it is a threat to hard-won order. For Britain, the war is a thankless burden, costly in money and men. And on all sides, cruelly wasted courage.

I relished British politicians—their love of free food and drink (they would linger three hours over lunch in our elegant little dining room atop the Time and Life Building in New Bond Street), the malicious wit of their comments about each other, the chatty familiarity: "Of course Harold, poor dear, didn't have a clue. . . ." And "so-and-so, old sod, was really caught out," and Denis this and Christopher that, and even the greatest, in all the clubby, gossipy talk, was simply "Winston." After Winston was succeeded by the Labourite Clement Attlee at the end of the war, it was said that he came into a Gents off the Commons lobby, his good friend Attlee already there, and stood several stalls away. When Clem asked why he was being so remote, Winston said (a true story, I was told), "Whenever you see anything big, you want to nationalize it." The casual brutality of British parliamentary life was a refreshing contrast to the flowery sentimentality of the American political style. Attlee dismissing one of his ministers: "Dear George: I am reorganizing the Cabinet, and I find I have no place for you. Faithfully yours, Clem." When an incumbent prime minister loses a general election, the moving van rolls up to Number 10 Downing Street the next morning; none of this lingering on from early November to mid-January.

I encountered all the British prime ministers from Anthony Eden on. Eden, if not a tragic figure, was a sad one. As successor-in-waiting to Churchill, he was ill-used by the old man—who saw him as a permanently promising young chap and stayed on too long—and ill-used by history, which brought him the Suez fiasco, wrecking his health and his career.

As people, my favorites were Sir Alec Douglas-Home, Scots aristocrat and enlightened Tory, and "Sunny Jim" Callaghan, ordinary seaman, Royal Navy, leader for a time of the sensible wing of Labour. Both were brighter than they let on.

Still brighter, and perfectly willing for it to be known, was Margaret Thatcher. When I first met her, over breakfast at Claridge's, she was Leader of the Opposition, and the PM was the somewhat shifty Harold Wilson. I was impressed with her robust appetite, as well as her clear, crisp view of what ailed Britain and how matters might be set right. The full Nanny-Headmistress style did not emerge until she had been in power for a while. And in ten years as PM—just her first ten years—she in fact accomplished much of what she ticked off over our breakfast: reducing taxes, breaking the paralyzing power of the unions, selling some of the state-owned enterprises back to the private sector, making it possible for people in "Council houses" to buy them, to become property owners.

But the most charming of the PMs was Harold Macmillan, Super Mac, as guileful a politician as any of them. In retirement, now styled Earl of Stockton, he became chancellor of Oxford, and in that cere-monial role he perfected a wonderful bit of theatrical business. As chancellor he was official Visitor to my old college, Hertford, and it was his duty to dine there at High Table at least once a year. I was lucky to be there once for an alumni dinner when the Visitor, now in his mid-eighties, was urged to speak. He kept waving off the principal, who was attempting to introduce him, shaking his head, murmuring, "No, no," huffing and puffing, harrumphing in protest. Eventually, exceedingly slowly, he did some unsteady shuffling about and you marveled that he had got to his feet and was even speaking a few halting words. You felt you should be ready to move on an instant's notice to help steady him. Within three sentences, he was in full voice and for the next half hour he delivered with great vigor, and no notes, the exact speech he had intended to deliver: a moving reminiscence of Oxford as it had been some seventy years earlier, and an eloquent summons to the work of the university in the latter years of the century. From the Hertford dining hall, the visitor moved on to the principal's lodgings, where he was staying overnight, received a liberal serving or two of the principal's whisky, and for a dozen of us told a deliciously wicked series, perhaps not totally verifiable, of British political tales. He was still at it when I left about 1 A.M.

The Britishness was part of what fascinated me when I first trav-eled to India. This was during World War II, and indeed the king of England was still emperor of India (as well as Defender of the Faith). In several visits to India after independence, I still marveled at the way Victorian law, administration, schooling, railroads, architecture, military style had been intruded into, and accepted into, the lush and fecund complexities of Indian culture. But India was more alien, for an American, than the USSR or Japan or China, and for me this, too, was part of the appeal. When American tourists complained of the insistent dirt and noise, the smells, dangerous water, beggars, and poverty, I wondered why they didn't just stay home, or maybe sightsee in Switzerland. For Westerners trying to do business there, or even for philanthropists such as the Ford and Rockefeller foundations trying to give away money there, India could indeed be maddening, as I heard in some detail: the mix of bureaucracy (perhaps the most tenacious in the world) and corruption, a strong Socialist strain coexisting with elitist privilege and ferociously acquisitive entrepreneurs. But I also saw some of the country's remarkable islands of advanced science and technology, some of the measures that led by the 1980s to self-sufficiency in food and one of the best economic growth rates in the Third World. And I thought journalists should notice that despite many predictions to the contrary (some wishful), this nation of scores of nations, and fourteen major languages, did not break up and through at least the first four decades of independence remained a democracy—a special sort of democracy, to be sure, since two-thirds of the people were still illiterate.

The first prime minister of India, effortlessly following upon the martyred Mahatma Gandhi, was Jawaharlal Nehru, and I felt lucky to have met him, showing off his gardens like an Oxbridge don with money, serving tea in his handsome high-ceilinged "bungalow" with excellent cross ventilation. I saw him overwhelm a touring party of American and Australian journalists with his elegance and erudition. I met Nehru's successor, the meek and charming little Lal Bahadur Shastri—not too meek, however, to lead India in its second war with Pakistan (a standoff). And his successor was Nehru's daughter, Indira Gandhi, as elegant and erudite as her father but more openly imperious—or so it seemed to me in interviews, once when she was in power, once out.

I heard her at a big lunch in New York, during the Q-and-A period, respond to somebody who wondered why there seemed to be squalid shantytown settlements in New Delhi—Wasn't there any program to give these people decent shelter? Yes, said the prime minister: "The programs are often quite effective in getting people out of these places, but then the trouble is, another lot moves in."

Imagine even Margaret Thatcher, supposedly heartless Darwinian, speaking in public of "another lot" of homeless. Imagine Golda Meir referring even to Palestinian rock-throwers as a "lot." There was an invincible snobbism in Indira.

Meir, Thatcher, Gandhi—surely the most formidable female politicians since Elizabeth I. To have had an acquaintance with all three was a quite special experience, though it did not leave me with a clear impression, alas, of what the first woman president of the United States will be like.

The first time I saw Japan, the businessmen were complaining about a recession. It was 1965, twenty years after V-J Day, and the gross national product was running only 8 percent ahead of the previous year. Over the previous five years, the annual increase had ranged from 10 to 12 percent. (In the United States, we are pleased, of course, with increases of 3 to 4 percent.)

If I had seen combat duty in the Pacific, I might have found postwar Japan a little hard to take. But if Japan had earned the ashes and rubble of 1945, as indeed it had, I was still awed by the energy, brains, and national cohesiveness that had created in two decades an economic powerhouse. And an equal miracle—for which the enlightened American occupation policies deserve much credit—was the conversion of the old Japan into a complete and genuine democracy. Genuine but with its own flavor, which included a somewhat nervous, introspective quality and a style of indirection that Westerners would find baffling. A refreshing aspect of interviewing Yasuhiro Nakasone (before he became prime minister) and Kakuei Tanaka (before he was indicted in a bribery trial) was their un-Japanese bluntness. Prime Minister Eisaku Sato was more characteristically opaque.

More memorable, however, was an audience with Emperor Hirohito in the Imperial Palace. While the empress engaged Dorothy in ladylike cultural topics, I toyed dangerously with protocol by asking the emperor a few questions of faintly political coloration, to which he offered exquisitely discreet answers. My audience had taken much more elaborate arranging than one that Luce had had shortly after the Japanese surrender. In Tokyo one morning, General Douglas MacArthur, winding up a conversation with Harry, asked him if he would like to see Hirohito. Since he was in town, Sure, why not, said Harry. The proconsul hit a button on his intercom and said to some unseen colonel, "The Emperor will receive Mr. Luce at 3 P.M." Harry had just enough time to think up a question that a journalist could have asked only once in all history (real history, not mythology): "How does it feel not to be God any more?" So Harry asked it, and, to his disappointment, the Japanese interpreter's English "conveniently failed at that moment." Some forty years later, I was speculating with Harry's lively sister, Elizabeth Moore, about what *would* have been a good answer if the interpreter had allowed Hirohito to hear the question. We quickly rejected "great" and "awful." A wise and public-spirited lady, Beth came up with the perfect formulation: "I still serve my people." Beth, as a matter of fact, would be a great empress of almost anywhere.

The emperor did give me one moment of glory. His annual garden party for the diplomatic corps and foreign journalists happened to come the day after my audience, and when the imperial party, moving along the winding paths, gravely nodding to their guests, reached the spot where Dorothy and I were standing, the chamberlain must have whispered to the nearsighted emperor that here was the editor he had seen just the day before. Hirohito uttered a loud "Hi!" and stopped to bow and beam. I hoped a dozen envious ambassadors were wondering who we were. The emperor was simply saying Yes to the chamberlain, of course, but Dorothy and I always preferred to think of it as an American Hi.

The emperor was perhaps the only Japanese who held his position by birth. There had been no truly dominant figure on the political landscape since MacArthur. Surprising numbers of those postwar political leaders whom I met were of modest origins; in one sequence of three prime ministers in the 1960s and 1970s, two were the sons of sake brewers and the third an unsuccessful horse dealer's son, all from the provinces. The Liberal Democratic (conservative) party and its business allies were the proprietors of the consensus. Within business, the old *Zaibatsu*—the Mitsui, Mitsubishi, and Sumitomo combines—swiftly reconstituted their financial and industrial power after the war.

At a dinner once in Osaka, the heads of half a dozen Sumitomo companies were politely questioning me about the American economy, and my impressions of the Japanese economy, so when it was my turn, I asked, "Who runs Japan?" A rather dreadful silence ensued. The men at the table would have been on the list. But like the senior politicians, they had advanced mainly by merit, loyalty to the organization, and a resolutely low profile.

. . . .

Our other ex-enemy sat in the middle of Europe. Germany (Italy didn't quite count as a full-blown enemy) and the Germans were always something to think about. And after 1945, it was good to have the Germans feeding my optimism instead of instructing me on the savagery a civilized state can commit. Indeed, one of the most hopeful events of the twentieth century is the construction of a sturdy German democracy on the ruins of the Third Reich.

One of the architects of that democracy was the somewhat autocratic Konrad Adenauer, former mayor of Cologne, twice arrested by the Nazis, postwar leader of the Christian Democratic party, first chancellor of the new Federal Republic of Germany. On the way to an interview with Adenauer, I was rehearsing a few questions with Jim Bell, our Bonn bureau chief, and I said with great self-assurance, "Let's see, now, we address him as Herr Reichskanzler?" Jim shuddered: "My God, no—Herr *Bundes*kanzler!" The title of "Reichskanzler" had been retired, as the sportswriters would say, with Adolf Hitler. "Der Alte" was eighty-five, the high cheekbones, wide-set hooded eyes, and yellowing skin making the face almost a death mask, but the mind was alert and utterly clear. He retired at eighty-seven and died at ninety-one.

I interviewed all his successors over the years. Ludwig Erhard was another of the Founding Fathers because as finance minister, he put through the currency reform that led to the economic "miracle." Erhard, as jolly a man as he looked, was less effective as chancellor, and his successor, the handsome Kurt Georg Kiesinger, was something of a nonentity. Then came the first Social Democratic chancellor, Willy Brandt, who as the defiant mayor of West Berlin had been a cold war hero, and now led the Federal Republic of Germany into dealings with East Germany and the Soviet Union that in effect recognized the partition of Germany. Ironically, he was forced to resign because one of his aides was exposed as an East German espionage agent. The bright and acerbic Helmut Schmidt followed, and I was on the receiving end, more than once, of his dissatisfactions with American policy. He was disdainful of Jimmy Carter but then could be harsh about Ronald Reagan. I once asked a friend in the German foreign ministry what on earth would be Helmut Schmidt's definition of a satisfactory U.S. president. After the briefest pause, he said, "Helmut Schmidt."

Along with the building of a democracy and a richly productive economy, postwar Germany became a good neighbor. Between 1870 and 1940, Germany had invaded France three times. That war between the two is now unthinkable does indeed suggest that human progress is possible.

France, of course, is coauthor of this accomplishment. Her postwar leaders—once de Gaulle's Fifth Republic created a strong presidency with a firm hold on foreign policy—were highly attentive to Germany. De Gaulle, who knew his Charlemagne, was prepared to like a Rhinelander and Catholic as the new Germany's first chancellor, and the fact that he and Adenauer were both aloof and paternalistic in political style was a point of compatibility. I found Georges Pompidou and his sly wit very likable, but Willy Brandt did not. Schmidt and the aristocratic Giscard d'Estaing, economists both, hit it off beautifully. I had known Giscard slightly before he became president—he once served me a three-star lunch in the finance minister's splendid suite in the Louvre Palace. At the Elysée Palace (no lunch), he was lively journalistic subject matter, always taking your questions and going somewhere with them. Q: How do you respond to the criticism that you value style more than substance? An American politician would doubtless answer, "Why that's not true at all, my opponent(s) must be feeling guilty because they worry so much about style." Giscard: "I attach great importance to style. Style is the aesthetic of action. . . . It is a compliment to be criticized for giving too much importance to style."

I never interviewed de Gaulle, though I once heard him speak, across a half-acre of white ties and evening gowns in the Grand Ballroom of the Waldorf-Astoria. (De Gaulle's press officer during much of World War II was André Laguerre, then enlisted in the "Free French," later in Time Inc. When de Gaulle came to New York, André, now managing editor of *Sports Illustrated*, paid a courtesy call. The general had a sardonic story suggestion: Did André realize a lineal descendant of the Marquis de Sade was living? Why not invite him to write an essay on "Cruelty as a Sporting Proposition"?)

I also saw Leonid Brezhnev from fifty meters or so, lined up with the rest of the Soviet Presidium to review a May Day parade. Foreign journalists and diplomats from their privileged enclosure on Red Square had hours to study who was standing next to whom. When some of the fedoras or generals' caps traded places, a lot of Kremlin-ology was thrown into chaos—or had the minister just gone to the men's room?

I once saw Stalin from an even greater distance. He had in fact been dead five years. Clad in his gray generalissimo's tunic (he had promoted himself from marshal), he was preserved under glass, lying alongside the glass-encased figure of Lenin (black business suit) in their somber granite shrine in Red Square. Stalin has since been demoted to a niche in the Kremlin wall, and the sole tenant of Lenin's Tomb is Lenin.

The Soviet Union: drab but mysterious and somehow magnetic, as the enemy can be. I had a profound curiosity about the place and made five visits over a span of twenty years. My standing question to myself was: In what sense, exactly, are these people our enemy?

Stalin, for all the savagery of his rule over the Soviet people, was relatively cautious in foreign policy. The lively, likable Nikita Khrush-chev, something of a "liberal" in domestic policy, was more of a saber-rattler on the world scene. He had more to rattle with, as the Soviet nuclear arsenal grew. In the interview he gave Dick Scammon, Cy Black, and me in our election-observing tour in 1958, Khrushchev was on his best behavior; he spoke of "annihilation" only once in ninety minutes—the fate of the West as well as the USSR in a nuclear war. On other occasions he had said, more dramatically, "The living would envy the dead," and the only survivors would be the cockroaches. But this did not stop him from precipitating the closest thing to a nuclear showdown the world has seen—the Cuban missile crisis of 1962.

Khrushchev liked his capitalists to be real capitalists, as he made clear to many visitors to Moscow and to American audiences. He was not impressed by arguments from Western liberals that the welfare state had tamed the old excesses of capitalism. He was much more interested in Thomas Watson of IBM than in Walter Reuther of the United Automobile Workers union.

An American arguing political systems with the apparatchiks was talking (as I wrote after my first visit) "across the widest chasm in the world today." But the Soviets were an appealing enemy, often touching in their desire to be respected by the West, and above all by America. I liked the people (who could not?), the pre-Revolutionary architecture, the haunting spaces, even the deep winter—the ideal season for a first visit—and all it evoked of Russian history and literature and the famous Slavic soul.

Harry Luce once asked me to comment on a speech draft by our colleague and stout cold warrior C. D. Jackson. "I agree with C. D. that war with the Soviet Union is thinkable," I wrote in 1959. "But to me it's also thinkable that things will improve peaceably in the U.S.S.R. It's also thinkable that things won't improve much, but there won't be any war either." The last of the "thinkables" turned out to be pretty good prophecy.

In 1963, I was wary of a naively dovish-sounding prospectus for a *Life* special issue on Russia. I wrote Luce that I thought it was perfectly okay for Hugh Moffett, the senior editor scouting the project,

> to have earnest conversations with the Soviets about "objectivity" if it leads to our getting some good pictures we otherwise wouldn't get. . . .
>
> I'm all in favor of honest reporting of "how people actually live" in the USSR. It is bound to show:
>
> a) They live somewhat more comfortably, and with less sense of an oppressive State, than the average American would suppose.
> b) They live better than they did 15 or 10 or 5 years ago.
> c) Their living standard is far, far below ours or Western Europe's. Moffett says we should "refrain from comparing everything they have with the U.S. counterpart." We do have to compare some things. Nothing could be more misleading and "non-objective" than a happy summertime picture of all those fairly well-dressed adults and beautifully dressed children taking their ease and ice cream in a Moscow park. Ideally, the balancing picture would show the six square meters of housing space per capita that they're going home to in the evening. But we probably won't get that picture. So captions and text will have to do most of the comparison work—prices, wages, purchasing power, etc.
>
> Nobody proposes that the issue should be one grand assault on Soviet ideology. That would be tedious indeed. But if the general theme is What's Russia Like Today, the issue should certainly include at least one serious political article—the present state of Communist theology, or the position of the intellectuals, or the latest dope on the Succession Problem.

The issue did get photographed, written, and published—maybe a little too nice to the Soviets, net, but packed with great pictures and interesting information most *Life* readers (me included) wouldn't have known.

In 1965, in a piece I wrote for *Panorama* (the magazine we co-published with Mondadori in Italy), I said, "Good Communists must still hope to see capitalism buried one day." Khrushchev had said this would happen. But if Communists wish capitalism buried, we must remember that "good Christians must hope to see all men redeemed. Communism is heavily armed, of course, while the church militant keeps no thermonuclear bombs. But the parallel is not entirely fanciful. How badly do the Communists want to see a Communist world, how soon, what would they risk to bring it about, what is their power to bring it about?"

In my visits to the Soviet Union in the 1960s and 1970s, I was always looking for what might have changed since the last time I was there. I saw modest improvements in living standards during the period—which lasted well into the 1960s—when the country was recovering from the devastation of World War II. Then improvements began to come harder, and the economy approached stagnation. In interviews, I heard a slight relaxation in expressed belligerence toward the West, and indeed in the days of détente, we all saw the photogenic bear-huggings between Brezhnev and, in sequence, Presidents Nixon, Ford, and Carter. But in cultural and political life, the "thaw" of the Khrushchev years gave way to a partial re-Stalinization under Brezhnev. I had imagined that the steady growth in the numbers of well-educated people would have forced greater internal change. It finally began to happen under Mikhail Gorbachev.

And always—just below the surface in so many of my conversations with Soviet officials—there was the enormously sensitive question of legitimacy. The "election" of the Communist party's hand-picked unopposed candidates for the Supreme Soviet—the elaborate charade I had watched as an official American "observer"—was of course an effort to beautify the party's dictatorship. But how could a real parliament, or even half-real, function alongside the party? If the party is not the sole vessel of truth about man and history, and if it is not the sole wielder of power within the state, then it is not "The Party" but merely a party. That heresy could bring down the whole system.

Without legitimacy, there was a fundamental moral instability in the Soviet system, and this, combined with the raw military power, could be frightening to think about. With sufficiently steady nerves (all our recent presidents, both parties, have had them), you could figure that those are rational men in Moscow, they love the power and perks the new ruling class has accumulated since 1917, and they love their grandchildren. As atheists, logically, they should love these carriers of their immortality even more than believers love their grandchildren. Suspicion arose from time to time, perhaps entirely unfair, that Khrushchev, and now Gorbachev, were not entirely immune to religious belief. But fortunately, the Russian Orthodox faith does not promise that martyrs will sleep in paradise tonight, as a reward for such ventures as charging Iraq machine-gun nests or blowing up American marines or Israeli bus passengers.

As the Soviet military buildup proceeded in the 1970s, however, I often wondered whether we were taking détente more seriously than they were. Tom Watson of IBM, a Time Inc. director, was a devout détente believer and gently reproached me, in a 1978 letter, for insufficient enthusiasm about SALT II.

I wrote Tom:

> I have some trouble with the argument that "there is no longer any way of getting ahead of the Russians." Are there ways the Russians could get ahead—or be perceived as getting ahead by other nations, maybe by themselves, maybe even by us?
>
> Isn't there a certain asymmetry in the way the two sides make use of being "ahead" or seeming to be ahead? We were miles ahead in the 1950s and made no aggressive use of that circumstance. As late as 1968, I suppose, we still had a meaningful edge, but we certainly didn't seek to apply it, even by remotest implication, in the case of Czechoslovakia. When you say, "one side or the other can get a quick and quite temporary military advantage," I can't help thinking that it is fundamentally more tempting to the Soviets to seek such an advantage than it is to us because we wouldn't do anything with it if we had it.

In my good-bye speech to the Time Inc. staff in 1979, I suggested a major journalistic effort at "figuring out the Russians." *Time* went right to work and obliged me with a special issue on the Soviet Union, which came out a year later. The U.S.–Soviet relationship, I had said, "is still the centerpiece of world politics and it is still, quite literally, a life-and-death matter. Just because that has been written so many times, one must not get too fatigued with the thought. . . . There has been an enormous turnover within the Soviet adult population since some of us formed our ideas about them. . . . With or without SALT II we are moving, both sides, toward a nuclear missile accuracy, maybe 50 meters after a flight of as much as 5,000 miles, that makes the disadvantage of receiving the first strike absolutely devastating. Can we trust the Soviets in any degree? Do they trust us? What sort of people have they become? Maybe they're still just like the old cold warriors think, and if so, that also is a useful thing to know."

The old cold warriors were already having to modify some of their ideas about Communist China. In 1976, the agile Deng Xiaoping, twice dropped from the top Communist leadership, made his second comeback. With the misleadingly modest title of vice premier, he began to lead the country away from the madness of Mao's "Cultural Revolution" and also into closer ties with the United States.

I had been trying to get into China ever since the Nixon-Kissinger opening led to visas for a few American journalists and for a hopelessly outmatched Ping-Pong team. My dozen or more applications got nowhere. I admired and envied the interviews with Mao and Chou En-lai that were granted James Reston of *The New York Times*. I cheered Scotty's thriftiness in turning an encounter with acupuncture, via an emergency appendectomy, into a lively piece of first-person journalism. When friends asked me why I hadn't been to China yet, was it because of the reputation of Henry Luce and the "China Lobby," I took the line that the Reds were afraid of my Ping-Pong (actually pretty good by American rumpus-room standards).

Then one day in January 1979, middle of the night New York time, I was notified that if I could be in Beijing in forty-eight hours, Deng would "probably" see me. I horrified Dick Duncan, chief of the Time-Life News Service, by saying I would have to think about it— I had been looking forward to going to the Super Bowl, and I was just back from a strenuous trip to the Middle East. In the morning, of course, I packed.

I was met by Marsh Clark, chief of our Hong Kong news bureau. Talking with Deng, Clark and I pressed for a speedy accreditation for a Time-Life bureau in Beijing (which soon came through). But to get to see Deng at all, after all the years and all the thousands of miles that had been traversed, we had to overcome one final bureaucratic difficulty: Discussions about the interview apparently were official business, but for some inscrutable reason, the interview itself was not. So when we called at Beijing offices to work out arrangements for the interview, we rated a foreign ministry car. Then on the morning of the interview, no official car showed up for us. Our hotel was not at all impressed that we were about to be late for a meeting with the leader himself. The taxi we finally captured gave us a memorable ride around and through the teeming bicycle traffic. We kept Deng waiting only three minutes, in the Sinkiang Room of the Great Hall of the People on Tienanmen Square.

Deng was to visit Washington the following week, the first Chinese leader to appear there since the Communists took power nearly thirty years earlier, and he used the interview to deliver a very blunt message. He knew what great store the Carter administration set by SALT II. He said the treaty was irrelevant to the "stark reality" facing the United States—and China. This was the Soviet drive for "global hegemony." Even as the Americans and Soviets talked of "détente and disarmament," the Soviets were moving aggressively in Africa, the Middle East, and, through their Vietnamese ally, in Southeast Asia. The Soviet military budget takes up around 20 percent of the gross national product, he told us (a better guess than the 11 to 15 percent the CIA was using at the time). "What does one do with all these things? With no war going on, the Soviet Union has increased its standing army in three years from 3 million to 4 million men. What does one do that for? . . . If one has so many things in one's hands, the day will come when one's fingers begin to itch. You can't eat those materials or wear them. You must use them somehow." Deng "very much approved" a manifesto signed by 170 retired American generals and admirals (many of them alumni of the old pro-Taiwan anti-Beijing "China Lobby") saying the Soviets were "heading for superiority not parity" in military power. "We consider that the true hotbed of war is the Soviet Union," Deng said, "not the U.S."

"The first characteristic of the Soviet Union is that it always adopts the attitude of bullying the soft and fearing the strong. The second characteristic of the Soviet Union is that it will go in and grab at every opportunity. . . . If we really want to be able to place curbs on the polar bear, the only realistic thing for us is to unite."

I had been wondering how to bring up the "Gang of Four" (not one of the topics cleared in advance with the foreign ministry), but Deng brought up the subject himself. The gang, he said, "looked upon people who didn't study as heroes, people who didn't work as heroes. We lost a whole generation as regards education, including science and technology."

I mentioned a *Time* interview in which Brezhnev had said he was tired of talking about the Chinese. I wondered, for fun, "if Brezhnev agreed not to talk about China, would you agree not to talk about the

Soviet Union?" Deng declined: "I am not tired of talking about them." Indeed, he sounded as if he could continue all morning, but our session had already gone far beyond the negotiated time.

The interview was published in *Time* the day Deng arrived in Washington. There he was more restrained in his public remarks about the Soviets. But he had made his point. In the *Times*, Reston, sensitive to State Department views but always generous to other journalists, called it a "provocative" interview that "said more for the enterprise of *Time* than for the diplomacy of China and Deputy Prime Minister Deng."

I got a kick out of being the conduit for Deng's peppery views. There was something in it (his first interview with a Western journalist) for each of us. And I got a kick out of the man himself—barely five feet tall, patriotically chain-smoking Chinese Panda cigarettes, at his feet a spacious spittoon worthy of a Southern senator of the 1930s. He was seventy-four when we talked. A decade later, he was still paramount leader, but now the very forces Deng had set in motion, with his introduction of market incentives and hospitality to foreign investment, were challenging his own regime. A breathtaking moment in world history: in May 1989, demonstrators by the hundreds of thousands demanding a democratic China. In time, the sickening moment: the crackdown, brutal reminder that "liberalization" is reversible.

History is of course more than "the biography of great men" (Thomas Carlyle didn't quite believe his famous dictum), but great men can surely give it a healthy shove. The idea permeated Time Inc. journalism: that much of the news could be conveyed through cover stories and profiles on great, near great, or simply interesting individual men and women, and some of them might be great in their capacity for evil.

On the cover of *Time*, January 2, 1950, instead of the usual Man of the Year, the magazine offered the Man of the Half-Century: Winston Churchill. If I had had a vote (*Fortune* writers didn't), I would have put up a case for Lenin or Hitler, the true World-Breakers of 1900–1950. And their credentials have stood up far into the second half of the century.

Both men led revolutions that were in no sense ordained by the forces of "history." Forces for political change were there in abundance, in the Russia of 1916–17 and the Germany of 1930–33, but it was the political genius of Lenin and Hitler that determined the destructive outcomes. The Bolshevik Revolution totally transformed society in the old domain of the czars and later spread its influence— by example, propaganda, or military occupation—to Eastern Europe, China, Southeast Asia, scattered outposts in the Middle East, Africa, Latin America. It was a potent presence in world politics for most of the twentieth century. Hitler fell nine hundred eighty-eight years short of building the Thousand-Year Reich, but during his brief reign he did create World War II, and we still live surrounded by the consequences. One of Hitler's chief consequences was indeed the aggrandizement of the Soviet state founded by Lenin. Perhaps (to adopt an occasional *Time* device) they should have been co-Men. The choice would have provoked angry letters and cancellations, of course, and *Time* would have had to explain once more that no accolade was implied; the criterion was impact on the news, for good or ill.

Churchill, great man that he was, owed part of his greatness to Hitler. Without World War II, he would have been remembered in Great Britain as a rather impulsive Tory politician not steady enough for PM, a romantic with a weakness for lost causes (e.g., his defense of Edward VIII during the abdication affair), and a flair for historical writing. But Churchill's reaction to Hitler was magnificent, and it made a difference in history. A different prime minister, just as brave and patriotic as Churchill, could have looked out on the same grim scene in 1940 and simply been unable to summon the words and bearing that would rally his countrymen to their "finest hour."

Franklin Roosevelt also owed something to Hitler (and of course to the Japanese militarists, though their boldness was in part the result of their German ally's successes in Europe and at sea). To me, Churchill was the more attractive figure—genuinely witty (as FDR was not), a far more inspiring speaker, much less devious as a politician. But Roosevelt was not only a highly effective war leader; unlike Churchill, he also left a very substantial legacy in domestic policy. His was a greatness of more breadth.

Since the days when I observed Roosevelt as a Washington reporter, and briefly glimpsed Churchill, I consider that I have met four other great political leaders: Adenauer, Sadat, Thatcher, Deng. If what Deng began helps others eventually to create a productive and humane system of government in China, he would rank, whatever the backsliding of his last years, among the century's true movers of history. "Our emperors," said one of the Beijing student demonstrators, "have never known how to leave."

. . . .

Since Roosevelt, America has not seen a great president. One reason could be my own line of work, journalism. The increasing intrusiveness, skepticism, and technical proficiency of the press today make it difficult for an American politician to look "great." Could George Washington, for that matter, have survived an ABC special on Valley Forge? Would *The New York Times* and the *Washington Post* have allowed Lincoln to get away with suspending *habeas corpus*? It could also be that the large expansion in the numbers of well-educated Americans in executive positions in private life makes respected "leaders" familiar figures in everybody's community—and admirers of these men and women will think some of them at least as able as the president of the moment.

Of our postwar presidents, Truman and Eisenhower came closest, as I saw them, to greatness—Truman making the most, and then some, of his plain and sturdy virtues, Eisenhower falling a bit short of his large potential. For all the differences in their biographies, philosophy, and style, and for all their separate shortcomings, these two Middle Westerners ran a generally strong and effective presidency for sixteen years. I don't rate any of their successors as highly.

Jack Kennedy had seemed a very likable fellow when I encountered him at a few Washington parties and touch football games in his early navy days, and that was still my impression when I talked with him after he became a congressman and a senator. He was too bright to be called a lightweight, but his six years in the House and eight in the Senate were not marked by any significant legislation or any discernible causes beyond his own advancement. In 1960, just like Richard Nixon, he wanted to be president for the sake of being president. I was not shocked that politicians on the national scene should aspire to the top job in their line of business, but I always hoped, looking at presidential candidates, for some mingling of ambition and public purpose, some vision of what they wanted to do with the presidency. Here, when you got past the public platitudes, Kennedy and Nixon both came up empty, though Kennedy did it with greater wit and grace.

I resented—I think it was more than envy—the way old Joe Kennedy's money had greased Jack's path into Congress, the Senate, and the Democratic presidential primaries of 1960. I was never bothered by the use of family money to free a young man to concentrate on a political career—as it did for Franklin Roosevelt (and Theodore)—

but the access to a private fortune to finance a whole campaign seemed an "unfair" advantage over a penniless competitor such as Hubert Humphrey. But then life, as Jack Kennedy noted on another occasion, *is* unfair. And in later years, I came to feel that if a candidate has to be obligated financially to somebody, better it should be his father or deceased grandfather than, say, the aircraft contractors or the Longshoremen's union.

But Kennedy was a fast learner, and as he matured in office, I came to think he had the potential to become a very successful, perhaps "great," president. And of course we never found out.

Lyndon Johnson had a far more impressive résumé, as he took the oath of office in Air Force One, heading back from Dallas to Washington, than John Kennedy did when he gave his Inaugural Address below the Capitol dome. Johnson had served twenty-four years on the Hill, the last six as Senate majority leader, in which role he wheeled, dealed, and legislated with a mastery not seen since. He and the Speaker, his fellow Texan Sam Rayburn, constructed a branch of government truly coequal with the president. I had first known him when he was a fast-talking, fanatically hard-working freshman congressman, highly accessible to reporters (even as junior as I), most of whom understood, without contradiction from Lyndon, that he was an FDR favorite. I saw him occasionally in his glory years in the Senate, and during the miseries of the vice presidency. In Paris once as VP, Johnson was granted an audience with Charles de Gaulle, who for openers asked: To what do I owe the honor of this visit? Johnson didn't like being shorter than de Gaulle (6 feet 3 inches versus 6 feet 4 inches), loathed the impotence of the VP role, loathed having to say things like: bring warmest greetings from President and Mrs. Kennedy, desire to express own deep respect for the president of the republic and our oldest ally, relationship never more vital, etc. De Gaulle proceeded to stress his urgent desire to have all American soldiers out of France—Johnson wished afterward that he had thought to ask, "Even the ones in the cemeteries?" Even after he became president, he was sometimes made to feel gauche by the Europeans.

During his administration, I was lodged somewhere on one of his lists of private citizens worth a little presidential cultivating. He was an expert cultivator. Does it affect the journalist's judgment to be on a first-name basis (one-way, of course, in the case of Mr. President) with the mighty? Possibly so; the trade-off, the journalist hopes, is extra insight into the mind and character of a public man.

It was Vietnam, of course, that destroyed Johnson's presidency, with his cooperation. The Vietnamese, South as well as North, destroyed his dreams of being remembered for his Great Society programs, above all his hopes for the widening of educational opportunities, which is something I had often heard him talk about most movingly. Instead, he became known mainly for an unsuccessful war. He was a monstrous man in some ways—vain, devious, secretive, as coarse in his ethics as in some of his conversation (he may have accumulated as much as $25 million in real estate and radio and TV properties during his legislative years). But he was also a deeply idealistic man and had the political skill to put spacious visions to work. I saw both Johnsons from fairly close up.

Johnson was to me a tragic figure and so was his successor, for the same reason: high promise undone. Richard Nixon had a first-rate intellect, coldly analytical, a résumé as good as Johnson's, and plenty of political moxie. Too much moxie—or not enough—as it transpired. But I felt a certain empathy with Nixon, as with Johnson and Hubert Humphrey, that I didn't feel with the rich kid, Jack Kennedy. The fact that Jack Kennedy was younger than I was also an irritant. These other fellows had the decency to be a bit older, and we were all sons of the Depression and knew Jack hadn't felt much of that.

As the 1968 election approached, I suggested to the Time Inc. editors that we had to weigh the old question of whether Nixon is "a principled man" against the question of whether Humphrey is "a man in full control of himself." Hubert's long-windedness had for years "been treated as a lovable minor failing, and so long as he was Senator or even Vice President there was no great harm done, except to some glassy-eyed audiences. [He could also be hard to stop one-on-one, as I knew firsthand.] But this year it has more and more frequently seemed the mark of a serious intellectual and emotional weakness. . . . In the past fortnight his wobbles all over the lot on Vietnam and on Daley and the Chicago police have been appalling. This has seemed not so much an opportunistic effort to get on all sides of issues as an honest chaos of ideas and words, the non-stop talking becoming a substitute for the harder work of thought and decision."

On the *Life* editorial page, we said both men had some impressive qualifications for the presidency, but it was time for a change, the Democrats having held the presidency (except for Eisenhower's relatively nonpartisan administration) for thirty-two years. When Nixon phoned me on a Sunday to express his thanks—he had not yet seen the text—I thought I should warn him it was a "measured" endorsement. Oh, that was fine—he was also a great admirer of Hubert.

As to Humphrey's garrulousness, I must in fairness record what happened when I signed him up as the eighth and last speaker at a dinner in Washington that *Time* gave in 1973 in honor of Congress. I asked each of these congressional eminences to speak no more than five minutes, which was daring of me, and it was still more daring of me to put Hubert on at what was certain to be a very late hour. In introducing him, I noted that only a man from the "famously taciturn state of Minnesota" could be trusted in the cleanup spot. He got in and out of his remarks in seven minutes! Several of his Senate colleagues came up to congratulate me.

Nixon was a fairly liberal, or at least centrist, Republican in his attitude on social-welfare issues. Spending on Lyndon Johnson's Great Society programs in fact increased more rapidly in Nixon's administration than in Jimmy Carter's. In several small gatherings, I heard him speak with apparent conviction of the potential significance of these measures, not only so Republicans could win elections but also as a matter of equity. He was much more sympathetic, instinctively, with lower-income people, and of course with Middle America, than with the "elite"—especially their Ivy League children. The sweaty side of Nixon's striving, the excessive eagerness to please—which I had first seen when he was a senator, then vice president—could still appear even when he was president. He was decidedly unliberal, indeed repressive, so far as civil liberties were concerned. Like Johnson before him, he tended to equate protest with treason. His civil-rights record was spotty.

Then there was the matter of Spiro Agnew. In a *Life* editorial in 1972, we suggested that Nixon unload him and choose a better-qualified VP. This led to a lunch, Agnew the host in his suite in the Executive Office Building, at which he berated eight or ten of us for the *Life* editorial and for the tone of *Time*'s coverage of his campaign. I'm afraid I berated him right back. At one time I considered walking out on the lunch, but I knew my colleagues would feel they must get up and follow me out, which—much as they deplored Agnew—might have given them uncomfortable yes-man sensations. Agnew would have been pleased at some of the mail *Life* was getting. "Your editorial," one man wrote from Shreveport, Louisiana, "confirms again what millions have known for some time: the national news media is so sick it cannot raise its head from the bed." A few weeks after the Nixon-Agnew victory, when *Life* had to fold, the vice president publicly gloated that the magazine deserved to be put out of business. In less than a year, of course, following his plea of *nolo contendere* to bribery charges, Spiro had to get out of business, or at least out of the vice-president business.

Notwithstanding Agnew and other unattractive aspects of Nixon's first administration, we endorsed him for reelection in a *Life* editorial. I was essentially casting a foreign-policy vote—as much against McGovernite isolationism as for Nixon. Though Nixon was too slow in extricating us from Vietnam, his bold initiatives vis-à-vis China and the Soviets were highly promising. Many of our editorial staff emphatically disagreed with the endorsement. I received petitions to that effect signed by about two-thirds of *Life*'s editorial staffers and substantial numbers of *Time*, *Fortune*, and Time-Life Books people. I put out no formal reply; in personal exchanges, I would only say, Thank you for being so frank, let's see how it goes.

How it went was Watergate. I never saw Nixon during his truncated second term. I did see his chief of staff, Al Haig, on the November day in 1973 when *Time* published an editorial, written by Henry Grunwald, saying Nixon should resign. He "has irredeemably lost his moral authority, the confidence of most of the country and his ability to govern effectively." Haig had gamely appeared at a long-planned lunch with *Time*'s editors—and we, too, had gamely appeared. Reading the editorial that morning "was like being hit in the face with a cold fish," he said. Had the president read it? "You may assume he has." I decided not to solicit further reader reaction from the White House. To date, it is the only head-on editorial *Time* has ever published. I think it may have had a little to do with preparing public opinion and perhaps the president himself—in the editorial we reminded him that Time Inc. had supported him in 1960, 1968, and 1972—to think of resignation as a possible outcome, that the country and the presidency need not undergo the impeachment ordeal.

Nixon loyalists were outraged at the editorial, among them Clare Luce. She had written me (in response to an earlier speech of mine calling Watergate "a subversion of the American political system") that the press, including Time Inc., was vastly inflating the importance of Watergate, that at worst it simply reflected the general moral condition of the country, induced in good part by the laxness of the "liberal point of view."

I had to send off a short lecture to Clare:

Having never considered myself a dues-paying member of the "liberal point of view," I have felt quite free to argue, out loud and in print, that individuals are responsible for their own acts. Far too much gets blamed on "poverty," "society," etc. The we-are-all-guilty line leads directly, of course, to nobody-is-guilty.

I did not vote for Linda Lovelace [Clare had cited *Deep Throat* as typical of the moral landscape] for President—I voted for Nixon (three times). I continue to believe that he is fully accountable for his own acts, and should be held to standards well above the worst things we see in the society around us.

In another letter, sent for publication in *Time*, she argued that it would be unconstitutional for Nixon to resign. I had already boned up on this—it doesn't take long—and conveyed to Clare that we would print her letter but follow it with an Editor's Note (in old-fashioned *Time*-speak): "Let Reader Luce re-read her U.S. Constitution, Article II, Section I, Paragraph 6, and the Twenty-fifth Amendment." She withdrew her letter. Nixon withdrew from the presidency, and Gerald Ford, his appointed vice president (replacing Spiro Agnew), succeeded.

Watergate was the biggest domestic news story since the Depression, and I was proud of *Time*'s coverage. I must also admit I enjoyed Watergate. The plot line was intricate, every revelation seemed to lead to another, and in the end, the American system won. Watergate did some temporary damage to the presidency as an institution, and to public trust in government. It could be seen as a triumphant vindication of the role of the press in a free society—or as proof of its excessive power. But it was not the press that "broke" Nixon—he did. Congress, the courts, and the press established the facts, and reaffirmed the basic constitutional principle that the president is not above the law. It was a personal tragedy for a politician of great capabilities, for his ever-loyal family, and for the Nixon men who had to go to jail, but I could not see Watergate as any sort of national tragedy.

I thought Gerald Ford was a good president, and I once said so to the man who beat him in 1976. Jimmy Carter agreed at once: "I thought so too." Carter, of course, wanted to think he had defeated a political figure of real stature—as he had—not the cartoonists' dummy banging his forehead on the exit hatch of Air Force One.

The context of the Carter comment was a conversation in the Oval Office in July 1979, a few weeks after I retired from Time Inc. Carter was urging me to become his "senior adviser," reporting directly to him with a charter to speak with total frankness about people and policies, foreign and domestic. It was an astonishing invitation. I was scarcely an intimate friend—I had seen Carter perhaps a dozen times during the years he was Georgia governor and a presidential candidate, and in the two and a half years since his election, I had been in the White House only once, along with two or three hundred other people at a Vladimir Horowitz recital in the East Room.

The president knew I was a political independent, but by way of reminding him, I said that in 1976 I couldn't decide how to vote until the Sunday evening before the election—my all-time record for political vacillation. My wife (also an independent, though increasingly allergic to Republicans) was strongly pro-Carter, but would not be able to vote because she was to have surgery that Monday morning. When I was shooed out of her hospital room, I went back to our New York apartment and attacked a mountainous pile of campaign speeches and materials I had been accumulating for weeks. The exercise did help take my mind off Dorothy's coming ordeal, and it had a salutary sedative effect, but while I could still keep my eyes open, I decided I would vote for Carter. I decided a Carter administration would be more interesting journalistically than four more years of Ford. I had promised Dorothy that if I decided for Ford, I would refrain from voting—she and I would be "paired" like opposing senators who had to miss some roll call. If I came down for Carter, I would drive out to our polling place on Sands Point, so he would get at least one Donovan vote. He liked this story well enough to repeat it to several people, adding that he admired Dorothy's judgment.

I did not repeat to the president what I told Sol Linowitz when he asked me the morning after how I liked the election results. "Fine," I said. "I just barely voted for him and he just barely won." (The choice had seemed so close I didn't think any Time Inc. endorsement was called for; there were no staff complaints.) It was Linowitz, I later learned, along with another Democratic pillar of the Washington bar, Clark Clifford, who urged the president to add me to his staff.

The presidential summons had something of the sound of a last-minute vacancy aboard the *Titanic*. This was the summer of the gas queues, dismally low ratings for Carter in the polls, his "crisis of confidence" speech, the abrupt firing of almost half the Cabinet. I accepted. My reasons, according to my rough notes to myself, included: "Maybe do a little for country?" and "Chance to see Govt. from inside." In the event, I fear I did little for the country. A "senior adviser" who is a political independent is something of an anomaly in a necessarily partisan White House. I had very limited influence, especially as the 1980 election approached. But I did indeed get a pretty good look at "Govt. from inside."

Ronald Reagan, when I saw him in his governor of California days and during his unsuccessful runs at the Republican nomination in 1968 and 1976, struck me as an affable lightweight. He was clearly a gifted vote-getter, but I simply couldn't see him sitting in the Oval Office. In this failure of imagination, I had a good deal of company, political and journalistic. His election, and reelection, and the considerable accomplishments of his administration, were cause for thought, to say the least. My own thought: What if a political leader of the same TV magnetism—and, equally important, the same firm fidelity to a few "simple" priorities—had also come equipped with a first-class intellect? Nightmare or New Jerusalem?

XVI

The Almost Apostolic Succession

I return to reflections on leadership in a more modest realm, in one American corporation. The publicly held corporation shares at least one problem with a dictatorship such as China or the Soviet Union: the succession can be ticklish business. It is not that the very legitimacy of the regime could be called into question, but the management is not about to invite "the people"—i.e., the shareholders or the employees—to elect the next CEO. And unless it is a family-controlled business with an heir-apparent—an entrepreneurial monarchy—we will see the hired executives of the corporation choose their successors, subject to the almost certain approval of a board of directors theoretically representing, but at some remove, the stockholders.

I started thinking fairly seriously about my successor at about the halfway point in my fifteen-year tenure as editor-in-chief. Andrew Heiskell began reviewing the possible candidates for his job. He was only a year younger than I, and Jim Shepley was just another year and a half younger than Heiskell. So if we all stayed on until age sixty-five, the company would undergo a complete turnover in top management in the years 1979 to 1981. Andrew and I discussed the possibility that one or both of us might retire early so the new appointments would not be so closely bunched. We tried out the idea on a few of the outside directors and on Roy Larsen, now Time Inc.'s elder statesman and everybody's uncle. (Roy was of course exempted from the age-sixty-five rule; he retired in 1979 at age eighty.) They were not enthusiastic, and I must admit we were easily dissuaded. But succession became a regular menu item when Heiskell and I were lunching alone, and we even exchanged slightly formal private memos from time to time, so each of us would have on record the other's up-to-date rankings of the brightest prospects. We shared these appraisals with the board of directors at least once a year.

I thought it especially important that the board should feel involved in the choice of the next editor-in-chief. The directors would involve themselves very naturally in the choice of the next CEO— boards feel at home with that decision. Most of the outside directors in fact were (or had been) CEOs of their own companies. But this semi-sacred office of editor-in-chief was another matter. A few of the directors, as previously noted, were not sure why the office was necessary at all—or, if it were, why it had to be lodged so high in the corporate hierarchy, right on the same level with CEO. But there I was, and I had received the seals of office from Henry Luce himself. The next editor-in-chief would not enjoy such august sponsorship. I wanted to make sure the board would feel the next editor-in-chief had been their choice as well as mine. I wanted to be in a position to present two names (at least) with an assurance to the board that each man was well qualified, and, with that understood, I would make my own recommendation. It would be the Apostolic Succession, Modified. Heiskell and I created many occasions for the rising editors and business-side executives to appear before the board, and we let the directors form their own judgments. If we needed a new CEO in a hurry, it was understood between Heiskell and me, and with the board, that Shepley would step in. As my backup, in case that Time Inc. "truck" came for me, I counted on Lou Banks, even after he had resigned as editorial director to become a professor in Cambridge. I'm not sure I ever asked Banks for permission to think of him in that role, but I had negotiated a seat on the board for him, and a consulting contract, so he kept in close touch with the company, and especially my editorial concerns. Heiskell agreed we had a sound medium-term insurance policy.

Meanwhile, I had that lively procession of acting deputies (mentioned in chapter IX) moving through my office. I kept up this experiment for almost three years. Then I decided that the upper editorial ranks (myself included) were entitled to a little relief from constructive confusion. In April 1976, I announced: "It is time now to stop rotating for a while, and I am appointing Ralph Graves to the office of Corporate Editor for all our publications." When *Life* folded, I wasn't going to allow Ralph to go down with his ship. He was appointed chief editorial liaison for our TV cable interests and for Time-Life films, then took a turn in my rotation of deputies, then went to the business side for a year's tour as associate publisher of *Time*.

The title Corporate Editor was a Heiskell inspiration. Thinking up titles had been a high executive art at Time Inc. from the beginning, but I was never very good at it. Too literal-minded perhaps (yes, but what does it *mean*?). In bringing Graves into my office, I didn't want to commit Editorial Director, which might imply the succession was settled, and I also had a hunch that that title could be a useful second prize when the succession did get settled. Corporate Editor was important-sounding in a noncommittal way. I knew Ralph would be a superb deputy, under whatever title, and I also wanted him in contention for my job.

Henry Grunwald would clearly be high in the running, on the strength of his masterly performance as managing editor of *Time*, and he would not have had to stir from that office. But I thought his credentials could be broadened if I brought him up to the thirty-fourth floor, so this meant preparing for the succession at his magazine. To set up these moves, I made an appointment in March 1976 that startled much of the staff and shocked *Time* traditionalists.

This was the transfer of Ray Cave from executive editor of *Sports Illustrated* to assistant managing editor of *Time*. I thought very highly of Cave's work at *S.I.*—he would have been an excellent M.E.—and he had performed well upstairs in my rotation of deputies. He had a fine feel for pictures and was an expert manager of *S.I.*'s intricate fast-color schedules. *Time* was about to invest in an expanded color program, and Grunwald put this new assistant M.E. in charge. I also wanted Cave there as a possible successor to Grunwald.

I wanted options at *Time* just as I thought the board deserved a genuine choice about my successor. The *Time* staff's favored candidate for M.E. was Jason McManus, a skillful editor with sharp news judgment and a manager of uncommon tact and patience. Cave survived a certain amount of new-boy hazing and impressed Grunwald, who came to feel that either Ray or Jason—in their very different ways—could handle the M.E. job. It was exactly the dilemma I had hoped for: two excellent candidates.* I thought *Time* habits needed shaking up, and this gave a slight edge to the "outsider." In September 1977,

---

*Wouldn't it be wonderful for us voters to have that problem in some presidential election?

426

I appointed Cave M.E., as Grunwald moved up to become a second corporate editor of Time Inc. The alphabet sometimes cooperates in delicate masthead arrangements; Graves, who had already been corporate editor for eighteen months, would be listed ahead of Grunwald.

At *Time*, there were some crucial supporters to be signed up for Cave. I made a one-day round trip to Cape Cod, where Edward Jamieson was vacationing, to tell him in advance of the Cave appointment. Ed was executive editor, in rank senior to the assistant M.E.s— Cave as well as McManus—sound, steady, much respected by the staff. He told me he had not considered himself in the running for M.E., and was sure he could work with Cave. He was an indispensable deputy.

McManus was keenly disappointed but agreed to stay on. In later years, he was gracious enough to say that for that stage in *Time*'s development, I had made the right decision. His own decision turned out well, too (see Epilogue). In a little memo to myself about the M.E. competition, I had counted it a plus for Jason that he was forty-three versus Ray's forty-eight, but on the other hand, "Jason has more time for future promotions."

Cave, who had not always been renowned for diplomacy in his *S.I.* days, now had a chance to sharpen that skill. He was generous in sharing not only responsibility with Jamieson and McManus, but also the credit for the considerable improvements in *Time* flow and looks over the next few years.

At the same time as we were sizing up the candidates for the top management of Time Inc., we were debating with some intensity the character of the company itself. The questions were of course intertwined: The company could be adapted to the talents of the managers, or managers could be found—some perhaps outside Time Inc.—to run the kind of company we wanted to become. Was it to be essentially a publishing company, the magazines the heart of the business, with an important sideline in cable TV? Or a more broadly conceived communications company in which TV and film could easily grow bigger than print? Or, still broader, a conglomerate including one or more businesses having nothing to do with information or entertainment?

These questions precipitated the only major disagreement I had with Andrew Heiskell during fifteen years of a very close partnership. At the time when *Life* was going down, and for two or three years afterward (until *People* was a certifiable hit), there was some gloom among our directors about the future of magazines in general. It was fed by the projections of several of our senior publishing executives, scarred by the *Life* experience but also concerned by the squeeze on *Time*'s profit margins. It wasn't that our magazines were going to drop one by one, but did they any longer add up to a "growth situation"?

In 1972, Heiskell became an ardent advocate of a Time Inc. merger with Temple Industries, a forest-products company based in the pine woods of East Texas. Heiskell was not a bottom-line man obsessed with the price Wall Street put on Time Inc. stock. He was as devoted as I to the belief that our journalism should serve the public interest. But he thought our magazines might need the protection of surrounding enterprises of greater growth potential and investment glamour.

And the Temple deal appealed to him on its own merits. He liked the "hedging" aspect—if rising paper prices were cutting into magazine profits, we could get some of our money back in the East Texas woods. Time Inc. already knew its way around those woods—because *Life* thirty-five years earlier had been so hungry for paper. A Time Inc. investment back then evolved into the East Texas Pulp and Paper Company, a highly profitable manufacturer that, as it happened, made almost no magazine paper because there was more money in other grades. Eastex timberlands were intermingled with the Temple properties, for a total of more than a million acres, and the two companies had long done business with each other; Eastex sold Temple saw logs (for building materials) and Temple sold Eastex chips and sawdust (for paper).

So the two Texas companies looked like a nice fit, and Heiskell felt that Arthur Temple himself, proprietor of his family company, was a nice fit with Time Inc. He was a first-rate businessman—he had expanded Temple's revenues by twenty-five times in twenty years—with a strong social conscience. He had desegregated the schools in the company town of Diboll, Texas, some years before the Supreme Court spoke, burned down company-owned tenements, and wangled federal help for the Diboll Housing Authority, which sold lots and decent houses to Temple employees at cut-rate prices.

I was against the deal. I thought it would indeed change the character of Time Inc., or at least perceptions of the character. The nonpublishing component of the company's revenues and earnings would increase, and the Temple family would own 15 percent of Time

Inc. stock—not a controlling interest, but a very significant chunk. I also questioned the business logic of a merger. The "hedging" argument always bothered me: It was nice if forest products and magazines could never be in serious trouble at the same time, but the corollary was that they could never be booming at the same time. We were not an insurance company, after all. I felt, too, that as long as Eastex was our wholly owned subsidiary, a relatively small part of our total business, well managed on the ground, it did not intrude much on anybody's time in New York. But doubling the size of our forest-products business, merging it right into Time Inc., and bringing Temple representatives onto the Time board imposed new demands on our management. Did a management that had grown up in publishing have any wisdom to contribute to forest products (not even including our kind of paper)? And did the forest have any useful advice for the magazines?

It had been my impression, first formed in *Fortune* reporting and editing days, that successful conglomerates depend on a central talent bank—sometimes no more than one entrepreneur and a small staff of exceptional managerial versatility—capable of applying their gifts to utterly unrelated lines of business. If the central talent bank owns or has access to enough money, it can also provide financial, technological, legal, accounting, advertising services of a quality the little bits and pieces could not afford on their own. But none of that was at work in the Time Inc.–Temple merger. It was the most awkward size of merger. We were injecting a substantial foreign business into Time Inc. but we were not really becoming a conglomerate (though that would be said). There were certainly no versatile-genius insights to be played back and forth across the two businesses.

I was outvoted—conversationally, which is how things were done. None of us would have brought a divided management to the board for resolution. Shepley, Larsen, and Jim Linen were generally sympathetic to the merger, though tougher about price than Heiskell was inclined to be. Andrew, normally cannier than the others about price, really wanted the deal, and he saw it as a major milestone in his management. I subsided, as I had some years earlier in the case of the MGM deal, thinking to myself: I have the last word on what goes into the magazines, which is what I care about. It's only fair to let Heiskell run Time Inc. as a business. The merger went through in 1973.

The magazine staffs were displeased, and we rode out the inevitable wave of Texas jokes and woodsy jokes. (A sign on a *Fortune* writer's door: "Vice President for Leaves, Twigs and Bark.") As things turned out, editorial integrity was not affected in the slightest. I found Temple himself as shrewd as his reputation, a likable man of bluff down-home style, impeccable in his respect for the independence of the magazines. I once had the pleasure of telling an audience of businessmen and politicians in Austin, Texas: "Arthur and I get along very well. He doesn't try to tell me how to put out magazines, and I don't tell him how to grow trees." The merger may indeed have fortified the independence of the magazines. At a time when the great surge of corporate raids and takeovers was just beginning, the addition of Temple gave Time Inc. some extra bulk. We became somewhat less digestible.

The deal did little for the bottom line. The building-materials business turned out to be even more cyclical than Time Inc. realized. Forest products became a serious claimant on Time Inc. capital and borrowing power at a time when our growing interest in cable TV also required heavy financing. Investment analysts were confused about the shape and direction of the company, and Time Inc. stock languished. By 1977, I was arguing that we had set in motion "a kind of negative synergism" in which the whole was less valuable than the sum of the parts. I wondered out loud whether we should spin off Temple-Eastex.

This was to some extent a counteroffensive against an idea that was developing strong support on the board: that magazine publishing be set up as a subsidiary company within Time Inc. There would be three other subsidiaries—Temple-Eastex, Books, and TV—and the parent company would be headed by *one boss*, the CEO, as in any proper corporation. I would be editor-in-chief of the magazine subsidiary, and, for an extra goodie, if I wished, chairman of magazines as well. I don't know how many thousands of man-hours were spent within management and the board in talking and memo writing about this question of "corporate structure." It might seem a silly bureaucratic squabble: Should we formally acknowledge that the company pretty much operated as four separate divisions, or should it continue proclaiming (pretending?) we were something different?

I insisted we were in fact different, and the difference was important. If the magazines were simply one of four (or, maybe some day, more) subsidiaries, their vitality and prestige, if not immediately their independence, was diminished. But the magazines had been the core of Time Inc., giving the company its fame and its intellectual and political weight. I thought it was dangerous to stockholders as well as readers to demote the magazines by one tier on the organization chart.

I once confided to my wife, who was as admiring of Andrew Heiskell as I, that I wished there were some way secretly to pay him twice as much as me, since his responsibilities extended across the whole of the company's activities and mine were only over about half. But the very "unfairness" of our equal salaries, published annually, said something important about Time Inc.: This is not an ordinary company. Dorothy thought that was a nice idea if it didn't mean a cut for me. (Fifteen or twenty years ago, I talked Heiskell into exercising some Time Inc. stock options he was about to let lapse because the option price was then barely below market. If he still has that stock, his paper profit would cover a good many years of the extra pay he didn't receive.)

I summed up my case against the magazine subsidiary in a long memo to Heiskell and Shepley on August 25, 1977. Though they had been inclined to favor the subsidiary structure, they were not disposed to have a fight about it. They liked a suggestion that I would draft a formal statement on the role of the editor-in-chief and his relationship with the board of directors, which had never been put in writing. In Harry Luce's eloquent but highly personal references to himself and me in a few speeches and memos, the board of directors received short shrift: The editor-in-chief was responsible to his Creator and/or his conscience. But the next editor-in-chief would need more than a ringing send-off speech from me. I wanted to get the board's agreement to a statement ensuring—so far as a piece of paper can—that my successor would exercise the office with the same freedom and authority I enjoyed. I fussed with several drafts; Shepley and Heiskell were helpful editors. When the three of us were entirely satisfied, I started lobbying the document through the board, almost director by director. My statement on "The Role of the Editor-in-Chief" was formally ratified on December 21, 1978, and enshrined in the minutes of the board. Some excerpts:

> The Board of Directors has the final responsibility for the editorial quality of Time Inc. publications, as it does for all other aspects of Time Inc. operations.
>
> The Board exercises its responsibility for Time Inc. editorial quality through its appointment of the Editor-in-Chief, who serves at the pleasure of the Board, and is responsible solely to the Board for editorial content.

The Board recognizes that Time Inc. as a corporation has been built upon the editorial quality of its publications, and that these publications have been intended, from the founding of the company, to advance the public interest as well as pay a competitive return on investment.

The Board, recognizing the special character of the editorial process, does not undertake to pass upon editorial content or positions, and delegates to the Editor-in-Chief the continuing appraisal and direction of the company's editorial work. If the Board finds editorial performance generally unsatisfactory over a significant period of time, it will appoint a new Editor-in-Chief, but it does not seek to supervise him month by month. The Editor-in-Chief is a member of the Board and of its Executive Committee. . . .

The Chief Executive Officer of Time Inc., by delegation of the Board, is responsible for the financial health of the company's publications. He is inevitably concerned with the quality of editorial performance, as the Editor-in-Chief must be concerned with the financial boundaries and consequences of the editorial effort. Where the responsibilities intersect, the C.E.O. and Editor-in-Chief are jointly responsible to the Board.

In non-publishing affairs of Time Inc., the Editor-in-Chief has the standing of a Time Inc. Board member. He has further responsibilities that may apply if non-publishing activities of Time Inc. seem to be in conflict with editorial positions of the company's publications. All Board members value the integrity of the Time Inc. publications; the Editor-in-Chief is not assumed to have special virtue in this regard, but he does have a full-time responsibility for editorial quality. Thus he has a specific obligation to the Board to express his concern, when such exists, to the C.E.O. and if necessary the Board, as to whether the good name of the Time Inc. publications might be affected unfavorably by some non-publishing activity of the company.

We had come down to the finals in the selection of the new editor-in-chief, with Henry Grunwald and Ralph Graves both serving as my deputies in 1978. They were each so well qualified that I never even considered looking "outside," and no director ever asked me if I had. I did share with the board my Dark Horse list: Ray Cave and Jason McManus on *Time* and Dick Stolley on *People*, first-rate editors in their forties, all with good growth potential and one management generation younger than Grunwald and Graves. The directors admired my thoroughness, but they were no more inclined than I to be bold just for the sake of being bold. Grunwald and Graves were given ample opportunities to impress the board—both did—and to get thoroughly fed up with each other and with me. And, so far as I knew, neither did. I was in more or less continuous consultation with Heiskell and Shepley about my choice, and about the parallel decisions coming up regarding their own successors.

One of the most difficult aspects of conveying to others your appraisal of two highly talented people is to do justice to the man who has just a little less of some desirable quality than the other fellow. Even for me in the word business, I found myself working very hard at the phrasing of these judgments. Grunwald and Graves, I told the board, were each utterly professional editors: men of integrity, courage, confidence, strong nerves, and physical stamina. Each had the complete respect of the editorial staffs. Each was of sound philosophical and political outlook—i.e., not too different from mine—though they were less cautious than I, and capable of interesting surprises. They were completely civilized characters who, as far as I could see, had done no unseemly jostling during a year that was awkward for them both. Graves was the better manager. Grunwald, by some indefinable margin, had the larger imagination and greater intellectual depth.

I recommended Grunwald as editor-in-chief, with the understanding that Graves would be invited to become editorial director— now was the day to spend that title. Grunwald, if somewhat negligent about managerial detail, grasped the big managerial point at once— he needed Graves. I'm not sure how I would have reacted if Henry Luce had said to me in 1964 that he wanted to make two appointments: me as editor-in-chief and Mr. X as my editorial director. I think I would have said, "Let's hold off on editorial director for a while." What would have happened next, I don't know. Nor did I know, fifteen years later, how I would handle things if Grunwald declined to be part of a "ticket." But I was pretty sure he would not decline. In announcing his appointment, I said, "Henry Grunwald (along with certain other virtues) is our Time Inc. edition of the lad born in a log cabin who becomes president. Henry started here as a copy boy. Let all copy boys, or copy persons, take heart, and, for that matter, all remaining politicians who were born in log cabins."

I was also able to announce that Ralph Graves was becoming editorial director by appointment of the board of directors—important nuance—and that he as well as Grunwald would join the board. Ralph, for his part, dealt gracefully with whatever disappointment he may have felt. "I have the highest regard and respect for Henry," he said at the staff dinner marking the changing of the guard, for "his mind, his wit, his extraordinary knowledge, his gentility. In fact, as I have told him, under different circumstances he would have made a hell of an Editorial Director."

Nice things were said about me at some length that evening. My combative old comrade Jim Shepley even likened me to General George Marshall. Jim had served on Marshall's staff for a year after World War II, four months "in very close proximity" in Chungking, China. Jim said that integrity was not uncommon, in Time Inc. and elsewhere, but he had known only two men of whom it could be said that "the most important aspect of their character was integrity, towering integrity." George Marshall was one, and I was the other. Marshall having been a hero of Jim's—and of mine from a greater distance—and Shepley being the hard-boiled fellow he was, this left me a little choked up. Luckily I didn't have to speak next.

I also treasured a pretty fantasy spun out that evening by Henry Grunwald, as an example of my "massive calm." When he was managing editor of *Time*, Henry said, he "often speculated what it would be like if we received the news of the Second Coming. I imagined that the phone would ring—not right away, but perhaps twenty-five minutes or so after the first flash. Trudi Lanz would say, 'Would you come up to see Mr. Donovan, please.' I would grasp my usual tranquilizing cigar and, braving the angry people in the elevator who hate cigars, would ride to the thirty-fourth floor. Hedley looks up from some useful reading, his face serene, while the sound of distant prayer rises from Sixth Avenue, along with lots of the prescribed wailing and gnashing of teeth. Hedley leans back in his chair and asks, 'Well, what are the plans? Do you think it's worth a cover?' "

Nothing succeeds, someone has said, like succession. No matter how greatly admired the old boss may have been, he had to have *some* faults, and it is mathematically impossible for the successor to have exactly the same faults. If the old boss has been in office as long as I was—fifteen years—there is something instantly invigorating in succession.

I was well aware of the heroic theory that the best thing an executive can do for his own reputation is to put in place a successor who will do better (even!) than he did. I was also aware of the nasty little secret of the departing boss—deep down, the utterly unworthy, not totally suppressible wish that his successor should do *almost* as well as he did. I am happy to rise above the baser side of executive nature and report that Grunwald did *at least* as well as I did. Having received the laying-on of hands from Donovan, not Luce, Henry had to earn much of his authority on the job. He did so brilliantly.

EPILOGUE

As Henry Grunwald's retirement date approached, he too took care that the board of directors should be well acquainted with the successor "field." Ralph Graves, who was only two years younger than Henry, had availed himself of early retirement at the end of 1983, after four and a half years as editorial director. I had thought Graves's managerial talents would be indispensable for at least the first couple of years of a Grunwald administration; anything more than that was sheer bonus. When Ralph left, Grunwald brought Ray Cave upstairs as corporate editor. Jason McManus moved from corporate editor to managing editor of *Time*, thus acquiring the only line his résumé had lacked—service in an M.E. chair. And Jason became Henry's choice as his successor, ratified by the board in April 1987. Henry himself made a very stylish exit, a couple of months before his sixty-fifth birthday, to become U.S. ambassador to Austria.

On the business side of the house, Heiskell and Shepley had been succeeded in 1980 by Ralph Davidson as chairman and J. Richard Munro as president. They were fitness fanatics (neither Heiskell nor I could be so characterized), and each had a fine Time Inc. track record. Davidson, among other things, had been publisher of *Time*, Munro publisher of *Sports Illustrated*, then VP in charge of Time-Life video. Reverting to a division of labor that had gone out of corporate fashion, the company designated the new president rather than the chairman as CEO, Davidson to be presiding officer of the board and "Mr. Outside."

The new management in the 1980s experienced an expensive series of disappointments in new ventures. I could share pride of authorship in the first of these: our acquisition in 1978, while I was still editor-in-chief, of the *Washington Star*. The *Star*, by far the richest and fattest paper in Washington back in the days when I worked for the *Post*, had fallen upon very thin times. We paid very little for it, which was fair enough, since the *Star* was losing money at a brisk clip. But it was still a first-rate paper, and the idea of a Time Inc. newspaper presence in the capital had powerful appeal to me and especially to Shepley, once a UP reporter in Washington and for nine years chief of our Washington bureau. And Heiskell, ex–*New York Herald Tribune*, had a little of the newspaper itch in him. He and I saw the chairmanship of the *Star* as a perfect role for Shepley, who was not going to be CEO of Time Inc. unless Andrew dropped dead. Shepley knew everybody in Washington and was already spending two or three days a week there as a high-level Time Inc. ambassador. He had done the close-in negotiating of the *Star* deal, and as chairman attacked the paper's problems with great energy. I asked Murray Gart, chief of the Time-Life News Service, to be Editor, and he moved down to Washington to do battle with the *Post*. I served on the *Star* board of directors even after I had left the Time board—as a subsidiary, the paper set its own retirement rules. I also sat in for a few weeks as "editor in residence," once wrote a very long piece for the Sunday paper, and generally enjoyed nostalgic sensations of having a Washington newspaper home again.

Gart and his valiant staff put out a lively paper, but the *Star* was more nearly competitive with the *Post* in editorial quality than in circulation or advertising revenue. We had not been so foolhardy as to think we could displace the *Post* as the number 1 paper in Washington. But we were foolhardy enough: We thought that in the large and affluent metropolitan Washington market there should be room for two profitable papers, and the *Star* could be the second. It cost Time Inc. $85 million (pretax) to learn otherwise. In 1981, the new Time Inc. management decided to close down the *Star*. Had I still held my old job, I probably would have concurred. Though I was generally inclined to stick longer with lost causes (*Life*, and luckily *Money*) than were my colleagues, the *Star*'s struggle against the *Post*'s overwhelming dominance had come to look hopeless.

Other publishing misadventures followed. In 1983, the company launched *TV-Cable Week*, a listings guide that folded after only seventeen issues. Another false start was *Picture Week*, which was test-marketed for four months in 1985–86, then dropped. Still another disappointment was *Discover*, a science monthly launched in 1980. It was designed to be less formidable than *Scientific American* and more comprehensive than the science coverage in the newsmagazines and the good newspapers. It ran an attractive mix of articles, well written and illustrated, but it never caught on. It was sold in 1987.

As these troubles unfolded, I was a distressed spectator up in the stands. Journalists working up stories on "Trouble in Luceland," always a popular theme in press coverage of our arrogant company, sought me out for comment on these Time Inc. miscalculations. I, of course, declined to cooperate. Management having long since given its own public critiques on these bad guesses, I can now toss mine in. I will confess that I never liked the *Picture Week* idea. The first test issues were embarrassingly tawdry but then the trial issues improved noticeably, and as they did, the magazine came to look too much like *People*. It could have become a serious competitor of *People*, I thought—and what was the point of that? As to *TV-Cable Week*, never having seen the memos, projections, presentations on which the decision to publish was based, I have no idea how I would have reacted. I like to think I would have intuited the terminal weaknesses in the business proposition, but I'm not sure I would have. And since it was a perfectly respectable service—if not exactly ground-breaking intellectually—that the magazine proposed to deliver, I would not have been disdainful of the buckets of money it was supposed to make (from out of which—a standard reflex of mine—more important things might have been funded). I admired the briskness of the Dick Munro management, when it was clear the thing wouldn't work, in closing it down. A huge embarrassment had to be swallowed—okay, get it over with.

The failure of *Discover*, with me still watching from the stands, bothered me more. *Discover*, my science allergy notwithstanding, had the intellectual heft of a Time Inc. magazine. It had been created by editors, not market-research people. But the editors could never put together a survivable magazine. Together, the three magazine failures cost the company (pretax) more than $100 million.

Amid these travails, the company stepped out smartly and put up half a billion dollars, more or less, to buy the Southern Progress Corporation of Birmingham, Alabama, proprietor of the lushly profitable *Southern Living* magazine and various offshoot publications. A North Carolina academic told me to page through some issues of *Southern Living*—"You won't see any blacks in those living rooms or gardens" (my friend was medium-liberal), "but don't let your fellows in New York try to change it, or you'll wreck it." They were no longer my fellows, of course, and I had to retreat into a somewhat detached consideration of whether Time Inc. should own publications whose attitudes might differ in some respects from Mother Church.

The woman's magazine that I failed to invent in the 1970s appeared under the company roof in interesting guise in 1986. Time Inc. purchased a half-interest in the 120-year-old *McCall's* and its offspring *Working Woman* and *Working Mother*, all monthlies. Time Inc. has not so far asserted any editorial voice.

The company's next publishing expansion gave me a bad case of sticker shock. Scott, Foresman, the textbook publisher, was bought in 1986 for $520 million cash. My first reaction was to look up the price we had paid in the early 1960s for another textbook publisher, Silver Burdett (a much smaller company, to be sure). I had the figure $15 million in mind, but that was the valuation put on the company when we merged it into the General Learning Corporation (see chapter IX) a few years later. Our actual cost was $6 million. My next reflex was to recall our purchase in the late 1960s of the fine old Boston house of Little, Brown. This cost $17 million in Time Inc. stock. All about as relevant, I suppose, as the fact that *Time* magazine once cost fifteen cents at the newsstand, and men's cotton undershorts were two for a dollar.

In 1984, to my gratification, Time Inc. had spun off Temple Industries, acknowledging that these were two quite distinct businesses that did not benefit from being under the same corporate roof, and indeed suffered in investor perceptions. As a result of the spin-off, and the purchase of Southern Progress and Scott, Foresman, Time Inc.'s business in 1988 was 59 percent in publishing (magazines and books) and 41 percent in cable TV. With publishing still predominant, I was entirely comfortable with the concept of a communications company broadly defined, dealing in entertainment as well as information. Certainly there were strong elements of entertainment in the Time Inc. magazines, especially *People* and *Sports Illustrated*, and even old print men had to concede that some information comes over the tube. As a stockholder, I was not shocked that management was openly attracted by the profit potentials in cable.

But my heaviest investment in Time Inc. was sentimental. Here the editorial quality of the magazines was the first thing I cared about, and to my prejudiced eye, it looked excellent. I suppressed the occasional urge to call up somebody and complain about a *Time* or

Fortune cover I didn't like. And behind the magazines were men and women and careers I cared about. It was a delight to see people I had first known as trainees in their mid-twenties reaching very senior editorial positions. To be sure, these comers were now, to my constant amazement, thirty-nine or forty-two or some such age.

There were some disappointments. Ray Cave and Jason McManus had been highly congenial colleagues as long as they were both in the running for editor-in-chief, but when that race was over, the relationship became strained. In little more than a year after McManus had become editor-in-chief, Cave was gone from Time Inc., to be succeeded as editorial director, in December 1988, by Dick Stolley.

Nor was all serene on the corporate side of the executive suite. Ralph Davidson, at age fifty-nine, gave up the board chairman's job in 1986, and later became chairman of the Kennedy Center in Washington. On his way out, he negotiated a $4 million "severance package," which even included the $18,500 fee he paid the lawyer who represented him in these dealings with the rest of Time Inc. management.

Andrew Heiskell and I, on our emeritus perches, were aghast. If I had been asked to leave my job earlier than I had planned, I couldn't imagine that I would have hired a lawyer to represent me "against" Time Inc. As I told Andrew, "It would be like suing myself." He and I sometimes mused that we were just as glad not to be out there in the American corporate culture of the late 1980s—Time Inc. very far from being the most vulgar exhibit—with the staggering parachute and golden-handshake deals for displaced executives, the mega billions being slung around in mergers and buyouts.

Talking with Andrew one evening in December 1988, I was reminiscing about my *Fortune* story of forty years earlier on Nabisco, which had just been bought out (it now included R. J. Reynolds) for the historic amount of $25 billion. I remembered "my" Nabisco, free-flowing source of Oreo cookies for the Donovan family, as having total annual *sales* of about $250 million. No, no, Andrew said, "You're forgetting how long ago that was—it would have been more like $100 million." A pity we didn't bet. I would have won $10, my standard proposition; cautious, I agree, but I have a lot of bets out there at any one time. Nabisco sales in 1947 were $264 million.

But I digress—not for the first time in this book, but almost the last. As Ralph Davidson departed, Dick Munro, already CEO of Time Inc., took the title of chairman as well, and Nicholas Nicholas, Harvard Business School '64, became president. Nick is a very sharp financial man with no magazine experience but an armful of combat stripes from the Time Inc. ventures in cable TV.

In March 1989, the Munro-Nicholas management announced a deal to merge Time Inc. with Warner Communications (movies, home video, recorded music). The resulting company, subject to approval by the S.E.C. and the stockholders of Time and Warner (and settlement of assorted lawsuits), would be the largest communications empire in the world. The stated rationale was that only very large media enterprises, vertically integrated, capable of competing aggressively in world markets, will thrive in the 1990s and beyond. While this deal was pending, Paramount Communications in June stepped in with an offer to buy Time stock, then trading in the 120s, at $175 a share. Time countered with a plan to buy Warner, rather than merge with it, a move that would probably not require stockholder approval. Paramount raised its offer to $200 a share. Other possible bidders were said to be on the prowl. Small armies of bankers, lawyers, take-over specialists, anti-takeover specialists hovered about the three principals. Other lawyers salivated at the potential for stockholder class-action suits. And week by week the "old" Time Inc. was disappearing, its magazines and books to become, at best, an important sideline in an entertainment company. Would Time Inc. journalism still flourish? My constitutional optimism was being sorely tried.

Back in the busyness of my editor-in-chief days, Dorothy once gave me an inspired wedding-anniversary present: a winter's sublease of an Upper East Side apartment. The idea was to see how we liked a life we had often talked about: three or four nights a week in the city, the weekends in Sands Point. We liked it. We bought a thirty-first-floor apartment on East 72nd Street. A spectacular view to the west and south was the luxury; otherwise, the rooms were unostentatious, and Dorothy resolutely referred to the place as "the pad," so nobody should think we thought it was any big deal. But it was a great enhancement of our lives. Every week from mid-September through June, there were at least one or two New York dinners where we should show up. One of Dorothy's many virtues—mine, too—was that we actually enjoyed almost all of these, and certainly more so when we could take a cab home to 72nd Street instead of staying at a hotel or driving to Sands Point at midnight. It was also great fun to walk out, spur of the moment, to a gallery, restaurant, film. It may have been a kind of delayed youth, since we had never before lived in Manhattan, single or young-married. We settled into a very happy pattern.

It was to last only a few years. Dorothy was stricken with cancer, survived three rounds of it, but the remissions grew shorter. Her mind stayed keen until just a little before the end. Once when she greeted me outside the radiation lab, where I was waiting to wheel her back to her room (therapy for the spouse), she said we must stop meeting like this, and she beamed like a proud teacher as I gave the answer, Yes, people are starting to talk. She died at Sloan-Kettering in July 1978.

When I retired the next year, Time Inc., as much from compassion, I think, as any need for my services, gave me a consultancy: an office in the Time and Life Building, which was a comforting home base, the continued services of the incomparable Trudi Lanz, my secretary of many years, and a retainer for "up to one-third" of my working time.

I didn't miss being editor-in-chief so much as I missed a working title—not necessarily a big one. "Associate Editor"—i.e., writer on *Fortune*—would have been fine. "Former" this and "former" that isn't entirely satisfying. At a White House correspondents' dinner in 1981, the *Washington Post* spotted Richard Helms, once head of the CIA, Henry Kissinger, and Hedley Donovan at the same table—"lots of formers." The *Post* called it the "memorial table." It was just as well the reporter didn't know what Kissinger and I were talking about: the Thirty Years War (1618–48). I think we were agreeing that it was more savage, per capita, than the world wars of this century.

While I was often asked, as a managing editor, editorial director, editor-in-chief, "What do you actually *do*?"—nobody ever asked me that about my consultancy. People were too tactful. I was not in fact entirely idle. I was glad to be taken to lunch when any editor wanted to try out some idea on me, as happened now and then. Mainly I wrote articles for *Fortune* and *Time*, about ten of them over four years.

I rather enjoyed being edited by my former juniors and hoped it was reasonably entertaining for them. The boss emeritus is entitled to a measure of respect, but it must not be overdone. Some of these youngsters could be brutal about space. I complained in a letter to a friend: "To give you some idea of what I am up against—this Essay [for *Time*] which Cave [Ray, the M.E.] originally thought of as two printed pages grew in an entirely graceful and natural way to six pages. So now they are asking me to cut one whole page—or 150 'lines' (that is the way they talk)—out of it. Think of the BTUs burned up in thinking up those 'lines.' At the same time, for obscure reasons of layout aesthetics, they want a few *more* lines here and there, in places where I have already said absolutely all there is to be said!" Nobody was so banal as to say, Welcome to the Club. One boy editor, Bill Rukeyser of *Fortune*, age forty-three or so, did remind me that he had heard me say more than once: "Anything can be cut."

I had intended to start writing a book—this one—as soon as I retired. But my year with Jimmy Carter, 1979–80, intervened, and when I returned to New York I had so many requests to write and speak about the White House experience that I decided to put aside the autobiography. I started a book on the Carter administration, eventually broadened it into *Roosevelt to Reagan: A Reporter's Encounters with Nine Presidents*, which Harper & Row published in 1985. When the presidents palled a little, I would switch to the memoir; when Donovan palled, back to the presidents.

Ralph Graves and I compared book-writing torments. He had written two novels as a young man; when he retired, he immediately wrote another, *August People*; in 1988 he finished a fourth, *Share of Honor*. He is also the author of Graves's Ten Laws on how to write a book. Among them:

2. Write every day. (Sunday is optional.)

3. Write at the same time every day. (Morning or afternoon or night, whatever works best, as long as it is always the same period.)

4. Write in the same place every day.

9. Children, colleagues, friends, and telephones are not permitted during writing hours. (This includes the President; you can always call him back.)

10. Have a martini at the end of each writing session.

I'm afraid I have repeatedly broken nine of Ralph's laws; I am in partial compliance with number 10.

Ralph has also given me one or two expensive lessons in backgammon. In betting on other sports, as well as elections and the stock market, I generally run a favorable balance with him. One evening, however, when we were on our way to the deservedly obscure Czech opera *Jenůfa*, Ralph asked me how many different operas I had seen, lifetime (suggesting he had had to listen to a lot of my opera name-dropping over the years). I guessed about fifty, and he bet me it was at least seventy-five. I spent a happy weekend researching the question—not working on either of my books—and came up with ninety-seven titles. As I wrote Ralph, "It was Verdi (16) and Wagner (11) who, as they say, broke the game wide open." I paid him $10.

I would have liked to compete with Ralph at the novel, too, but at least as of early 1989, I hadn't come up with any plot. My closest approach to *belles lettres* came in a few haiku I submitted in a contest sponsored in 1988 by Japan Air Lines. The prize was two first-class tickets to Tokyo, and $1,000 spending money, which at the prevailing yen-dollar exchange might have lasted through midafternoon of the first day. Considering that the prize would have been taxable, and that my guest and I might have wanted to stay for more than one day, it would have been an expensive victory. Still, I wanted it. My entries (among some 40,000 JAL received):

> *Papers from a life*
> *those to burn, those to keep*
> *and these?*

(This was inspired by the scene in my Sands Point study, where much of the raw material for this book was spread out.)

> *Forty floors*
> *above the street*
> *snow is falling up!*

> *Ruined walls, old pots and coins,*
> *a lizard.*
> *Some famous empire.*

> *Politicians speaking*
> *wind rising.*
> *The nation sighs.*

Inexplicably, I failed to win.

One of the great clichés about retirement is: "I'll bet you're busier than ever!" Especially objectionable when spoken by some hyperactive fifty-year-old, just in from jogging, but partway true. (I have noted earlier the tendency of clichés to contain some truth.) In my case, the extra workload came not from a flurry of new boards and causes, pressed upon the defenseless freshman senior citizen, but from an athletic urge to try a couple of things I had never done before. One was book writing, the other university teaching. A confession to the stockholders of Time Inc. is in order here. In the last five years, say, of my fifteen years as editor-in-chief, I had had so much practice at the job, and I had so many first-class people working for me, that I could have performed the essentials in a couple of hours a day. I never arrived in the office with the slightest doubt that I could deal with the problems I knew about—or the ones I didn't that were about to break. Since I liked my work, however, I continued to put in very long hours at it, but now I am including in "work" all sorts of events, excursions, millings-around that many might consider sheer recreation. As did I—hence my definition of a wonderful job: one in which it is impossible to say this is work and that is fun.

All very different from arriving, at age sixty-six, in a classroom in the Kennedy School of Government, Harvard University, on a raw March afternoon, for my first performance as a professor. I had butterflies. Do I have the faintest idea how to do this? It would be very different from showing up on a campus as a slightly prominent outside speaker, as I had done so many times: Give my talk, handle the Q and A (a contest I loved), and get out of town. Now I was undertaking to give a seminar on—modest topic—"The Press and Society," two-hour sessions once a week for seven weeks. It was a credit-bearing course, and I had to devise reading lists and term-paper topics, read the papers, and give grades. Graham Allison, dean of the Kennedy School, designated me a "Fellow of the Faculty of Government." When I told him I was achieving this dignity forty-five years after unsuccessful job searching in academia, he said, "Better late than never."

My students were mainly people in government—federal, state, or local—who had come back to the campus in their thirties for a graduate degree in public administration. The aim of my course was not to convert them into journalists but to convey to these people in other professions some idea of how the press operates and why it acts the way it does. Such courses are commonplace today, but in 1981, when I first gave my seminar, it was one of the few in the country.

In one Harvard field exercise, I would ask for a volunteer to act as White House press spokesman when we met the next week. The amateur spokesman could spend a nervous week trying to anticipate what questions would come up. The rest of the class could enjoy themselves thinking up the questions. One classroom "Larry" (at the time when Larry Speakes was parrying with the press) was a very bright and articulate fellow who in real life was clearly no Ronald Reagan fan. He dealt manfully with a long string of tough questions but finally floundered in trying to explain some exceptionally muddled pronouncement by the president. "Larry" broke up in helpless laughter, simply said, "Oh, shit," and fled our classroom podium. I said desertion in the face of the enemy was a serious matter, but for previous gallantry I would give him a B+ anyway.

My favorite moment in the Speakes game followed by a day or two the White House announcement that Margaret Heckler, then secretary of Health and Human Services, the largest civilian department in the government, was being "promoted" to ambassador to Ireland. Our new "Larry" fielded the questions ingeniously, but again there came one too many. "Larry," piped up somebody, "we understand the post of Ambassador to Iceland will soon be vacant. Are there any other Cabinet officers in line for promotion?" I felt my students were learning.

But I was doubtless better at the editor-in-chief business than at impersonating a professor. Jason McManus, in his inaugural in October 1987 as fourth editor-in-chief of Time Inc., paid me a wildly extravagant compliment, saying, "Columnist James Brady wrote me a note after the announcement of my new job that said, 'I'll bet you never thought you'd grow up to be Henry Luce.' I replied, 'Sure, I did. It was growing up to be Hedley Donovan that sometimes seemed problematical.' "

Here and elsewhere in this autobiography, I am reminded of a brief book review once uttered by Roy Howard of Scripps-Howard and the United Press. He had read the memoirs of his fellow Hoosier and wire-service competitor, Kent Cooper, general manager of the Associated Press. Someone who had also read the book asked him how he liked it: "Well," said Roy, "the guy didn't give himself any the worst of it, did he?"

INDEX